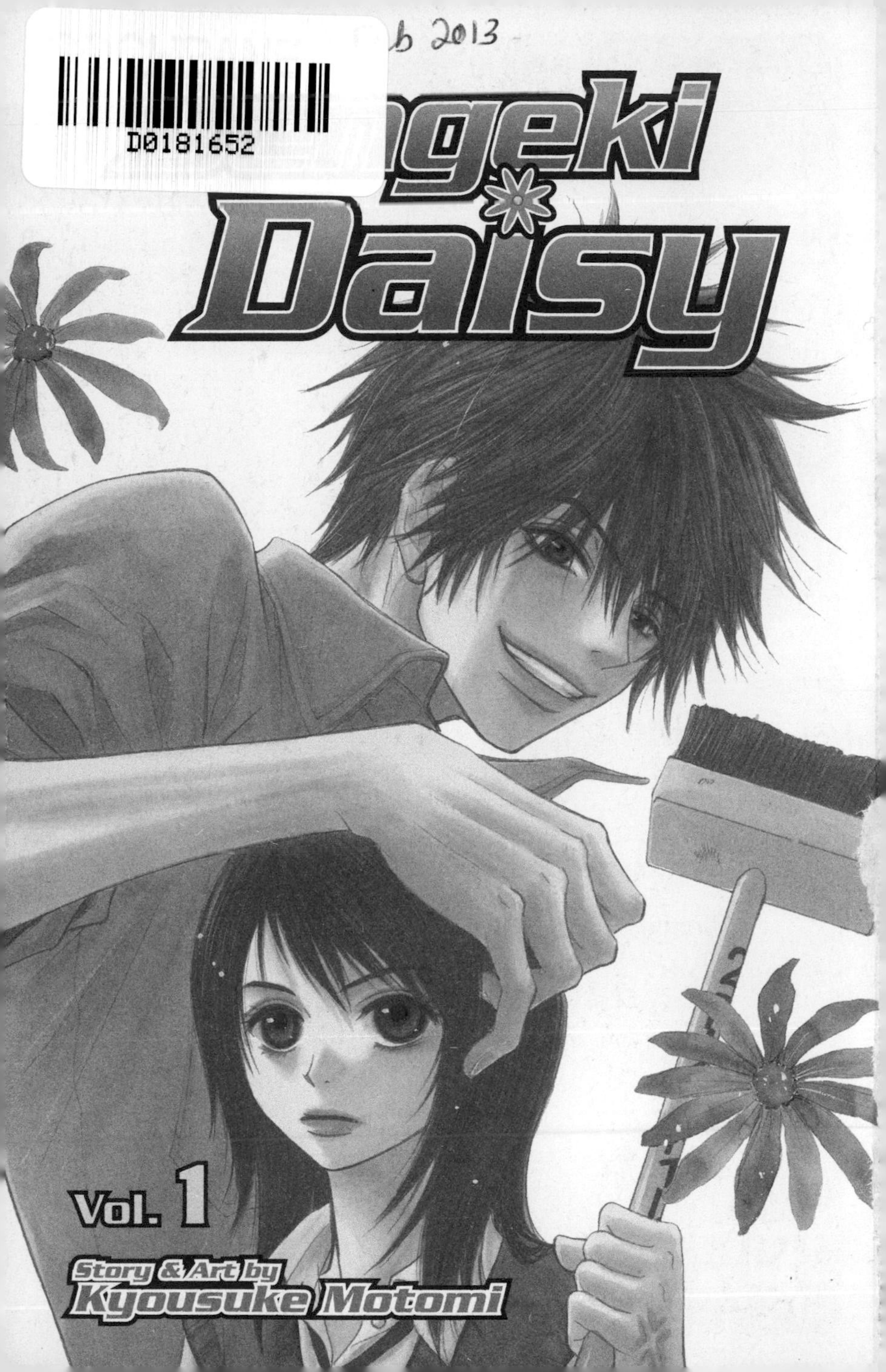
ageki
Daisy
Vol. 1
Story & Art by
Kyousuke Motomi

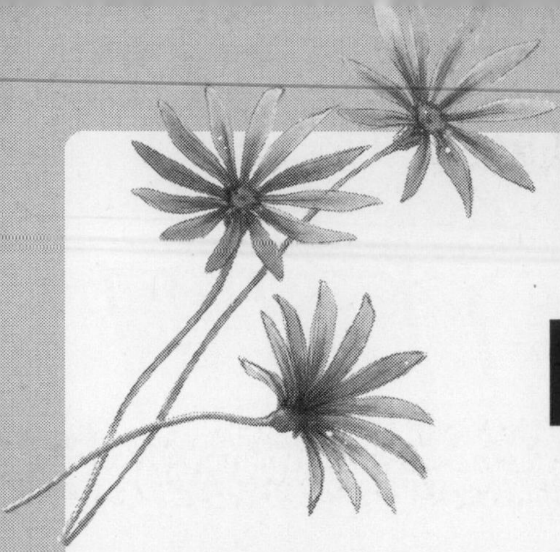

Dengeki Daisy

Volume 1 CONTENTS

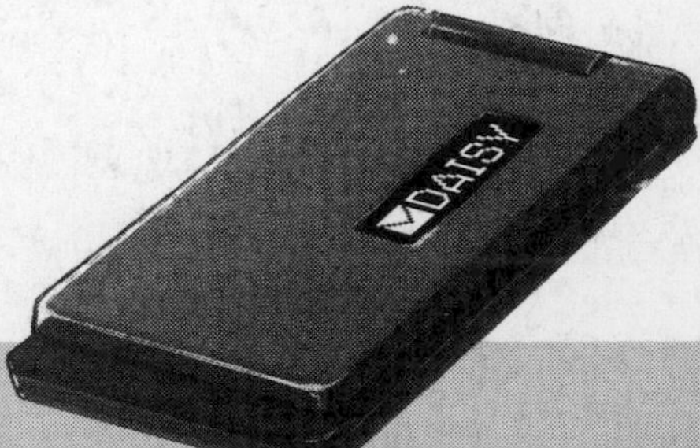

DAISY

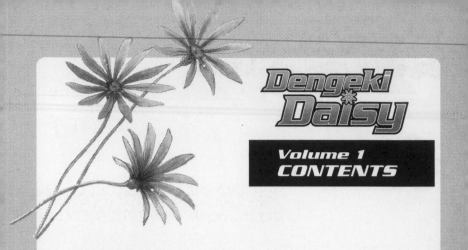

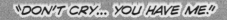
"DON'T CRY... YOU HAVE ME!"

"I'LL ALWAYS BE ON YOUR SIDE!"

"NO MATTER WHAT HAPPENS, I'LL PROTECT YOU!"

"I WILL ALWAYS—"

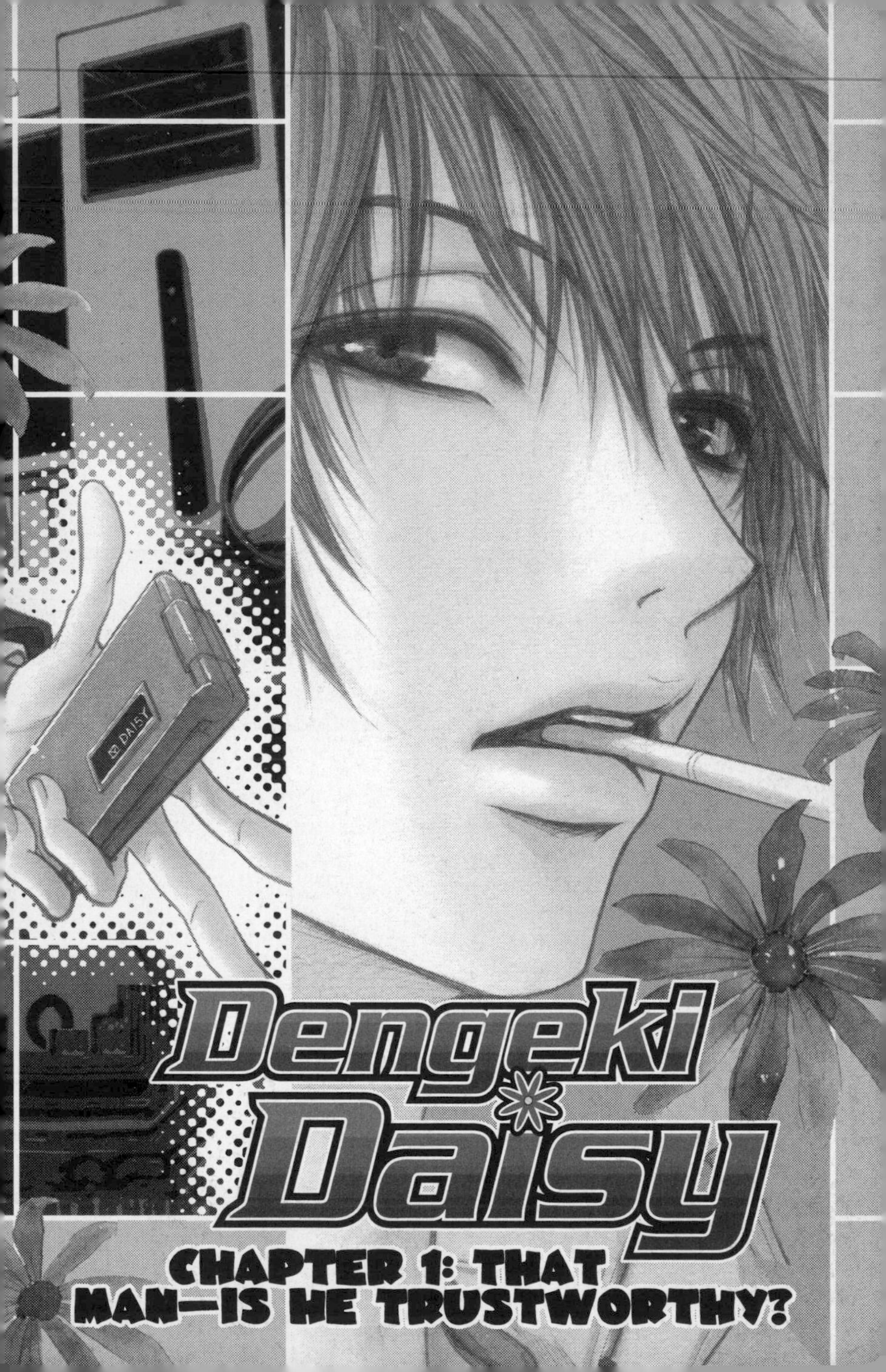
DAISY
Dengeki Daisy
CHAPTER 1: THAT MAN—IS HE TRUSTWORTHY?

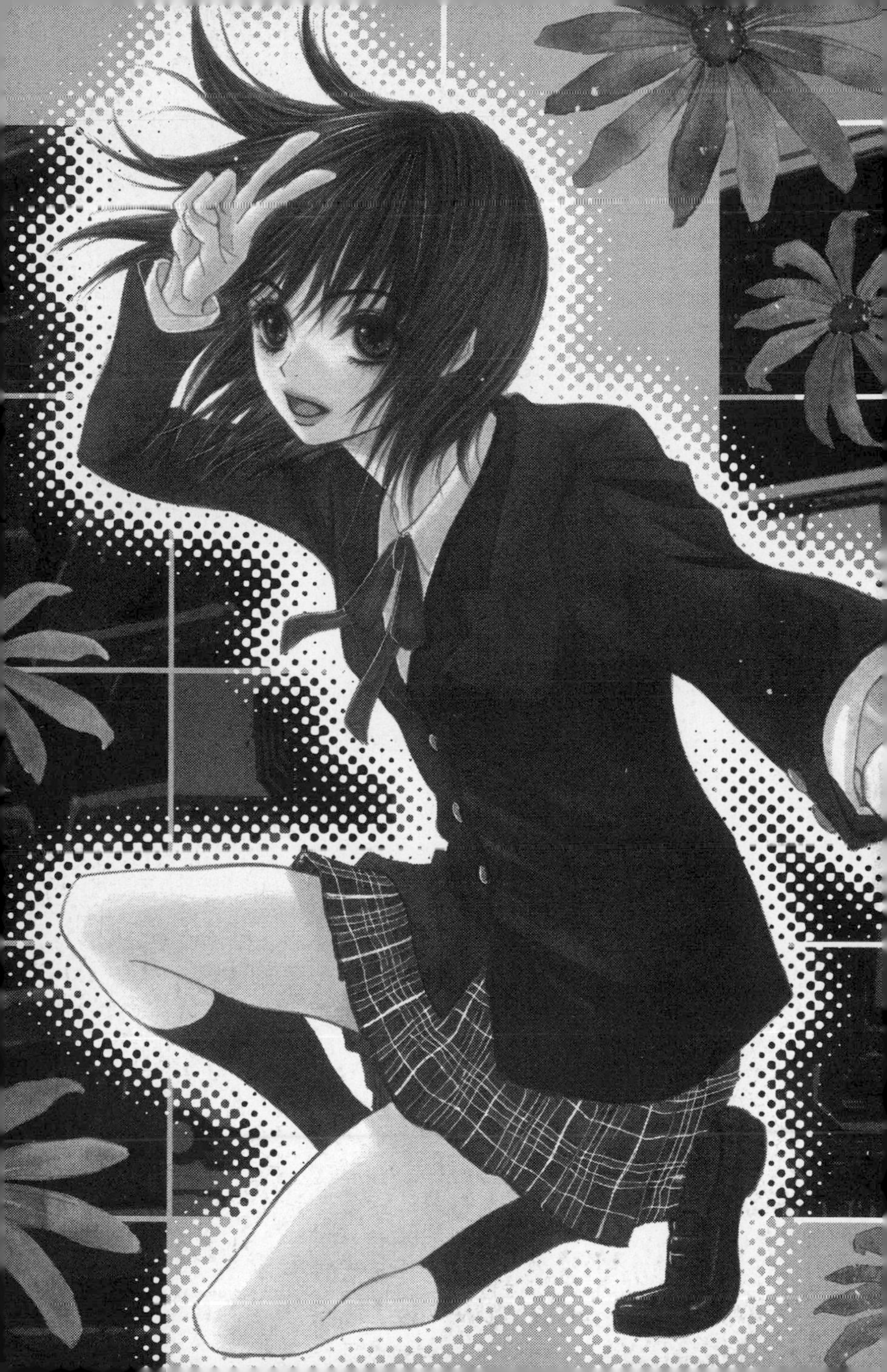

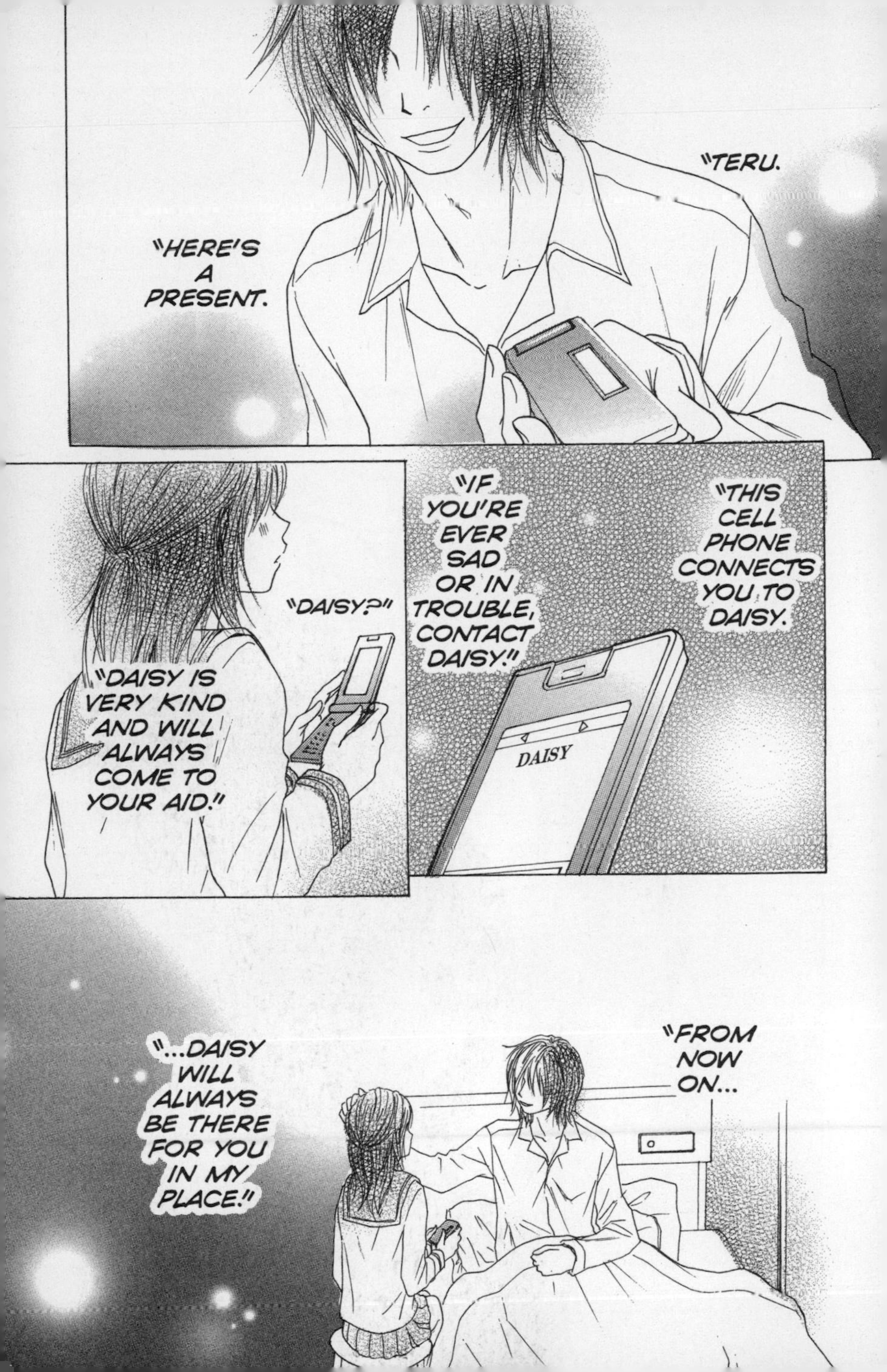
"TERU.
"HERE'S A PRESENT.
"THIS CELL PHONE CONNECTS YOU TO DAISY.
"IF YOU'RE EVER SAD OR IN TROUBLE, CONTACT DAISY!"
DAISY
"DAISY?"
"DAISY IS VERY KIND AND WILL ALWAYS COME TO YOUR AID!"
"FROM NOW ON...
"...DAISY WILL ALWAYS BE THERE FOR YOU IN MY PLACE!"

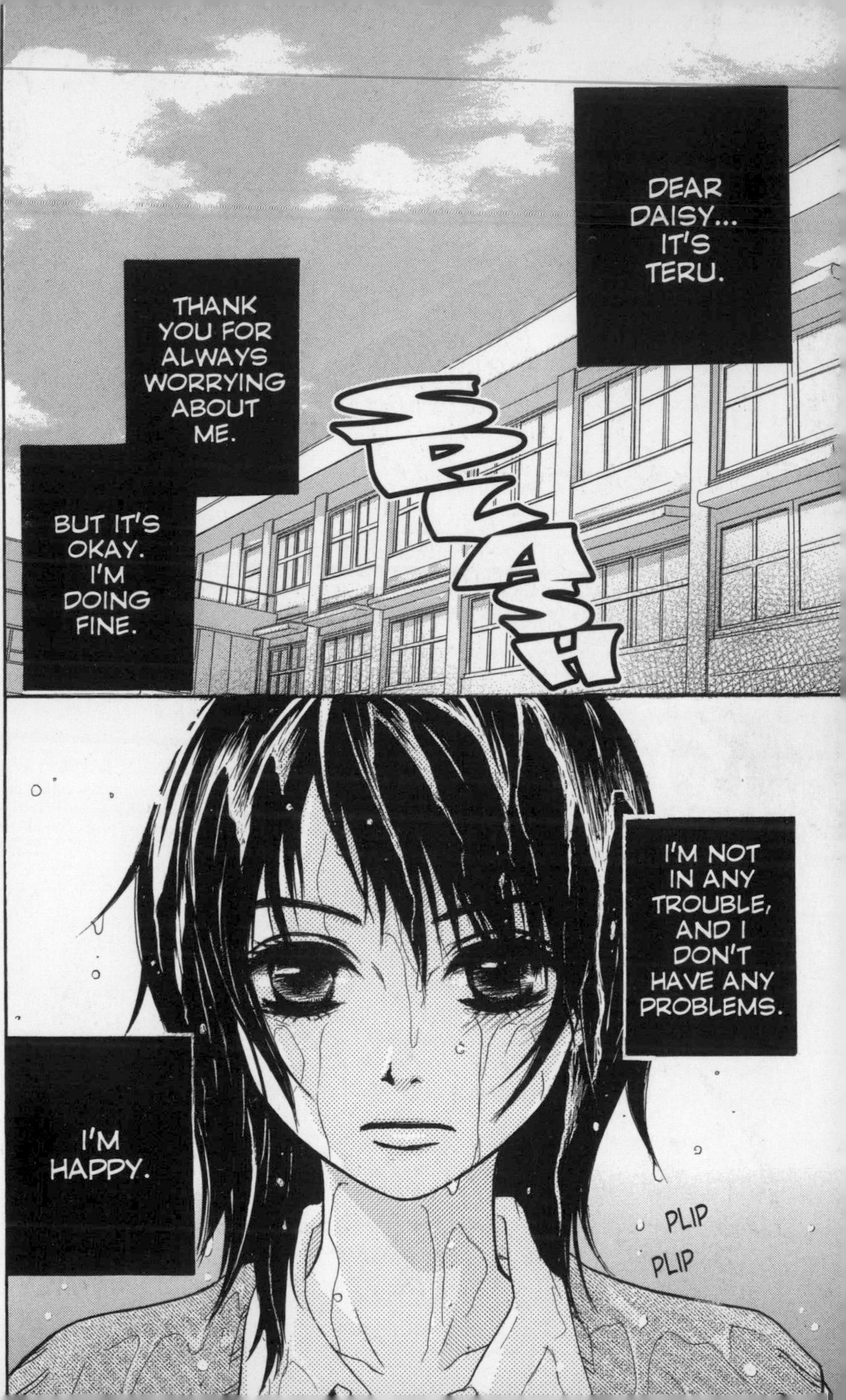
DEAR DAISY... IT'S TERU.
THANK YOU FOR ALWAYS WORRYING ABOUT ME.
BUT IT'S OKAY. I'M DOING FINE.
SPLASH
I'M NOT IN ANY TROUBLE, AND I DON'T HAVE ANY PROBLEMS.
I'M HAPPY.
PLIP
PLIP

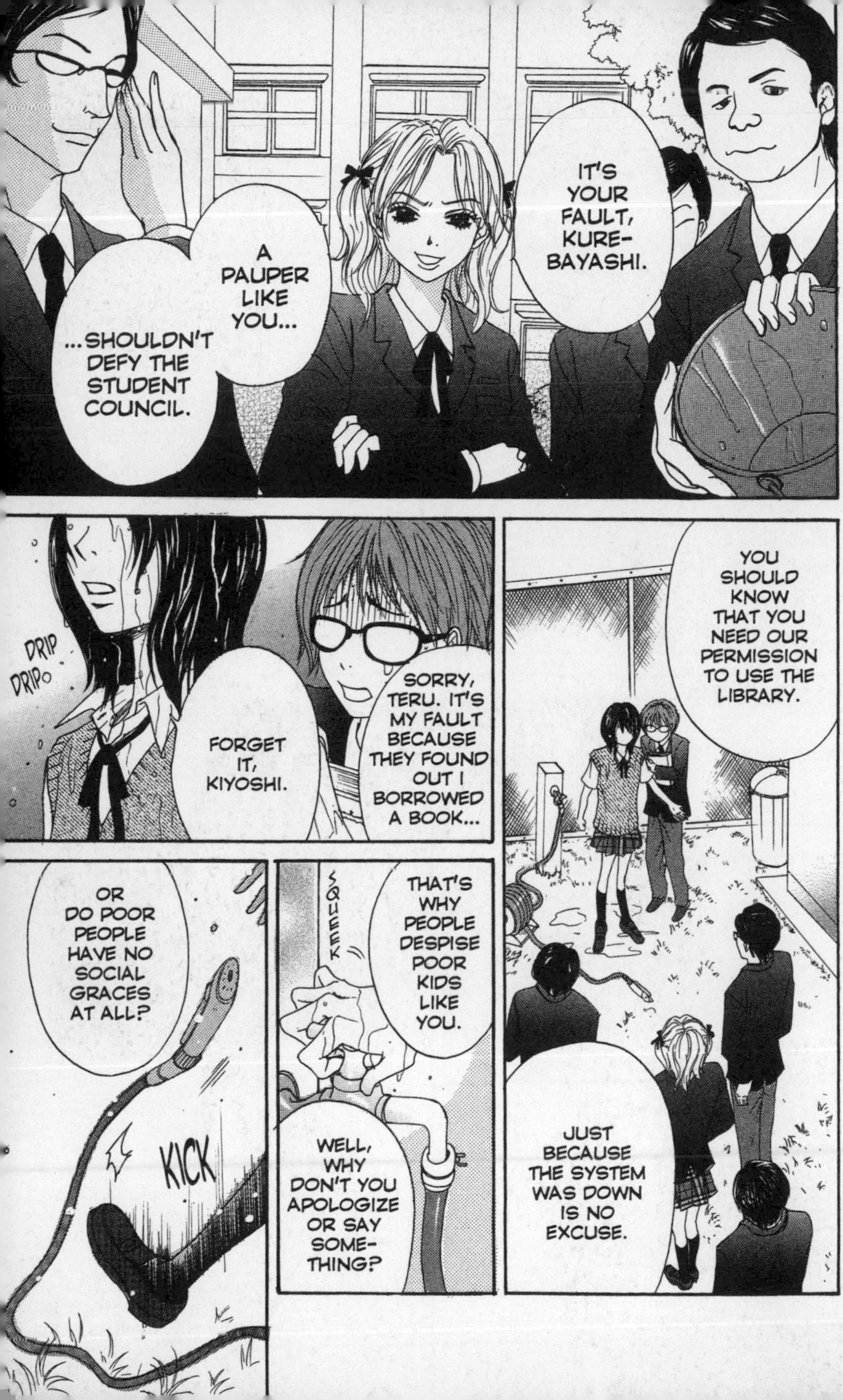
IT'S YOUR FAULT, KURE-BAYASHI.
A PAUPER LIKE YOU...
...SHOULDN'T DEFY THE STUDENT COUNCIL.
YOU SHOULD KNOW THAT YOU NEED OUR PERMISSION TO USE THE LIBRARY.
JUST BECAUSE THE SYSTEM WAS DOWN IS NO EXCUSE.
SORRY, TERU. IT'S MY FAULT BECAUSE THEY FOUND OUT I BORROWED A BOOK...
FORGET IT, KIYOSHI.
DRIP DRIP
THAT'S WHY PEOPLE DESPISE POOR KIDS LIKE YOU.
SQUEEK
WELL, WHY DON'T YOU APOLOGIZE OR SAY SOME-THING?
OR DO POOR PEOPLE HAVE NO SOCIAL GRACES AT ALL?
KICK

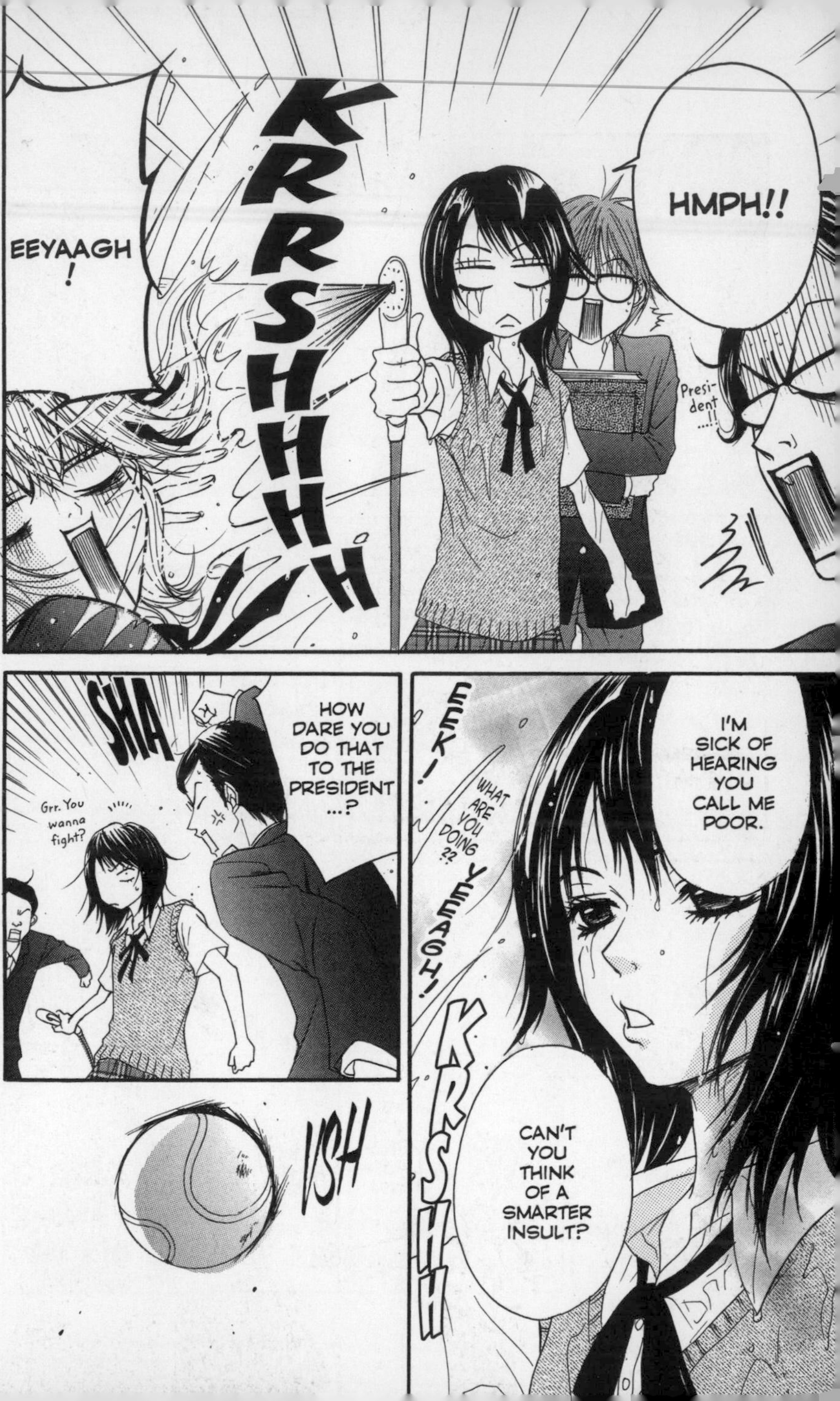
HMPH!!
President...!!
KRRSHHHHH
EEYAAGH!
I'M SICK OF HEARING YOU CALL ME POOR.
EEK!
WHAT ARE YOU DOING??
YEEAGH!
KRSHHHH
CAN'T YOU THINK OF A SMARTER INSULT?
SHA
HOW DARE YOU DO THAT TO THE PRESIDENT...?
Grr. You wanna fight?
VSH

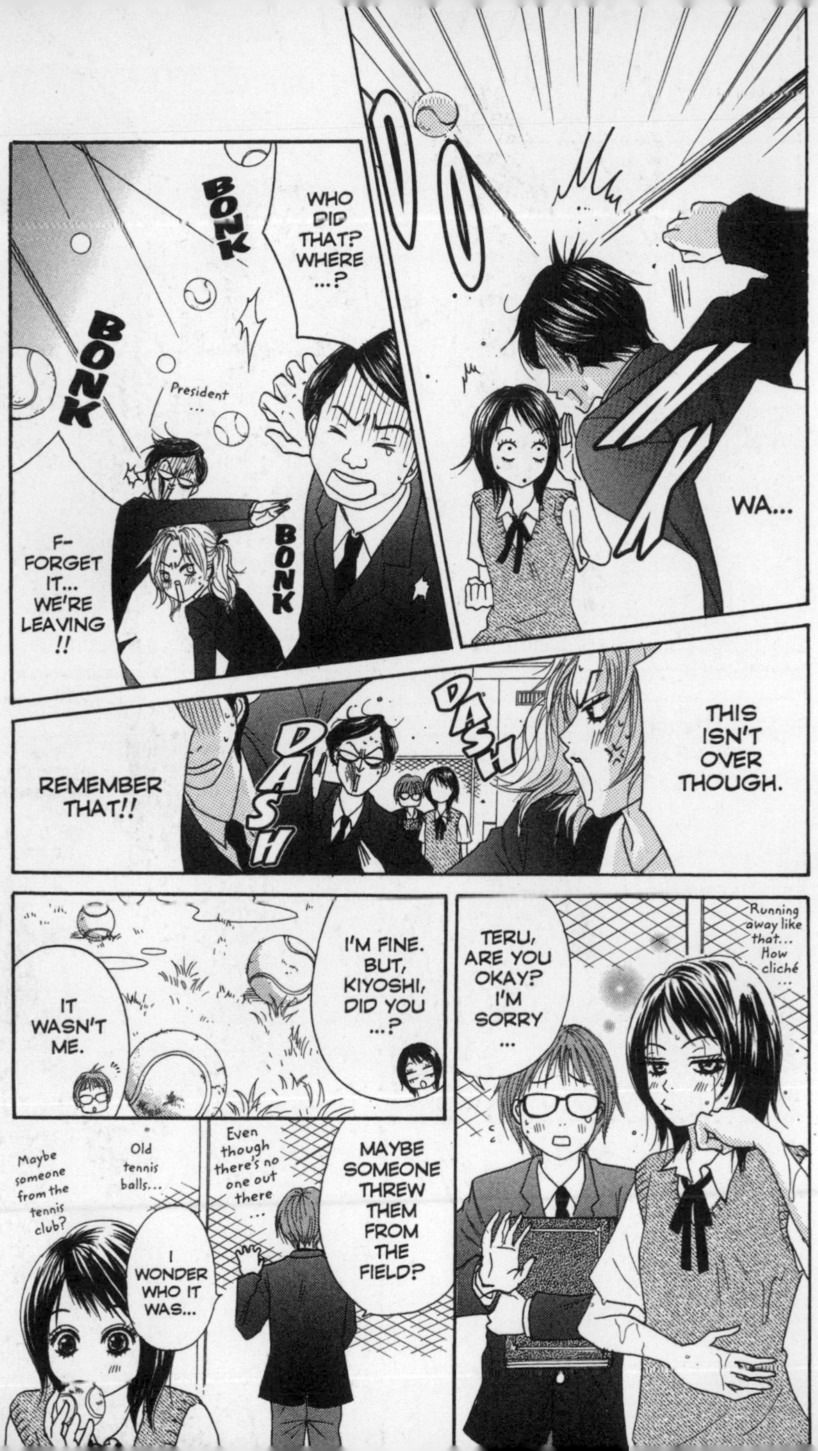
WA...
WHO DID THAT? WHERE ...?
BONK
BONK
President ...
BONK
F-FORGET IT... WE'RE LEAVING!!
THIS ISN'T OVER THOUGH.
DASH
DASH
REMEMBER THAT!!
Running away like that... How cliché ...
TERU, ARE YOU OKAY? I'M SORRY ...
I'M FINE. BUT, KIYOSHI, DID YOU ...?
IT WASN'T ME.
MAYBE SOMEONE THREW THEM FROM THE FIELD?
Even though there's no one out there ...
Old tennis balls...
I WONDER WHO IT WAS...
Maybe someone from the tennis club?

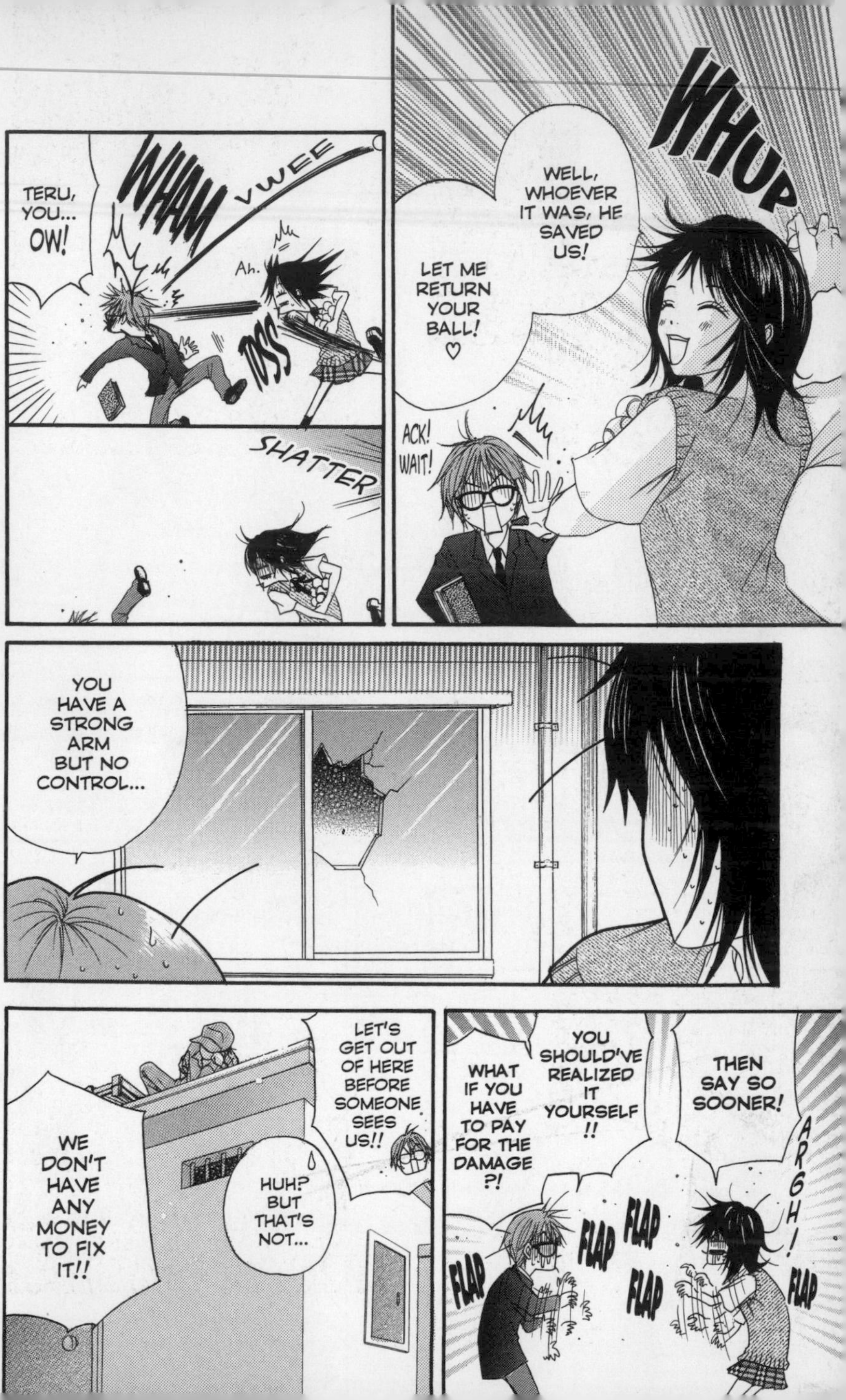
WHUP
WELL, WHOEVER IT WAS, HE SAVED US!
LET ME RETURN YOUR BALL! ♡
ACK! WAIT!
VWEE
WHAM
Ah.
TERU, YOU... OW!
TOSS
SHATTER
YOU HAVE A STRONG ARM BUT NO CONTROL...
THEN SAY SO SOONER!
ARGH!
YOU SHOULD'VE REALIZED IT YOURSELF!!
WHAT IF YOU HAVE TO PAY FOR THE DAMAGE?!
FLAP
FLAP
FLAP
FLAP
FLAP
LET'S GET OUT OF HERE BEFORE SOMEONE SEES US!!
HUH? BUT THAT'S NOT...
WE DON'T HAVE ANY MONEY TO FIX IT!!

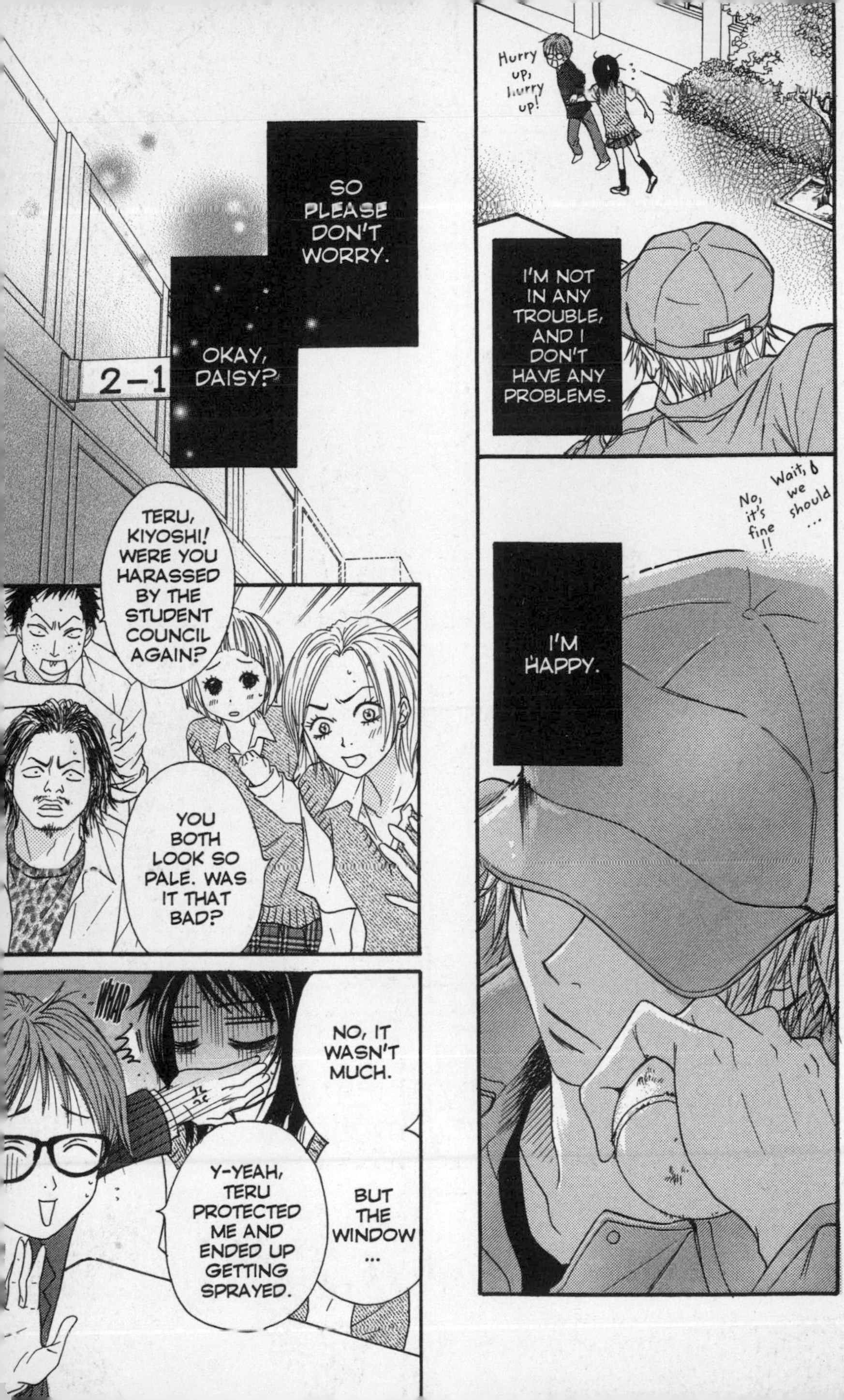
Hurry up, hurry up!
I'M NOT IN ANY TROUBLE, AND I DON'T HAVE ANY PROBLEMS.
Wait, we should...
No, it's fine!!
I'M HAPPY.
SO PLEASE DON'T WORRY.
OKAY, DAISY?
2-1
TERU, KIYOSHI! WERE YOU HARASSED BY THE STUDENT COUNCIL AGAIN?
YOU BOTH LOOK SO PALE. WAS IT THAT BAD?
WHAP
NO, IT WASN'T MUCH.
BUT THE WINDOW...
Y-YEAH, TERU PROTECTED ME AND ENDED UP GETTING SPRAYED.

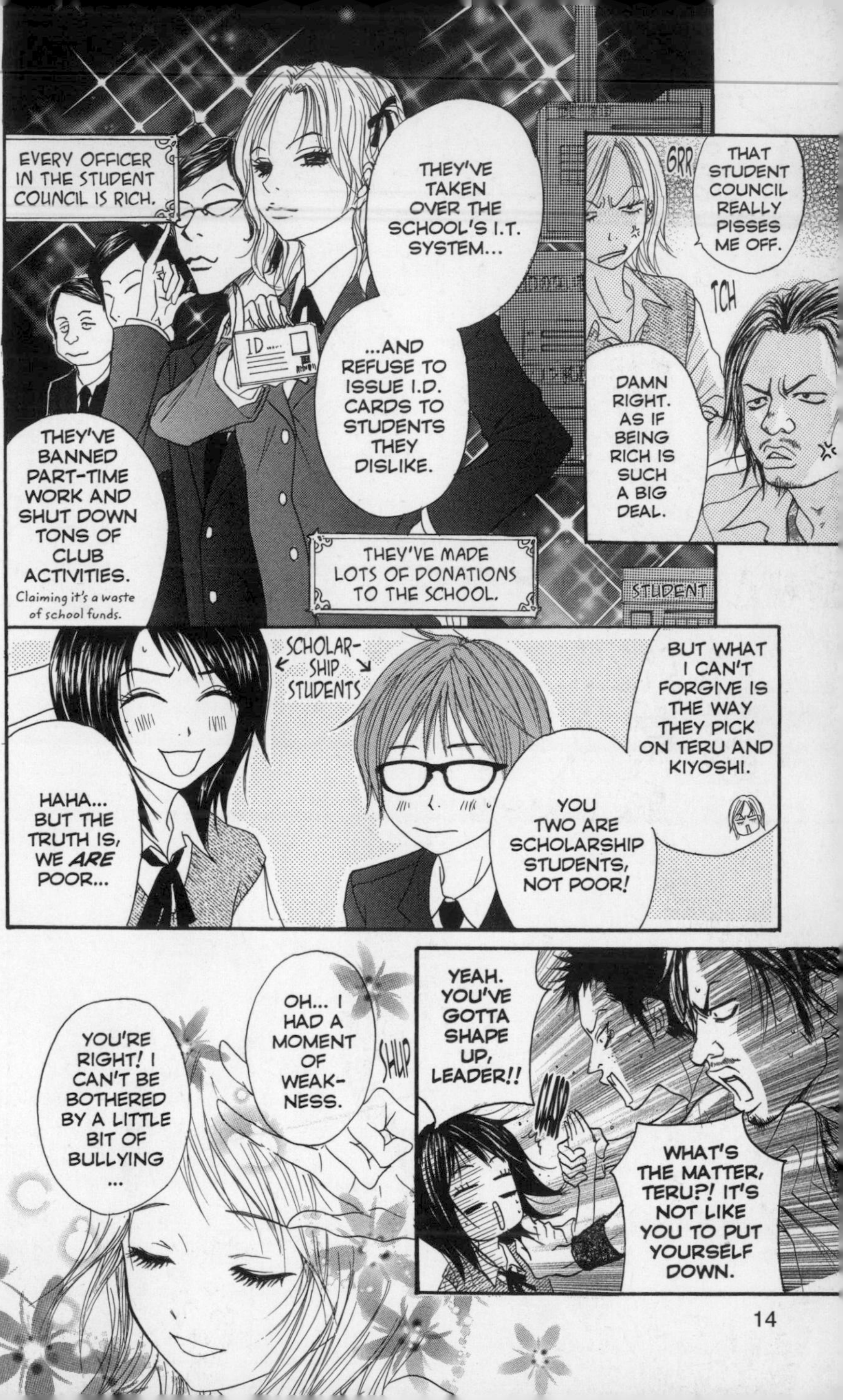
GRR
THAT STUDENT COUNCIL REALLY PISSES ME OFF.
TCH
DAMN RIGHT. AS IF BEING RICH IS SUCH A BIG DEAL.
THEY'VE TAKEN OVER THE SCHOOL'S I.T. SYSTEM...
EVERY OFFICER IN THE STUDENT COUNCIL IS RICH.
...AND REFUSE TO ISSUE I.D. CARDS TO STUDENTS THEY DISLIKE.
THEY'VE BANNED PART-TIME WORK AND SHUT DOWN TONS OF CLUB ACTIVITIES.
Claiming it's a waste of school funds.
THEY'VE MADE LOTS OF DONATIONS TO THE SCHOOL.
STUDENT
BUT WHAT I CAN'T FORGIVE IS THE WAY THEY PICK ON TERU AND KIYOSHI.
SCHOLAR-SHIP STUDENTS
YOU TWO ARE SCHOLARSHIP STUDENTS, NOT POOR!
HAHA... BUT THE TRUTH IS, WE *ARE* POOR...
YEAH. YOU'VE GOTTA SHAPE UP, LEADER!!
WHAT'S THE MATTER, TERU?! IT'S NOT LIKE YOU TO PUT YOURSELF DOWN.
OH... I HAD A MOMENT OF WEAK-NESS.
SHUP
YOU'RE RIGHT! I CAN'T BE BOTHERED BY A LITTLE BIT OF BULLYING ...

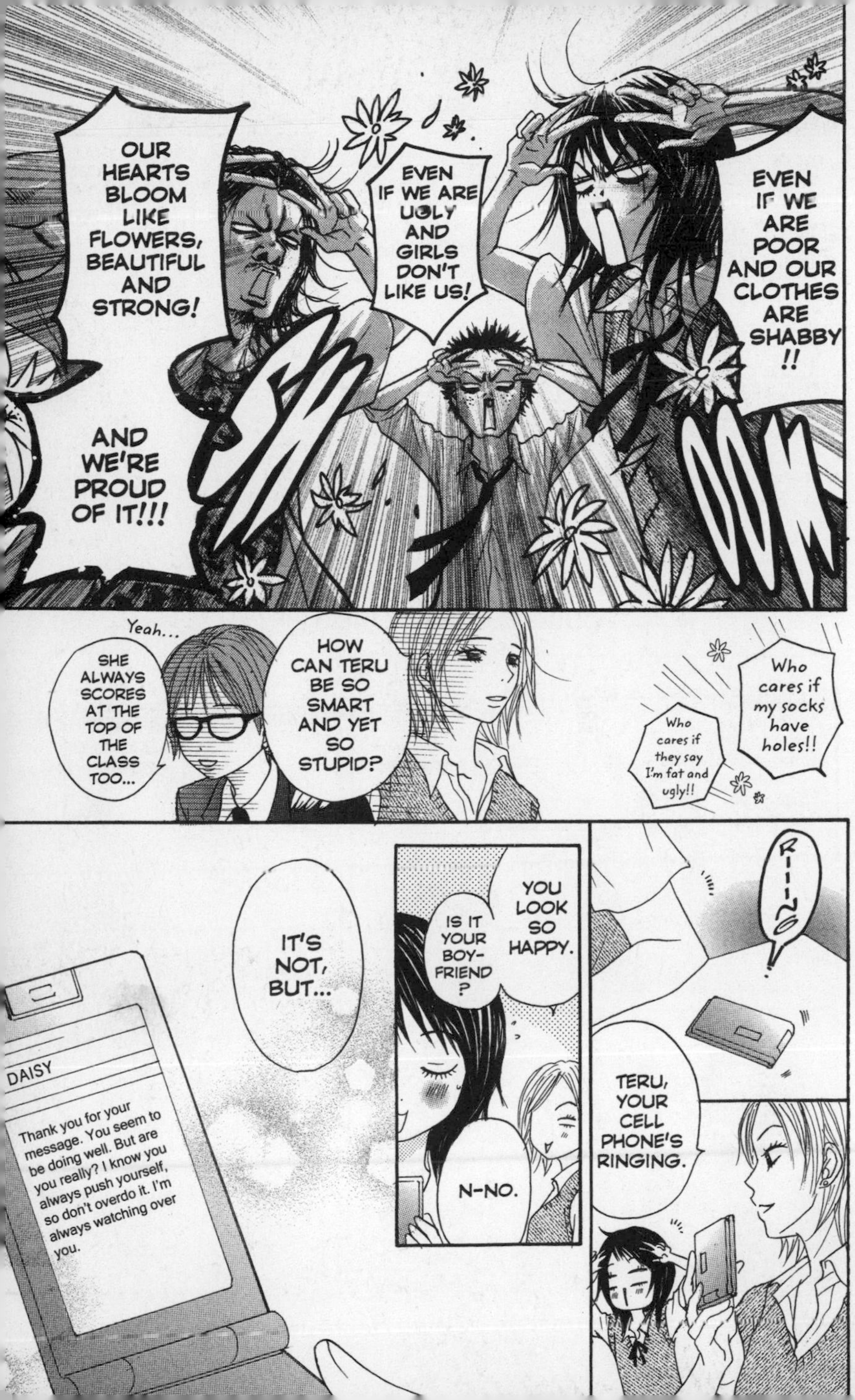
EVEN IF WE ARE POOR AND OUR CLOTHES ARE SHABBY!!
EVEN IF WE ARE UGLY AND GIRLS DON'T LIKE US!
OUR HEARTS BLOOM LIKE FLOWERS, BEAUTIFUL AND STRONG!
AND WE'RE PROUD OF IT!!!
Who cares if my socks have holes!!
Who cares if they say I'm fat and ugly!!
HOW CAN TERU BE SO SMART AND YET SO STUPID?
SHE ALWAYS SCORES AT THE TOP OF THE CLASS TOO...
Yeah...
RIIING!
TERU, YOUR CELL PHONE'S RINGING.
YOU LOOK SO HAPPY.
IS IT YOUR BOY-FRIEND?
N-NO.
IT'S NOT, BUT...
DAISY
Thank you for your message. You seem to be doing well. But are you really? I know you always push yourself, so don't overdo it. I'm always watching over you.

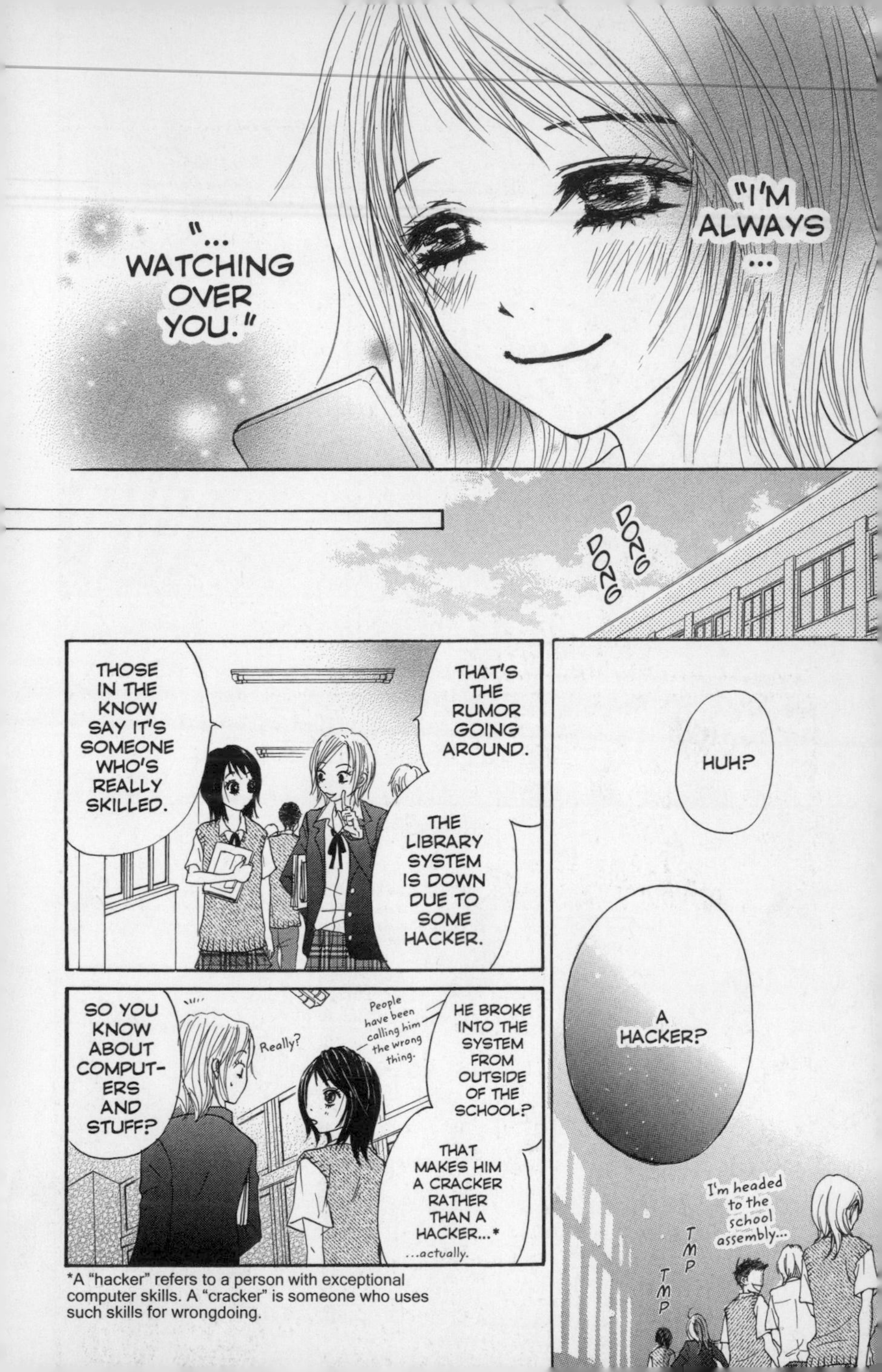
"I'M ALWAYS ...
"... WATCHING OVER YOU."
DONG DONG
HUH?
A HACKER?
I'm headed to the school assembly...
TMP TMP
THAT'S THE RUMOR GOING AROUND.
THE LIBRARY SYSTEM IS DOWN DUE TO SOME HACKER.
THOSE IN THE KNOW SAY IT'S SOMEONE WHO'S REALLY SKILLED.
HE BROKE INTO THE SYSTEM FROM OUTSIDE OF THE SCHOOL?
People have been calling him the wrong thing.
THAT MAKES HIM A CRACKER RATHER THAN A HACKER...*
...actually.
Really?
SO YOU KNOW ABOUT COMPUTERS AND STUFF?

*A "hacker" refers to a person with exceptional computer skills. A "cracker" is someone who uses such skills for wrongdoing.

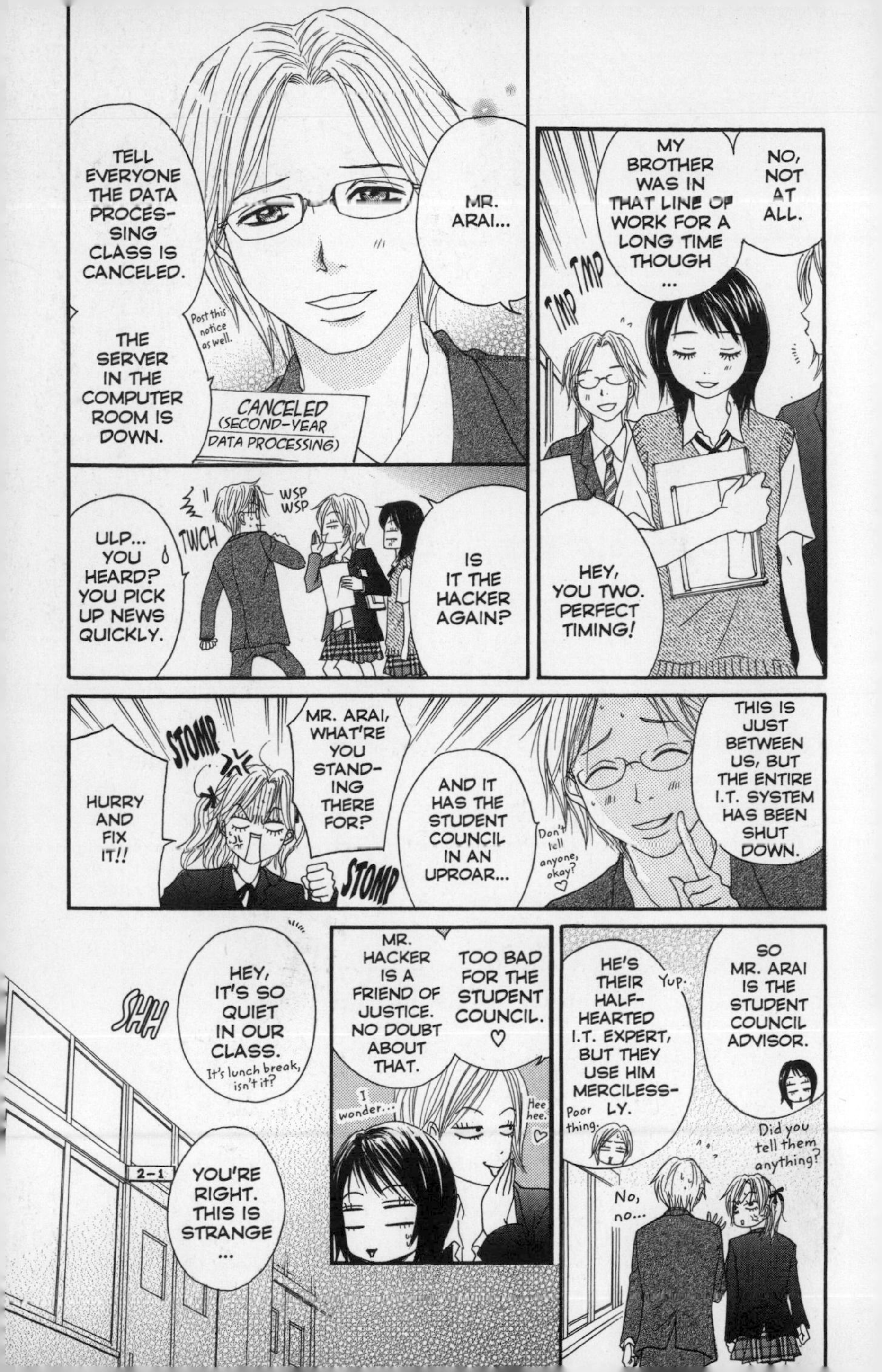
NO, NOT AT ALL.
MY BROTHER WAS IN THAT LINE OF WORK FOR A LONG TIME THOUGH ...
TMP TMP
HEY, YOU TWO. PERFECT TIMING!
MR. ARAI...
TELL EVERYONE THE DATA PROCES-SING CLASS IS CANCELED.
Post this notice as well.
THE SERVER IN THE COMPUTER ROOM IS DOWN.
CANCELED (SECOND-YEAR DATA PROCESSING)
IS IT THE HACKER AGAIN?
WSP WSP
TWCH
ULP... YOU HEARD? YOU PICK UP NEWS QUICKLY.
THIS IS JUST BETWEEN US, BUT THE ENTIRE I.T. SYSTEM HAS BEEN SHUT DOWN.
Don't tell anyone, okay? ♡
AND IT HAS THE STUDENT COUNCIL IN AN UPROAR...
MR. ARAI, WHAT'RE YOU STANDING THERE FOR?
STOMP
STOMP
HURRY AND FIX IT!!
SO MR. ARAI IS THE STUDENT COUNCIL ADVISOR.
Yup.
HE'S THEIR HALF-HEARTED I.T. EXPERT, BUT THEY USE HIM MERCILESS-LY.
Poor thing.
Did you tell them anything?
No, no...
TOO BAD FOR THE STUDENT COUNCIL. ♡
MR. HACKER IS A FRIEND OF JUSTICE. NO DOUBT ABOUT THAT.
Hee hee. ♡
I wonder...
HEY, IT'S SO QUIET IN OUR CLASS.
It's lunch break, isn't it?
SHH
2-1
YOU'RE RIGHT. THIS IS STRANGE ...

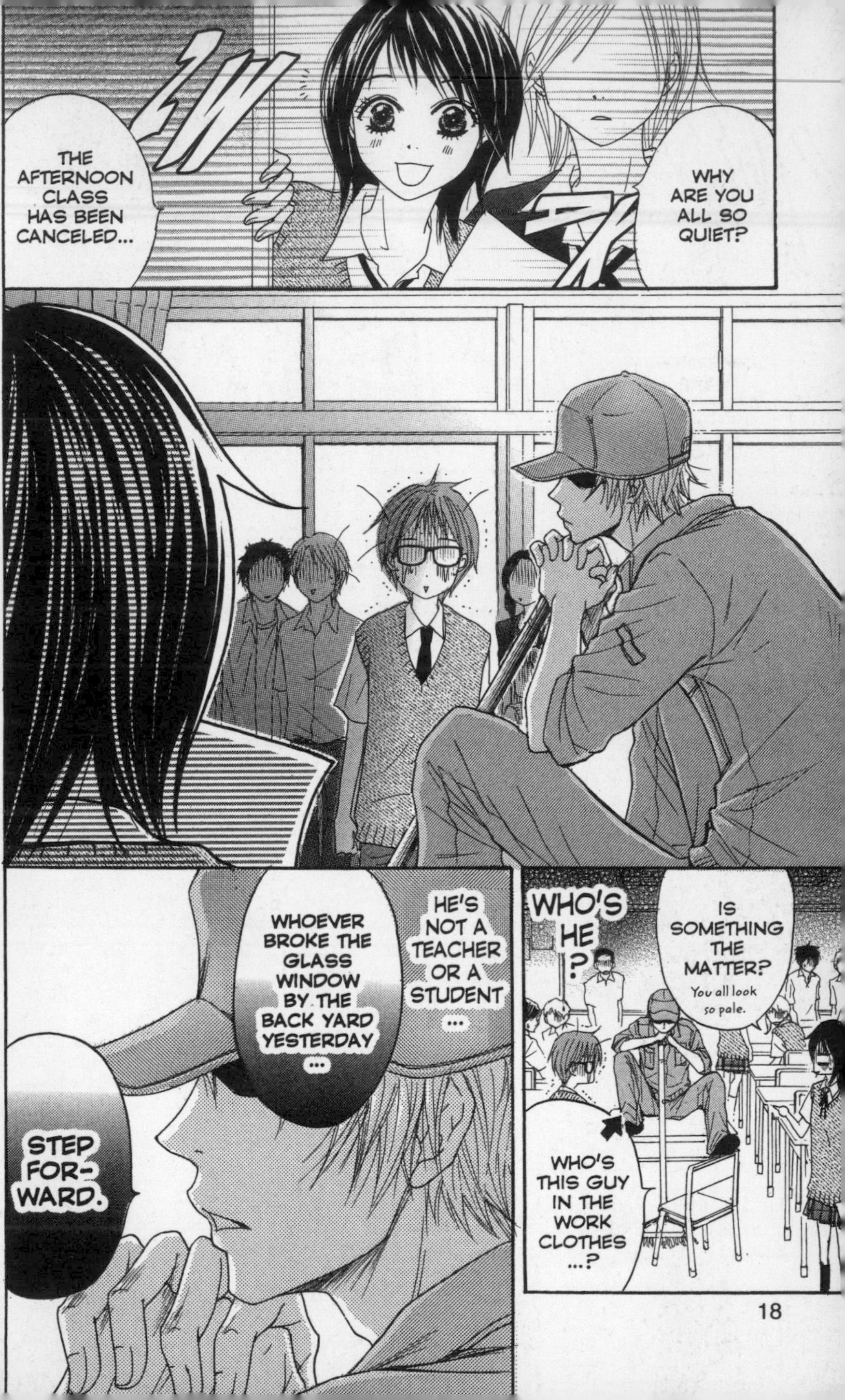
WHY ARE YOU ALL SO QUIET?
THE AFTERNOON CLASS HAS BEEN CANCELED...
IS SOMETHING THE MATTER?
You all look so pale.
WHO'S HE?
WHO'S THIS GUY IN THE WORK CLOTHES...?
HE'S NOT A TEACHER OR A STUDENT...
WHOEVER BROKE THE GLASS WINDOW BY THE BACK YARD YESTERDAY...
STEP FOR-WARD.

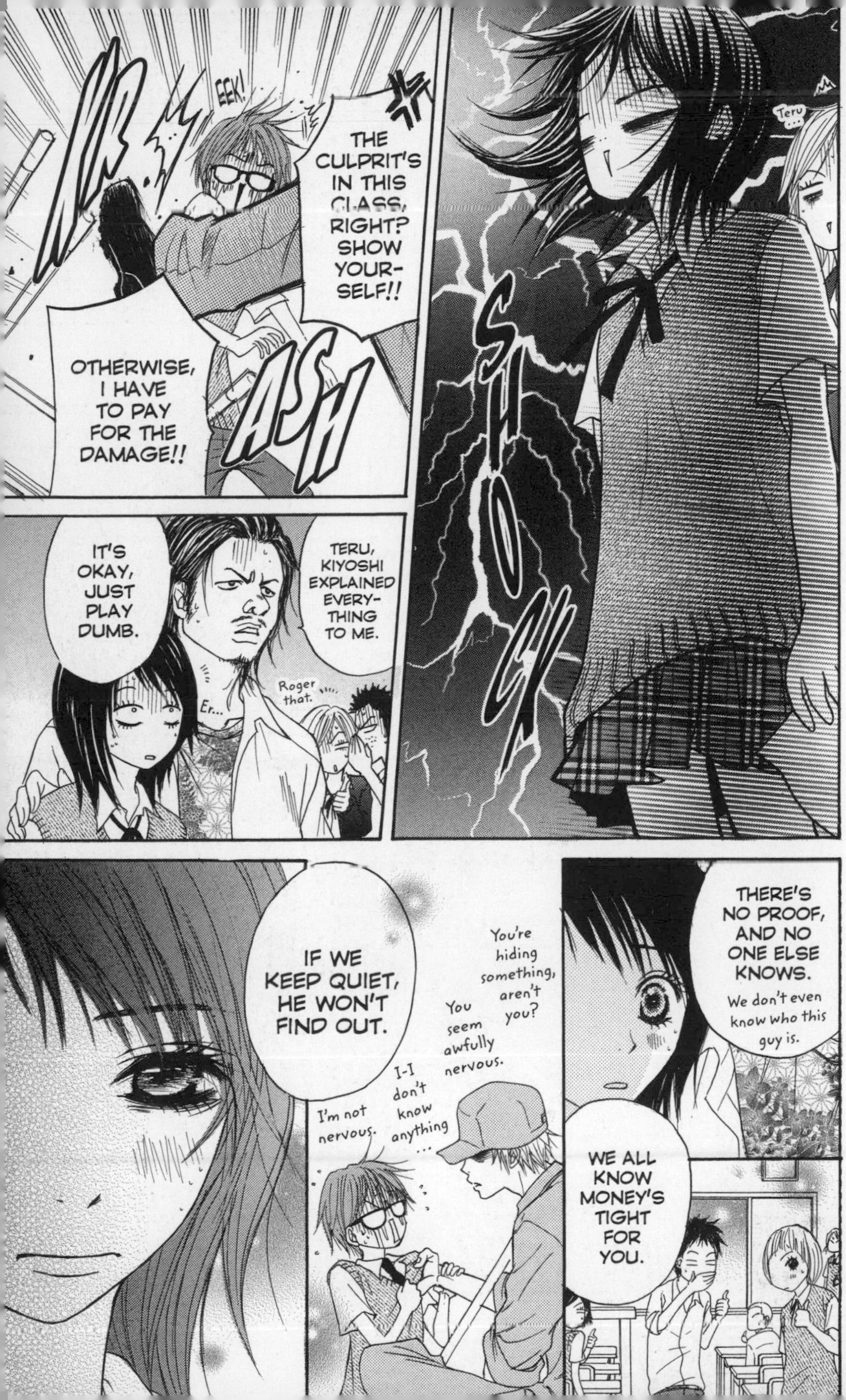
Teru...
SHOCK
EEK!
THE CULPRIT'S IN THIS CLASS, RIGHT? SHOW YOURSELF!!
ASH
OTHERWISE, I HAVE TO PAY FOR THE DAMAGE!!
TERU, KIYOSHI EXPLAINED EVERYTHING TO ME.
Roger that.
IT'S OKAY, JUST PLAY DUMB.
Er...
THERE'S NO PROOF, AND NO ONE ELSE KNOWS.
We don't even know who this guy is.
WE ALL KNOW MONEY'S TIGHT FOR YOU.
You're hiding something, aren't you?
You seem awfully nervous.
I-I don't know anything...
I'm not nervous.
IF WE KEEP QUIET, HE WON'T FIND OUT.

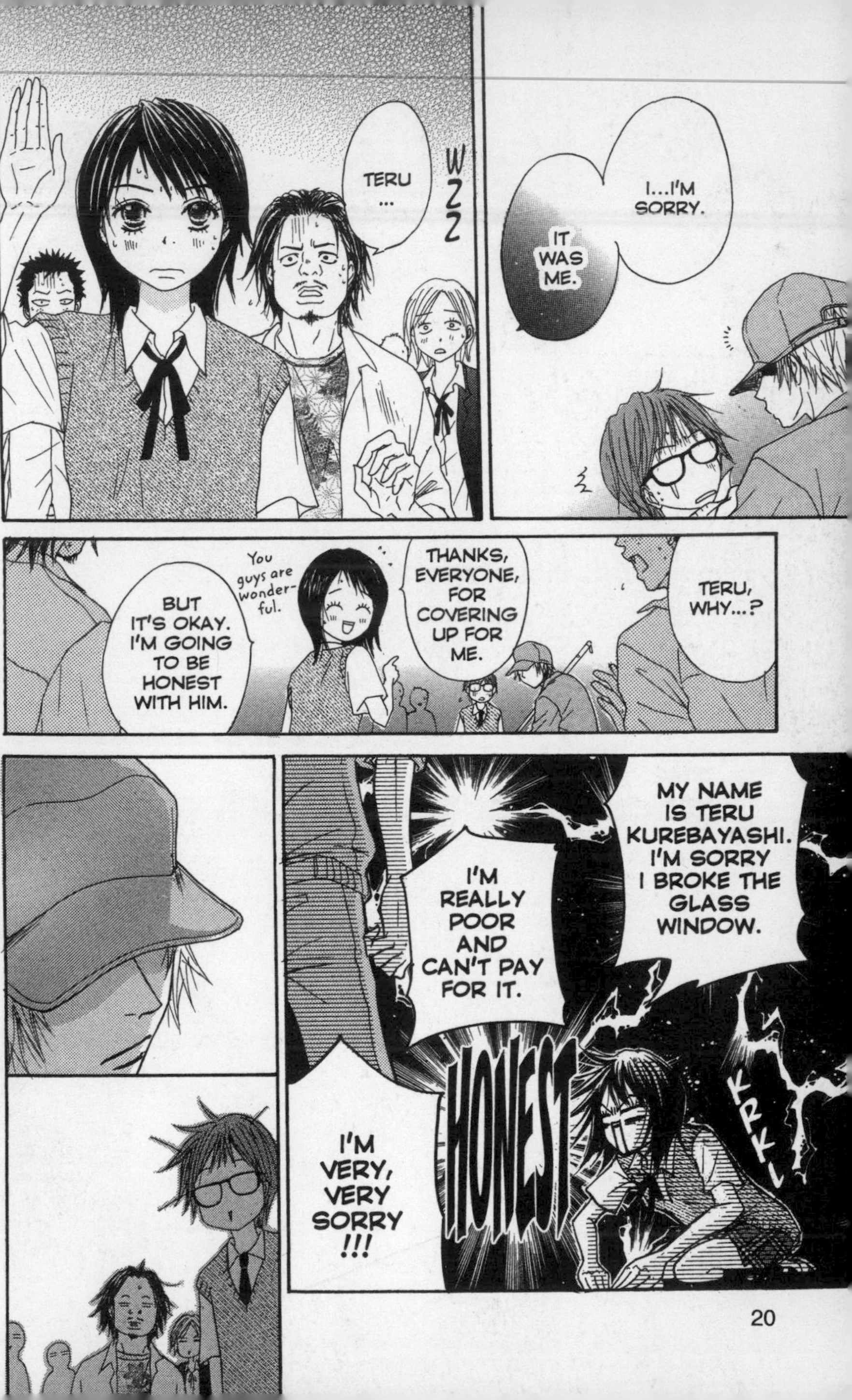
I...I'M SORRY.
IT WAS ME.
TERU ...
WZZ
TERU, WHY...?
THANKS, EVERYONE, FOR COVERING UP FOR ME.
You guys are wonderful.
BUT IT'S OKAY. I'M GOING TO BE HONEST WITH HIM.
MY NAME IS TERU KUREBAYASHI. I'M SORRY I BROKE THE GLASS WINDOW.
I'M REALLY POOR AND CAN'T PAY FOR IT.
KRK
HONEST
I'M VERY, VERY SORRY!!!

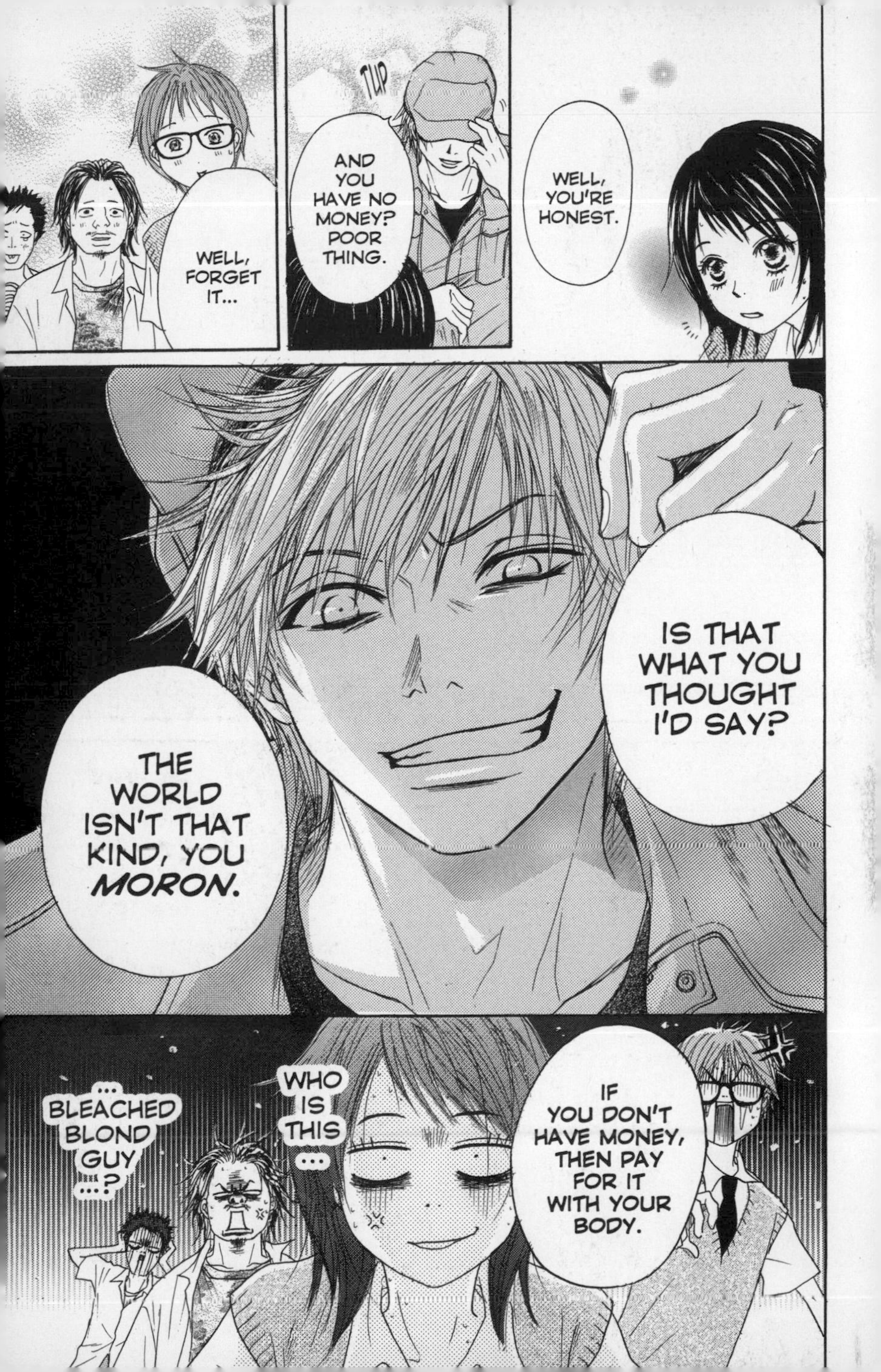
WELL, YOU'RE HONEST.
TUP
AND YOU HAVE NO MONEY? POOR THING.
WELL, FORGET IT...
IS THAT WHAT YOU THOUGHT I'D SAY?
THE WORLD ISN'T THAT KIND, YOU *MORON*.
IF YOU DON'T HAVE MONEY, THEN PAY FOR IT WITH YOUR BODY.
WHO IS THIS ...
... BLEACHED BLOND GUY ...?

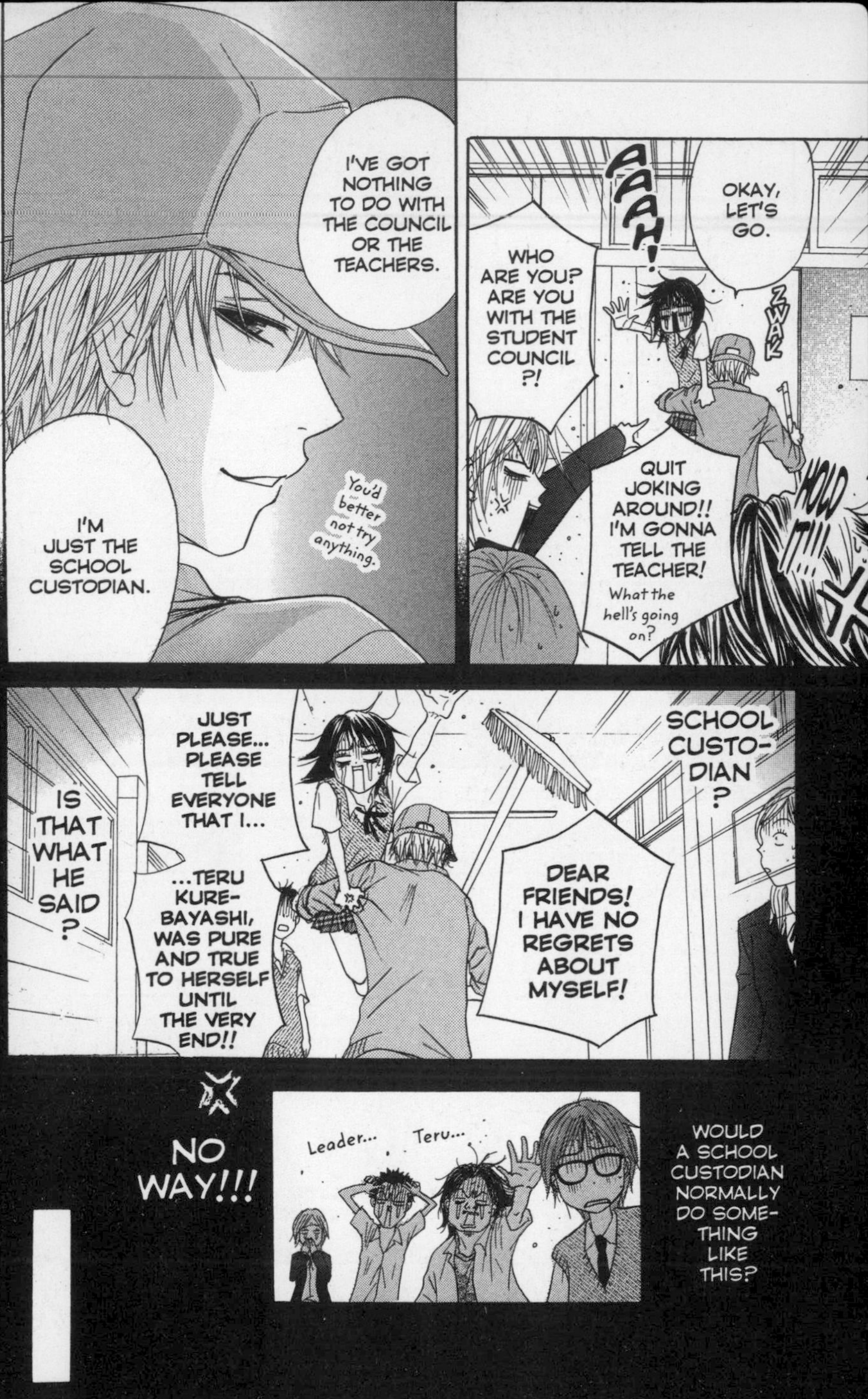
OKAY, LET'S GO.
AAAH!
ZWAK
WHO ARE YOU? ARE YOU WITH THE STUDENT COUNCIL ?!
HOLD IT!!
QUIT JOKING AROUND!! I'M GONNA TELL THE TEACHER!
What the hell's going on?
I'VE GOT NOTHING TO DO WITH THE COUNCIL OR THE TEACHERS.
You'd better not try anything.
I'M JUST THE SCHOOL CUSTODIAN.
SCHOOL CUSTO-DIAN ?
DEAR FRIENDS! I HAVE NO REGRETS ABOUT MYSELF!
JUST PLEASE... PLEASE TELL EVERYONE THAT I...
...TERU KURE-BAYASHI, WAS PURE AND TRUE TO HERSELF UNTIL THE VERY END!!
IS THAT WHAT HE SAID ?
WOULD A SCHOOL CUSTODIAN NORMALLY DO SOME-THING LIKE THIS?
Teru...
Leader...
NO WAY!!!

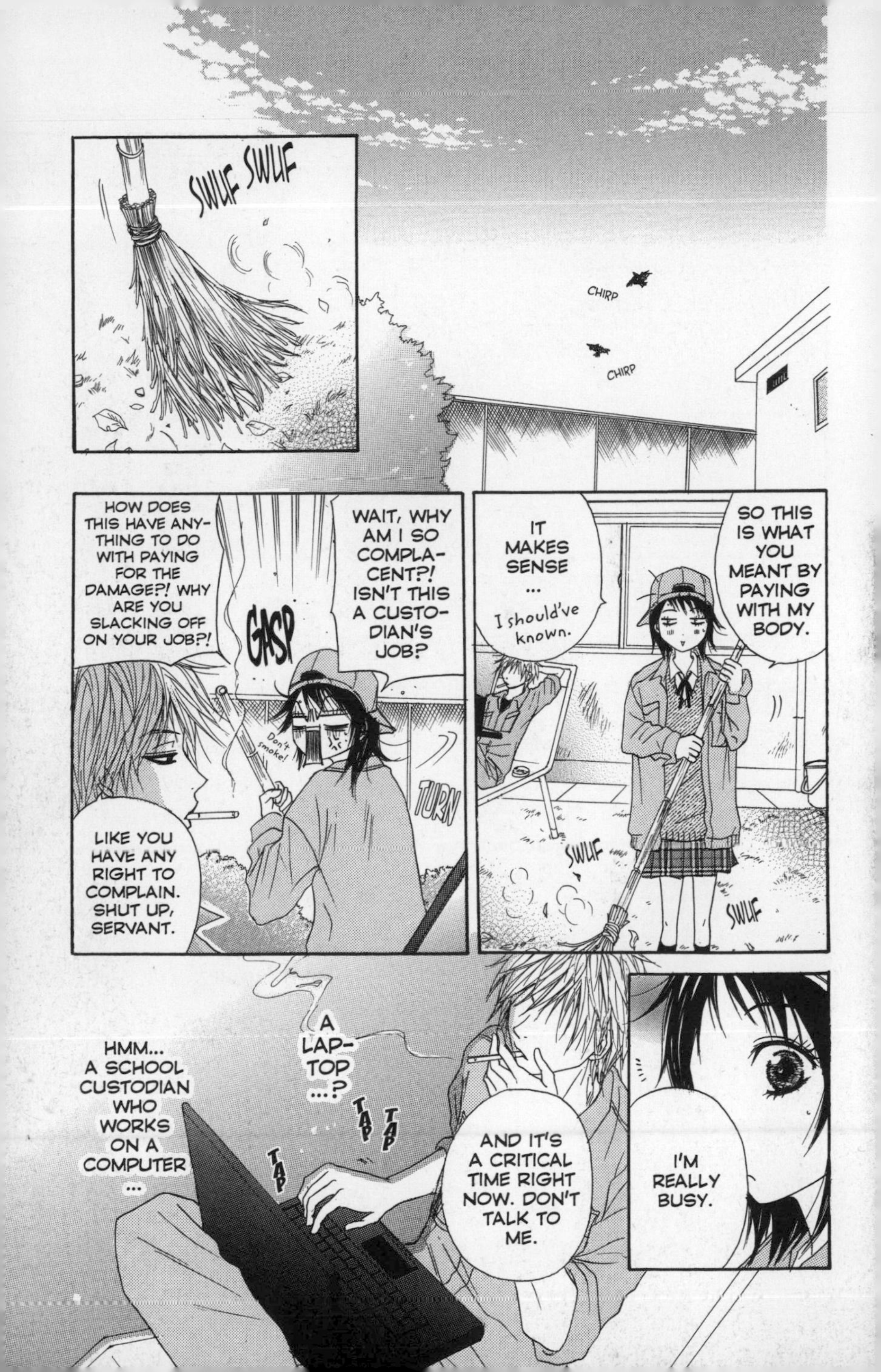
SWUF SWUF
CHIRP
CHIRP
SO THIS IS WHAT YOU MEANT BY PAYING WITH MY BODY.
IT MAKES SENSE ...
I should've known.
SWUF
SWUF
WAIT, WHY AM I SO COMPLACENT?! ISN'T THIS A CUSTODIAN'S JOB?
GASP
HOW DOES THIS HAVE ANYTHING TO DO WITH PAYING FOR THE DAMAGE?! WHY ARE YOU SLACKING OFF ON YOUR JOB?!
TURN
Don't smoke!
LIKE YOU HAVE ANY RIGHT TO COMPLAIN. SHUT UP, SERVANT.
I'M REALLY BUSY.
AND IT'S A CRITICAL TIME RIGHT NOW. DON'T TALK TO ME.
A LAPTOP ...?
TAP TAP
HMM... A SCHOOL CUSTODIAN WHO WORKS ON A COMPUTER ...
TAP

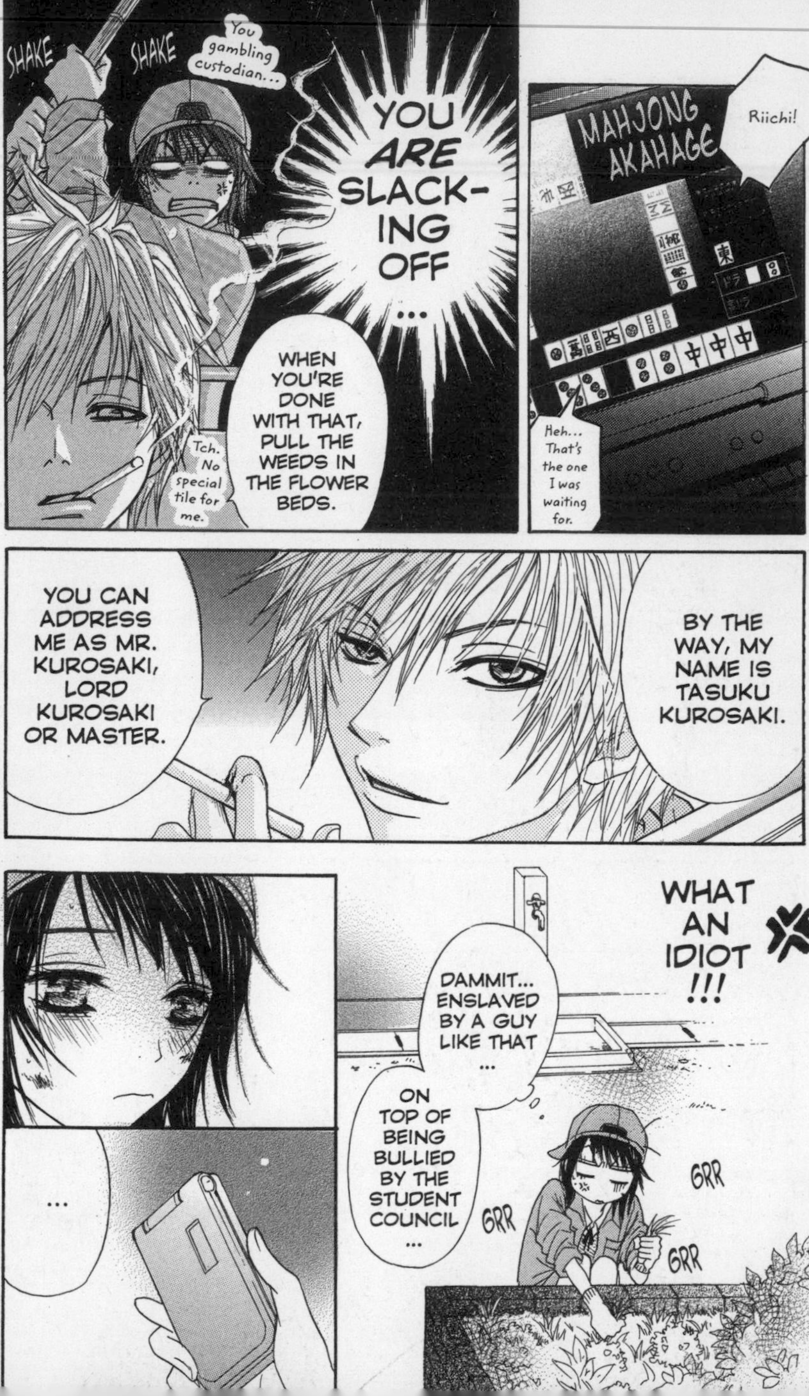
MAHJONG AKAHAGE
Riichi!
Heh... That's the one I was waiting for.
YOU ARE SLACKING-ING OFF...
You gambling custodian...
SHAKE
SHAKE
WHEN YOU'RE DONE WITH THAT, PULL THE WEEDS IN THE FLOWER BEDS.
Tch. No special tile for me.
BY THE WAY, MY NAME IS TASUKU KUROSAKI.
YOU CAN ADDRESS ME AS MR. KUROSAKI, LORD KUROSAKI OR MASTER.
WHAT AN IDIOT!!!
DAMMIT... ENSLAVED BY A GUY LIKE THAT...
ON TOP OF BEING BULLIED BY THE STUDENT COUNCIL...
GRR
GRR
GRR
...

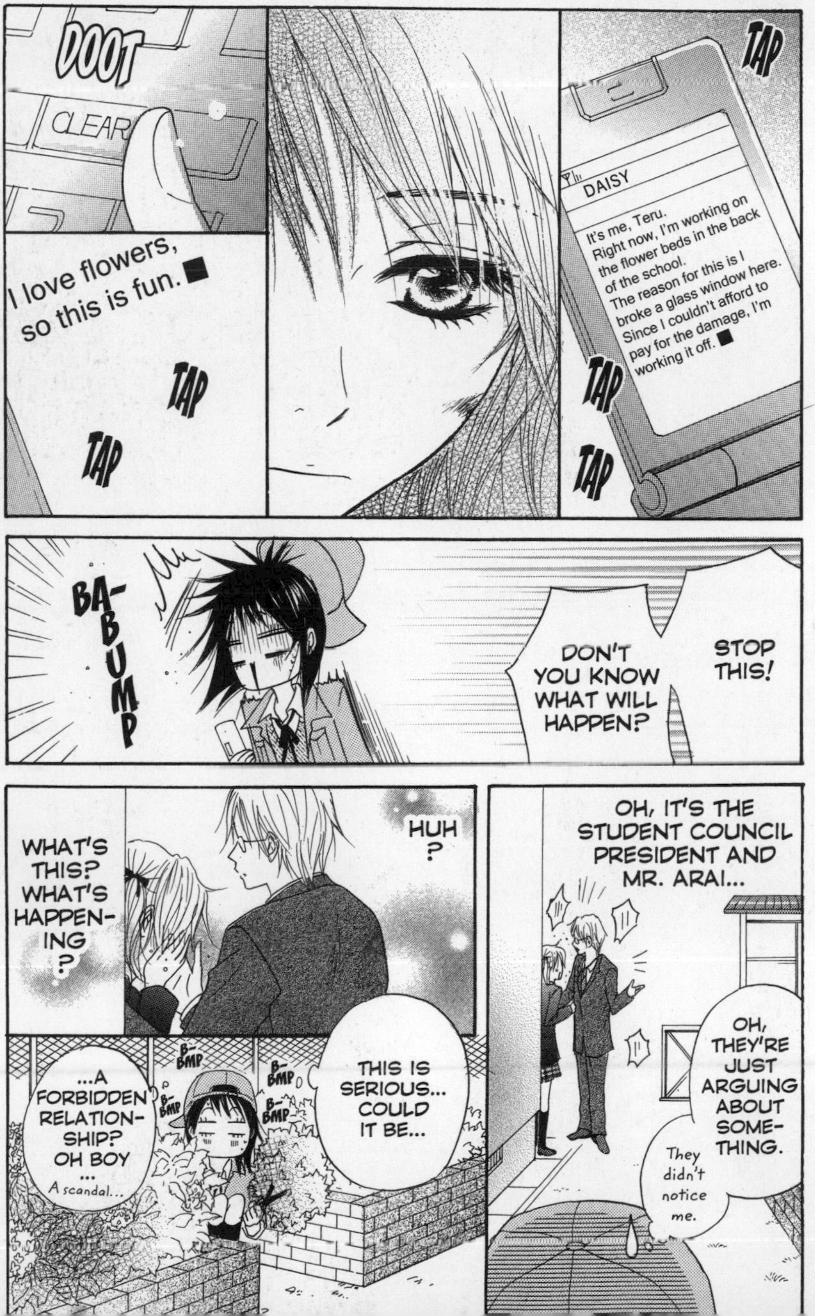
TAP
DAISY
It's me, Teru.
Right now, I'm working on the flower beds in the back of the school.
The reason for this is I broke a glass window here.
Since I couldn't afford to pay for the damage, I'm working it off. ■
TAP
TAP
DOOT
CLEAR
I love flowers, so this is fun. ■
TAP
TAP
STOP THIS!
DON'T YOU KNOW WHAT WILL HAPPEN?
BA-BUMP
OH, IT'S THE STUDENT COUNCIL PRESIDENT AND MR. ARAI...
OH, THEY'RE JUST ARGUING ABOUT SOMETHING.
They didn't notice me.
HUH?
WHAT'S THIS? WHAT'S HAPPENING?
THIS IS SERIOUS... COULD IT BE...
B-BMP
B-BMP
B-BMP
B-BMP
...A FORBIDDEN RELATIONSHIP? OH BOY...
A scandal...

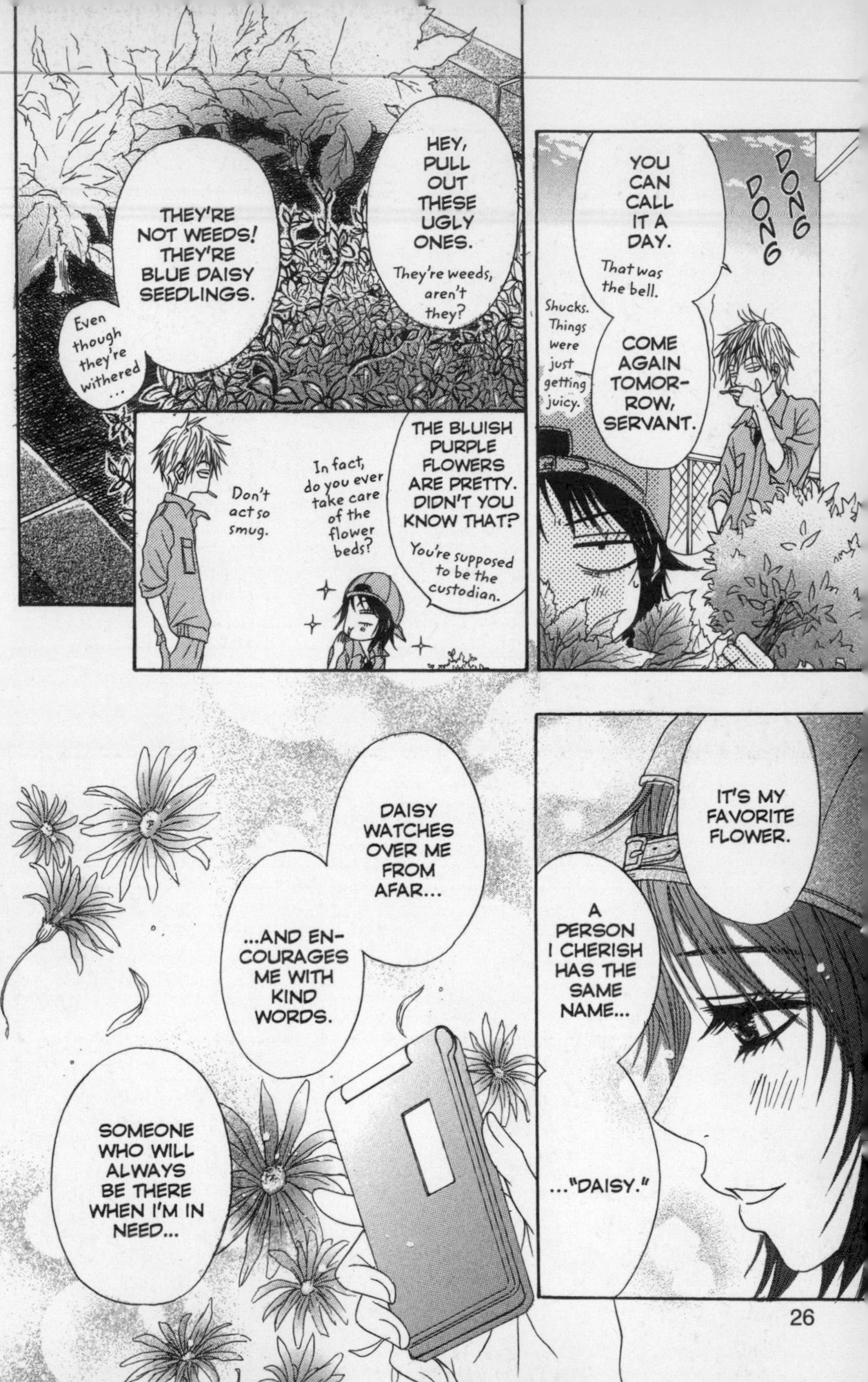
HEY, PULL OUT THESE UGLY ONES.
They're weeds, aren't they?
THEY'RE NOT WEEDS! THEY'RE BLUE DAISY SEEDLINGS.
Even though they're withered...
THE BLUISH PURPLE FLOWERS ARE PRETTY. DIDN'T YOU KNOW THAT?
You're supposed to be the custodian.
In fact, do you ever take care of the flower beds?
Don't act so smug.
DONG DONG
YOU CAN CALL IT A DAY.
That was the bell.
COME AGAIN TOMORROW, SERVANT.
Shucks. Things were just getting juicy.
IT'S MY FAVORITE FLOWER.
A PERSON I CHERISH HAS THE SAME NAME...
..."DAISY."
DAISY WATCHES OVER ME FROM AFAR...
...AND ENCOURAGES ME WITH KIND WORDS.
SOMEONE WHO WILL ALWAYS BE THERE WHEN I'M IN NEED...

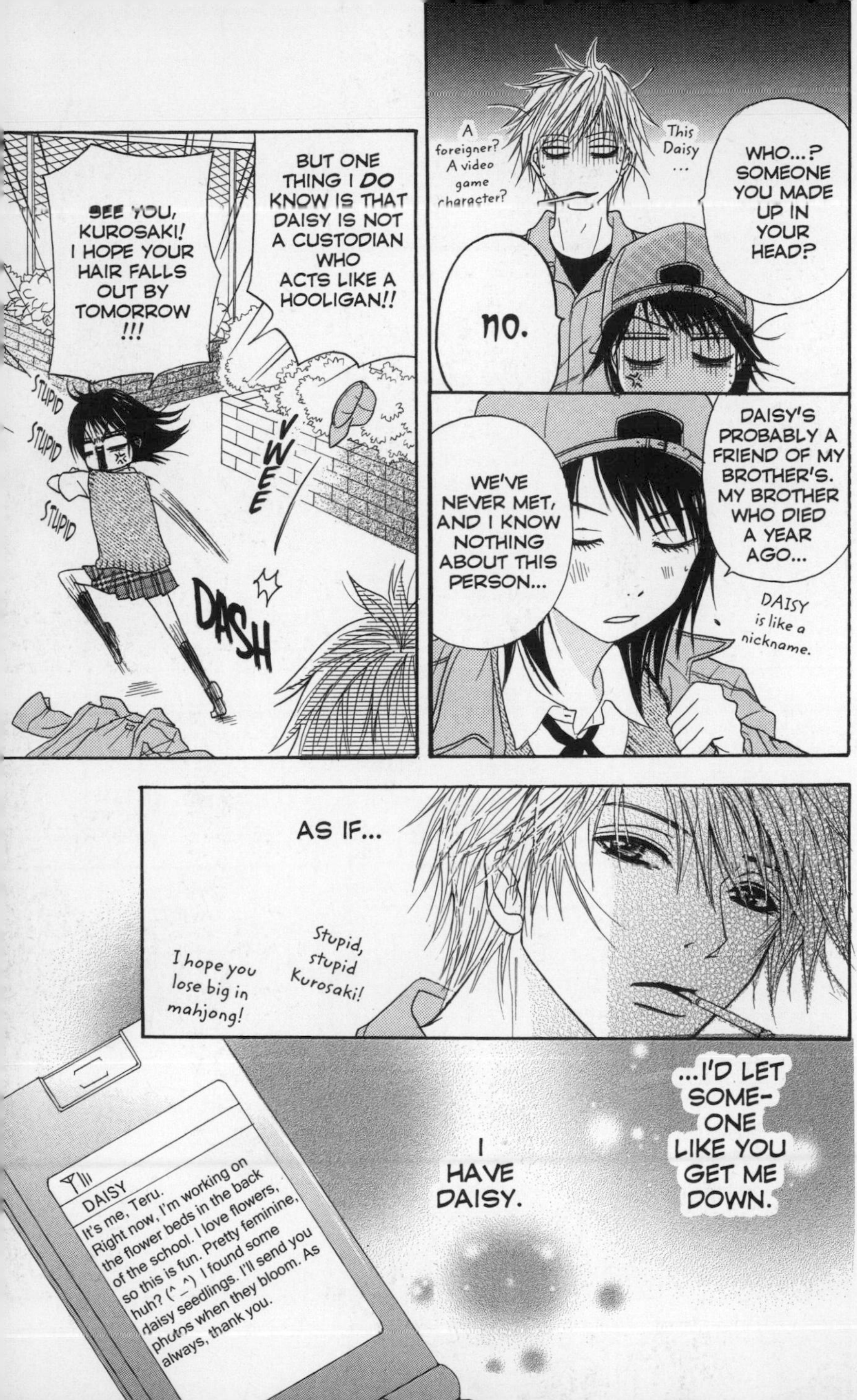
WHO...? SOMEONE YOU MADE UP IN YOUR HEAD?
This Daisy ...
A foreigner? A video game character?
no.
DAISY'S PROBABLY A FRIEND OF MY BROTHER'S. MY BROTHER WHO DIED A YEAR AGO...
WE'VE NEVER MET, AND I KNOW NOTHING ABOUT THIS PERSON...
DAISY is like a nickname.
BUT ONE THING I *DO* KNOW IS THAT DAISY IS NOT A CUSTODIAN WHO ACTS LIKE A HOOLIGAN!!
SEE YOU, KUROSAKI! I HOPE YOUR HAIR FALLS OUT BY TOMORROW !!!
VWEE
STUPID
STUPID
STUPID
DASH
AS IF...
Stupid, stupid Kurosaki!
I hope you lose big in mahjong!
...I'D LET SOME-ONE LIKE YOU GET ME DOWN.
I HAVE DAISY.
DAISY
It's me, Teru. Right now, I'm working on the flower beds in the back of the school. I love flowers, so this is fun. Pretty feminine, huh? (^_^) I found some daisy seedlings. I'll send you photos when they bloom. As always, thank you.

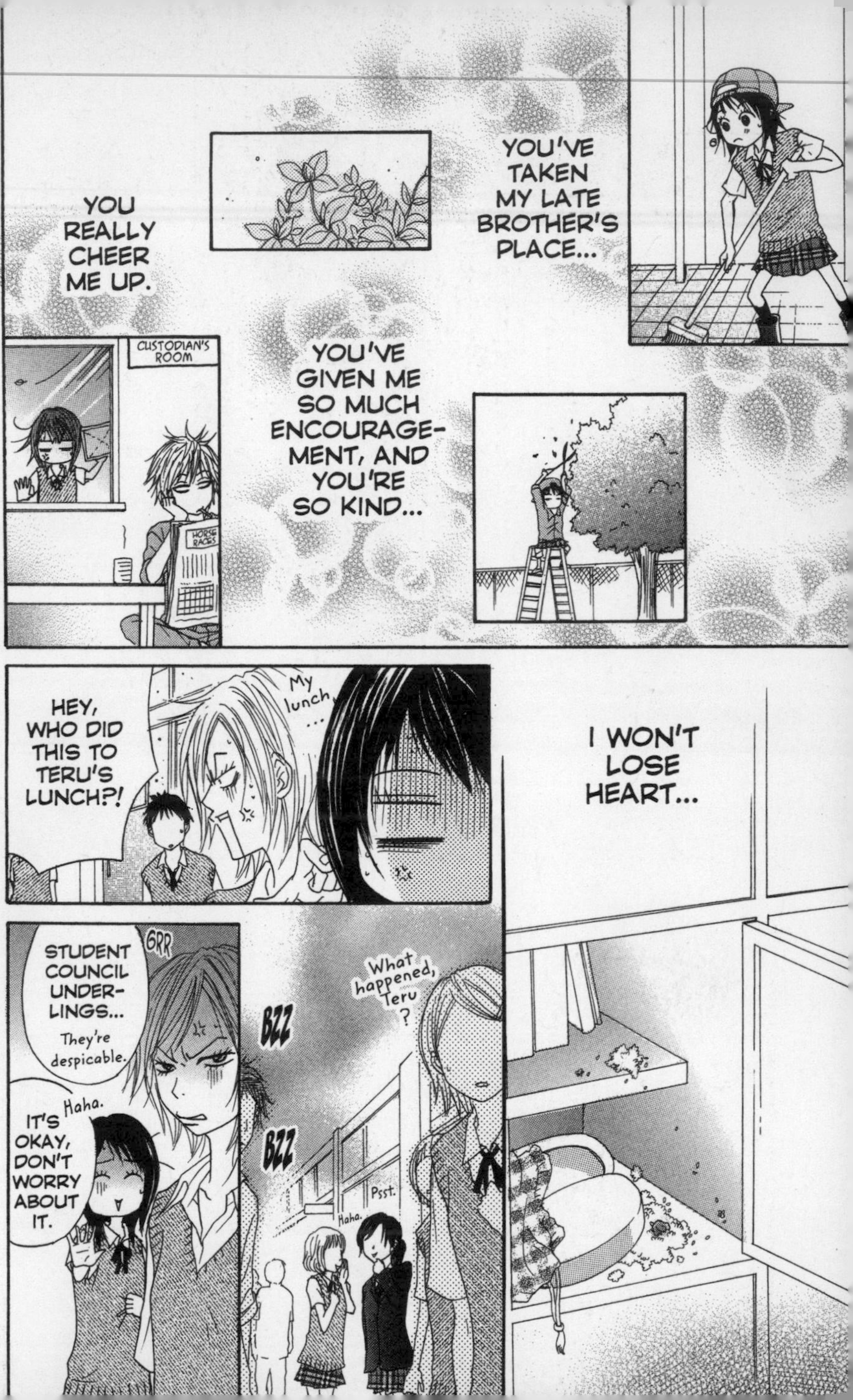
YOU'VE TAKEN MY LATE BROTHER'S PLACE...
YOU REALLY CHEER ME UP.
YOU'VE GIVEN ME SO MUCH ENCOURAGE- MENT, AND YOU'RE SO KIND...
CUSTODIAN'S ROOM
HORSE RACES
I WON'T LOSE HEART...
My lunch...
HEY, WHO DID THIS TO TERU'S LUNCH?!
What happened, Teru?
BZZ
BZZ
Psst.
Haha.
GRR
STUDENT COUNCIL UNDER- LINGS...
They're despicable.
Haha.
IT'S OKAY, DON'T WORRY ABOUT IT.

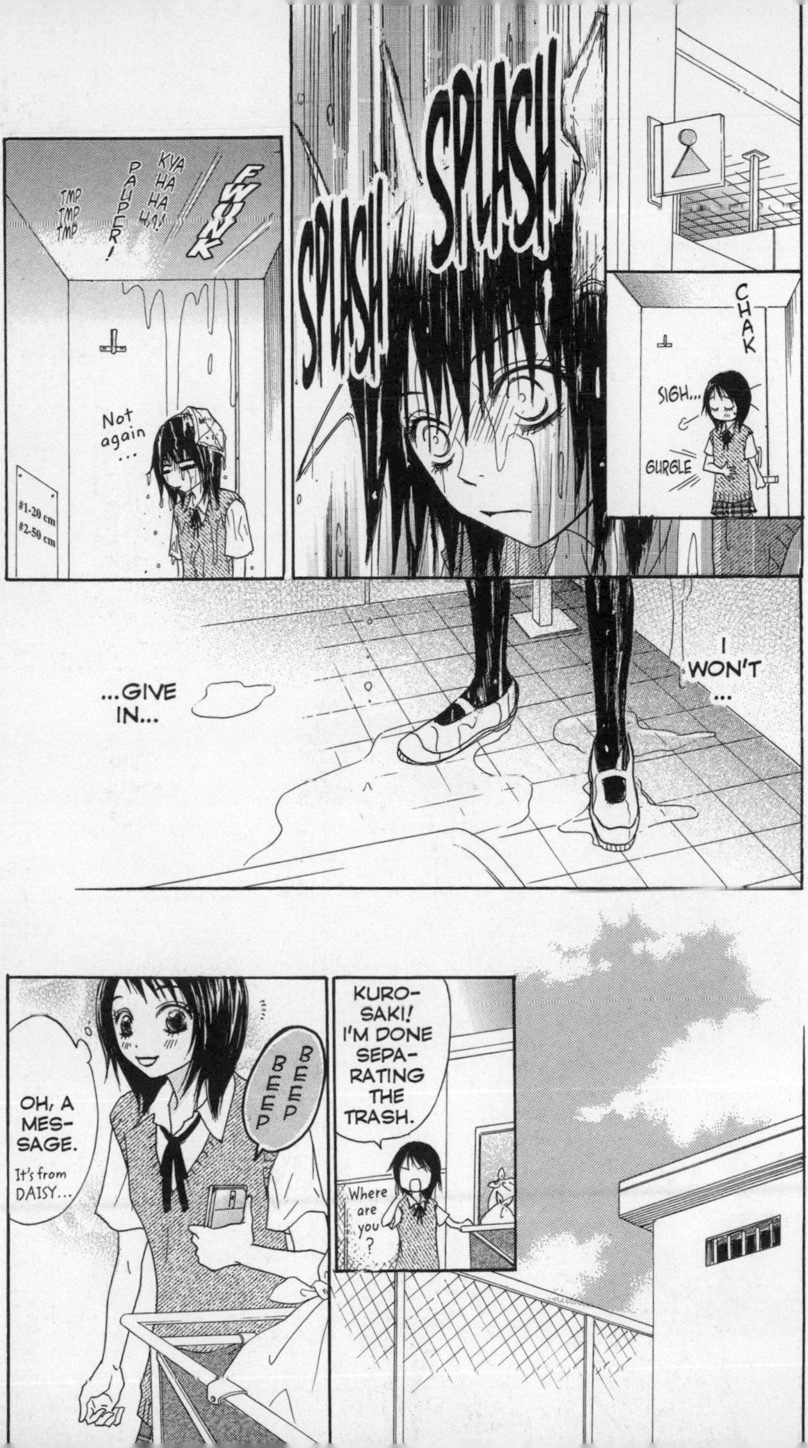
CHAK
SIGH...
GURGLE
SPLASH
SPLASH
FWUNK
KYA HA HA H?!
PAUPER!
TMP TMP TMP
Not again ...
#1-20 cm
#2-50 cm
I WON'T ...
...GIVE IN...
KURO-SAKI! I'M DONE SEPA-RATING THE TRASH.
Where are you ?
BEEP BEEP
OH, A MES-SAGE.
It's from DAISY...

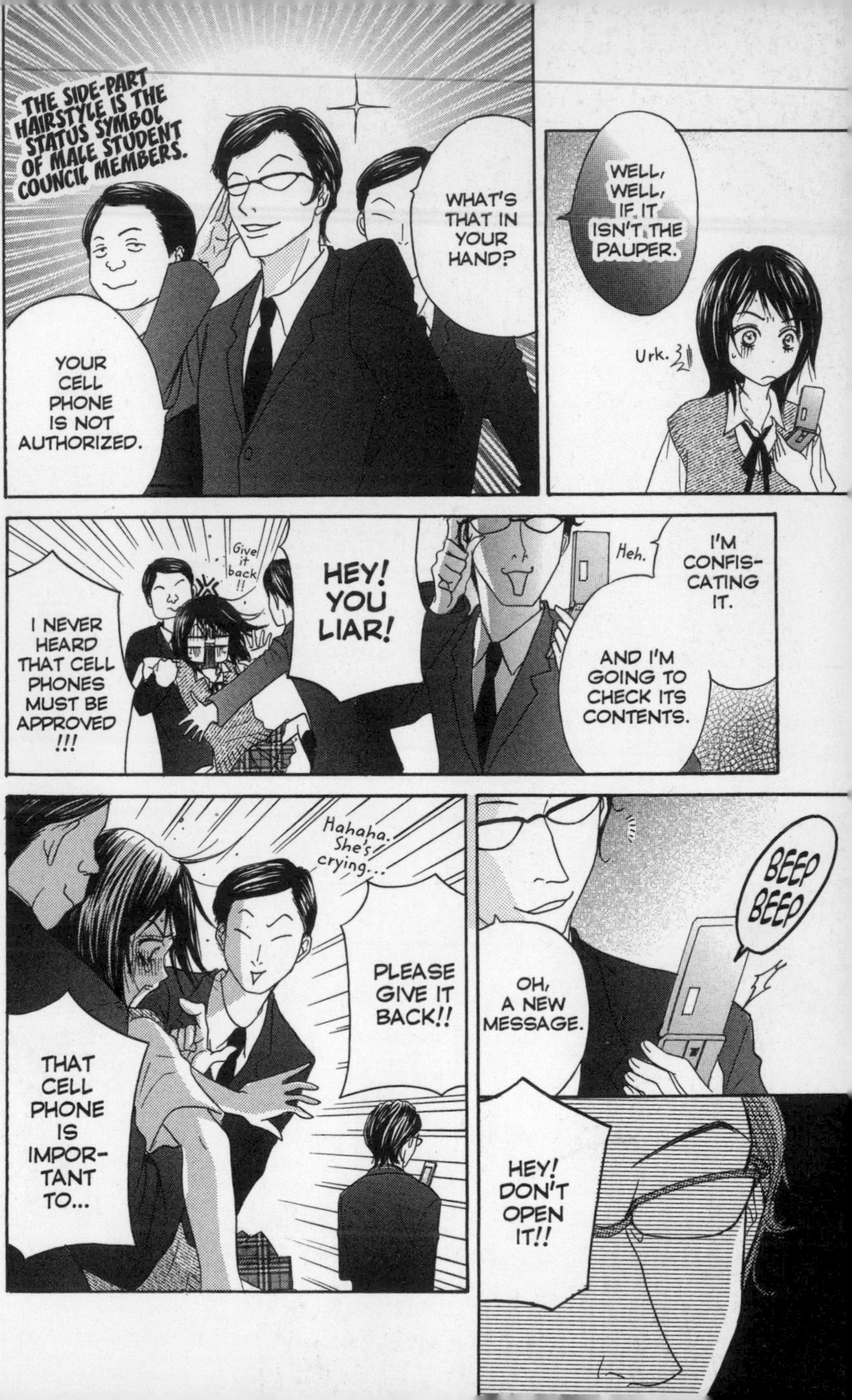
WELL, WELL, IF IT ISN'T THE PAUPER.
Urk.
WHAT'S THAT IN YOUR HAND?
THE SIDE-PART HAIRSTYLE IS THE STATUS SYMBOL OF MALE STUDENT COUNCIL MEMBERS.
YOUR CELL PHONE IS NOT AUTHORIZED.
Heh.
I'M CONFISCATING IT.
AND I'M GOING TO CHECK ITS CONTENTS.
HEY! YOU LIAR!
Give it back!!
I NEVER HEARD THAT CELL PHONES MUST BE APPROVED!!!
BEEP BEEP
OH, A NEW MESSAGE.
HEY! DON'T OPEN IT!!
Hahaha. She's crying...
PLEASE GIVE IT BACK!!
THAT CELL PHONE IS IMPORTANT TO...

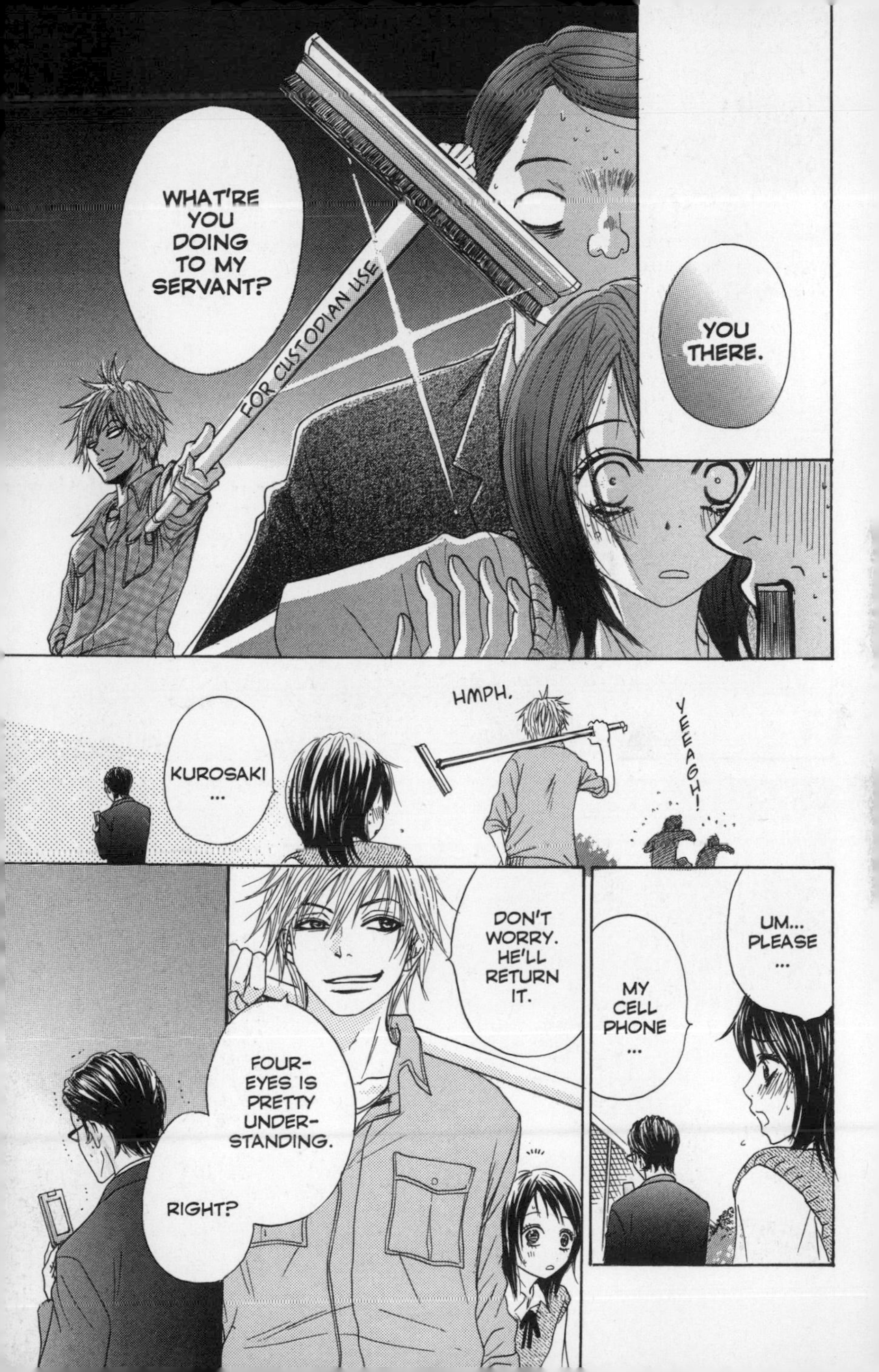
YOU THERE.
WHAT'RE YOU DOING TO MY SERVANT?
FOR CUSTODIAN USE
YEEAGH!
HMPH.
KUROSAKI ...
UM... PLEASE ...
MY CELL PHONE ...
DON'T WORRY. HE'LL RETURN IT.
FOUR-EYES IS PRETTY UNDER-STANDING.
RIGHT?

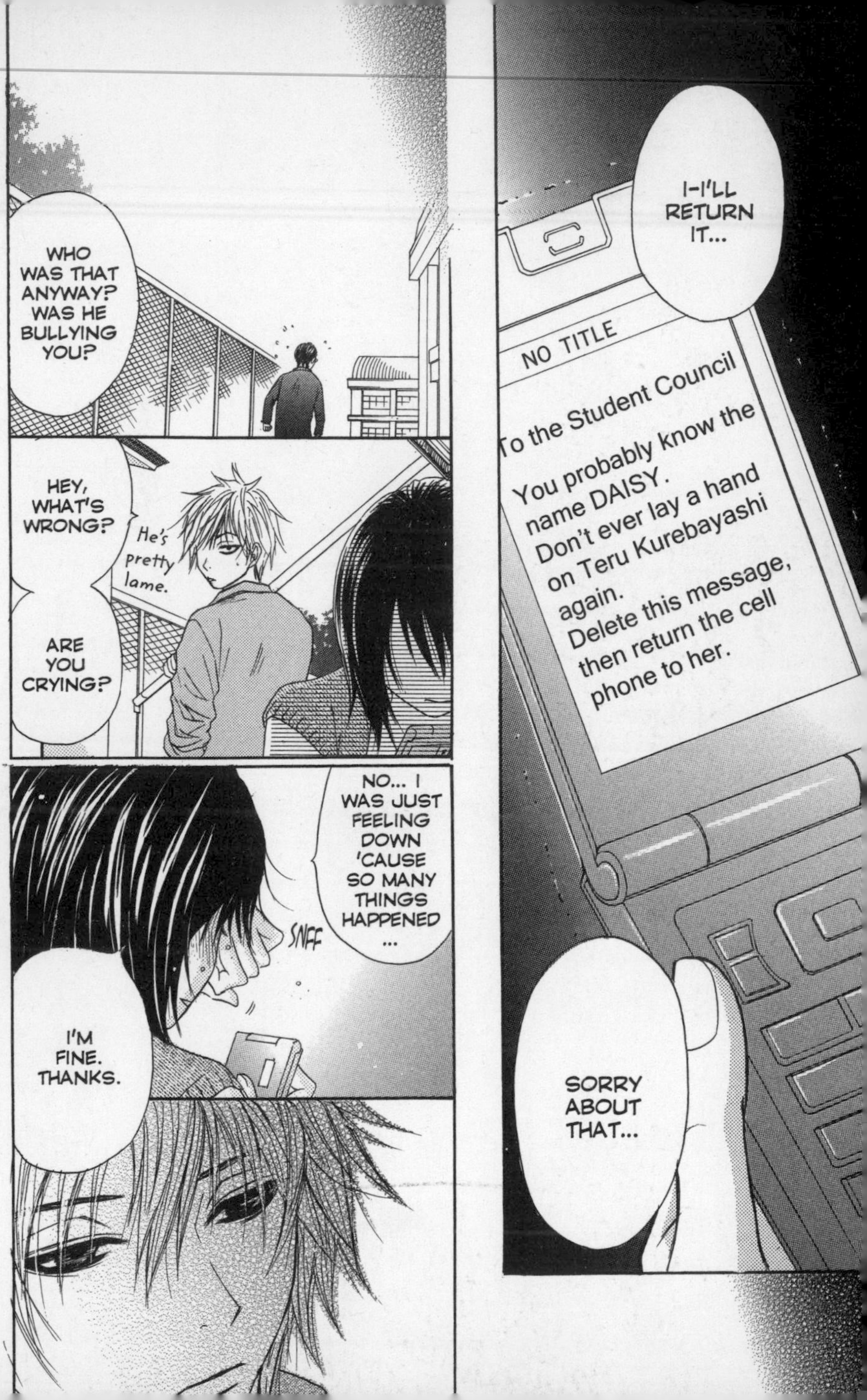
I-I'LL RETURN IT...
NO TITLE
To the Student Council
You probably know the name DAISY.
Don't ever lay a hand on Teru Kurebayashi again.
Delete this message, then return the cell phone to her.
SORRY ABOUT THAT...
WHO WAS THAT ANYWAY? WAS HE BULLYING YOU?
HEY, WHAT'S WRONG?
He's pretty lame.
ARE YOU CRYING?
NO... I WAS JUST FEELING DOWN 'CAUSE SO MANY THINGS HAPPENED ...
SNIFF
I'M FINE. THANKS.

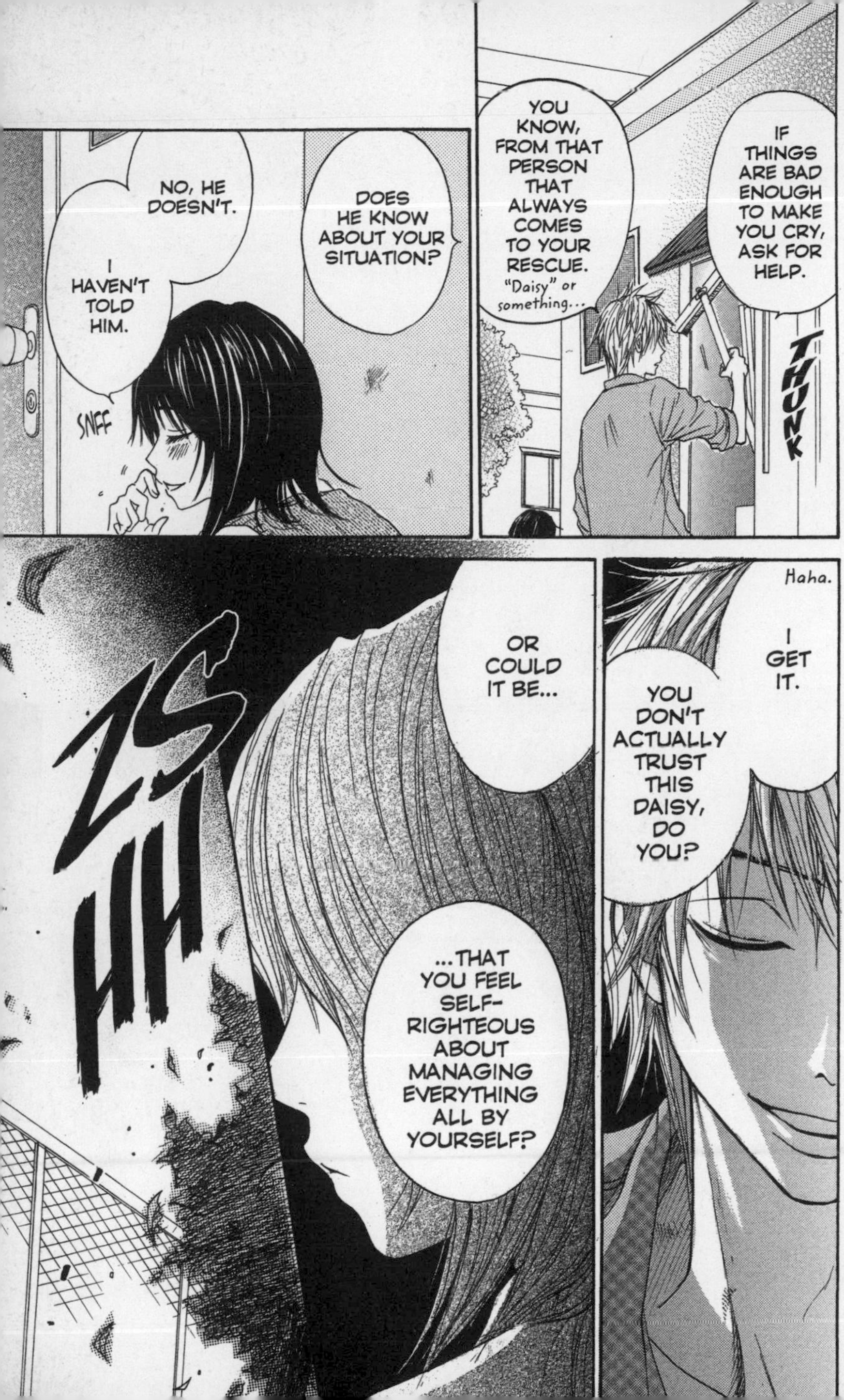
IF THINGS ARE BAD ENOUGH TO MAKE YOU CRY, ASK FOR HELP.
YOU KNOW, FROM THAT PERSON THAT ALWAYS COMES TO YOUR RESCUE.
“Daisy” or something...
THUNK
DOES HE KNOW ABOUT YOUR SITUATION?
NO, HE DOESN'T.
I HAVEN'T TOLD HIM.
SNFF
Haha.
I GET IT.
YOU DON'T ACTUALLY TRUST THIS DAISY, DO YOU?
OR COULD IT BE...
...THAT YOU FEEL SELF-RIGHTEOUS ABOUT MANAGING EVERYTHING ALL BY YOURSELF?
ZSHH

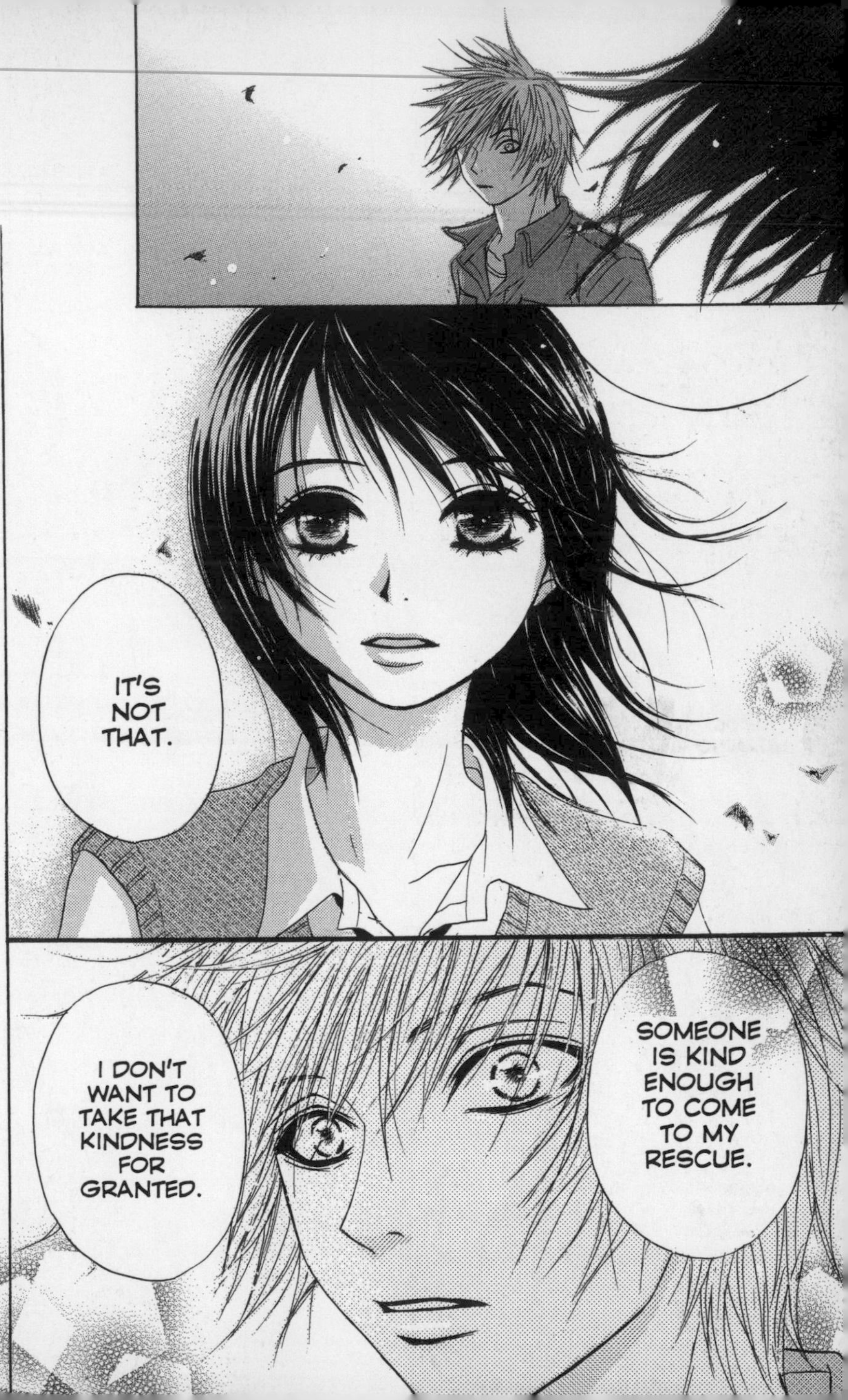
IT'S NOT THAT.
SOMEONE IS KIND ENOUGH TO COME TO MY RESCUE.
I DON'T WANT TO TAKE THAT KINDNESS FOR GRANTED.

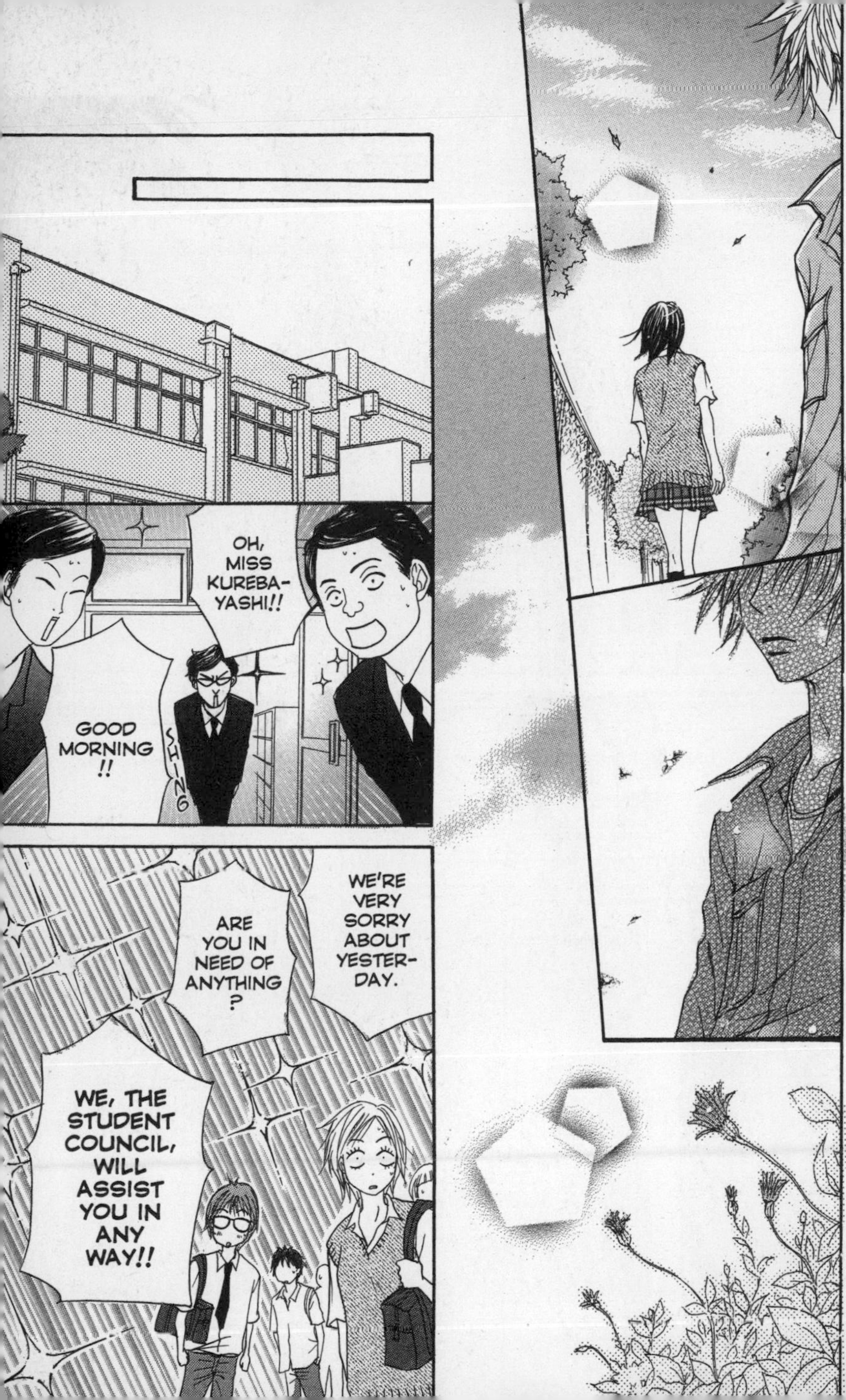
OH, MISS KUREBA-YASHI!!
SHING
GOOD MORNING!!
WE'RE VERY SORRY ABOUT YESTER-DAY.
ARE YOU IN NEED OF ANYTHING?
WE, THE STUDENT COUNCIL, WILL ASSIST YOU IN ANY WAY!!

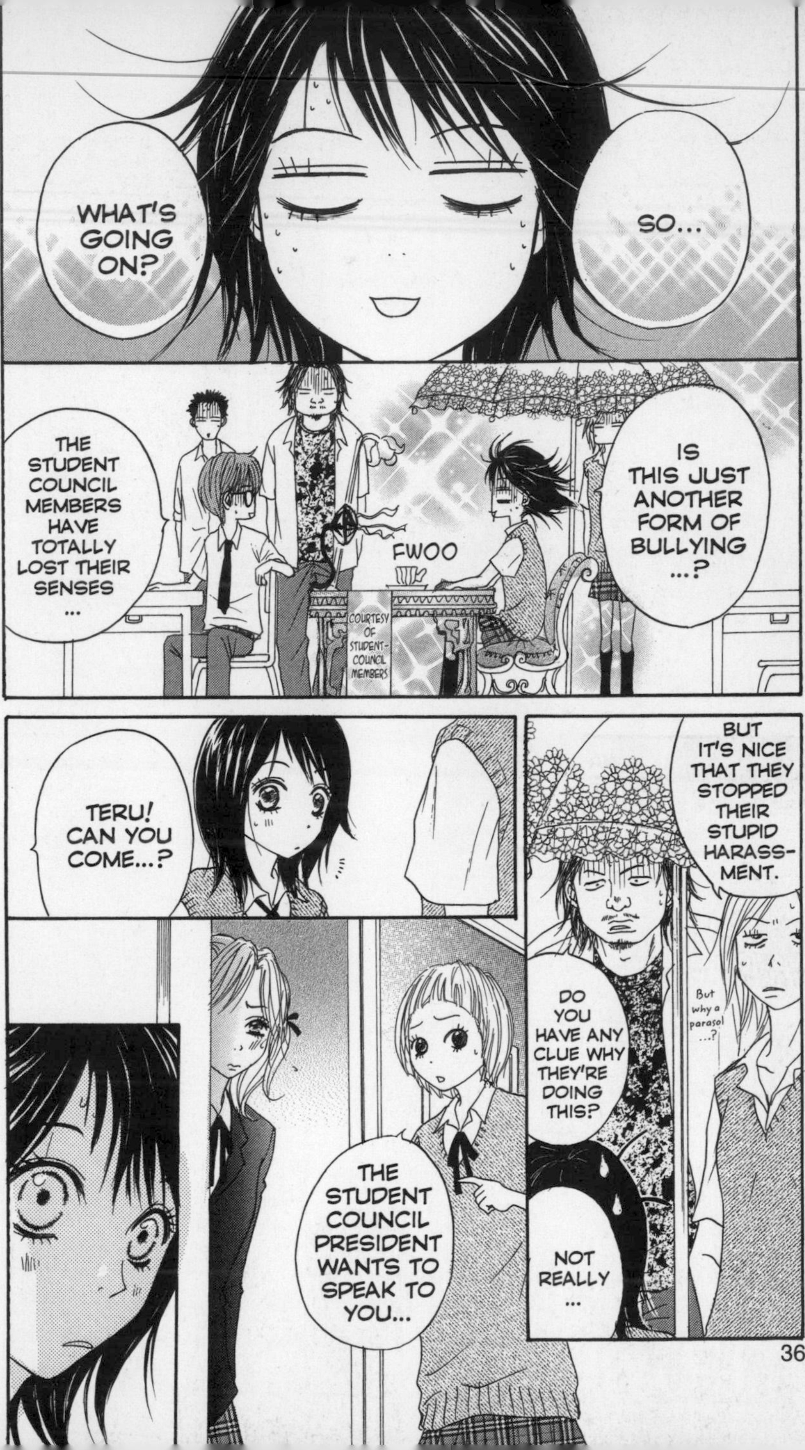
SO...
WHAT'S GOING ON?
IS THIS JUST ANOTHER FORM OF BULLYING...?
FWOO
COURTESY OF STUDENT-COUNCIL MEMBERS
THE STUDENT COUNCIL MEMBERS HAVE TOTALLY LOST THEIR SENSES...
BUT IT'S NICE THAT THEY STOPPED THEIR STUPID HARASS-MENT.
But why a parasol...?
DO YOU HAVE ANY CLUE WHY THEY'RE DOING THIS?
NOT REALLY...
TERU! CAN YOU COME...?
THE STUDENT COUNCIL PRESIDENT WANTS TO SPEAK TO YOU...

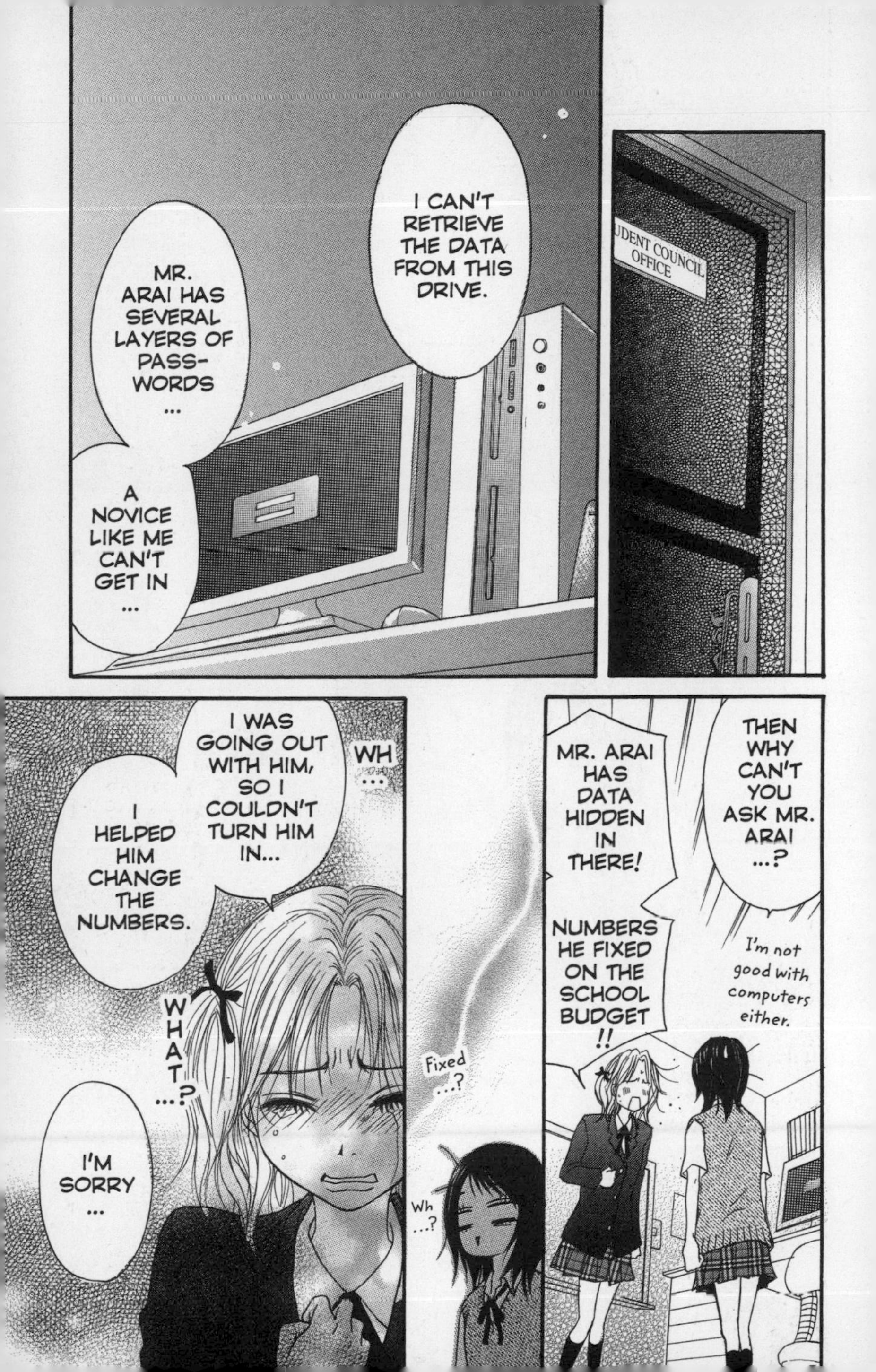
UDENT COUNCIL OFFICE
I CAN'T RETRIEVE THE DATA FROM THIS DRIVE.
MR. ARAI HAS SEVERAL LAYERS OF PASS-WORDS...
A NOVICE LIKE ME CAN'T GET IN...
THEN WHY CAN'T YOU ASK MR. ARAI...?
I'm not good with computers either.
MR. ARAI HAS DATA HIDDEN IN THERE!
NUMBERS HE FIXED ON THE SCHOOL BUDGET!!
Fixed...?
Wh...?
WH...
I WAS GOING OUT WITH HIM, SO I COULDN'T TURN HIM IN...
I HELPED HIM CHANGE THE NUMBERS.
WHAT...?
I'M SORRY...

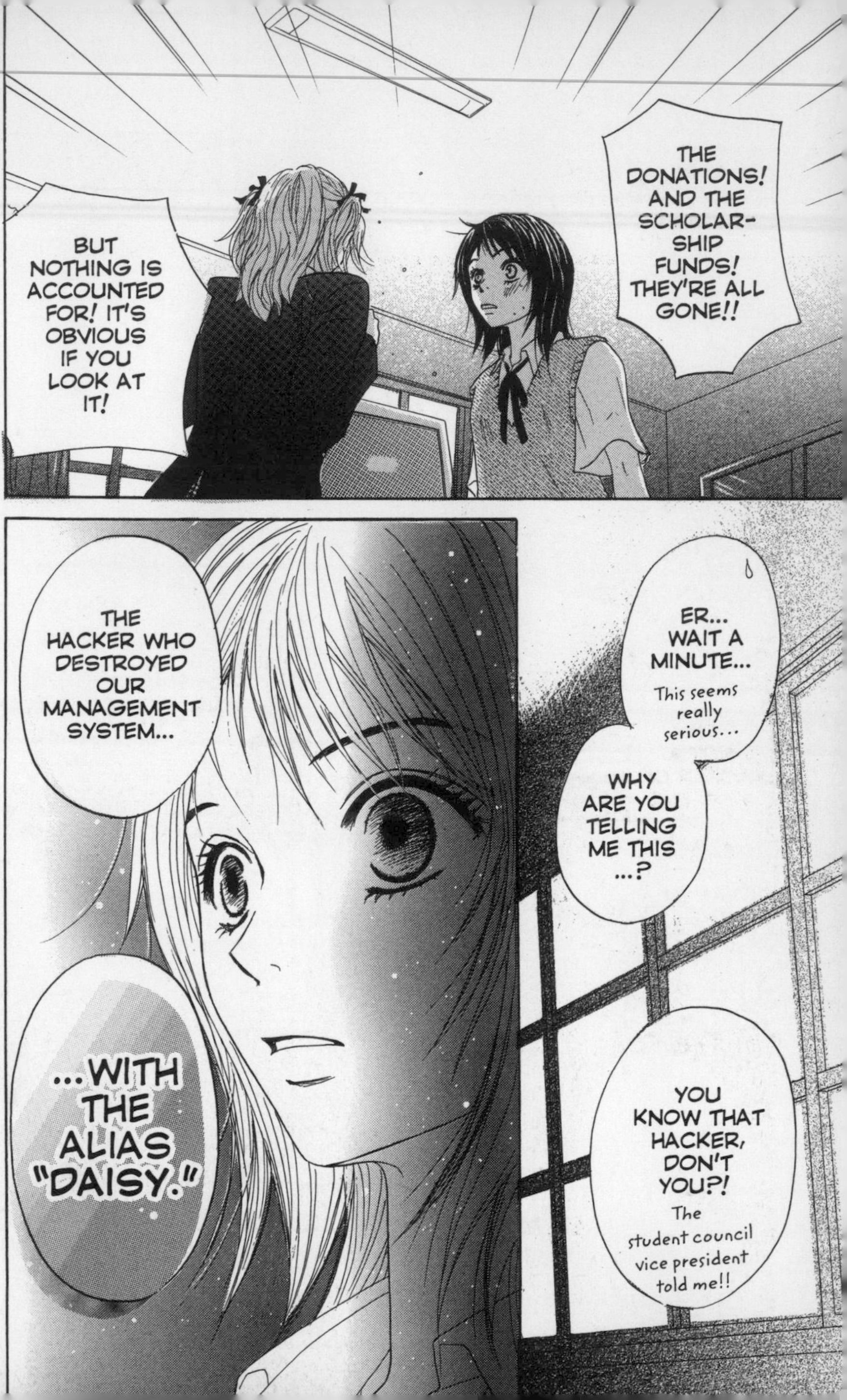
THE DONATIONS! AND THE SCHOLARSHIP FUNDS! THEY'RE ALL GONE!!
BUT NOTHING IS ACCOUNTED FOR! IT'S OBVIOUS IF YOU LOOK AT IT!
ER... WAIT A MINUTE...
This seems really serious...
WHY ARE YOU TELLING ME THIS...?
THE HACKER WHO DESTROYED OUR MANAGEMENT SYSTEM...
...WITH THE ALIAS "DAISY."
YOU KNOW THAT HACKER, DON'T YOU?!
The student council vice president told me!!

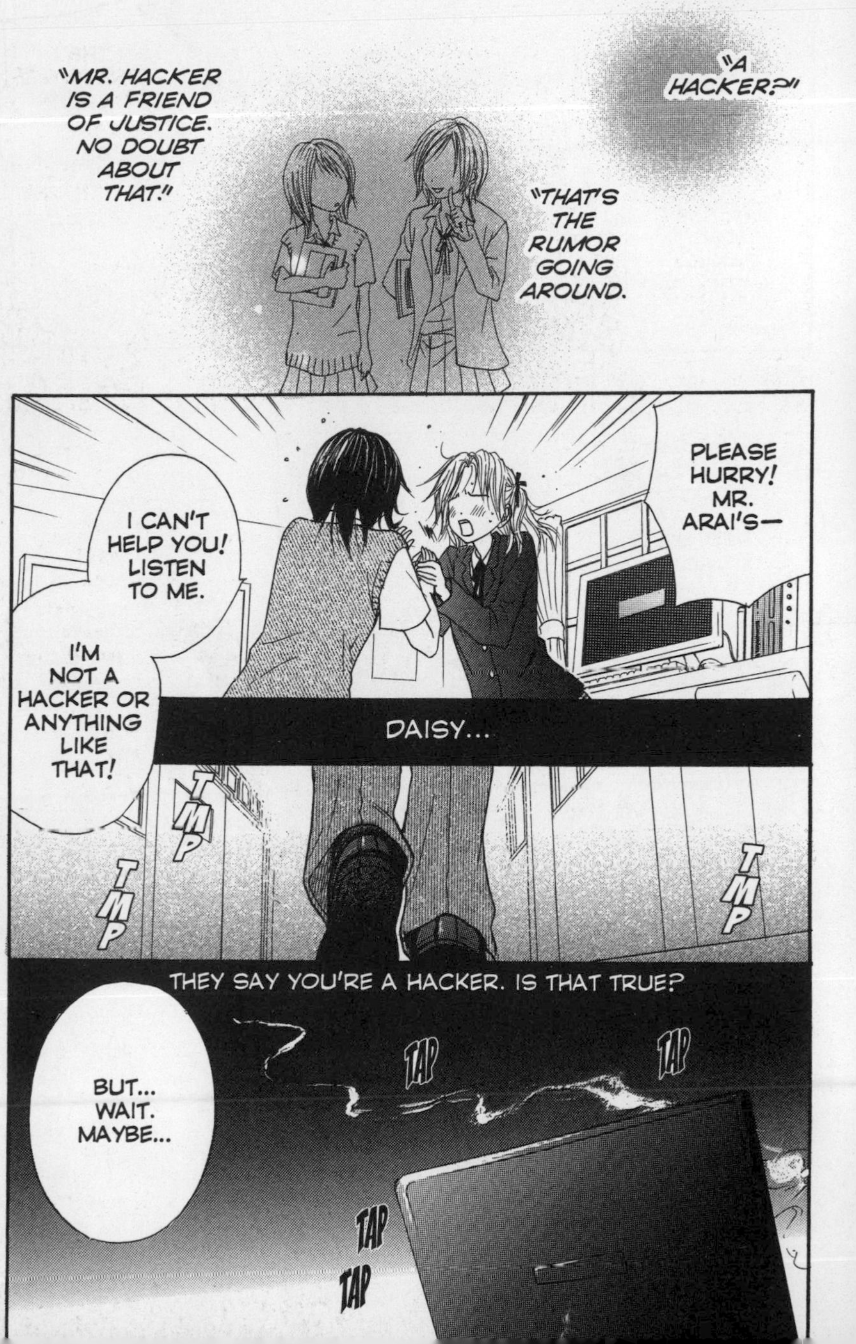
"A HACKER?"
"THAT'S THE RUMOR GOING AROUND.
"MR. HACKER IS A FRIEND OF JUSTICE. NO DOUBT ABOUT THAT."
PLEASE HURRY! MR. ARAI'S—
I CAN'T HELP YOU! LISTEN TO ME.
I'M NOT A HACKER OR ANYTHING LIKE THAT!
DAISY...
TMP
TMP
TMP
THEY SAY YOU'RE A HACKER. IS THAT TRUE?
TAP
TAP
BUT... WAIT. MAYBE...
TAP
TAP

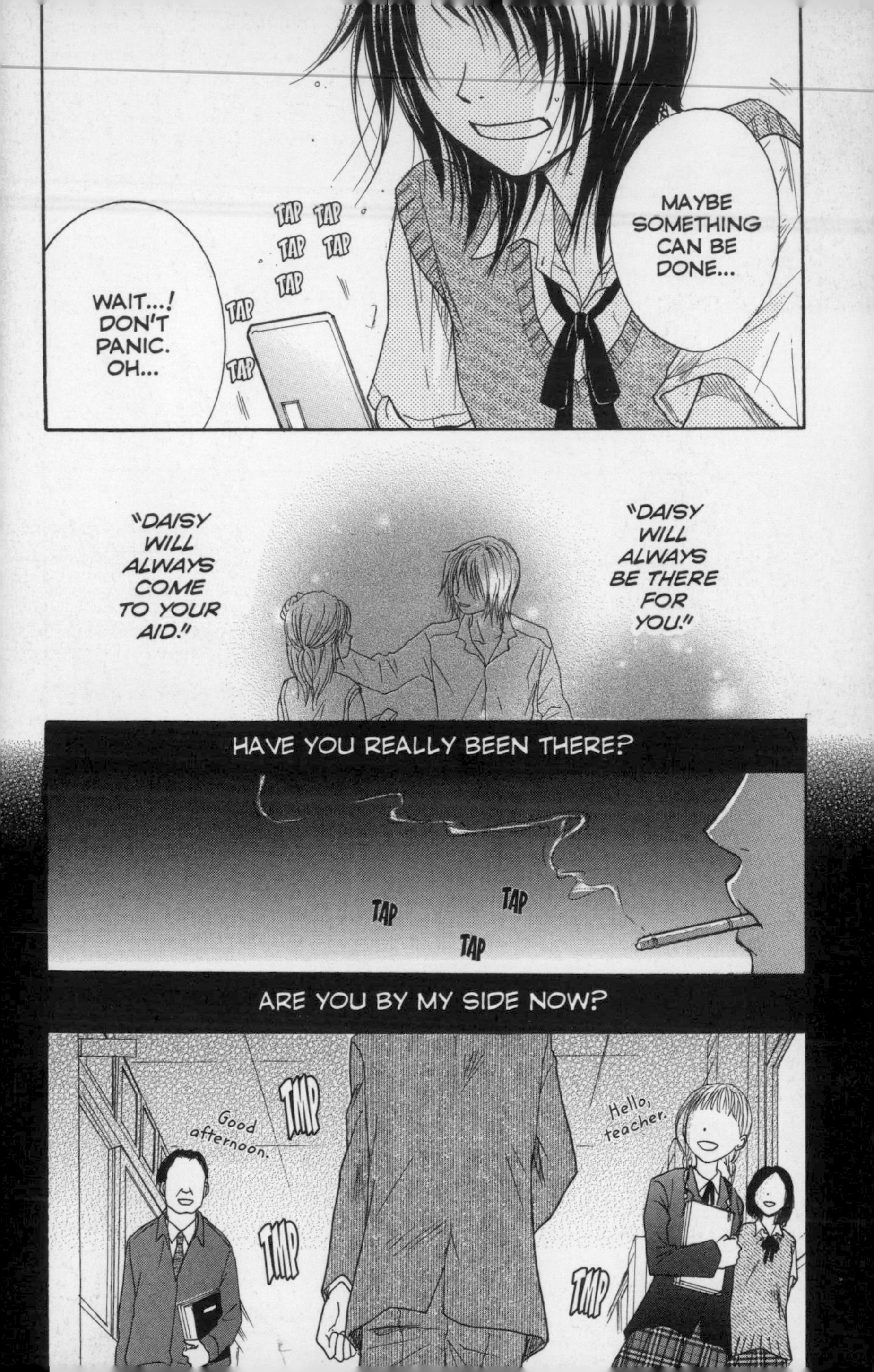
MAYBE SOMETHING CAN BE DONE...
TAP TAP TAP TAP TAP TAP TAP
WAIT...! DON'T PANIC. OH...
"DAISY WILL ALWAYS BE THERE FOR YOU."
"DAISY WILL ALWAYS COME TO YOUR AID."
HAVE YOU REALLY BEEN THERE?
TAP TAP TAP
ARE YOU BY MY SIDE NOW?
Hello, teacher.
TMP
TMP
Good afternoon.
TMP

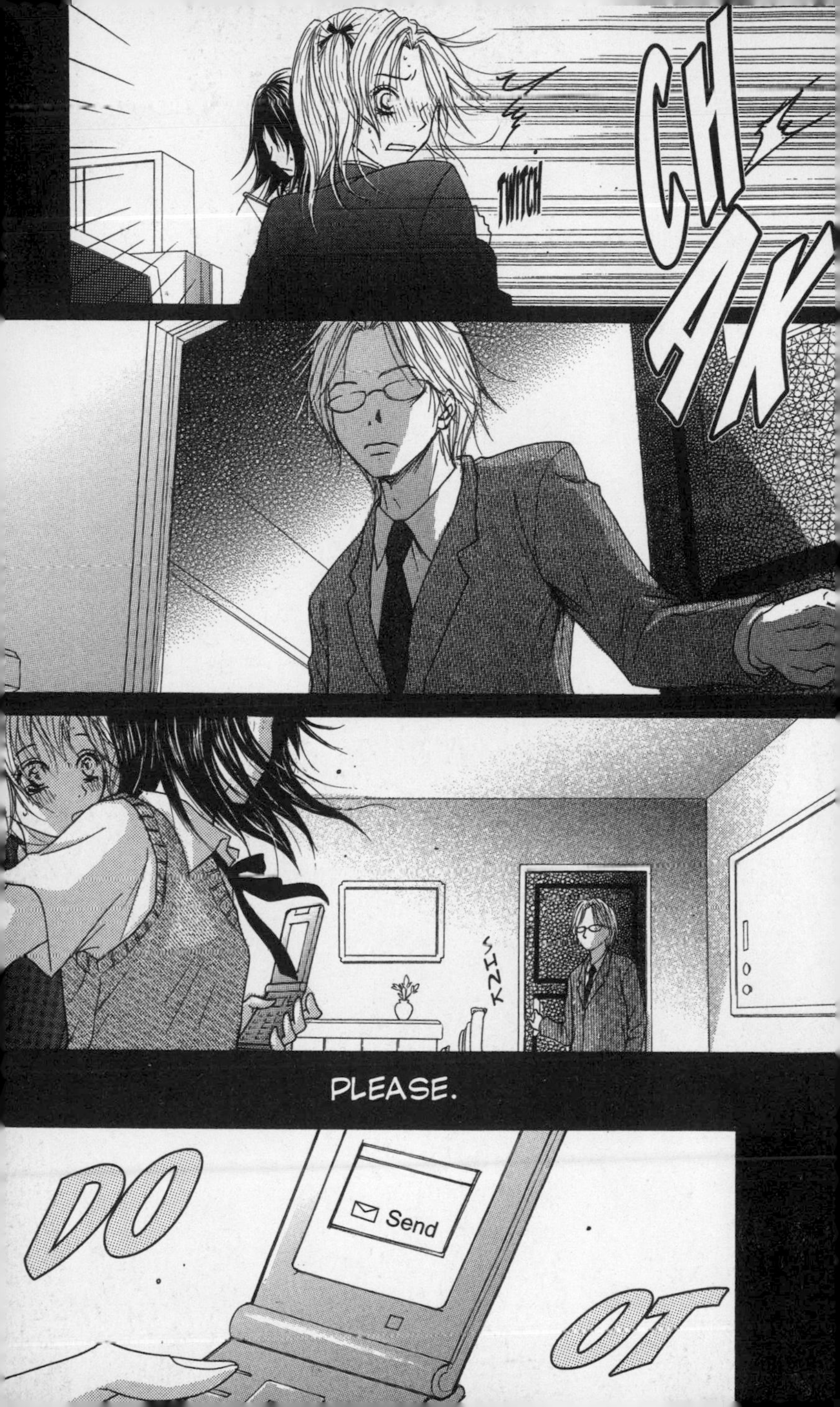
CHAK
TWITCH
SHINK
PLEASE.
Send
DOOT

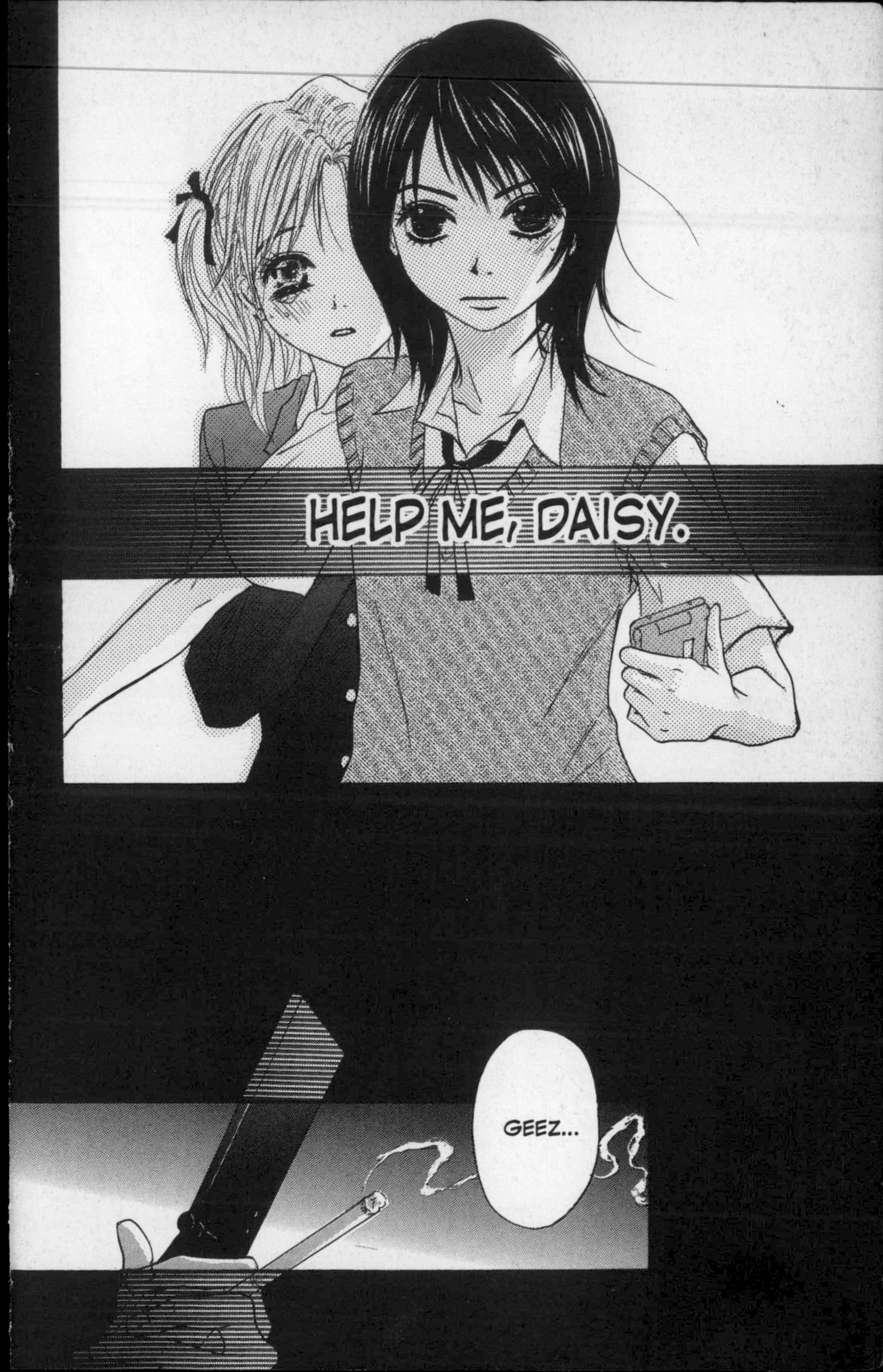
HELP ME, DAISY.
GEEZ...

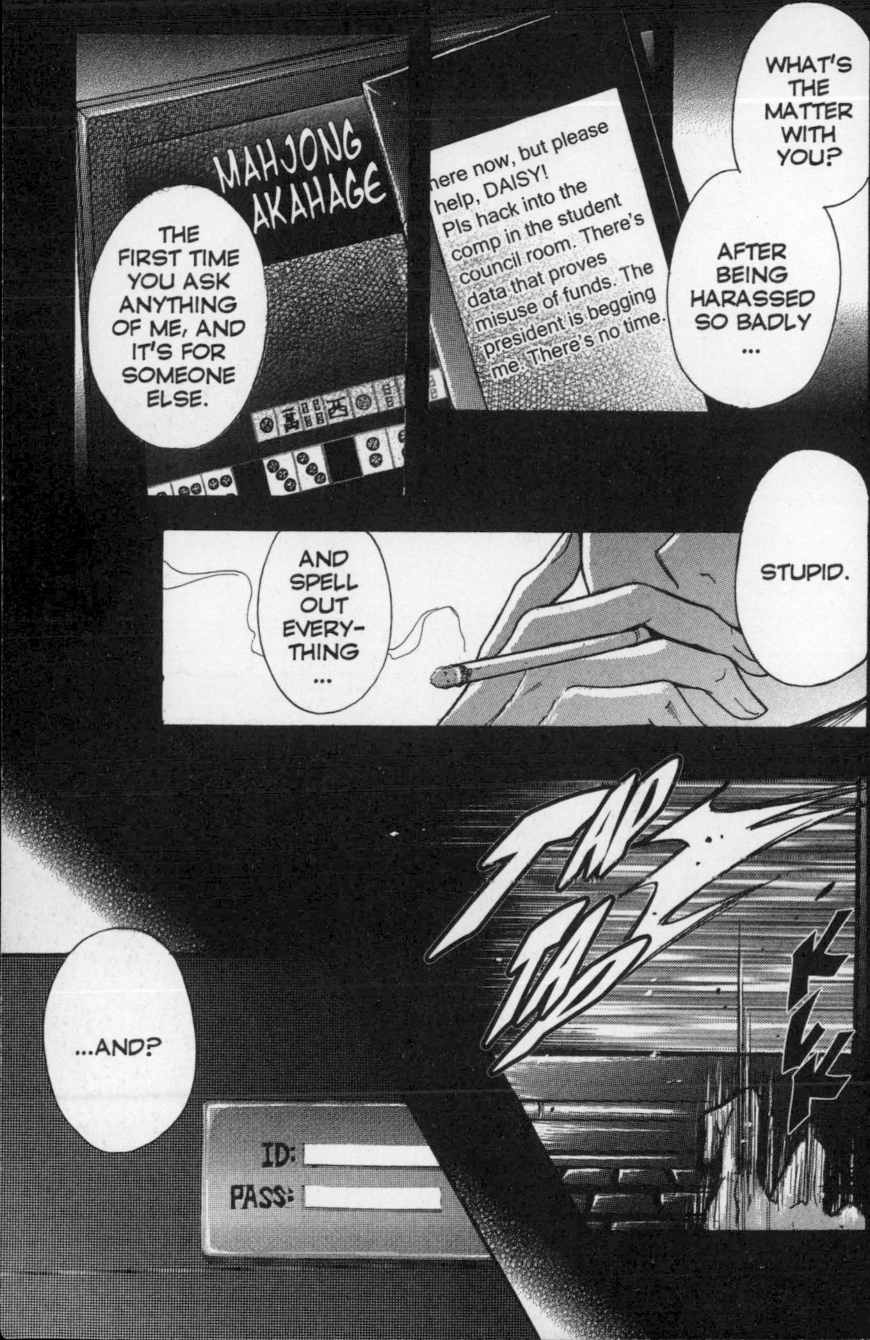
here now, but please help, DAISY! PIs hack into the comp in the student council room. There's data that proves misuse of funds. The president is begging me. There's no time.
WHAT'S THE MATTER WITH YOU?
AFTER BEING HARASSED SO BADLY ...
MAHJONG AKAHAGE
THE FIRST TIME YOU ASK ANYTHING OF ME, AND IT'S FOR SOMEONE ELSE.
STUPID.
AND SPELL OUT EVERY-THING ...
TAP TAP
...AND?
ID:
PASS:

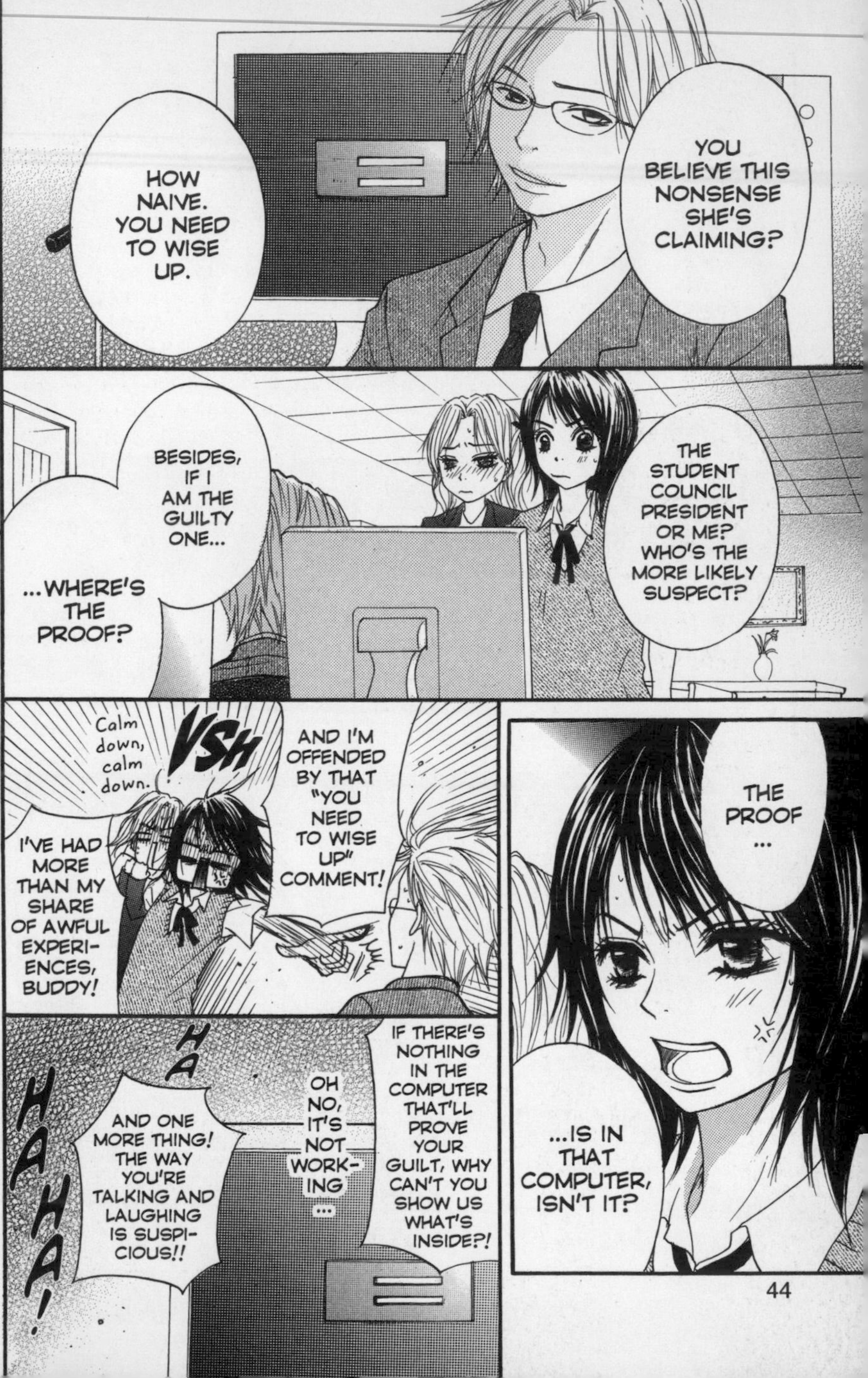
YOU BELIEVE THIS NONSENSE SHE'S CLAIMING?
HOW NAIVE. YOU NEED TO WISE UP.
THE STUDENT COUNCIL PRESIDENT OR ME? WHO'S THE MORE LIKELY SUSPECT?
BESIDES, IF I AM THE GUILTY ONE...
...WHERE'S THE PROOF?
THE PROOF ...
...IS IN THAT COMPUTER, ISN'T IT?
AND I'M OFFENDED BY THAT "YOU NEED TO WISE UP" COMMENT!
VSH
Calm down, calm down.
I'VE HAD MORE THAN MY SHARE OF AWFUL EXPERIENCES, BUDDY!
IF THERE'S NOTHING IN THE COMPUTER THAT'LL PROVE YOUR GUILT, WHY CAN'T YOU SHOW US WHAT'S INSIDE?!
OH NO, IT'S NOT WORKING ...
HA
AND ONE MORE THING! THE WAY YOU'RE TALKING AND LAUGHING IS SUSPICIOUS!!
HAHAHA!

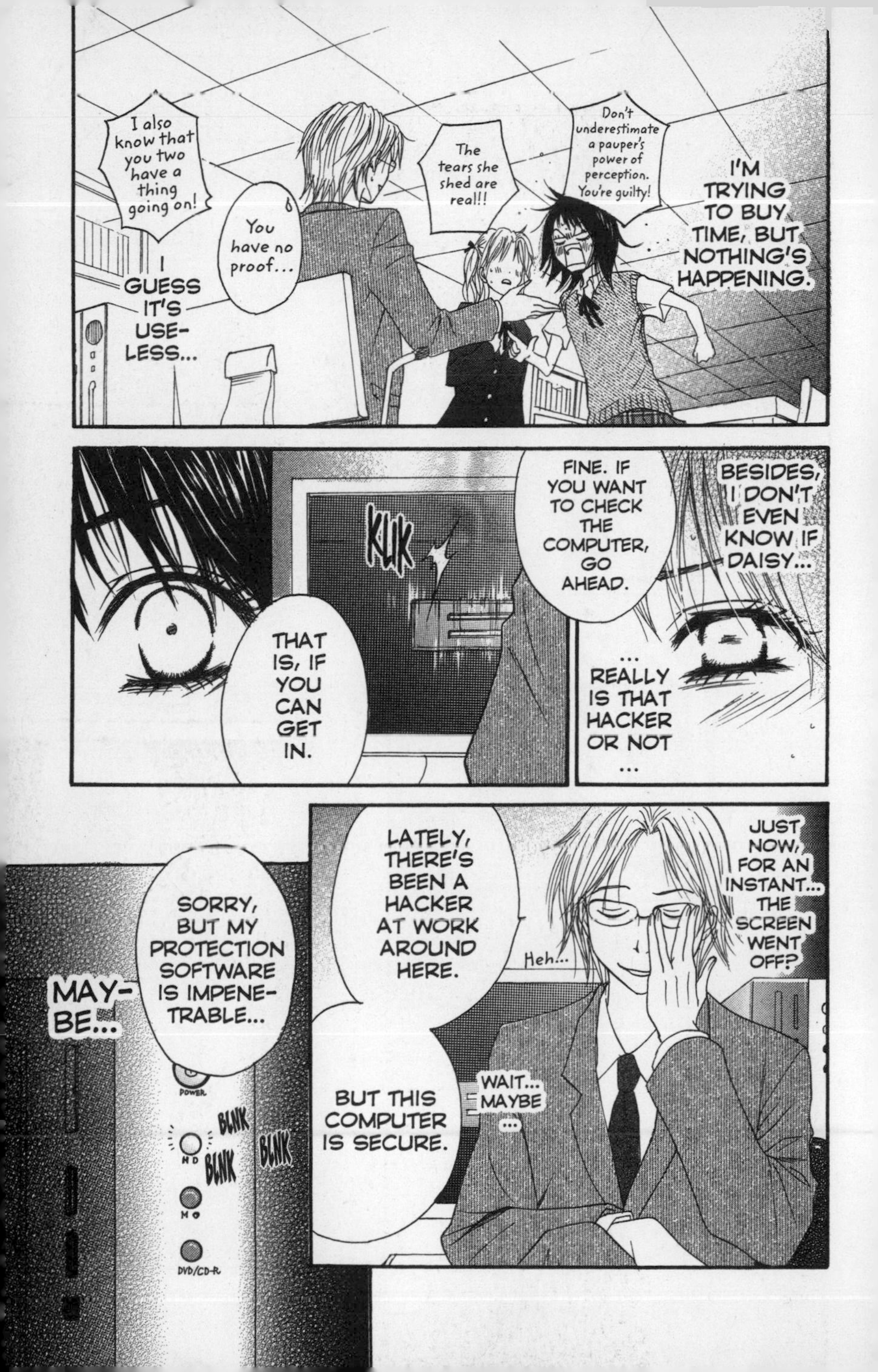
I'M TRYING TO BUY TIME, BUT NOTHING'S HAPPENING.
Don't underestimate a pauper's power of perception. You're guilty!
The tears she shed are real!!
I also know that you two have a thing going on!
You have no proof...
I GUESS IT'S USELESS...
BESIDES, I DON'T EVEN KNOW IF DAISY...
...REALLY IS THAT HACKER OR NOT...
FINE. IF YOU WANT TO CHECK THE COMPUTER, GO AHEAD.
KLIK
THAT IS, IF YOU CAN GET IN.
JUST NOW, FOR AN INSTANT... THE SCREEN WENT OFF?
LATELY, THERE'S BEEN A HACKER AT WORK AROUND HERE.
Heh...
WAIT... MAYBE...
BUT THIS COMPUTER IS SECURE.
SORRY, BUT MY PROTECTION SOFTWARE IS IMPENETRABLE...
MAYBE...
POWER
BLNK
BLNK
BLNK
HD
MO
DVD/CD-R

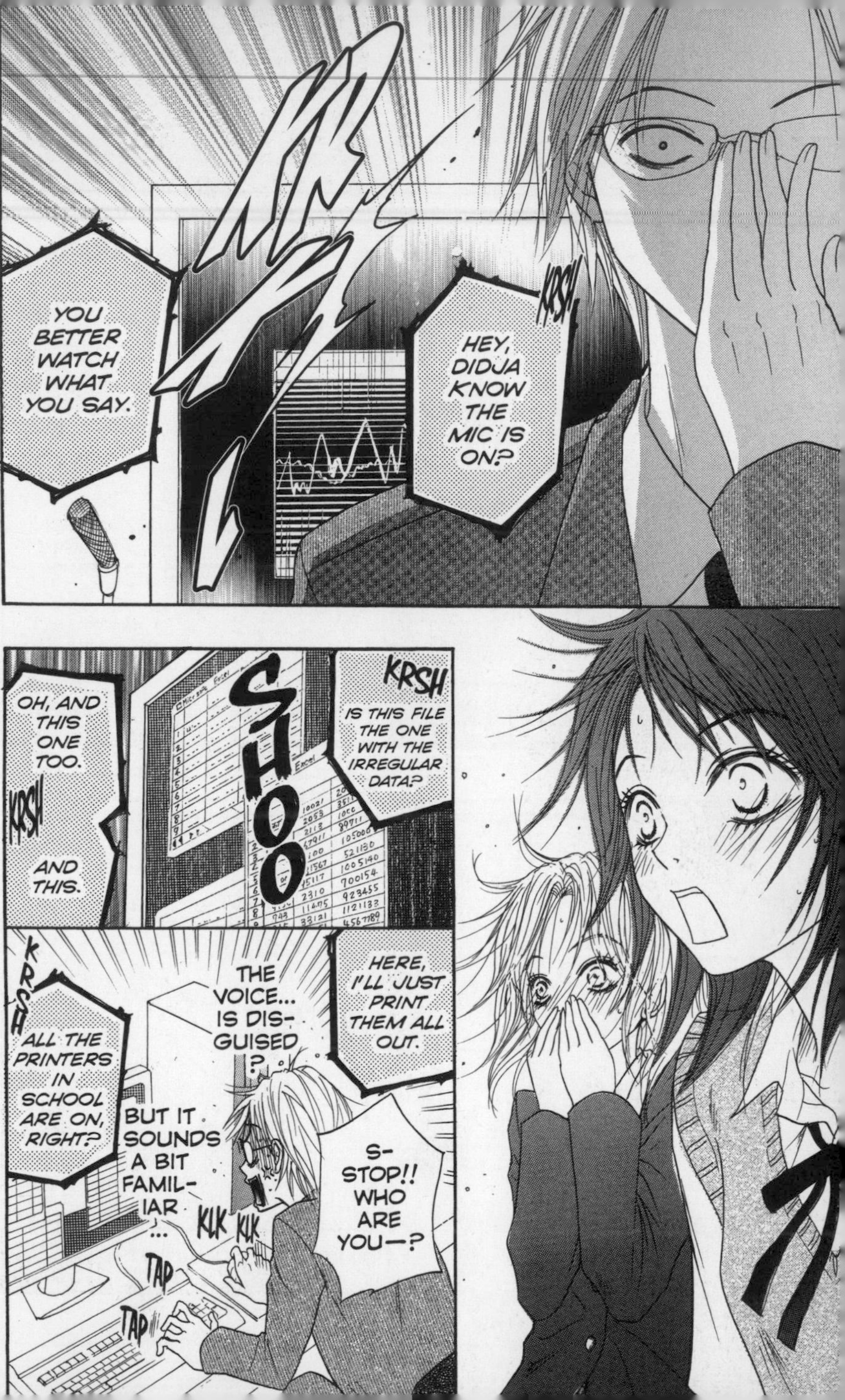
KRSH
HEY, DIDJA KNOW THE MIC IS ON?
YOU BETTER WATCH WHAT YOU SAY.
KRSH
IS THIS FILE THE ONE WITH THE IRREGULAR DATA?
SHOO
OH, AND THIS ONE TOO.
KRSH
AND THIS.
HERE, I'LL JUST PRINT THEM ALL OUT.
THE VOICE... IS DISGUISED!?
KRSH
ALL THE PRINTERS IN SCHOOL ARE ON, RIGHT?
BUT IT SOUNDS A BIT FAMILIAR...
S-STOP!! WHO ARE YOU—?
KLK KLK
TAP
TAP

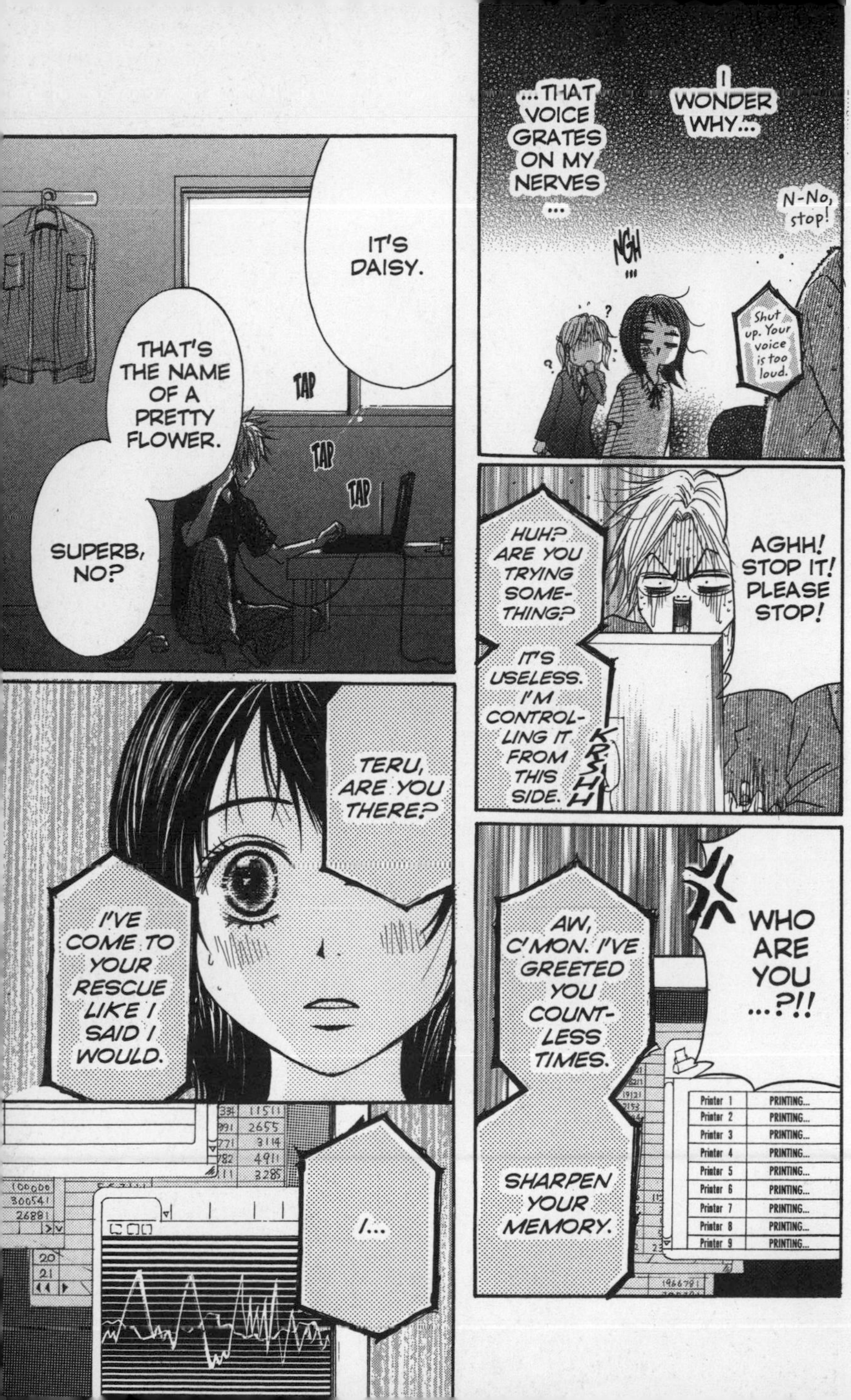
I WONDER WHY...
...THAT VOICE GRATES ON MY NERVES ...
N-No, stop!
NGH!!!
Shut up. Your voice is too loud.
AGHH! STOP IT! PLEASE STOP!
HUH? ARE YOU TRYING SOMETHING?
IT'S USELESS. I'M CONTROLLING IT FROM THIS SIDE.
KRSHH
WHO ARE YOU ...?!!
AW, C'MON. I'VE GREETED YOU COUNTLESS TIMES.
SHARPEN YOUR MEMORY.
Printer 1 PRINTING...
Printer 2 PRINTING...
Printer 3 PRINTING...
Printer 4 PRINTING...
Printer 5 PRINTING...
Printer 6 PRINTING...
Printer 7 PRINTING...
Printer 8 PRINTING...
Printer 9 PRINTING...
IT'S DAISY.
THAT'S THE NAME OF A PRETTY FLOWER.
TAP
TAP
TAP
SUPERB, NO?
TERU, ARE YOU THERE?
I'VE COME TO YOUR RESCUE LIKE I SAID I WOULD.
I...

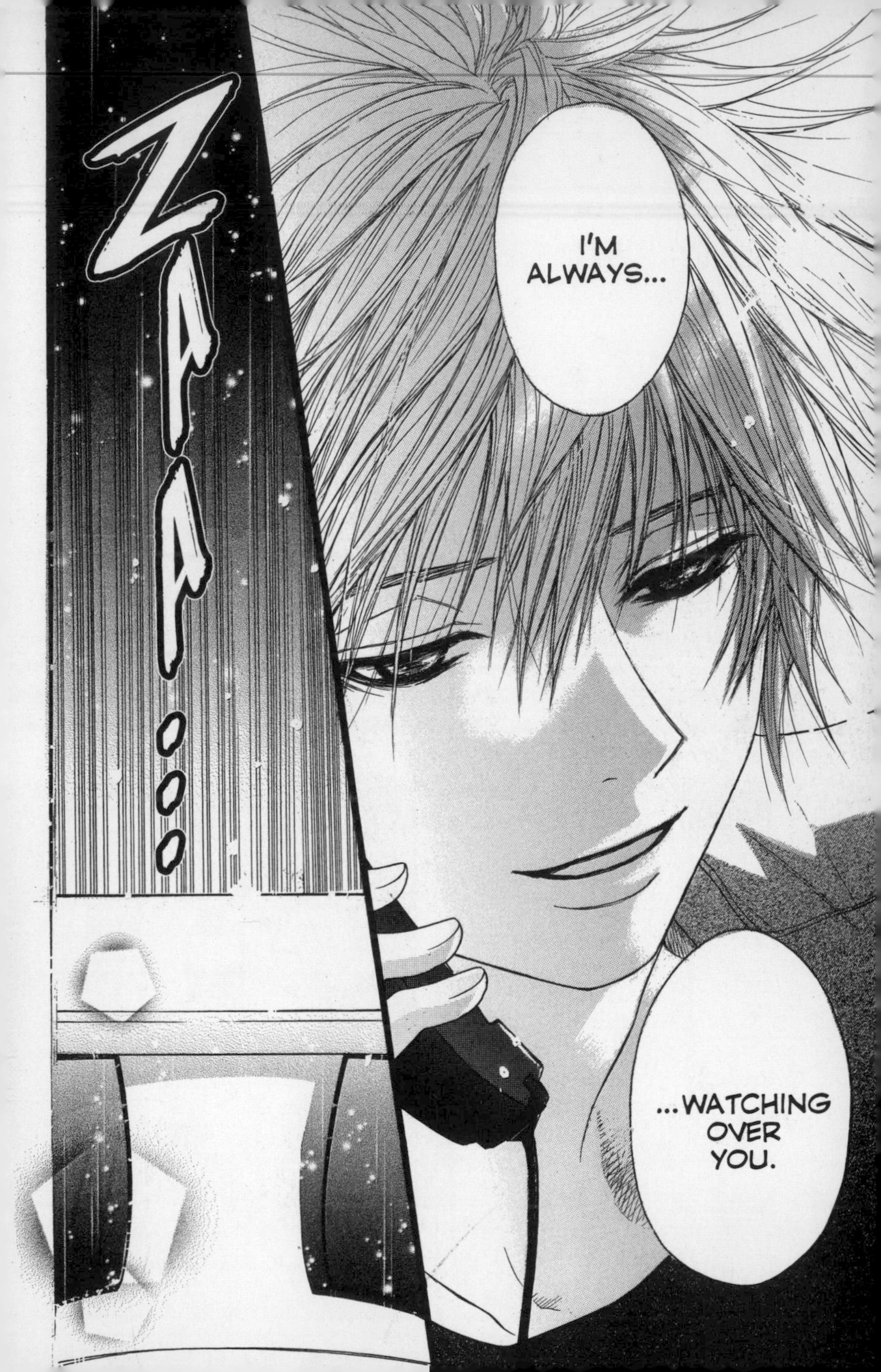
I'M ALWAYS...
...WATCHING OVER YOU.
ZAP...

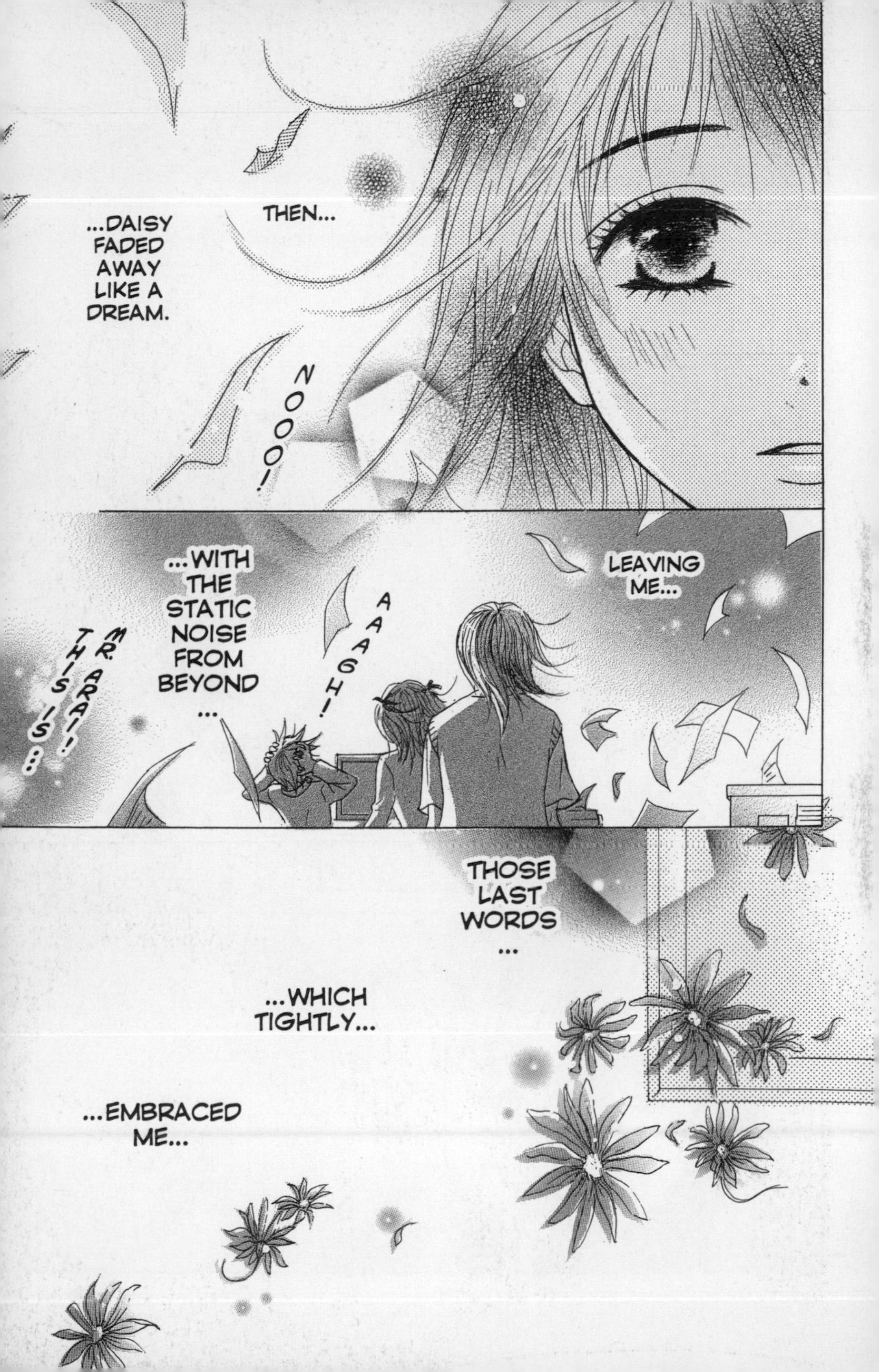
THEN...
...DAISY FADED AWAY LIKE A DREAM.
NOOOO!
LEAVING ME...
...WITH THE STATIC NOISE FROM BEYOND...
AAAGH!
MR. ARAI! THIS IS...
THOSE LAST WORDS...
...WHICH TIGHTLY...
...EMBRACED ME...

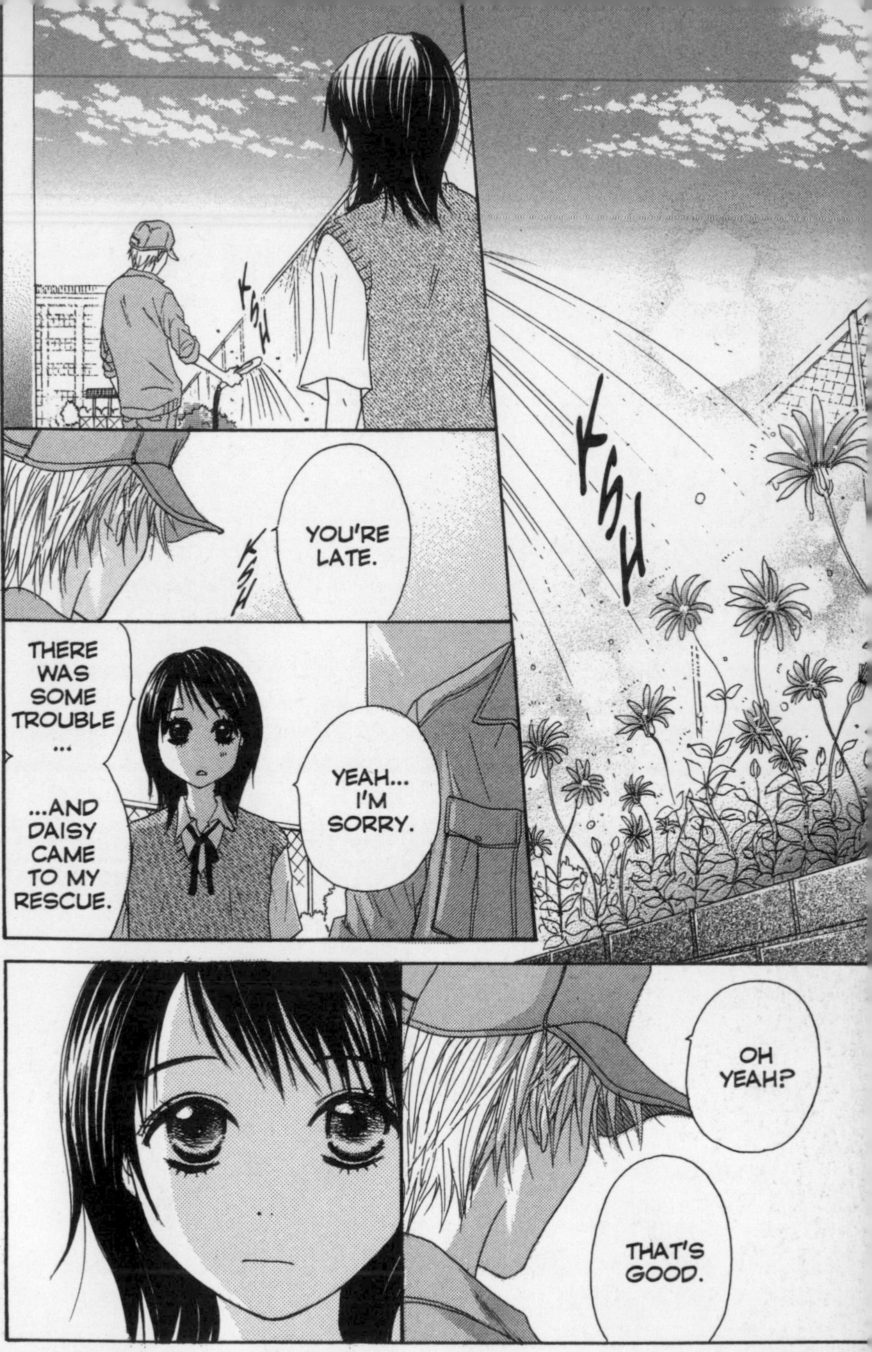
KSH
KSH
YOU'RE LATE.
KSH
YEAH... I'M SORRY.
THERE WAS SOME TROUBLE...
...AND DAISY CAME TO MY RESCUE.
OH YEAH?
THAT'S GOOD.

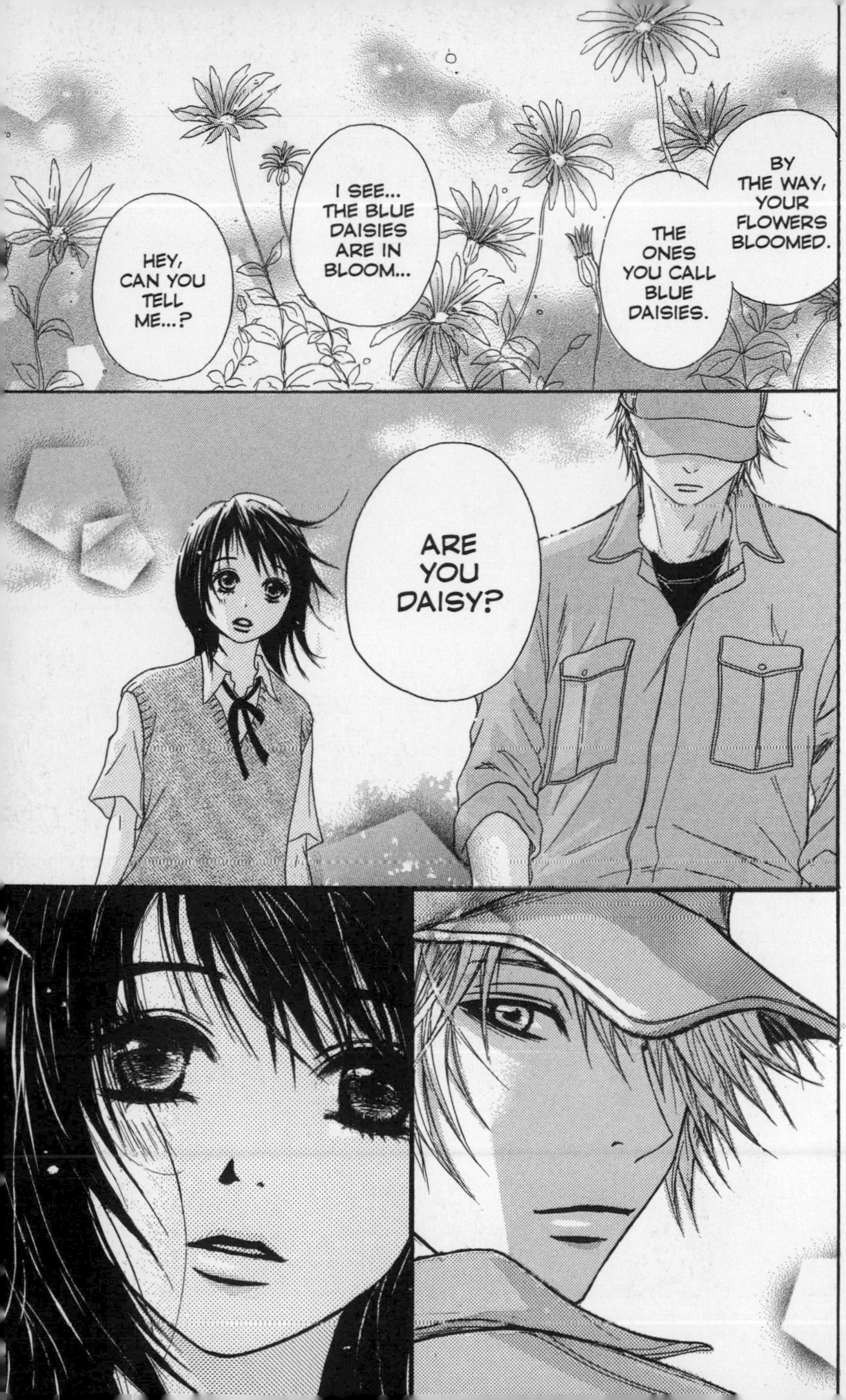
BY THE WAY, YOUR FLOWERS BLOOMED.
THE ONES YOU CALL BLUE DAISIES.
I SEE... THE BLUE DAISIES ARE IN BLOOM...
HEY, CAN YOU TELL ME...?
ARE YOU DAISY?

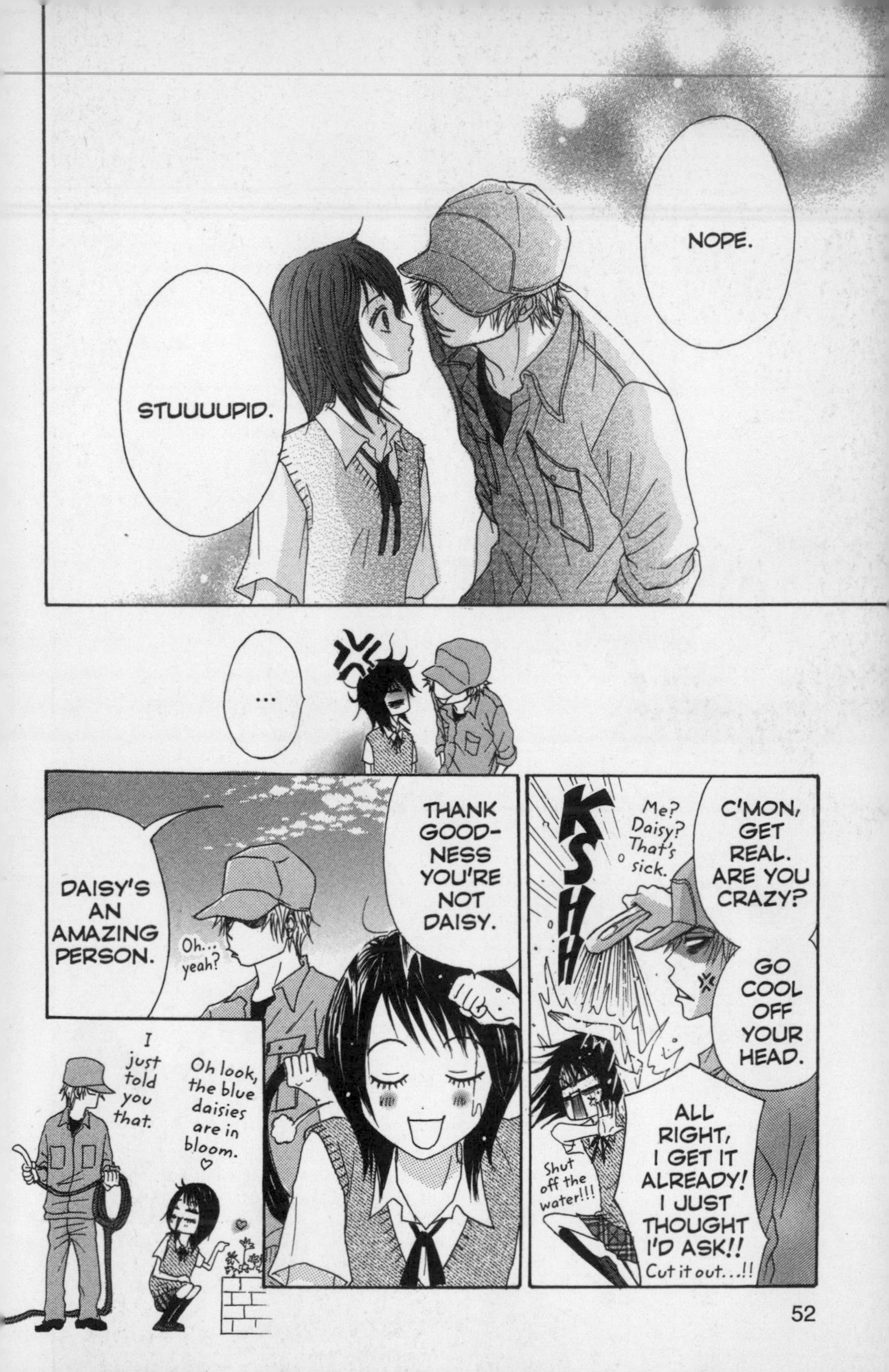
NOPE.
STUUUUPID.
...
C'MON, GET REAL. ARE YOU CRAZY?
Me? Daisy? That's sick.
KSHH
GO COOL OFF YOUR HEAD.
ALL RIGHT, I GET IT ALREADY! I JUST THOUGHT I'D ASK!!
Cut it out...!!
Shut off the water!!!
THANK GOODNESS YOU'RE NOT DAISY.
Oh... yeah?
DAISY'S AN AMAZING PERSON.
Oh look, the blue daisies are in bloom. ♡
I just told you that.

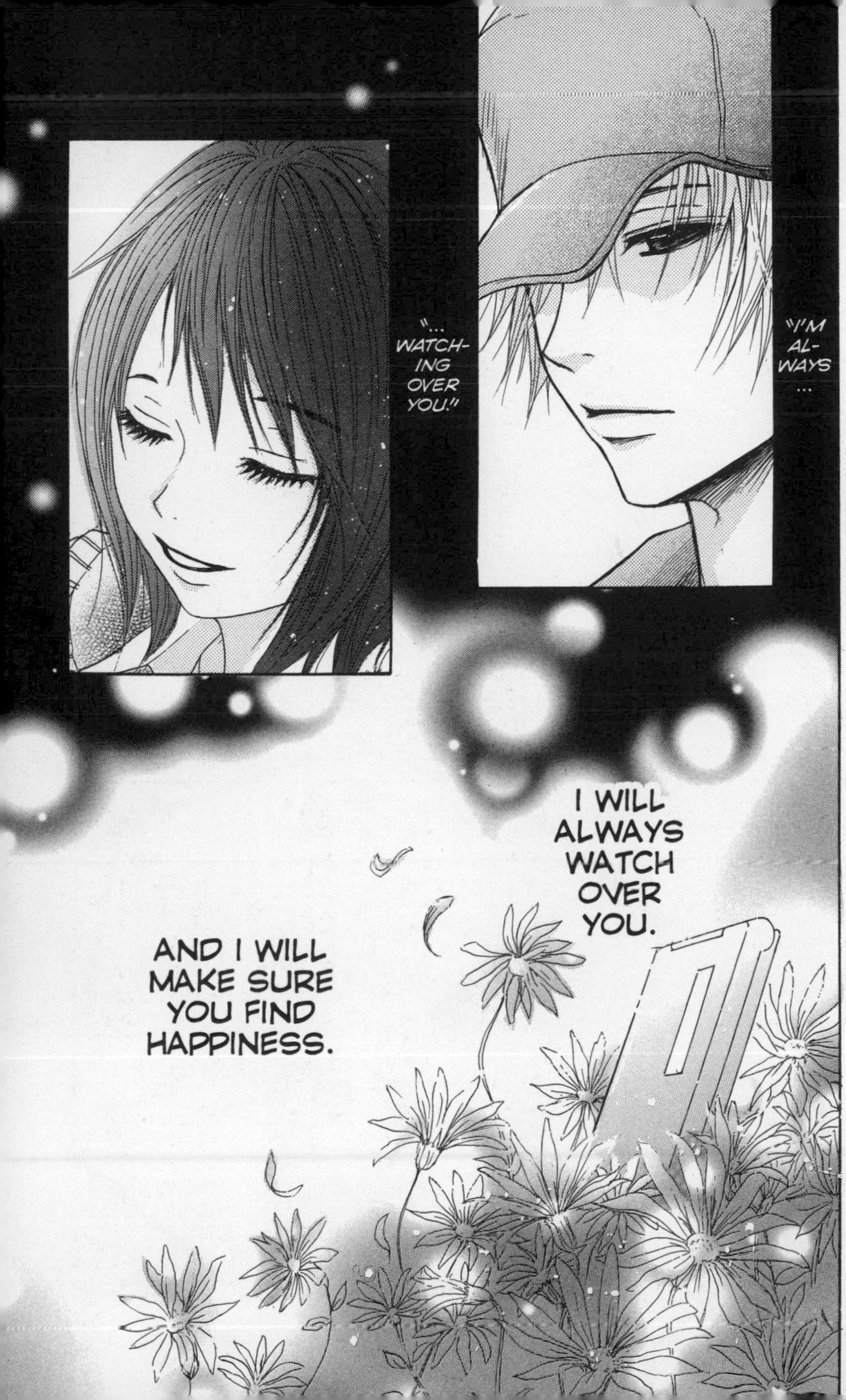
"I'M ALWAYS...
"...WATCHING OVER YOU."
I WILL ALWAYS WATCH OVER YOU.
AND I WILL MAKE SURE YOU FIND HAPPINESS.

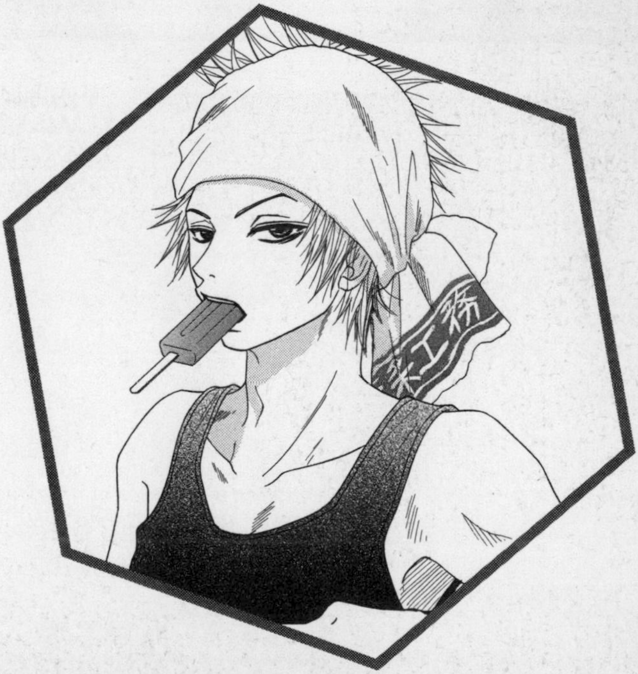
工務

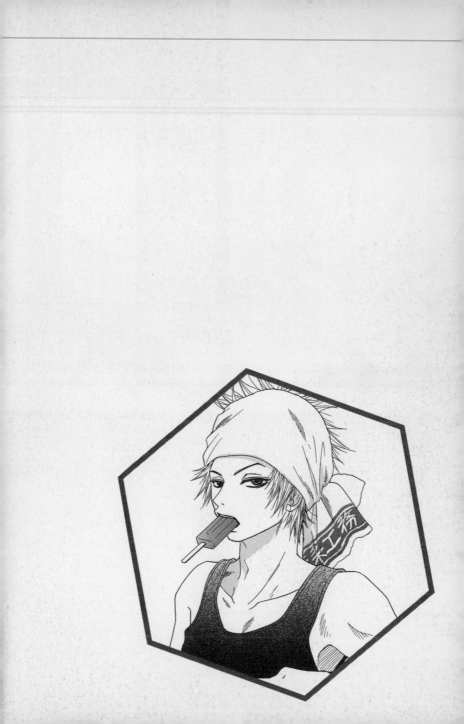

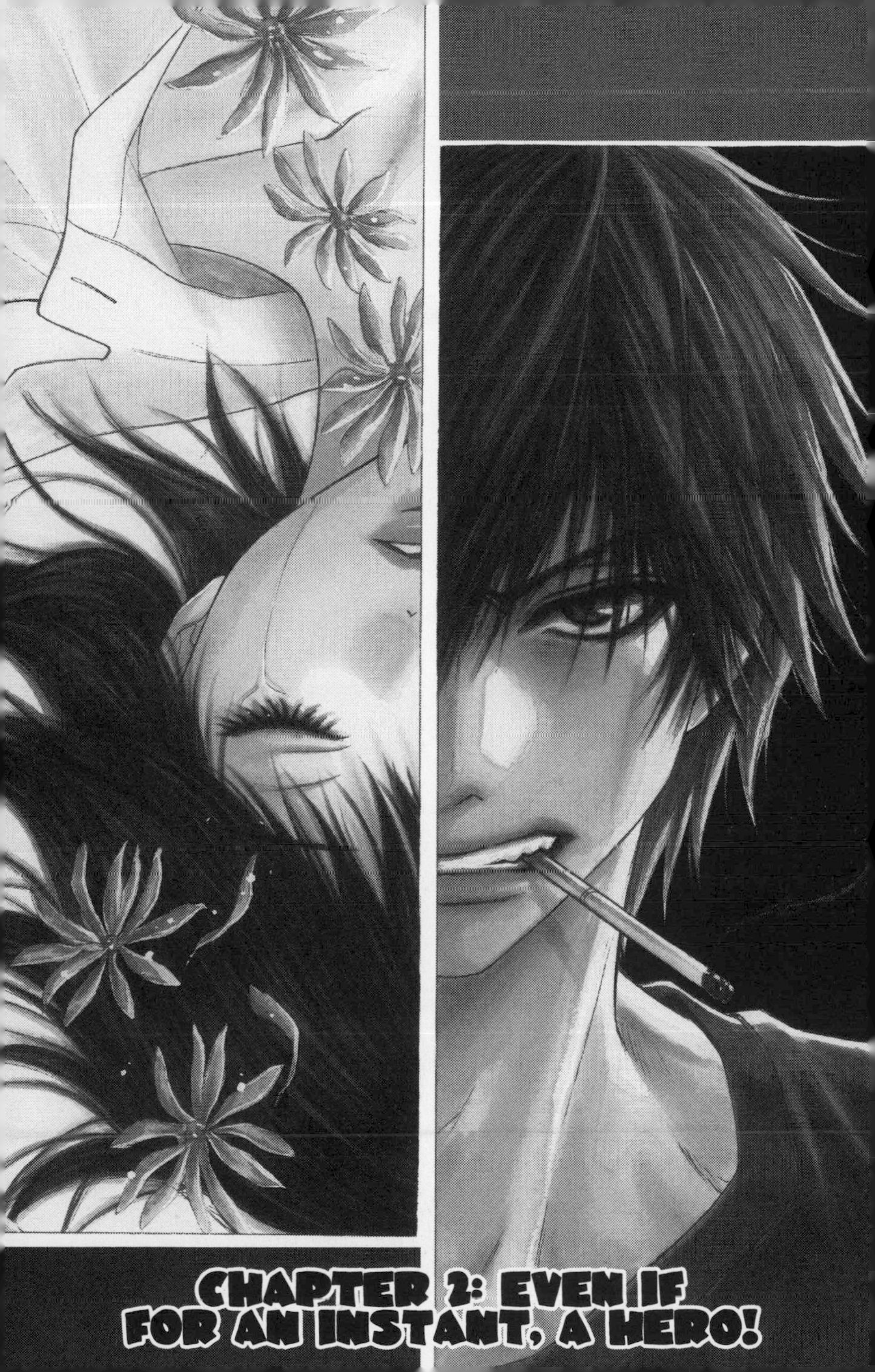
CHAPTER 2: EVEN IF
FOR AN INSTANT, A HERO!

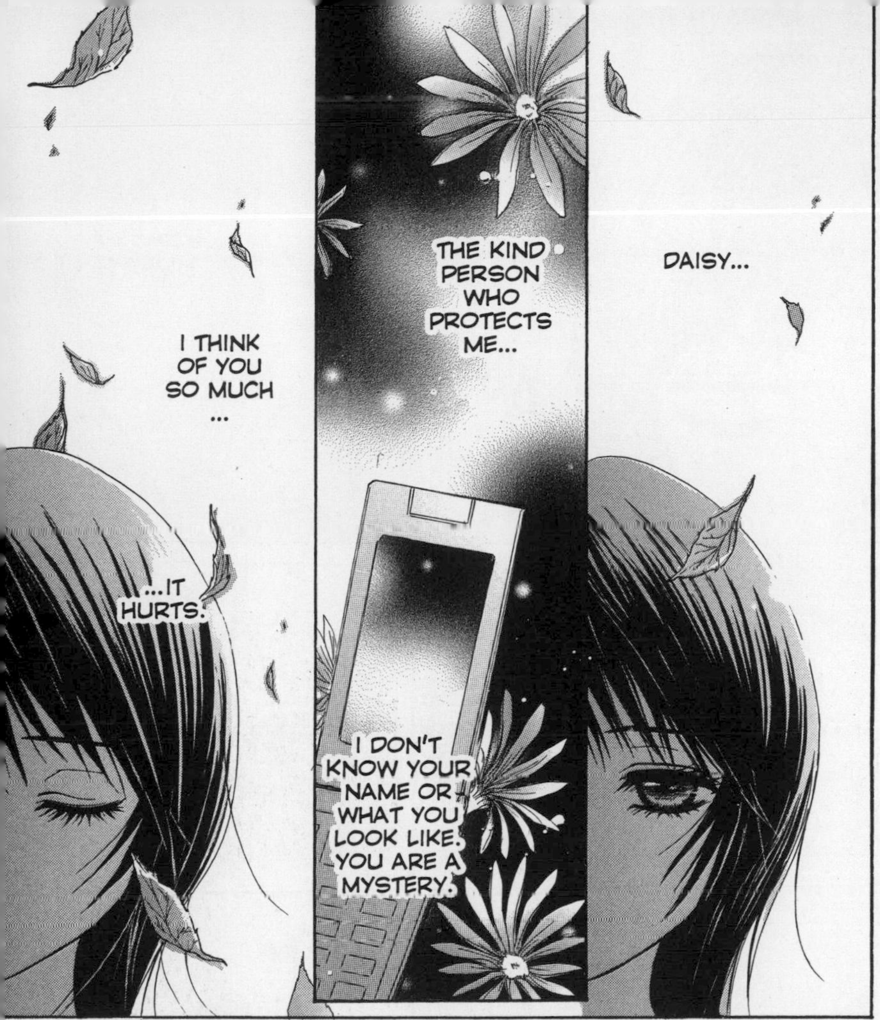
DAISY...
THE KIND PERSON WHO PROTECTS ME...
I DON'T KNOW YOUR NAME OR WHAT YOU LOOK LIKE. YOU ARE A MYSTERY.
I THINK OF YOU SO MUCH ...
...IT HURTS.

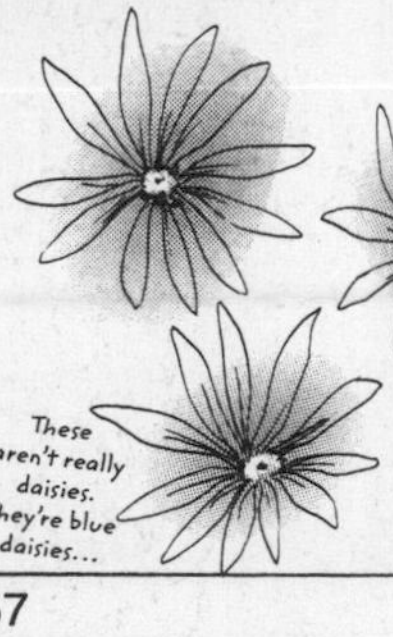
These aren't really daisies. They're blue daisies...

I'M SORRY THIS IS SUCH A SMALL SECTION. HELLO, EVERYONE. I'M KYOUSUKE MOTOMI. THANK YOU FOR READING *DENGEKI DAISY*!!

THIS MANGA HAS LOTS OF TEDIOUS DETAILS TO DRAW, LIKE COMPUTERS AND ALL THE FLOWERS, BUT THE THING THAT'S THE MOST TEDIOUS TO DRAW IS KUROSAKI'S HAIR. ...Go bald!!!

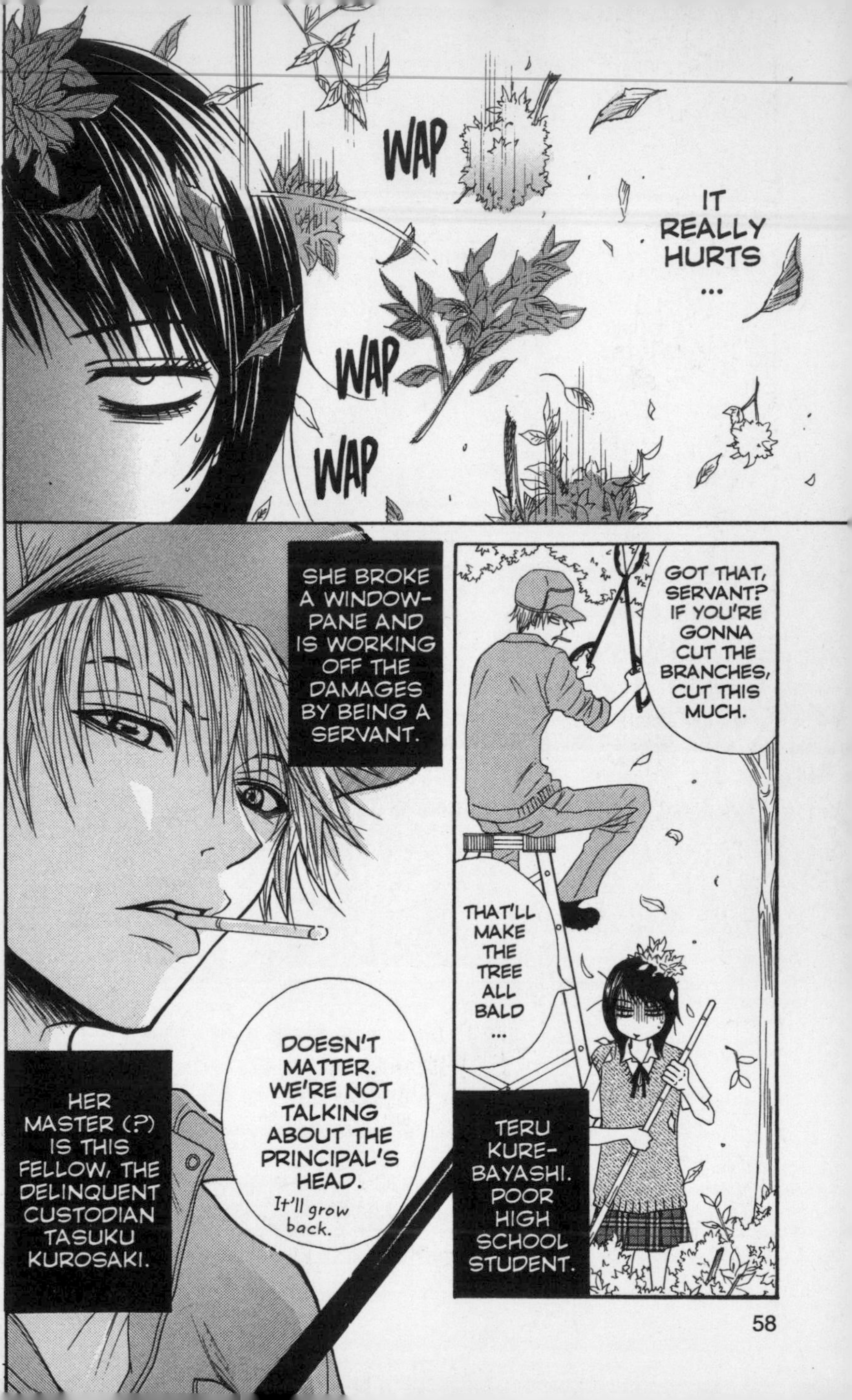
IT REALLY HURTS ...
WAP
WAP
WAP
GOT THAT, SERVANT? IF YOU'RE GONNA CUT THE BRANCHES, CUT THIS MUCH.
THAT'LL MAKE THE TREE ALL BALD ...
TERU KURE-BAYASHI. POOR HIGH SCHOOL STUDENT.
SHE BROKE A WINDOW-PANE AND IS WORKING OFF THE DAMAGES BY BEING A SERVANT.
DOESN'T MATTER. WE'RE NOT TALKING ABOUT THE PRINCIPAL'S HEAD.
It'll grow back.
HER MASTER (?) IS THIS FELLOW, THE DELINQUENT CUSTODIAN TASUKU KUROSAKI.

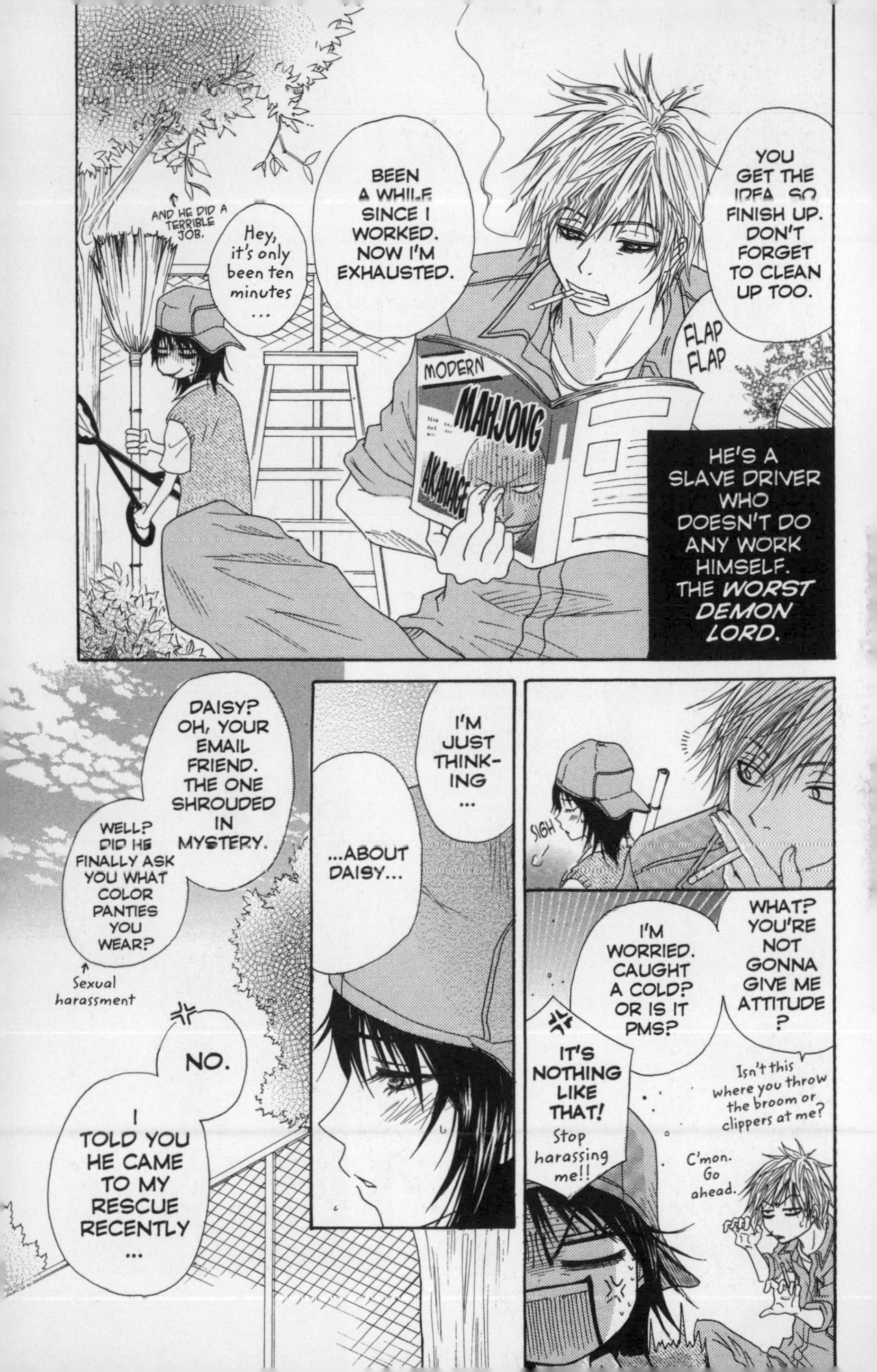
YOU GET THE IDEA, SO FINISH UP. DON'T FORGET TO CLEAN UP TOO.
FLAP FLAP
BEEN A WHILE SINCE I WORKED. NOW I'M EXHAUSTED.
Hey, it's only been ten minutes...
AND HE DID A TERRIBLE JOB.
MODERN MAHJONG
AKAHAGE
HE'S A SLAVE DRIVER WHO DOESN'T DO ANY WORK HIMSELF. THE *WORST DEMON LORD*.
SIGH
WHAT? YOU'RE NOT GONNA GIVE ME ATTITUDE?
I'M WORRIED. CAUGHT A COLD? OR IS IT PMS?
IT'S NOTHING LIKE THAT! Stop harassing me!!
Isn't this where you throw the broom or clippers at me?
C'mon. Go ahead.
I'M JUST THINKING...
...ABOUT DAISY...
DAISY? OH, YOUR EMAIL FRIEND. THE ONE SHROUDED IN MYSTERY.
WELL? DID HE FINALLY ASK YOU WHAT COLOR PANTIES YOU WEAR?
Sexual harassment
NO.
I TOLD YOU HE CAME TO MY RESCUE RECENTLY...

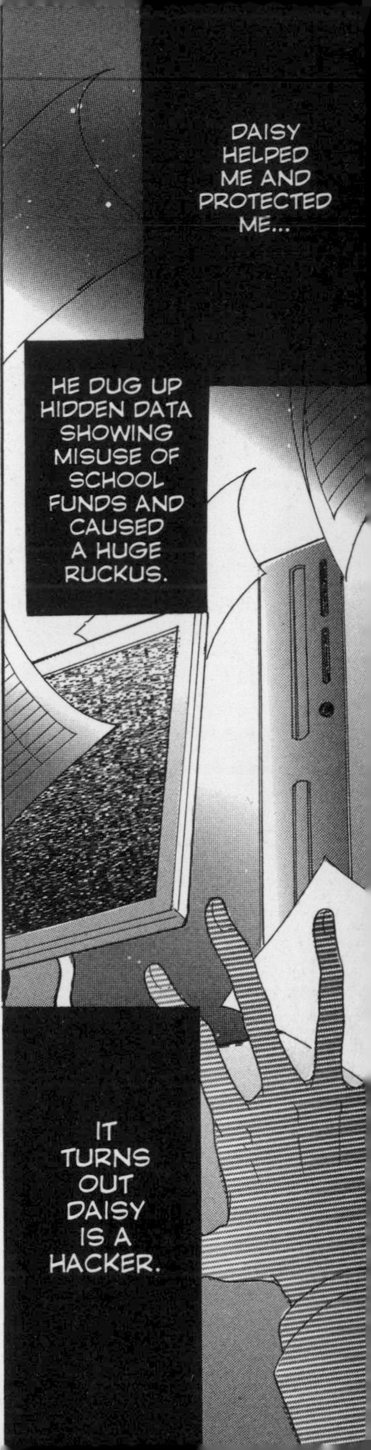
DAISY HELPED ME AND PROTECTED ME...
HE DUG UP HIDDEN DATA SHOWING MISUSE OF SCHOOL FUNDS AND CAUSED A HUGE RUCKUS.
IT TURNS OUT DAISY IS A HACKER.

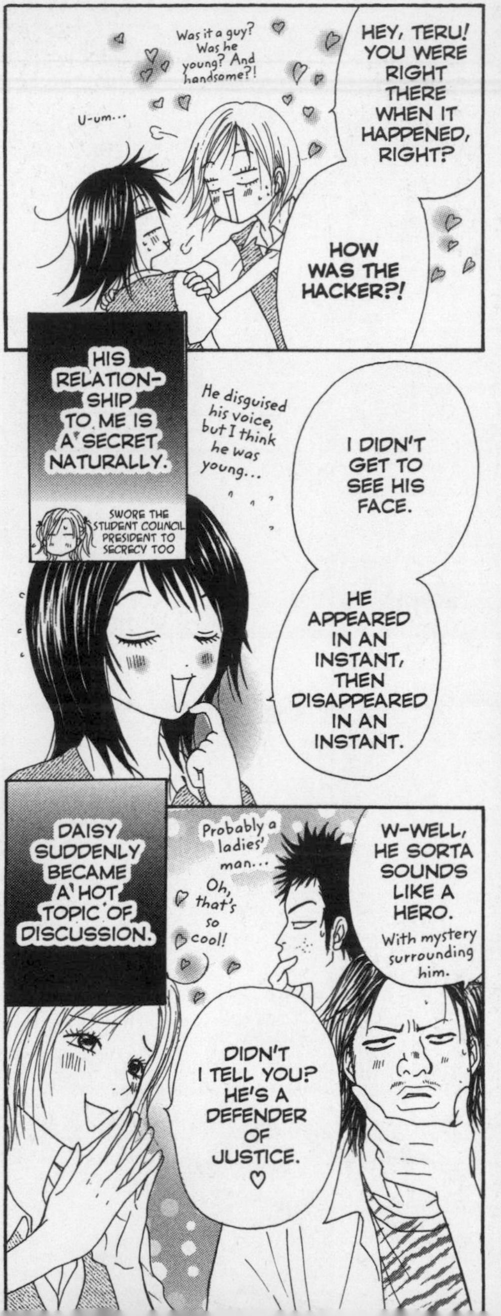
HEY, TERU! YOU WERE RIGHT THERE WHEN IT HAPPENED, RIGHT?
HOW WAS THE HACKER?!
Was it a guy? Was he young? And handsome?!
U-um...
HIS RELATIONSHIP TO ME IS A SECRET NATURALLY.
SWORE THE STUDENT COUNCIL PRESIDENT TO SECRECY TOO
I DIDN'T GET TO SEE HIS FACE.
He disguised his voice, but I think he was young...
HE APPEARED IN AN INSTANT, THEN DISAPPEARED IN AN INSTANT.
DAISY SUDDENLY BECAME A HOT TOPIC OF DISCUSSION.
W-WELL, HE SORTA SOUNDS LIKE A HERO.
With mystery surrounding him.
Probably a ladies' man...
Oh, that's so cool!
DIDN'T I TELL YOU? HE'S A DEFENDER OF JUSTICE. ♡

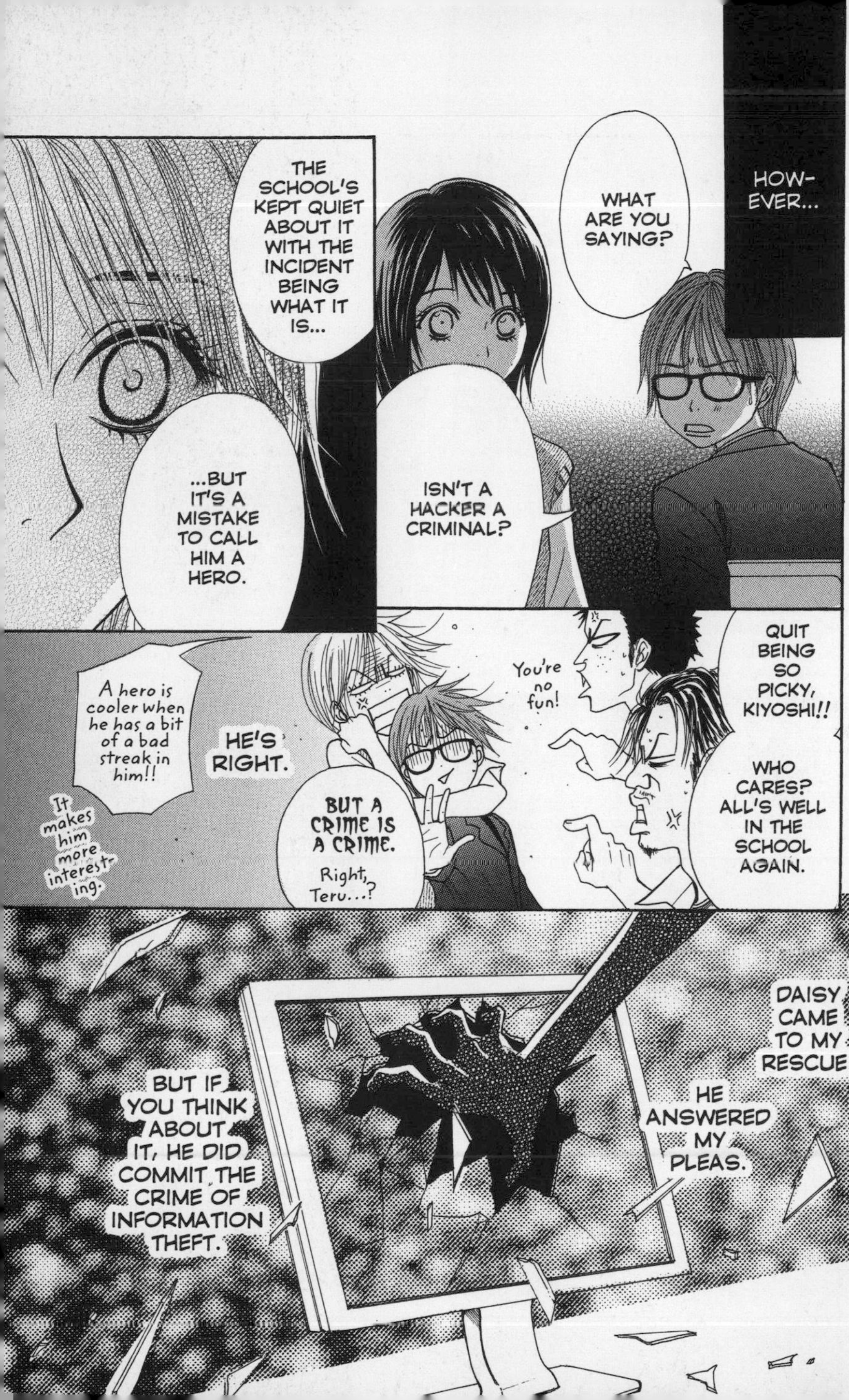
HOW-EVER...
WHAT ARE YOU SAYING?
ISN'T A HACKER A CRIMINAL?
THE SCHOOL'S KEPT QUIET ABOUT IT WITH THE INCIDENT BEING WHAT IT IS...
...BUT IT'S A MISTAKE TO CALL HIM A HERO.
QUIT BEING SO PICKY, KIYOSHI!!
WHO CARES? ALL'S WELL IN THE SCHOOL AGAIN.
You're no fun!
BUT A CRIME IS A CRIME.
Right, Teru...?
HE'S RIGHT.
A hero is cooler when he has a bit of a bad streak in him!!
It makes him more interesting.
DAISY CAME TO MY RESCUE.
HE ANSWERED MY PLEAS.
BUT IF YOU THINK ABOUT IT, HE DID COMMIT THE CRIME OF INFORMATION THEFT.

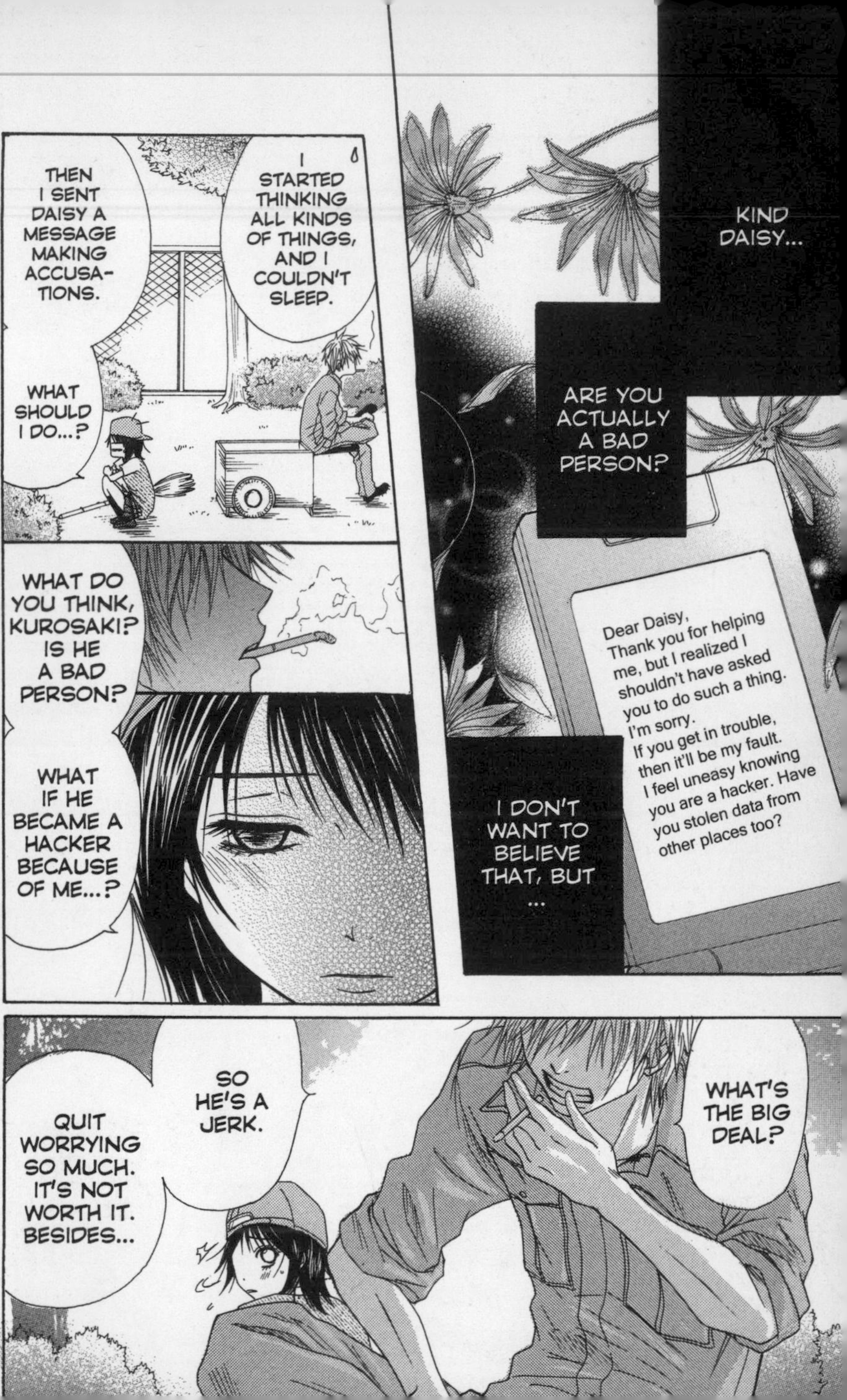
KIND DAISY...
ARE YOU ACTUALLY A BAD PERSON?
Dear Daisy,
Thank you for helping me, but I realized I shouldn't have asked you to do such a thing.
I'm sorry.
If you get in trouble, then it'll be my fault.
I feel uneasy knowing you are a hacker. Have you stolen data from other places too?
I DON'T WANT TO BELIEVE THAT, BUT ...
I STARTED THINKING ALL KINDS OF THINGS, AND I COULDN'T SLEEP.
THEN I SENT DAISY A MESSAGE MAKING ACCUSATIONS.
WHAT SHOULD I DO...?
WHAT DO YOU THINK, KUROSAKI? IS HE A BAD PERSON?
WHAT IF HE BECAME A HACKER BECAUSE OF ME...?
WHAT'S THE BIG DEAL?
SO HE'S A JERK.
QUIT WORRYING SO MUCH. IT'S NOT WORTH IT. BESIDES...

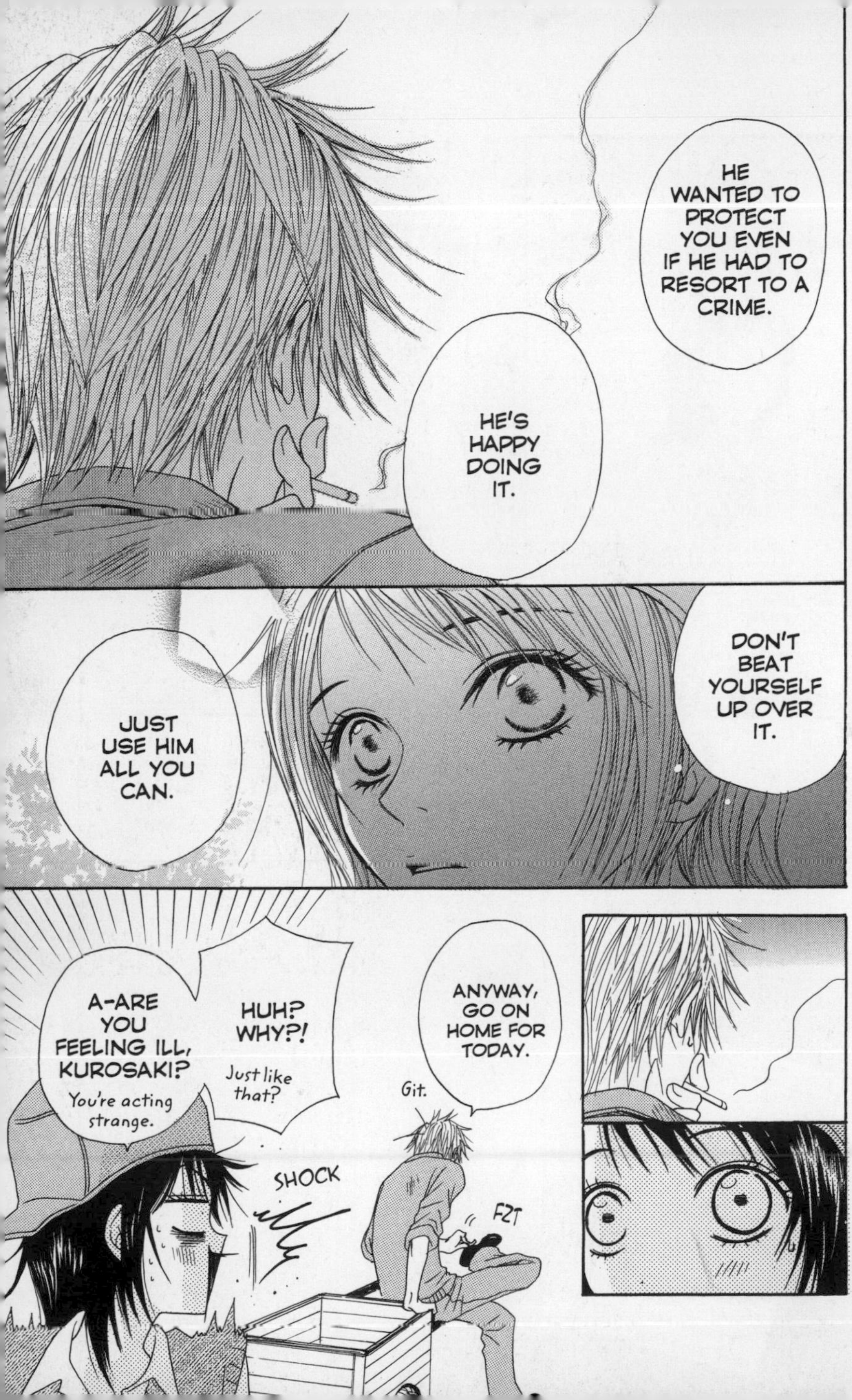
HE WANTED TO PROTECT YOU EVEN IF HE HAD TO RESORT TO A CRIME.
HE'S HAPPY DOING IT.
DON'T BEAT YOURSELF UP OVER IT.
JUST USE HIM ALL YOU CAN.
ANYWAY, GO ON HOME FOR TODAY.
Git.
HUH? WHY?!
Just like that?
A-ARE YOU FEELING ILL, KUROSAKI?
You're acting strange.
FZT
SHOCK

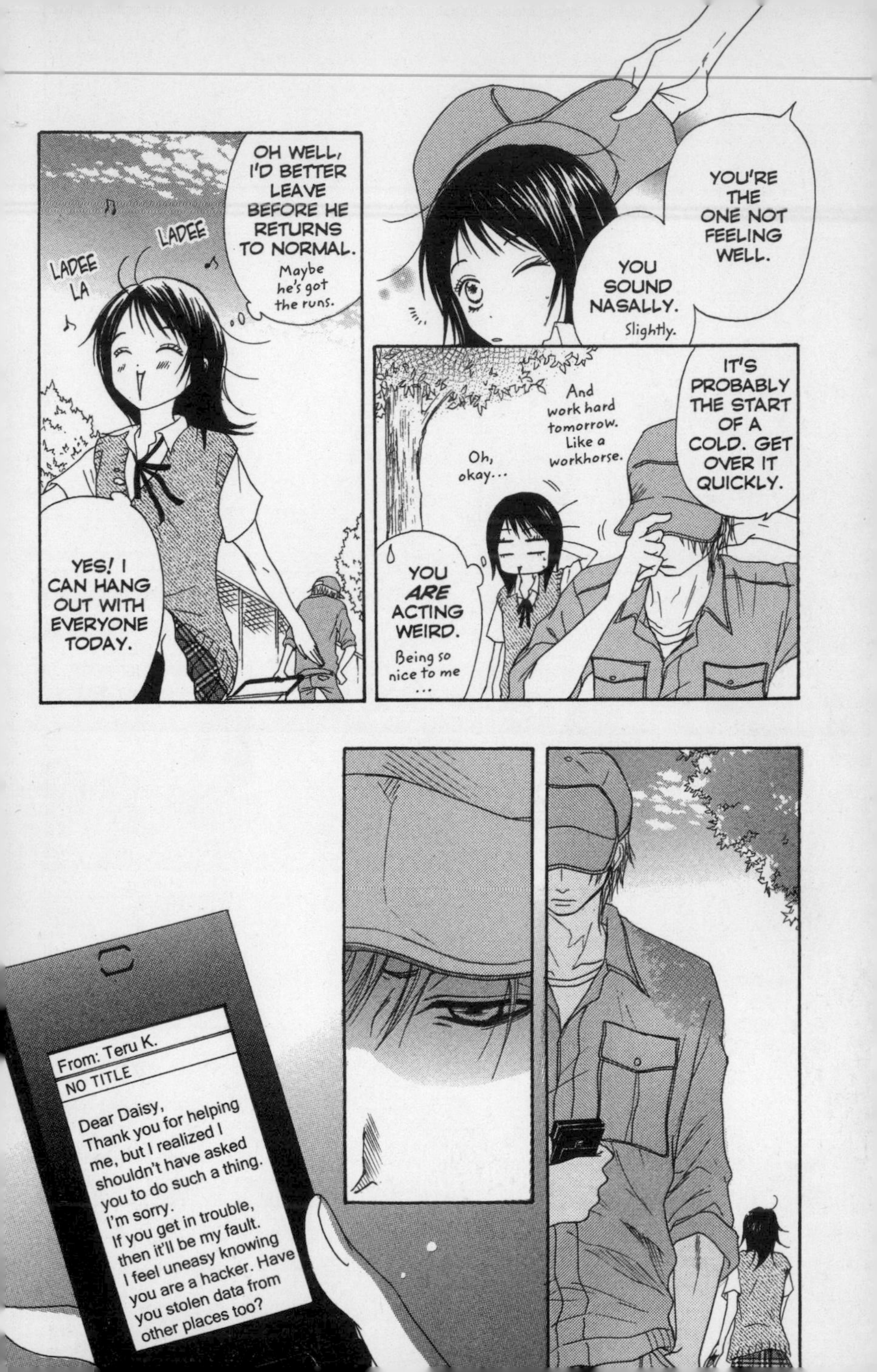
YOU'RE THE ONE NOT FEELING WELL.
YOU SOUND NASALLY.
Slightly.
IT'S PROBABLY THE START OF A COLD. GET OVER IT QUICKLY.
And work hard tomorrow. Like a workhorse.
Oh, okay...
YOU *ARE* ACTING WEIRD.
Being so nice to me ...
OH WELL, I'D BETTER LEAVE BEFORE HE RETURNS TO NORMAL.
Maybe he's got the runs.
LADEE
LADEE LA
YES! I CAN HANG OUT WITH EVERYONE TODAY.
From: Teru K.
NO TITLE
Dear Daisy,
Thank you for helping me, but I realized I shouldn't have asked you to do such a thing. I'm sorry.
If you get in trouble, then it'll be my fault.
I feel uneasy knowing you are a hacker. Have you stolen data from other places too?

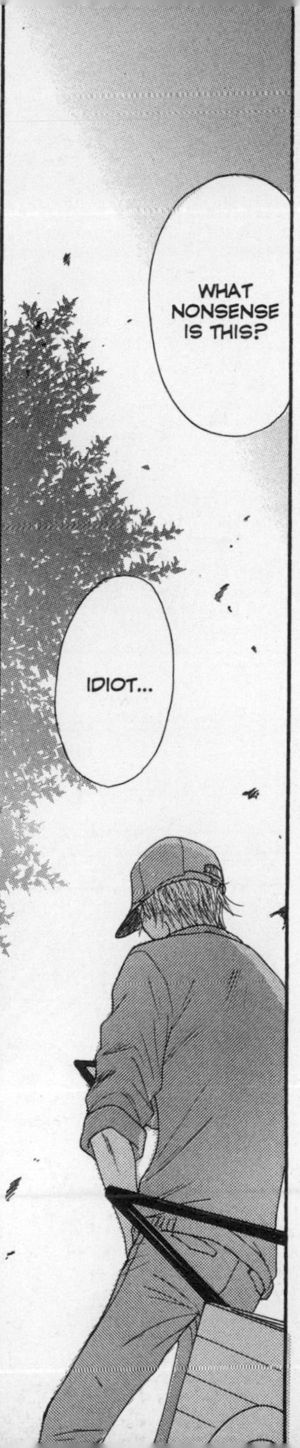
WHAT NONSENSE IS THIS?
IDIOT...

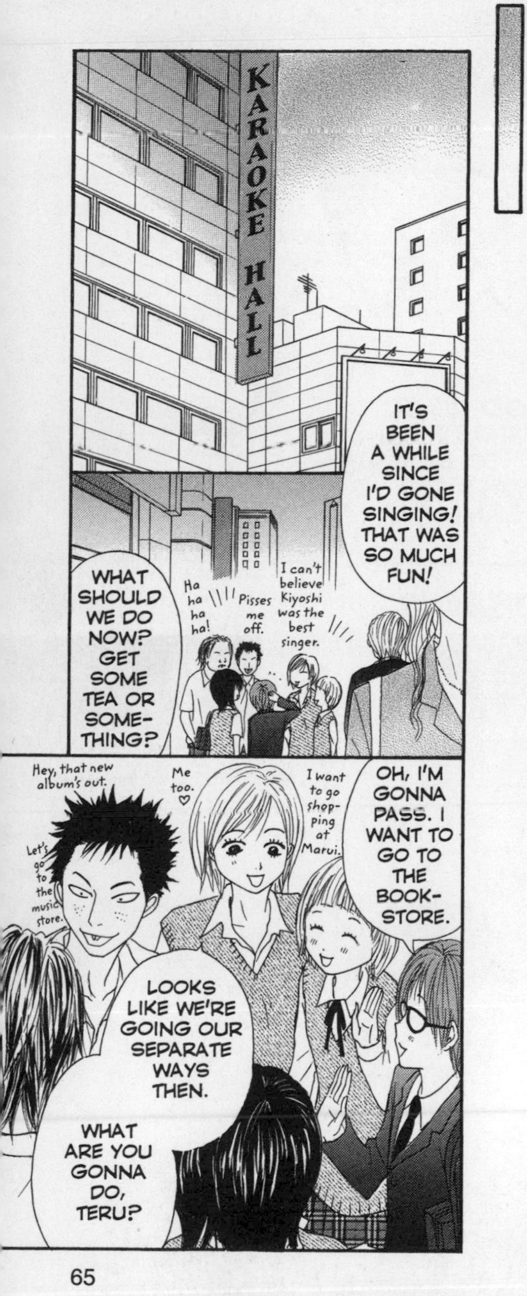
KARAOKE HALL
IT'S BEEN A WHILE SINCE I'D GONE SINGING! THAT WAS SO MUCH FUN!
I can't believe Kiyoshi was the best singer.
Pisses me off.
Ha ha ha!
WHAT SHOULD WE DO NOW? GET SOME TEA OR SOME-THING?
OH, I'M GONNA PASS. I WANT TO GO TO THE BOOK-STORE.
I want to go shop-ping at Marui.
Me too ♡
Hey, that new album's out.
Let's go to the music store.
LOOKS LIKE WE'RE GOING OUR SEPARATE WAYS THEN.
WHAT ARE YOU GONNA DO, TERU?

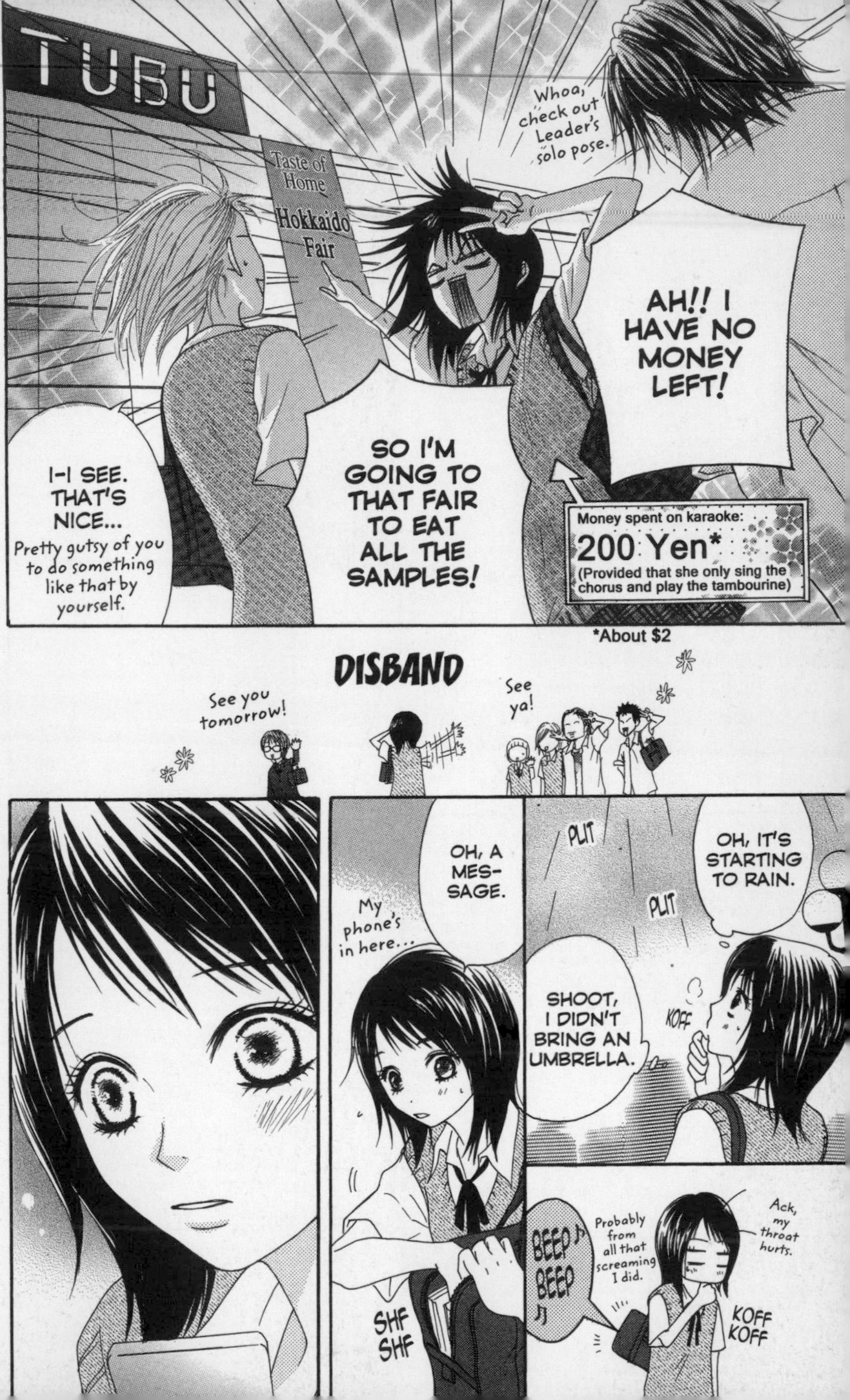
TUBU
Whoa, check out Leader's solo pose.
AH!! I HAVE NO MONEY LEFT!
Money spent on karaoke:
200 Yen*
(Provided that she only sing the chorus and play the tambourine)
Taste of Home
Hokkaido Fair
SO I'M GOING TO THAT FAIR TO EAT ALL THE SAMPLES!
I-I SEE. THAT'S NICE...
Pretty gutsy of you to do something like that by yourself.
*About $2
DISBAND
See ya!
See you tomorrow!
OH, IT'S STARTING TO RAIN.
PLIT
PLIT
SHOOT, I DIDN'T BRING AN UMBRELLA.
KOFF
Ack, my throat hurts.
Probably from all that screaming I did.
KOFF KOFF
BEEP BEEP
OH, A MESSAGE.
My phone's in here...
SHF SHF

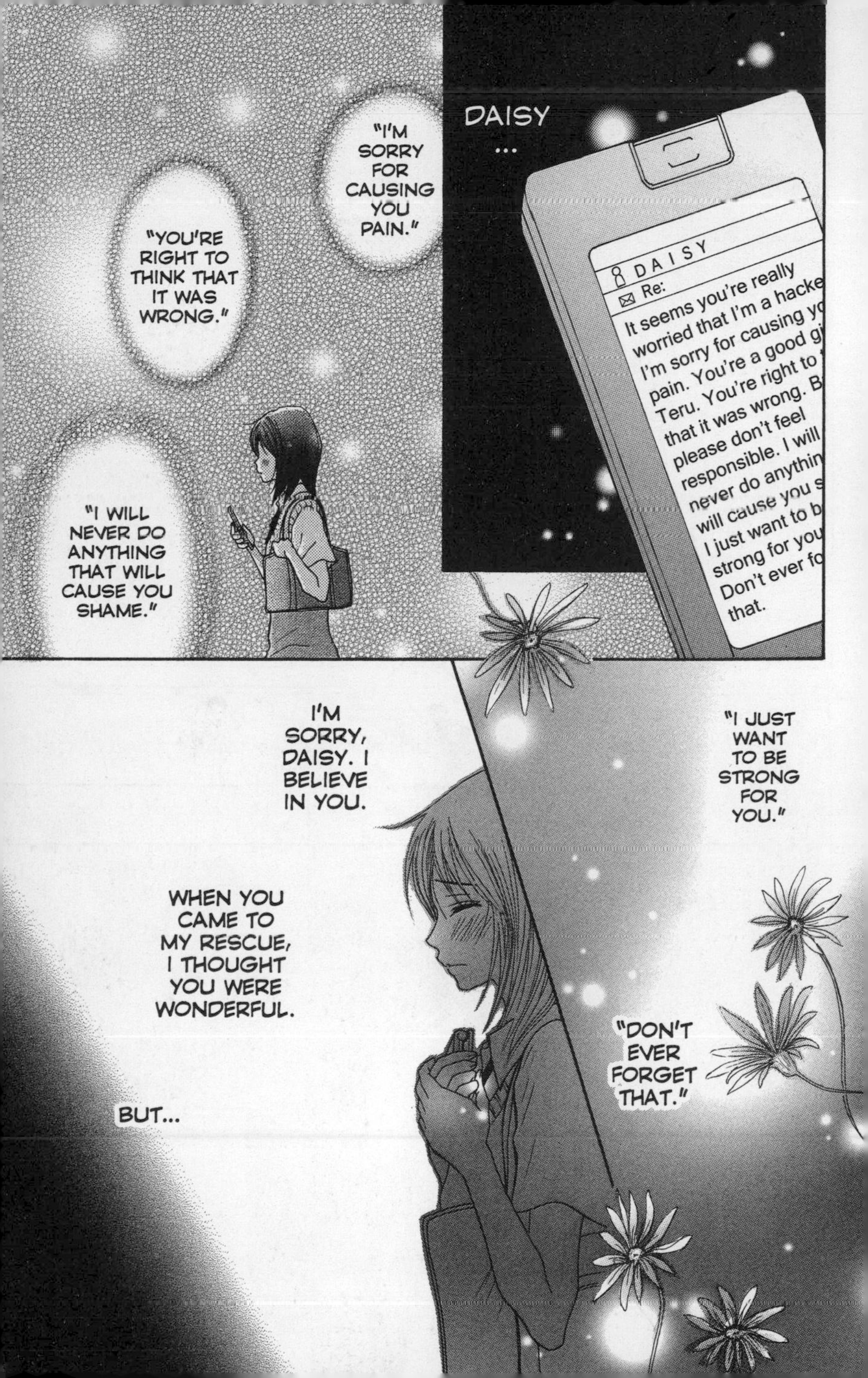
DAISY ...
DAISY
DAISY
Re:
It seems you're really
worried that I'm a hacke
I'm sorry for causing yo
pain. You're a good gi
Teru. You're right to
that it was wrong. B
please don't feel
responsible. I will
never do anythin
will cause you s
I just want to b
strong for you
Don't ever fo
that.
"I'M SORRY FOR CAUSING YOU PAIN."
"YOU'RE RIGHT TO THINK THAT IT WAS WRONG."
"I WILL NEVER DO ANYTHING THAT WILL CAUSE YOU SHAME."
"I JUST WANT TO BE STRONG FOR YOU."
"DON'T EVER FORGET THAT."
I'M SORRY, DAISY. I BELIEVE IN YOU.
WHEN YOU CAME TO MY RESCUE, I THOUGHT YOU WERE WONDERFUL.
BUT...

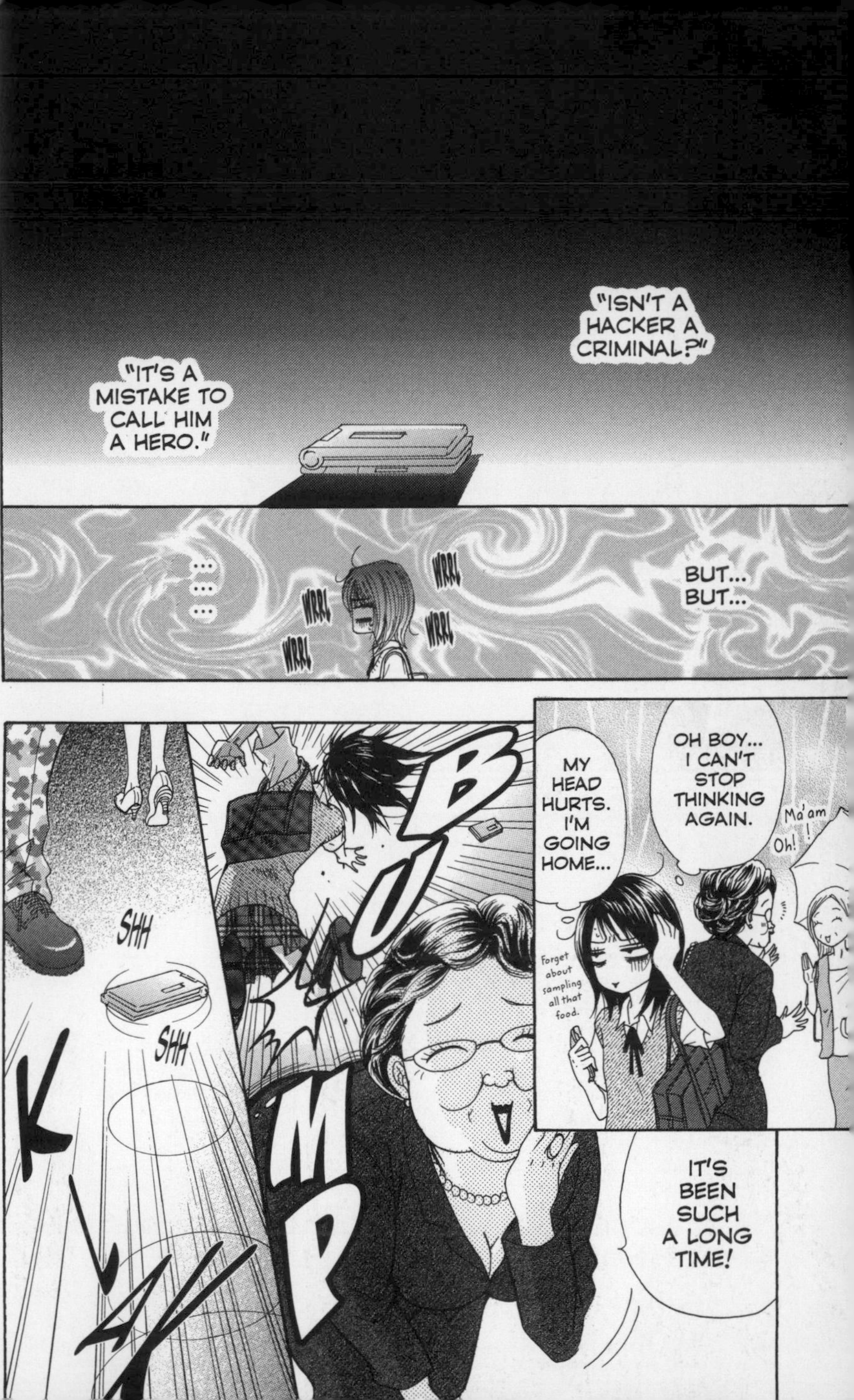
"ISN'T A HACKER A CRIMINAL?"
"IT'S A MISTAKE TO CALL HIM A HERO."
BUT... BUT...
......
WRRL
WRRL
WRRL
WRRL
OH BOY... I CAN'T STOP THINKING AGAIN.
MY HEAD HURTS. I'M GOING HOME...
Ma'am
Oh!
Forget about sampling all that food.
BUMP
IT'S BEEN SUCH A LONG TIME!
SHH
SHH
KLAK

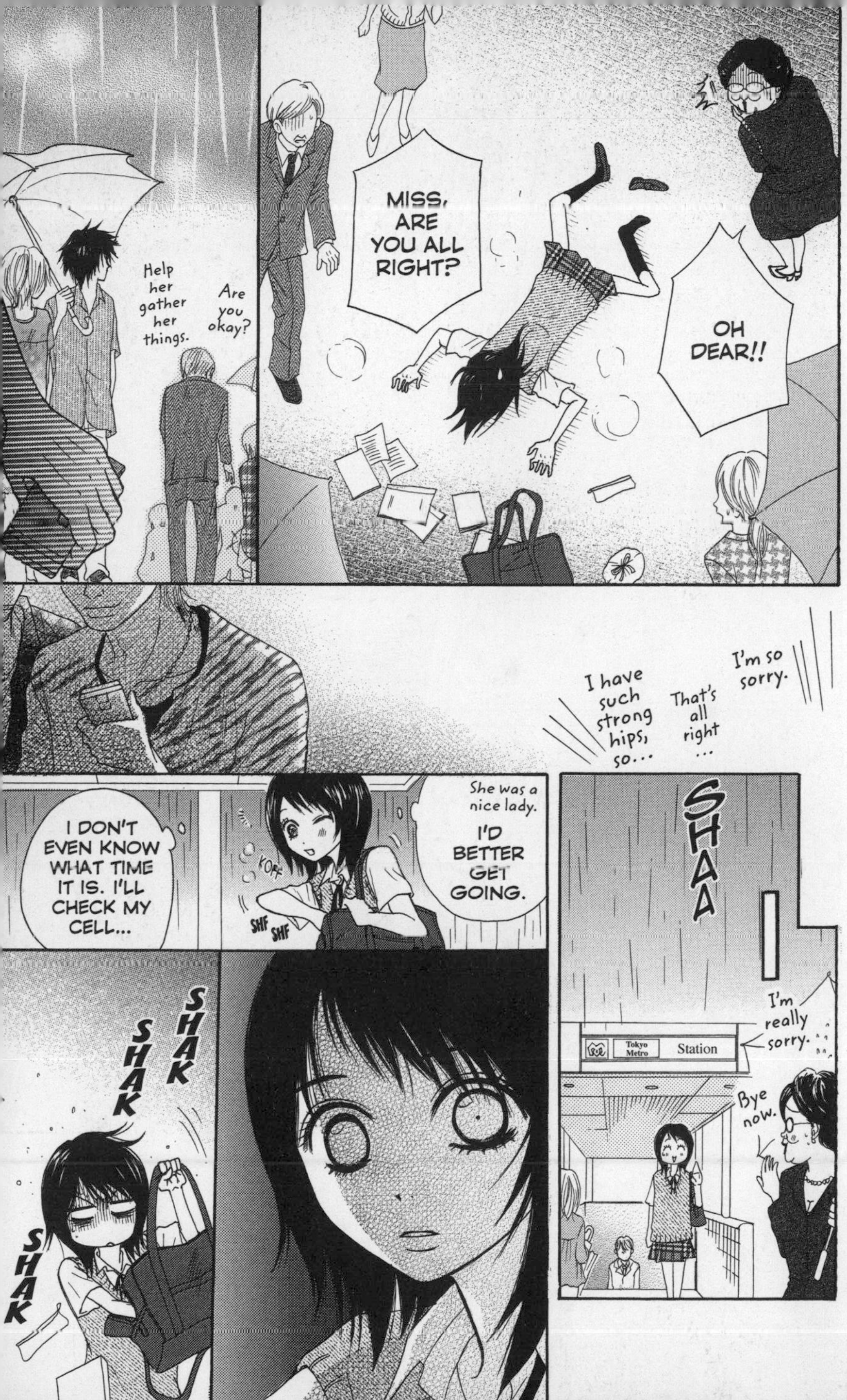
OH DEAR!!
MISS, ARE YOU ALL RIGHT?
Are you okay?
Help her gather her things.
I'm so sorry.
That's all right...
I have such strong hips, so...
SHAA
I'm really sorry.
Tokyo Metro Station
Bye now.
She was a nice lady.
I'D BETTER GET GOING.
KOFF
SHF SHF
I DON'T EVEN KNOW WHAT TIME IT IS. I'LL CHECK MY CELL...
SHAK SHAK SHAK

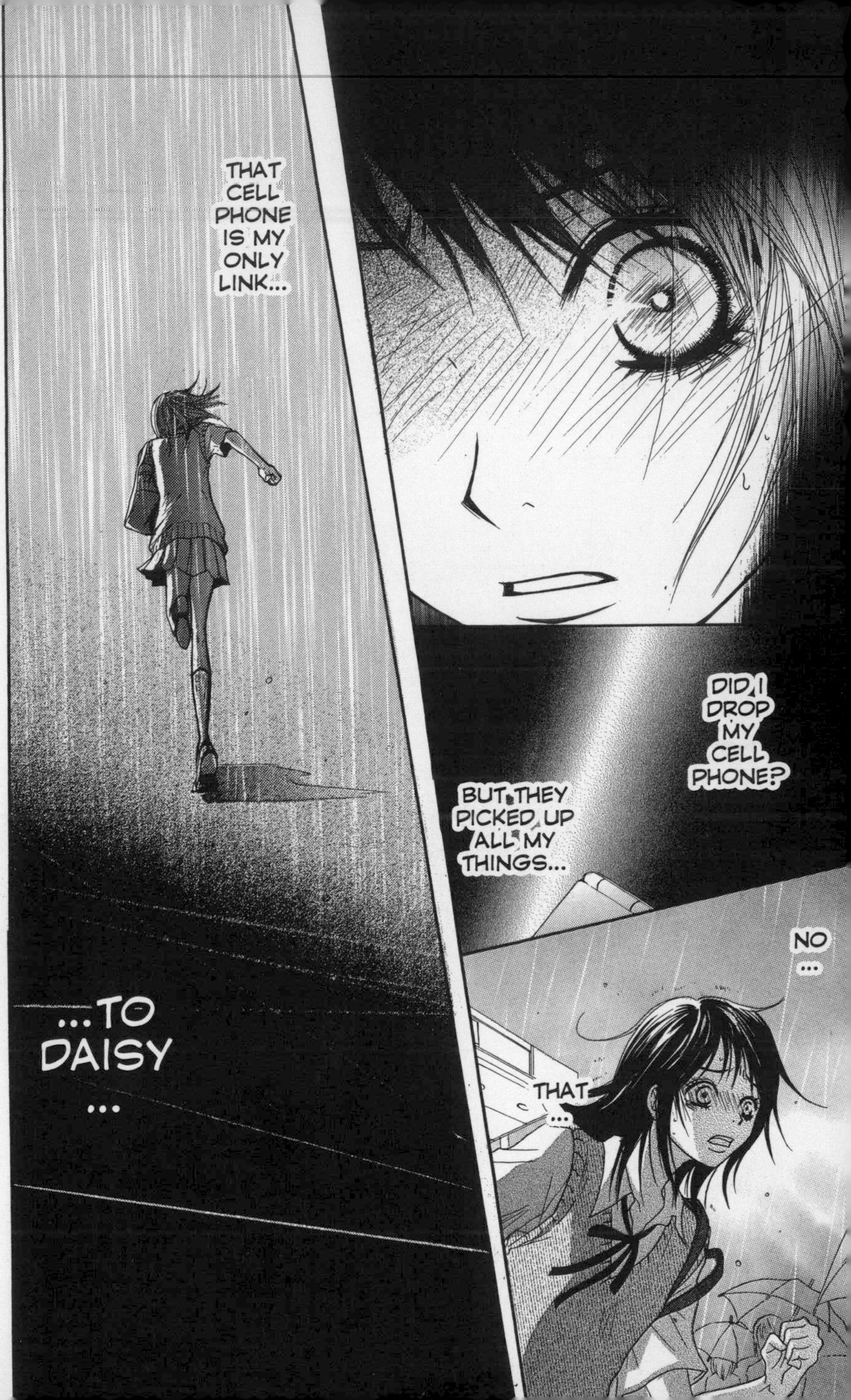
DID I DROP MY CELL PHONE?
BUT THEY PICKED UP ALL MY THINGS...
NO...
THAT...
THAT CELL PHONE IS MY ONLY LINK...
...TO DAISY...

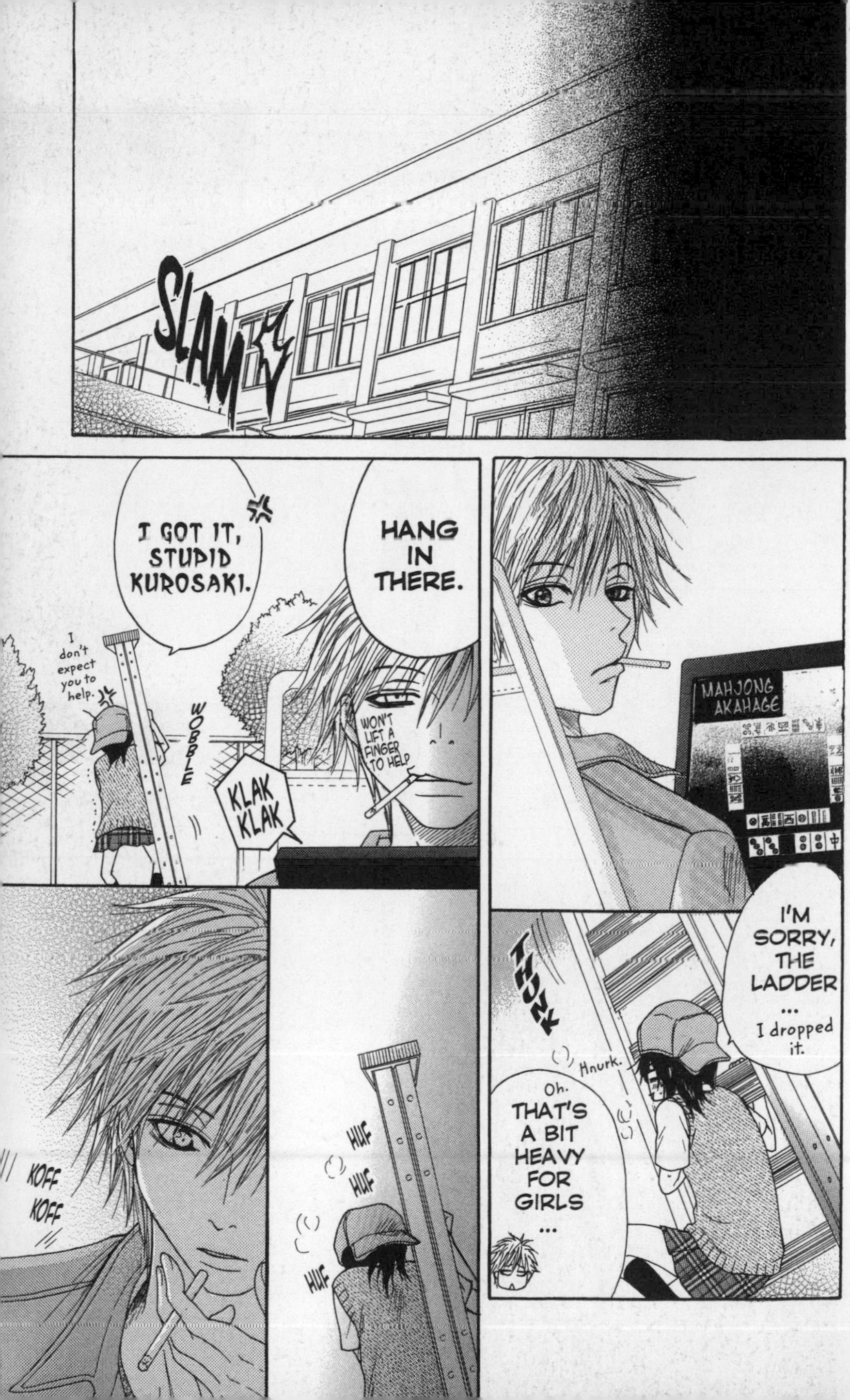
SLAM
MAHJONG AKAHAGE
HANG IN THERE.
I GOT IT, STUPID KUROSAKI.
WON'T LIFT A FINGER TO HELP
I don't expect you to help.
WOBBLE
KLAK KLAK
I'M SORRY, THE LADDER ... I dropped it.
THUNK
Hnurk.
Oh. THAT'S A BIT HEAVY FOR GIRLS ...
HUF
HUF
HUF
KOFF KOFF

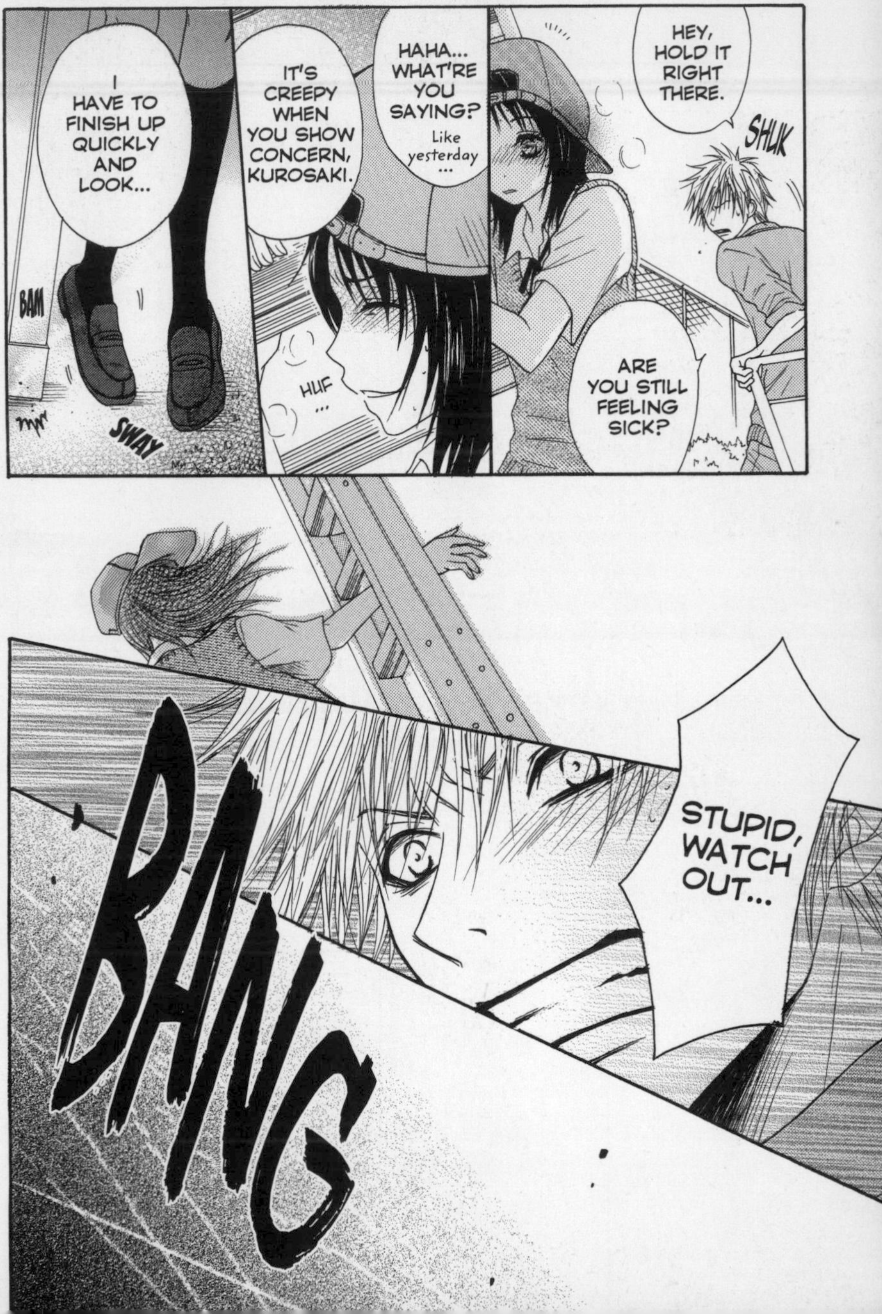
HEY, HOLD IT RIGHT THERE.
SHUK
ARE YOU STILL FEELING SICK?
HAHA... WHAT'RE YOU SAYING?
Like yesterday...
IT'S CREEPY WHEN YOU SHOW CONCERN, KUROSAKI.
HUF...
I HAVE TO FINISH UP QUICKLY AND LOOK...
BAM
SWAY
STUPID, WATCH OUT...
BANG

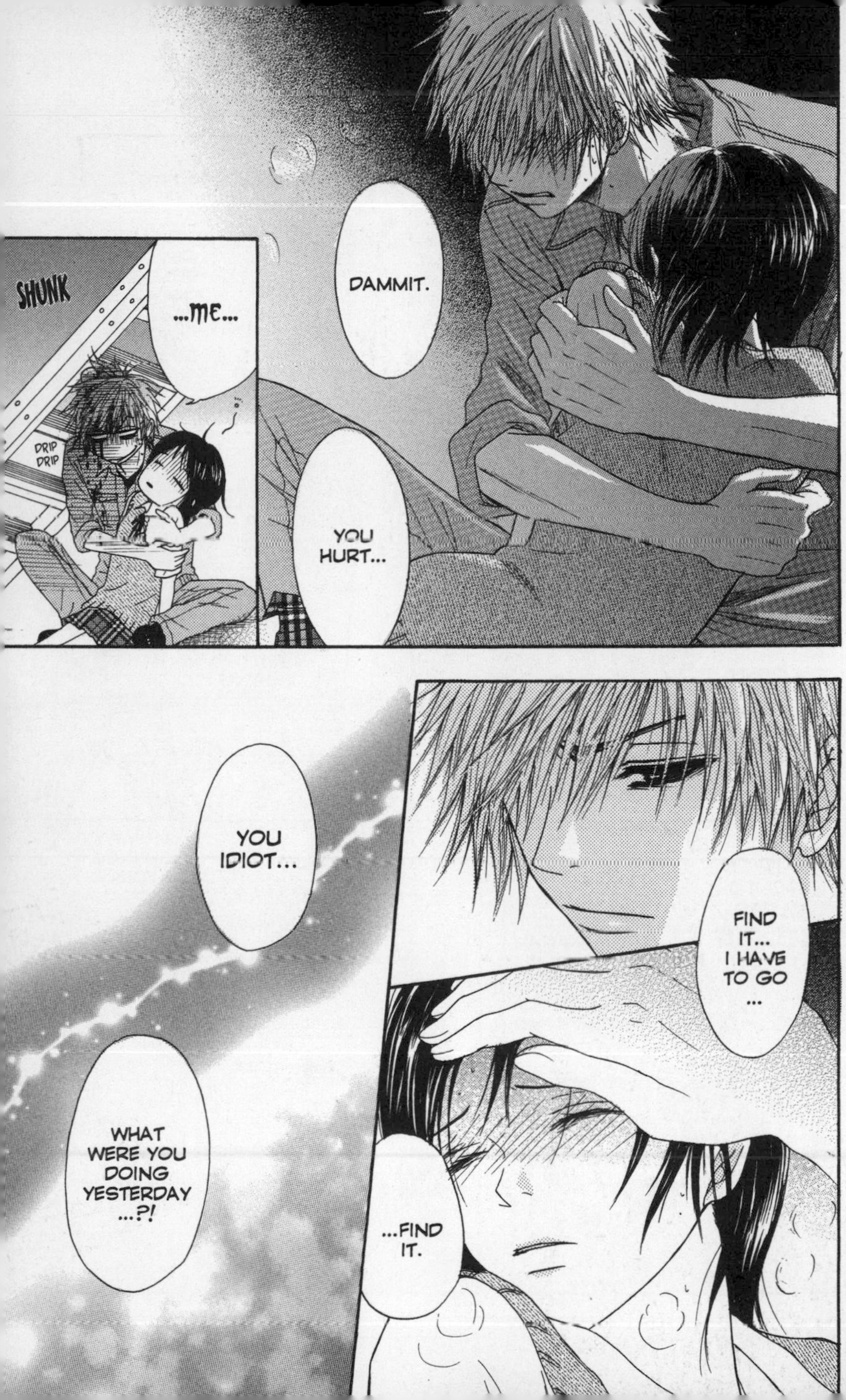
DAMMIT.
YOU HURT...
SHUNK
...ME...
DRIP DRIP
FIND IT... I HAVE TO GO ...
...FIND IT.
YOU IDIOT...
WHAT WERE YOU DOING YESTERDAY ...?!

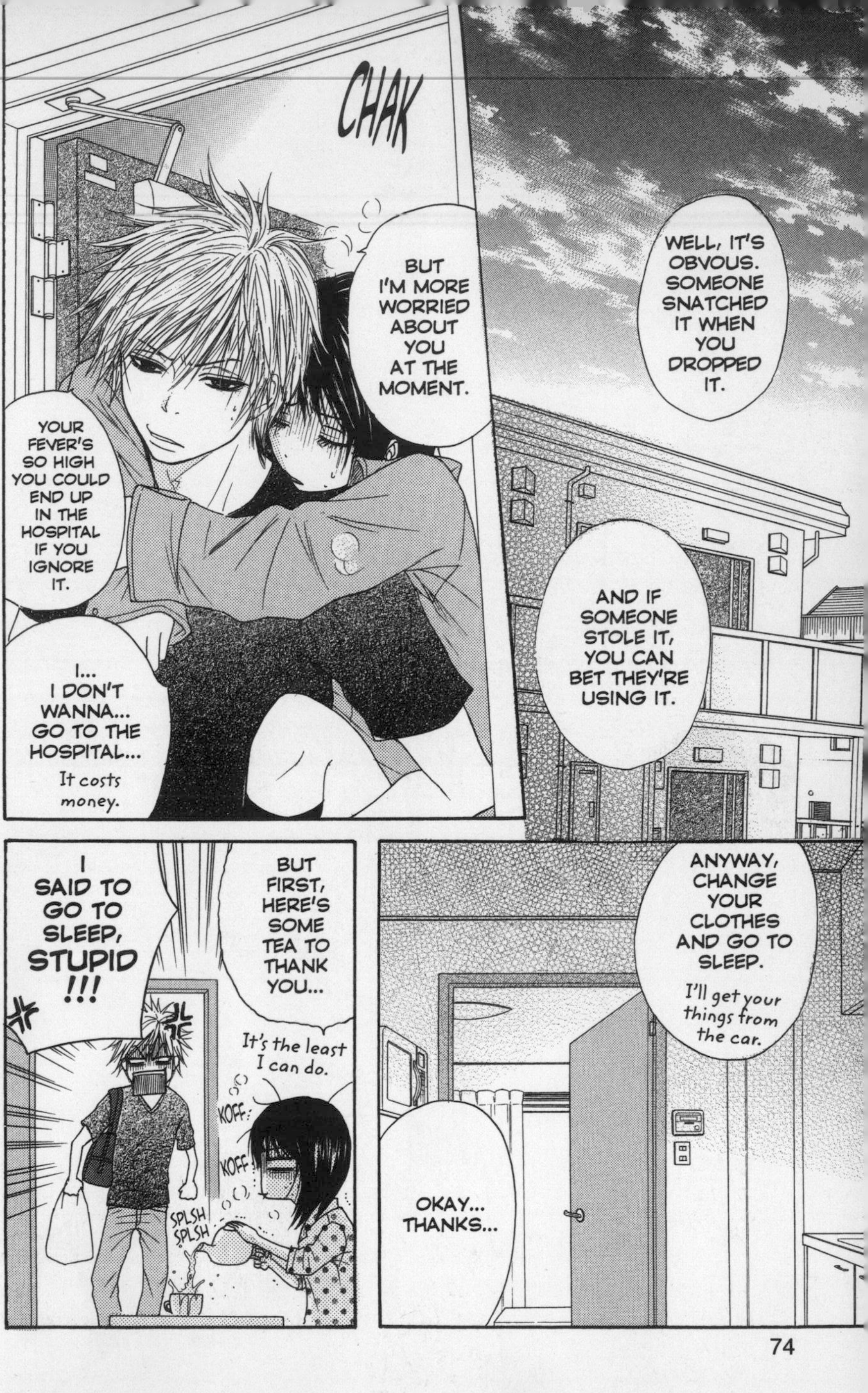
WELL, IT'S OBVOUS. SOMEONE SNATCHED IT WHEN YOU DROPPED IT.
AND IF SOMEONE STOLE IT, YOU CAN BET THEY'RE USING IT.
CHAK
BUT I'M MORE WORRIED ABOUT YOU AT THE MOMENT.
YOUR FEVER'S SO HIGH YOU COULD END UP IN THE HOSPITAL IF YOU IGNORE IT.
I... I DON'T WANNA... GO TO THE HOSPITAL...
It costs money.
ANYWAY, CHANGE YOUR CLOTHES AND GO TO SLEEP.
I'll get your things from the car.
OKAY... THANKS...
BUT FIRST, HERE'S SOME TEA TO THANK YOU...
It's the least I can do.
KOFF
KOFF
SPLSH SPLSH
I SAID TO GO TO SLEEP, STUPID!!!

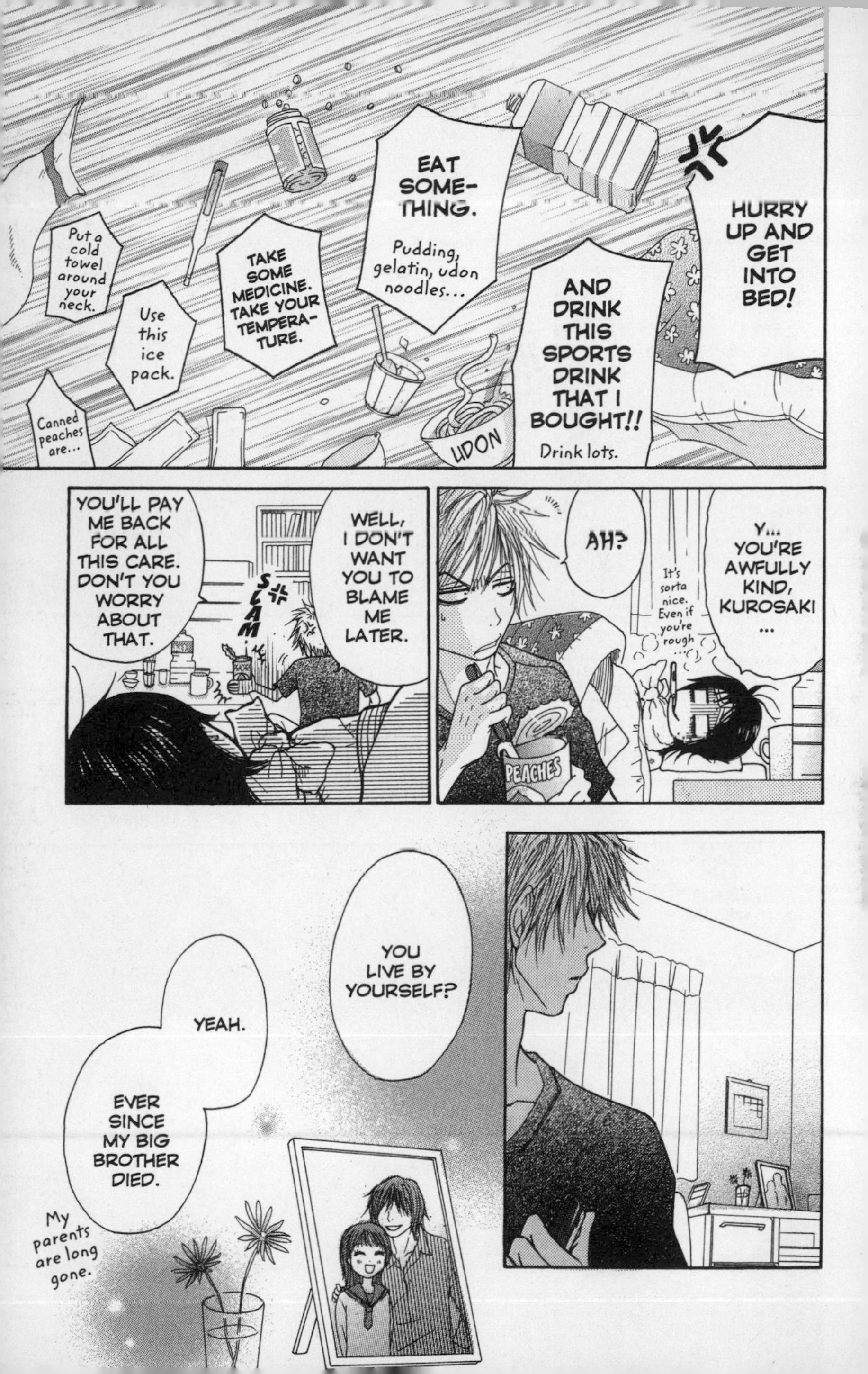
HURRY UP AND GET INTO BED!
AND DRINK THIS SPORTS DRINK THAT I BOUGHT!!
Drink lots.
EAT SOMETHING.
Pudding, gelatin, udon noodles...
UDON
TAKE SOME MEDICINE. TAKE YOUR TEMPERATURE.
Use this ice pack.
Put a cold towel around your neck.
Canned peaches are...
Y... YOU'RE AWFULLY KIND, KUROSAKI...
It's sorta nice. Even if you're rough...
AH?
PEACHES
WELL, I DON'T WANT YOU TO BLAME ME LATER.
SLAM
YOU'LL PAY ME BACK FOR ALL THIS CARE. DON'T YOU WORRY ABOUT THAT.
YOU LIVE BY YOURSELF?
YEAH.
EVER SINCE MY BIG BROTHER DIED.
My parents are long gone.

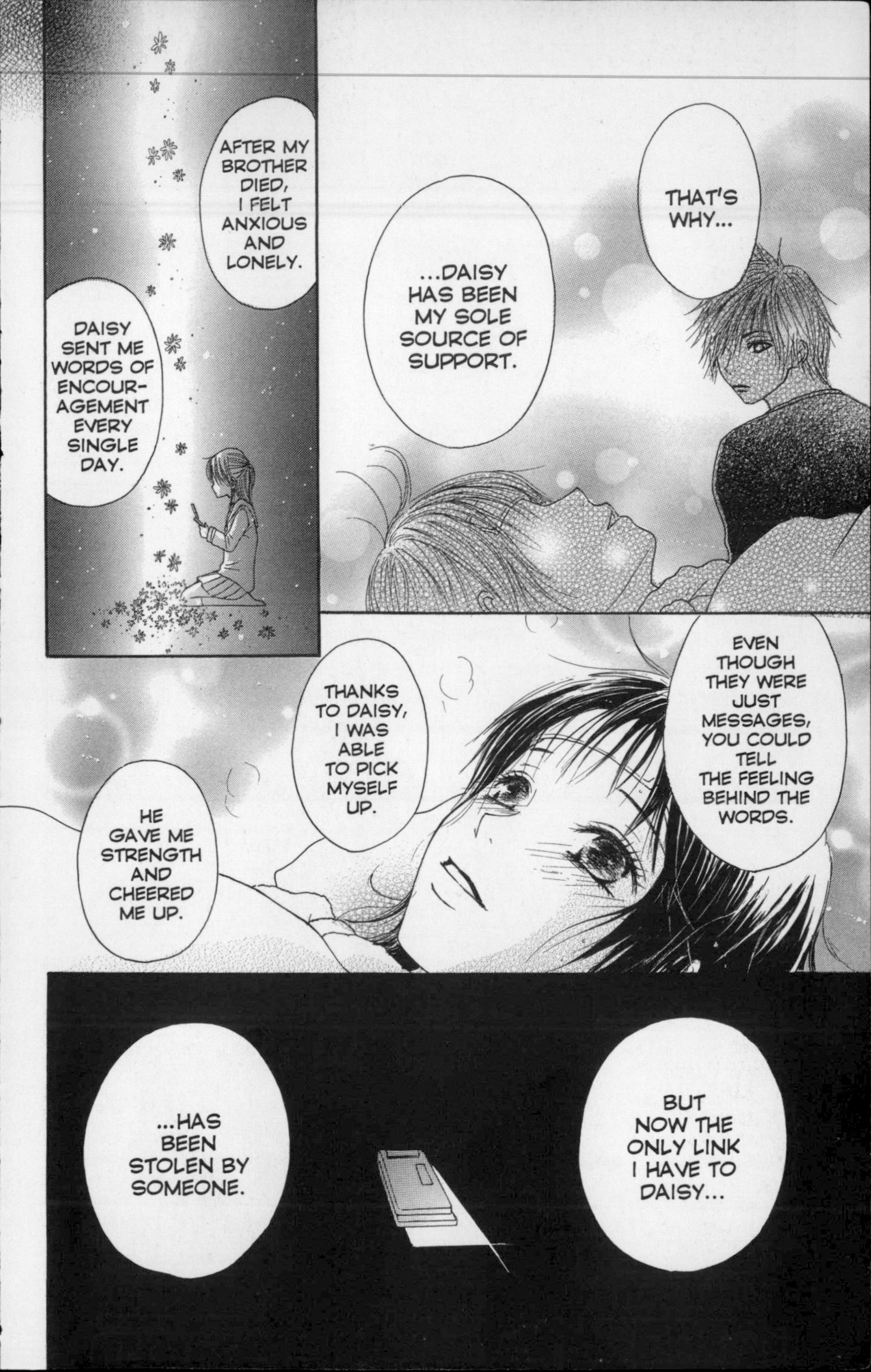
THAT'S WHY...
...DAISY HAS BEEN MY SOLE SOURCE OF SUPPORT.
AFTER MY BROTHER DIED, I FELT ANXIOUS AND LONELY.
DAISY SENT ME WORDS OF ENCOUR-AGEMENT EVERY SINGLE DAY.
EVEN THOUGH THEY WERE JUST MESSAGES, YOU COULD TELL THE FEELING BEHIND THE WORDS.
THANKS TO DAISY, I WAS ABLE TO PICK MYSELF UP.
HE GAVE ME STRENGTH AND CHEERED ME UP.
BUT NOW THE ONLY LINK I HAVE TO DAISY...
...HAS BEEN STOLEN BY SOMEONE.

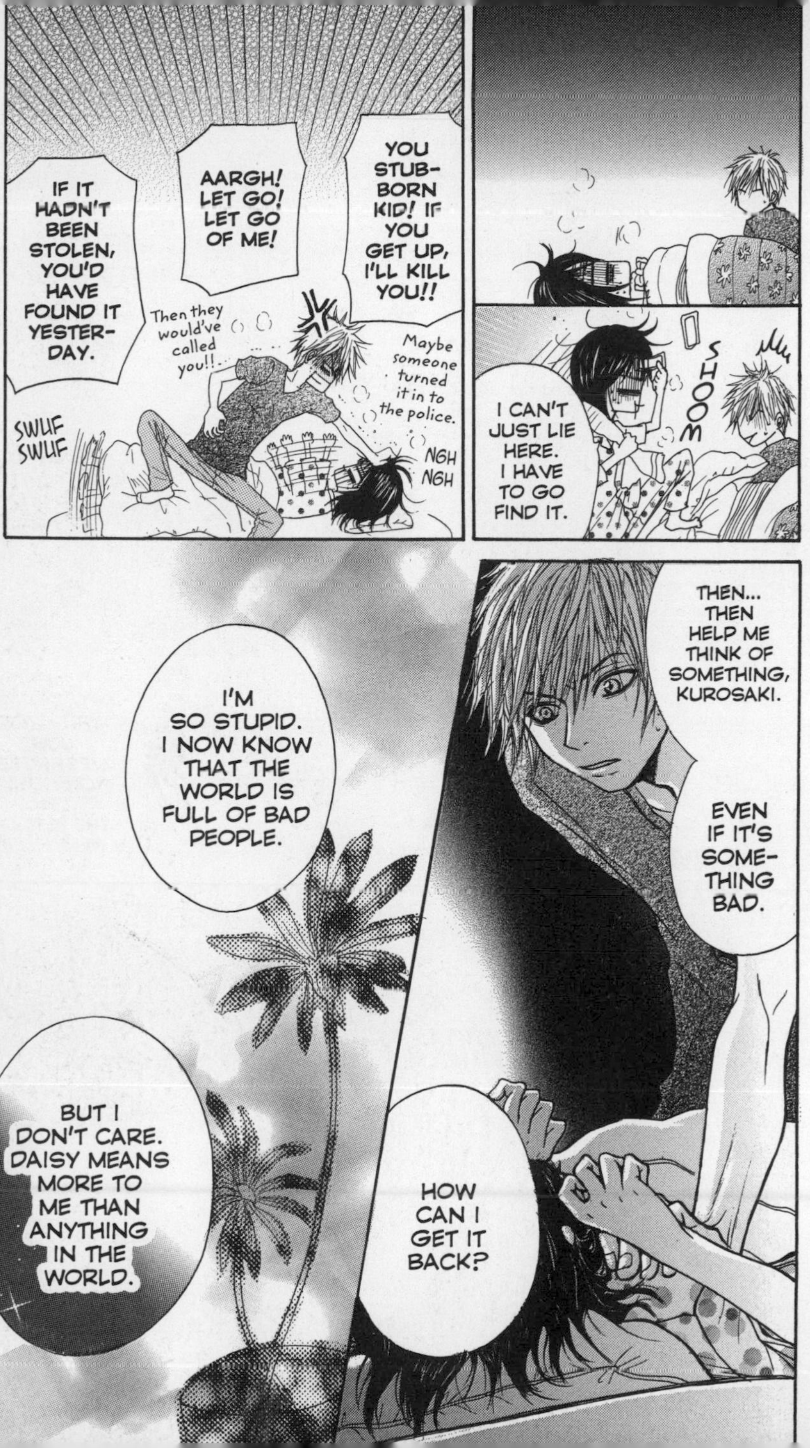
SHOOM
I CAN'T JUST LIE HERE. I HAVE TO GO FIND IT.
YOU STUBBORN KID! IF YOU GET UP, I'LL KILL YOU!!
AARGH! LET GO! LET GO OF ME!
IF IT HADN'T BEEN STOLEN, YOU'D HAVE FOUND IT YESTERDAY.
Maybe someone turned it in to the police.
Then they would've called you!!
NGH NGH
SWUF SWUF
THEN... THEN HELP ME THINK OF SOMETHING, KUROSAKI.
EVEN IF IT'S SOMETHING BAD.
HOW CAN I GET IT BACK?
I'M SO STUPID. I NOW KNOW THAT THE WORLD IS FULL OF BAD PEOPLE.
BUT I DON'T CARE. DAISY MEANS MORE TO ME THAN ANYTHING IN THE WORLD.

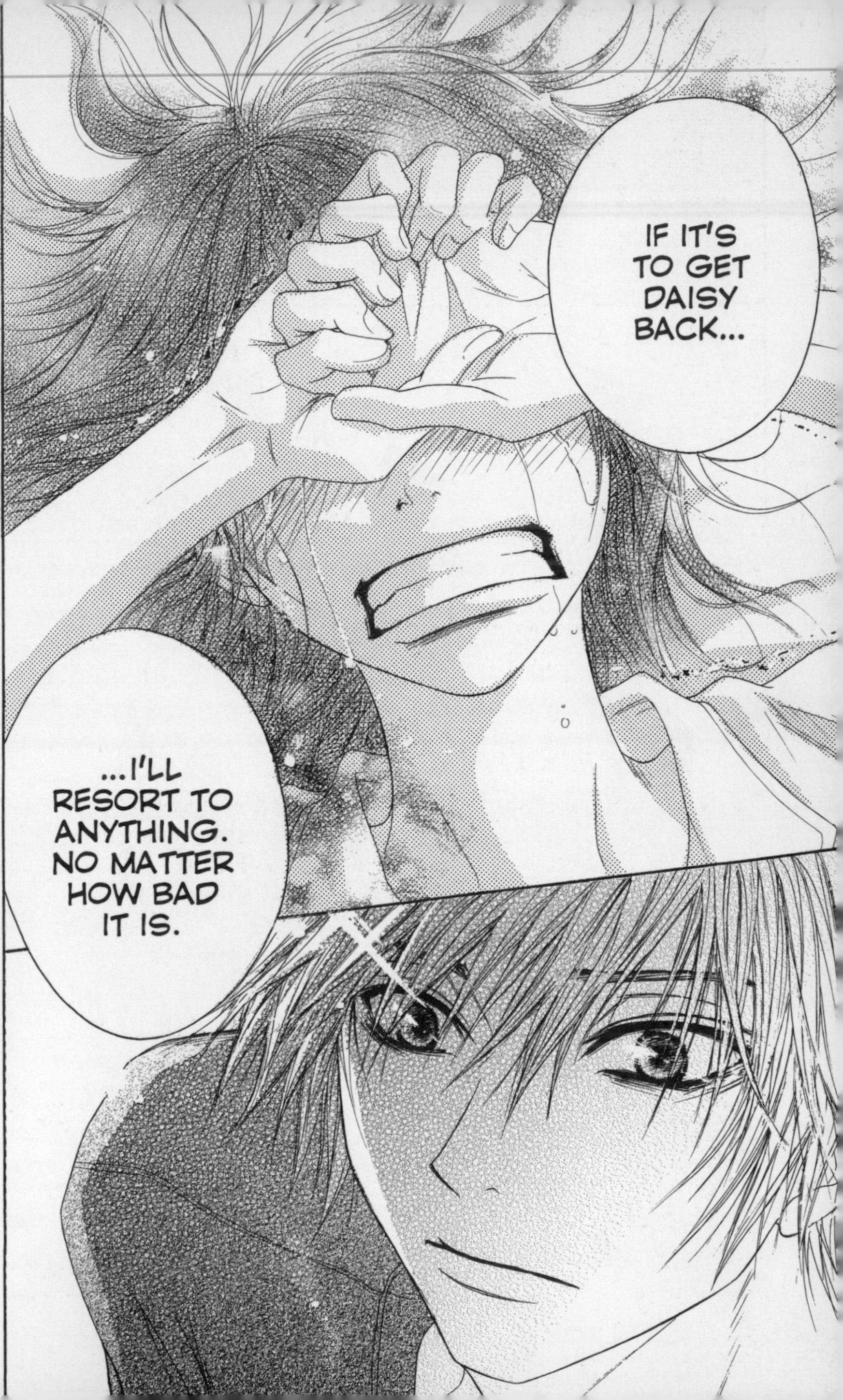
IF IT'S TO GET DAISY BACK...
...I'LL RESORT TO ANYTHING. NO MATTER HOW BAD IT IS.

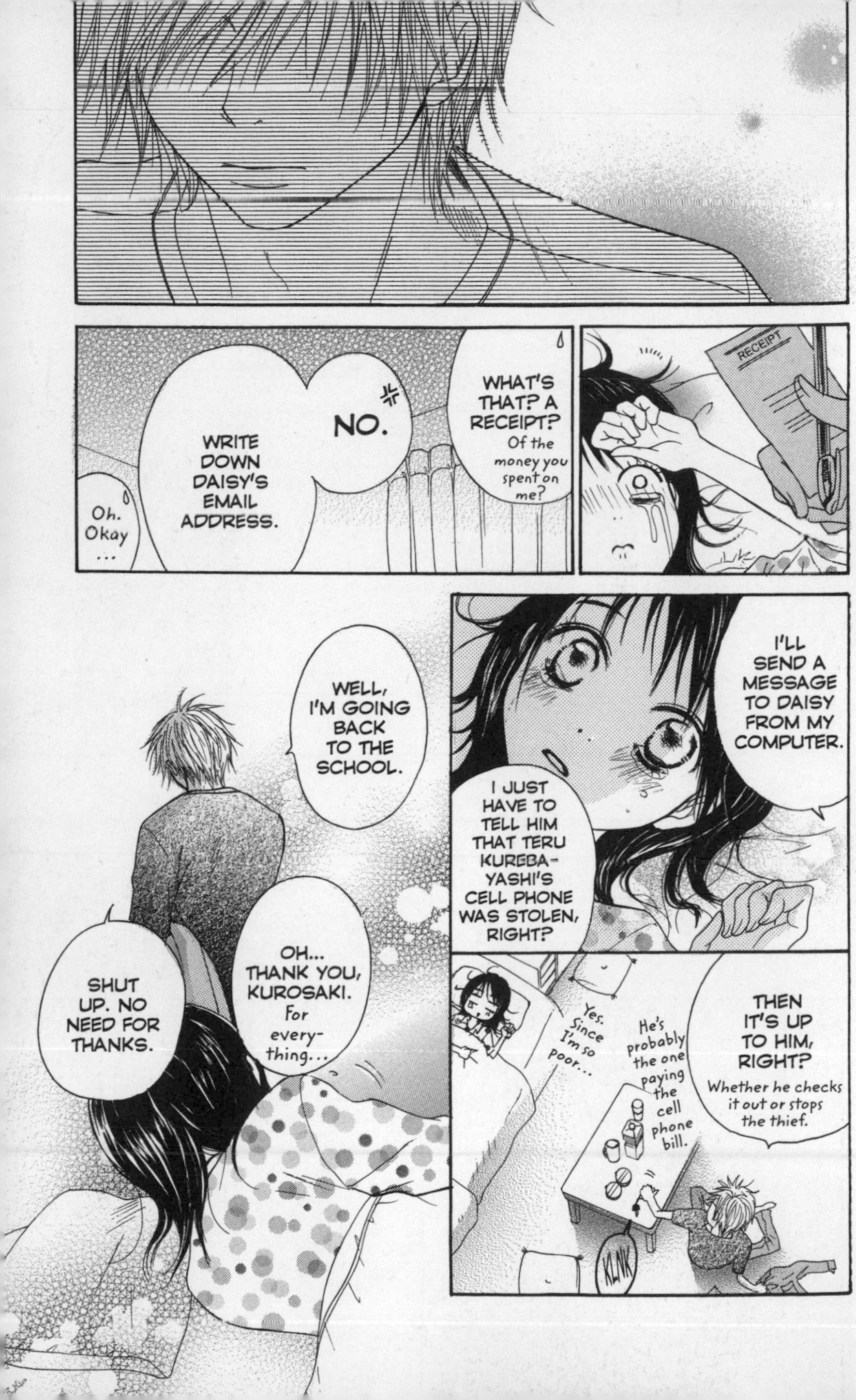
RECEIPT
WHAT'S THAT? A RECEIPT? Of the money you spent on me?
NO.
WRITE DOWN DAISY'S EMAIL ADDRESS.
Oh. Okay...
I'LL SEND A MESSAGE TO DAISY FROM MY COMPUTER.
I JUST HAVE TO TELL HIM THAT TERU KUREBA-YASHI'S CELL PHONE WAS STOLEN, RIGHT?
THEN IT'S UP TO HIM, RIGHT? Whether he checks it out or stops the thief.
He's probably the one paying the cell phone bill.
Yes. Since I'm so poor...
KLNK
WELL, I'M GOING BACK TO THE SCHOOL.
OH... THANK YOU, KUROSAKI. For every-thing...
SHUT UP. NO NEED FOR THANKS.

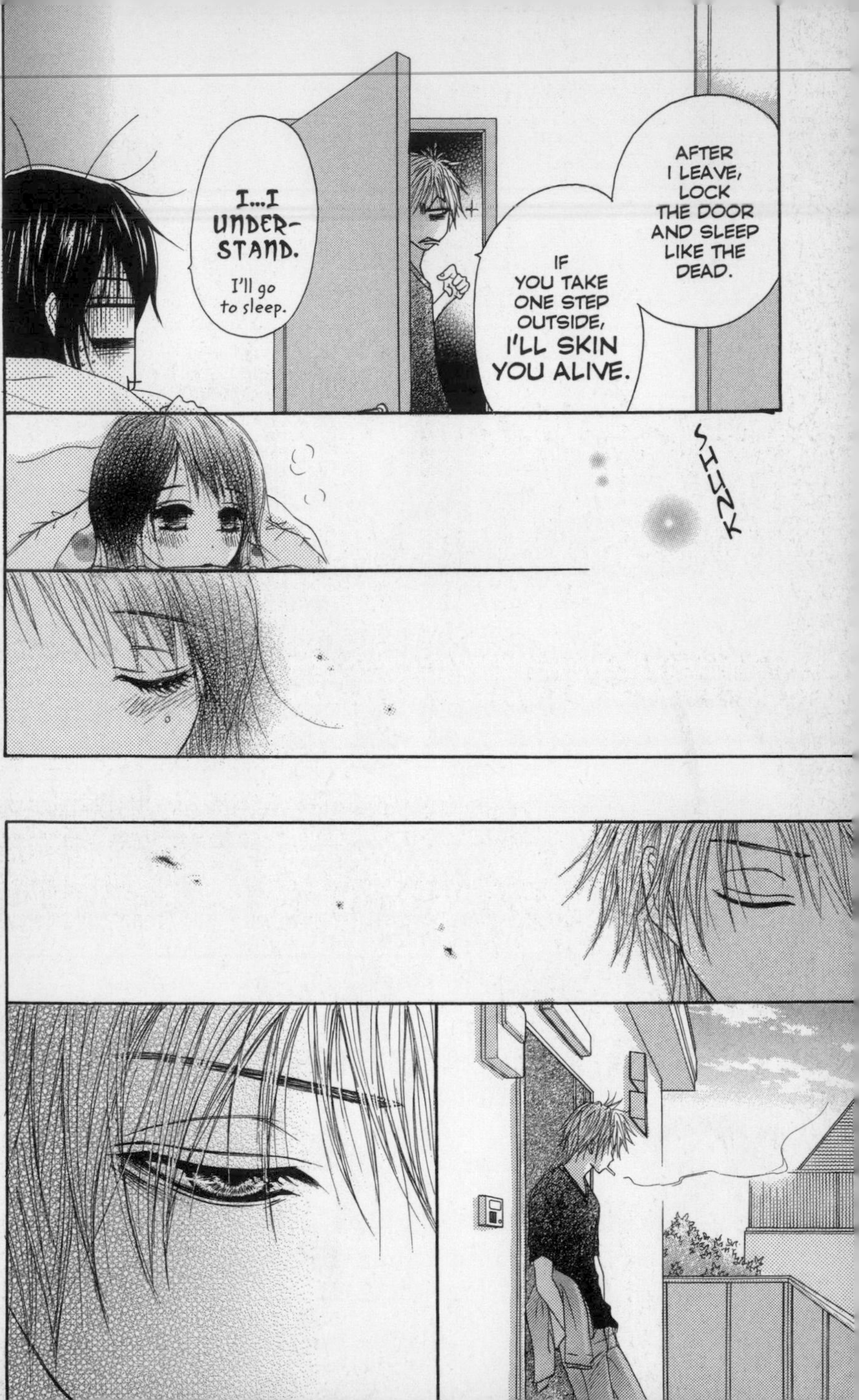
AFTER I LEAVE, LOCK THE DOOR AND SLEEP LIKE THE DEAD.
IF YOU TAKE ONE STEP OUTSIDE, I'LL SKIN YOU ALIVE.
I...I UNDER-STAND.
I'll go to sleep.
SHUNK

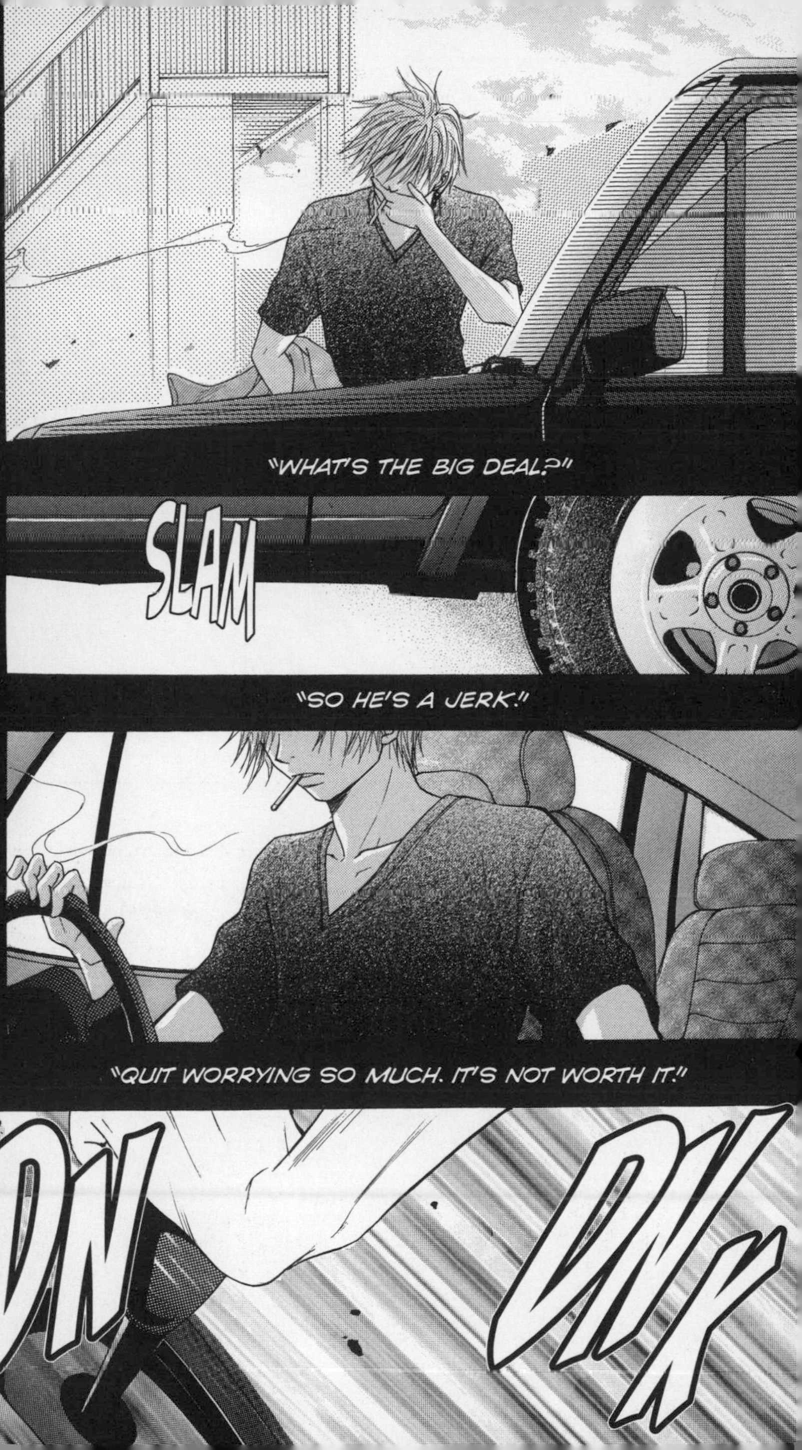
"WHAT'S THE BIG DEAL?"
SLAM
"SO HE'S A JERK."
"QUIT WORRYING SO MUCH. IT'S NOT WORTH IT."
DN DNK

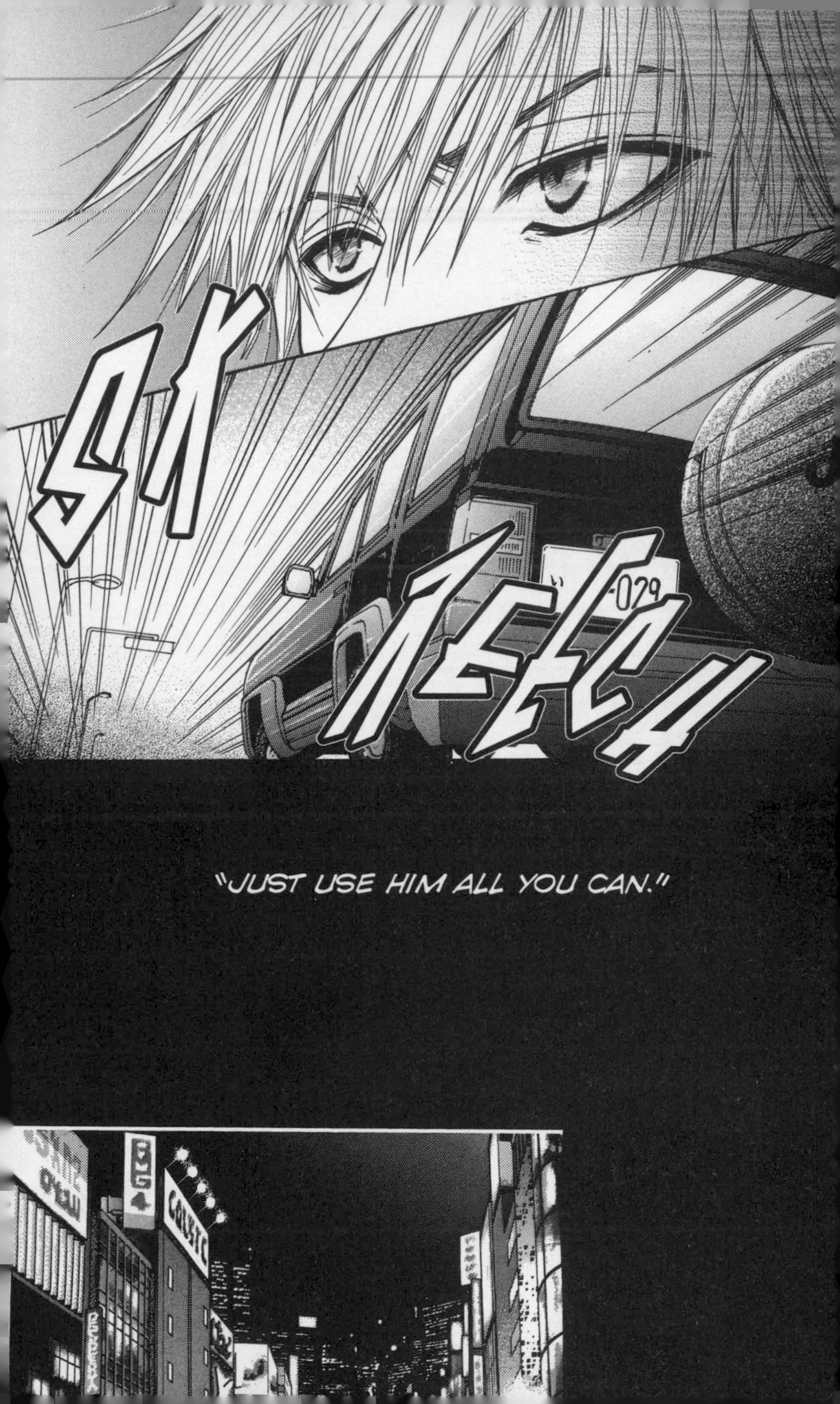
SKREECH
"JUST USE HIM ALL YOU CAN."

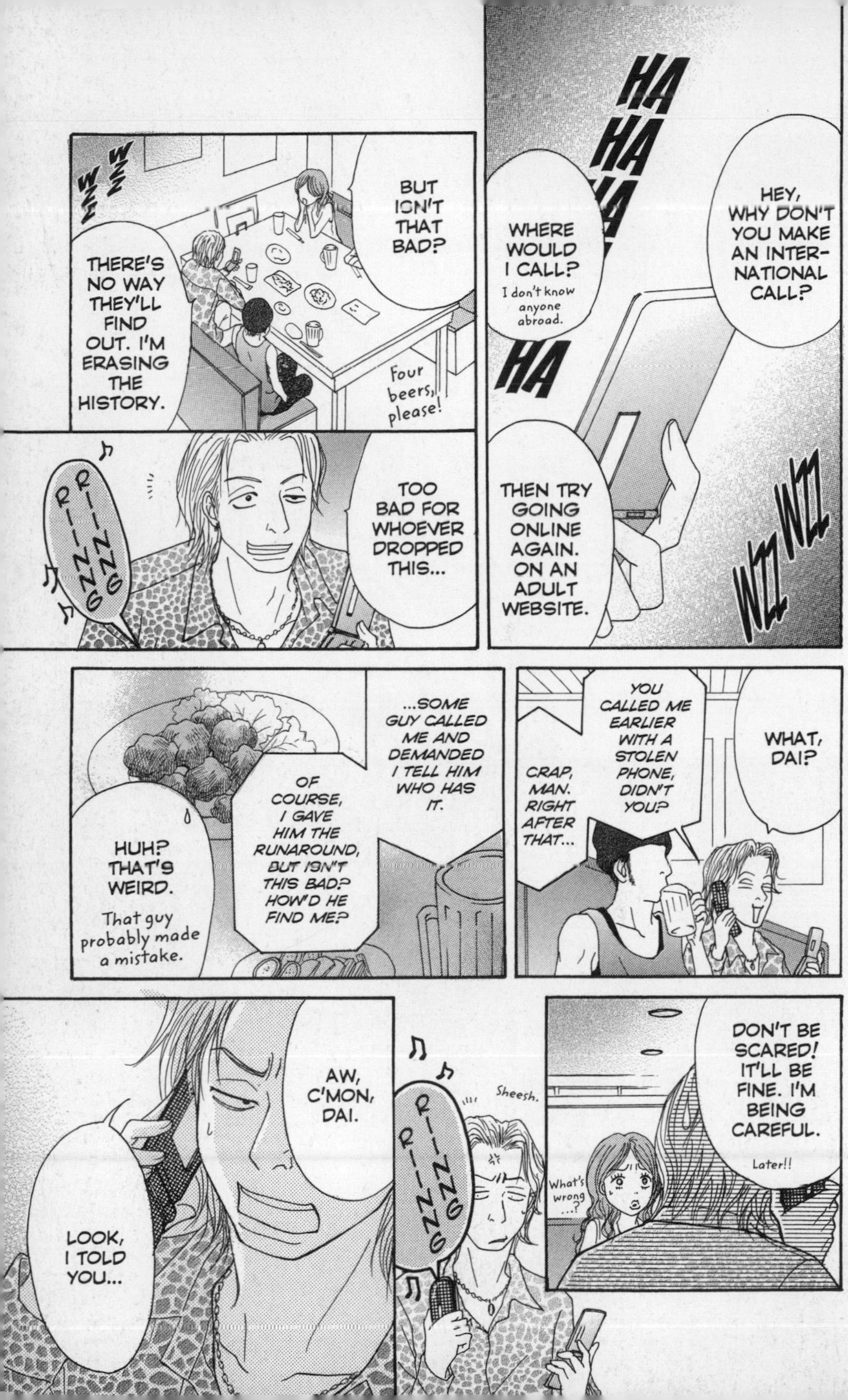
HEY, WHY DON'T YOU MAKE AN INTER-NATIONAL CALL?
HA HA HA HA HA
WHERE WOULD I CALL?
I don't know anyone abroad.
THEN TRY GOING ONLINE AGAIN. ON AN ADULT WEBSITE.
WZZ WZZ
BUT ISN'T THAT BAD?
Four beers, please!
THERE'S NO WAY THEY'LL FIND OUT. I'M ERASING THE HISTORY.
WZZ WZZ
TOO BAD FOR WHOEVER DROPPED THIS...
RIINNG RIINNG
WHAT, DAI?
YOU CALLED ME EARLIER WITH A STOLEN PHONE, DIDN'T YOU?
CRAP, MAN. RIGHT AFTER THAT...
...SOME GUY CALLED ME AND DEMANDED I TELL HIM WHO HAS IT.
OF COURSE, I GAVE HIM THE RUNAROUND, BUT ISN'T THIS BAD? HOW'D HE FIND ME?
HUH? THAT'S WEIRD.
That guy probably made a mistake.
DON'T BE SCARED! IT'LL BE FINE. I'M BEING CAREFUL.
Later!!
What's wrong ...?
AW, C'MON, DAI.
Sheesh.
RIINNG RIINNG
LOOK, I TOLD YOU...

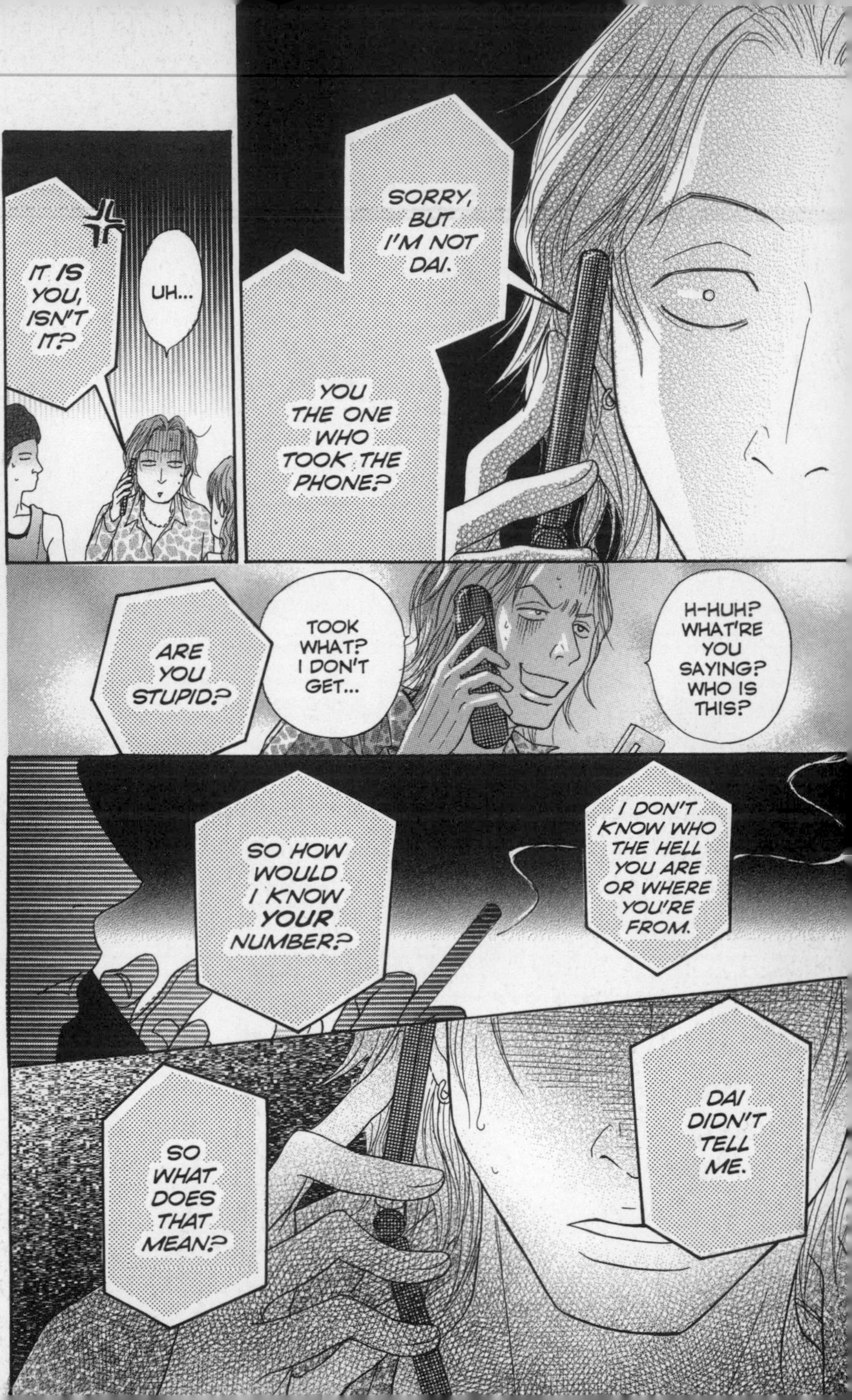
SORRY, BUT I'M NOT DAI.
YOU THE ONE WHO TOOK THE PHONE?
UH...
IT IS YOU, ISN'T IT?
H-HUH? WHAT'RE YOU SAYING? WHO IS THIS?
TOOK WHAT? I DON'T GET...
ARE YOU STUPID?
I DON'T KNOW WHO THE HELL YOU ARE OR WHERE YOU'RE FROM.
SO HOW WOULD I KNOW YOUR NUMBER?
DAI DIDN'T TELL ME.
SO WHAT DOES THAT MEAN?

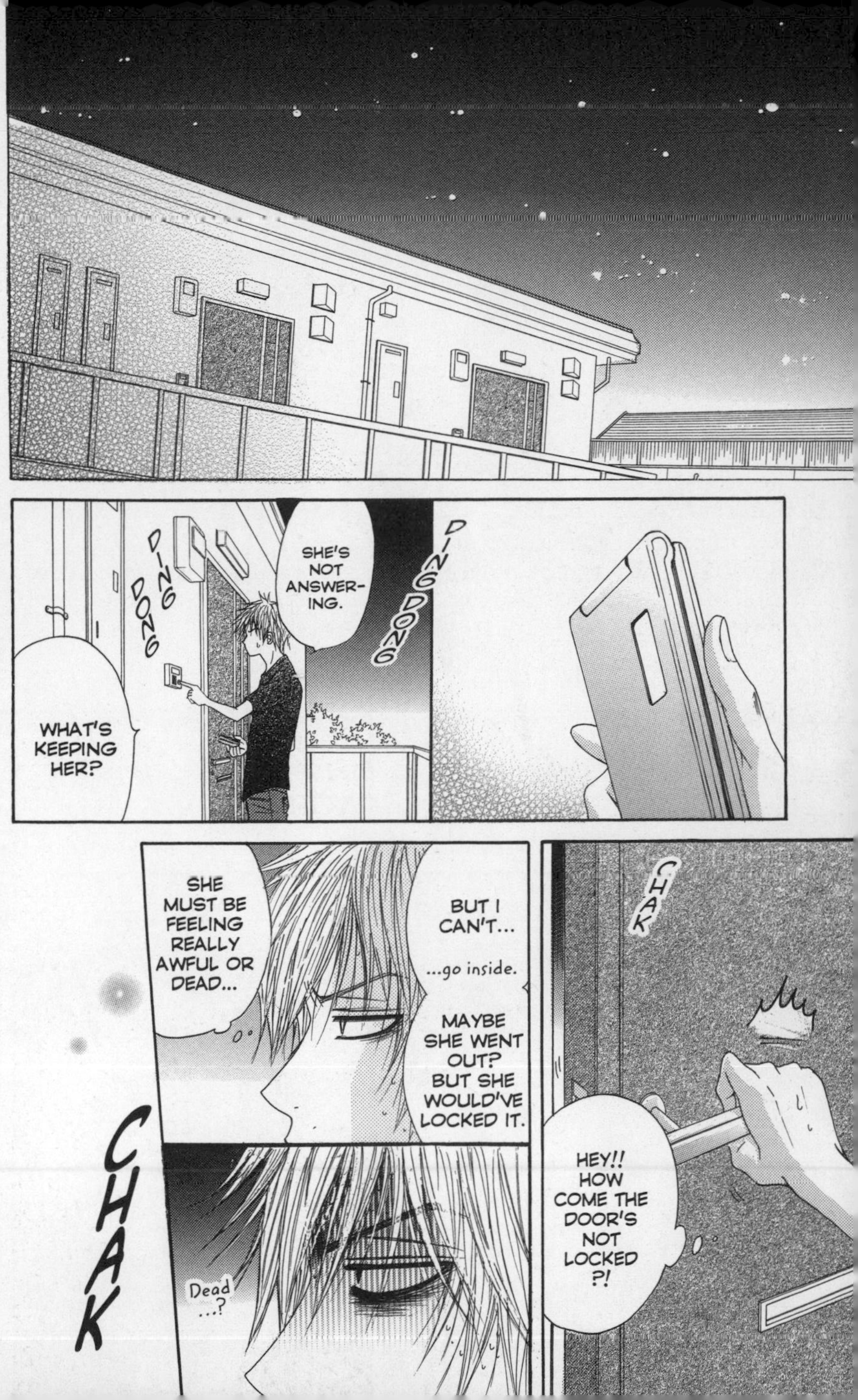
DING DONG
SHE'S NOT ANSWERING.
DING DONG
WHAT'S KEEPING HER?
CHAK
HEY!! HOW COME THE DOOR'S NOT LOCKED?!
BUT I CAN'T...
...go inside.
MAYBE SHE WENT OUT? BUT SHE WOULD'VE LOCKED IT.
SHE MUST BE FEELING REALLY AWFUL OR DEAD...
Dead ...?
CHAK

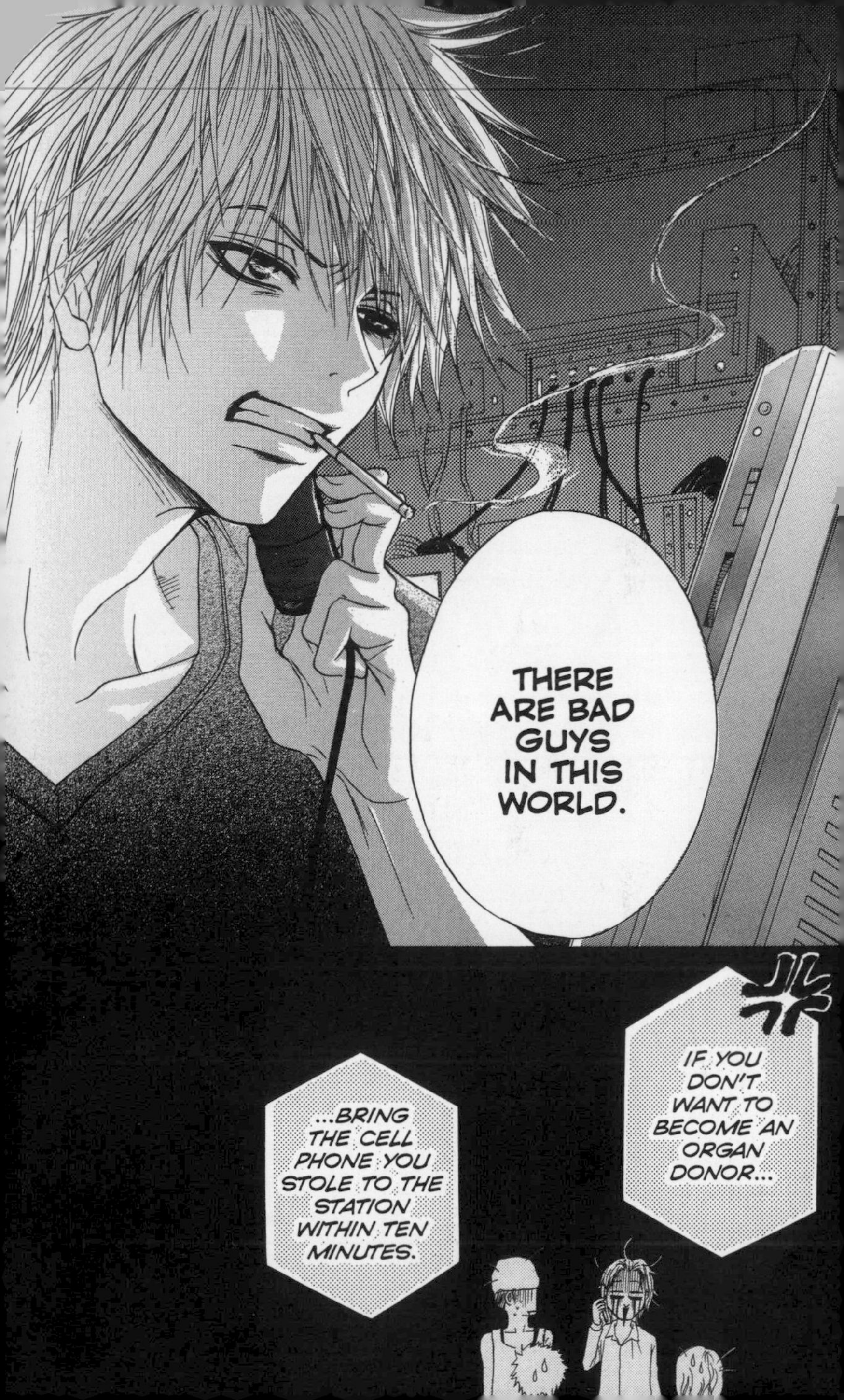
THERE ARE BAD GUYS IN THIS WORLD.
IF YOU DON'T WANT TO BECOME AN ORGAN DONOR...
...BRING THE CELL PHONE YOU STOLE TO THE STATION WITHIN TEN MINUTES.

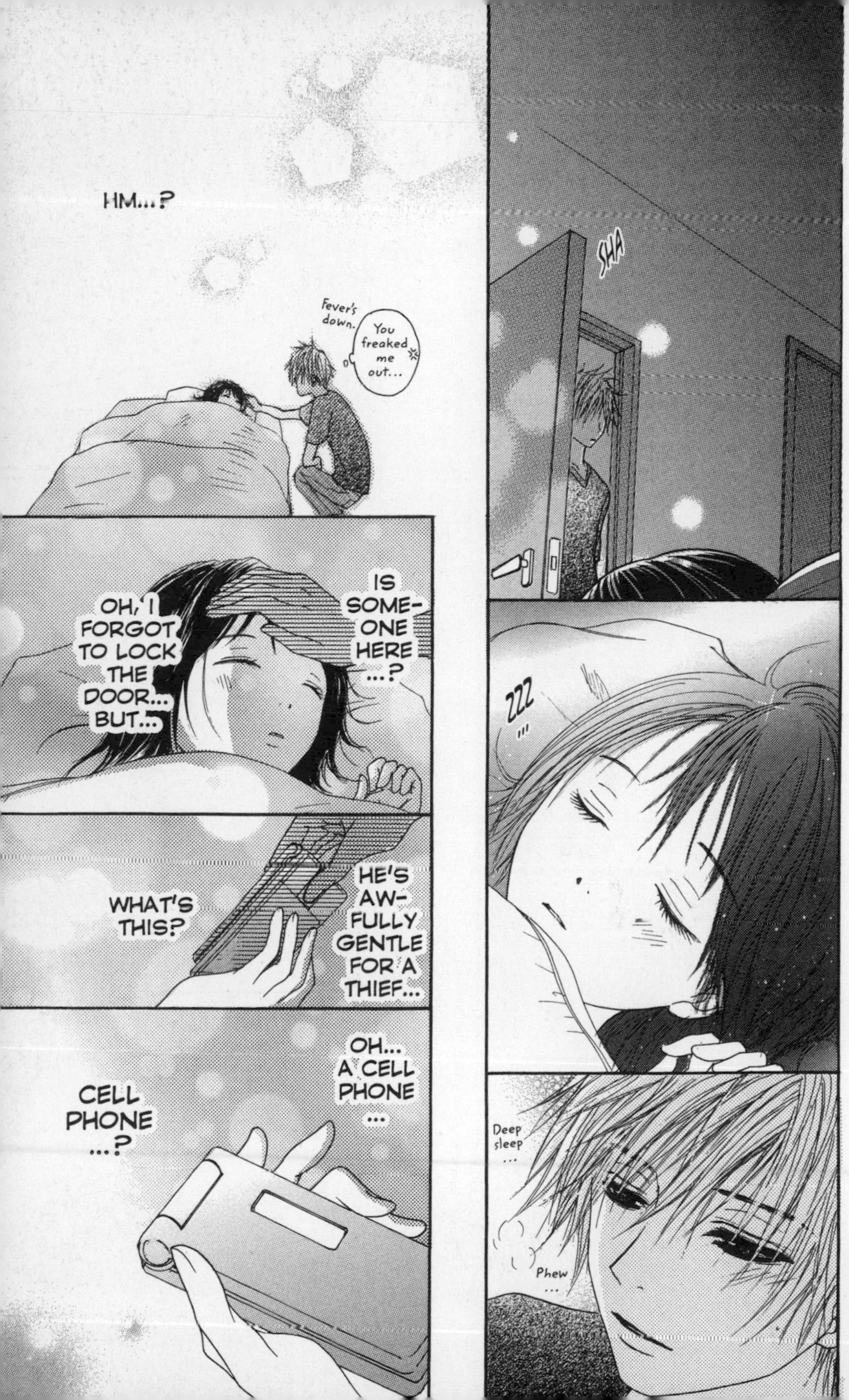
SHA
ZZZ
...
Deep sleep...
Phew...
HM...?
Fever's down.
You freaked me out...
IS SOMEONE HERE...?
OH, I FORGOT TO LOCK THE DOOR... BUT...
HE'S AWFULLY GENTLE FOR A THIEF...
WHAT'S THIS?
OH... A CELL PHONE...
CELL PHONE...?

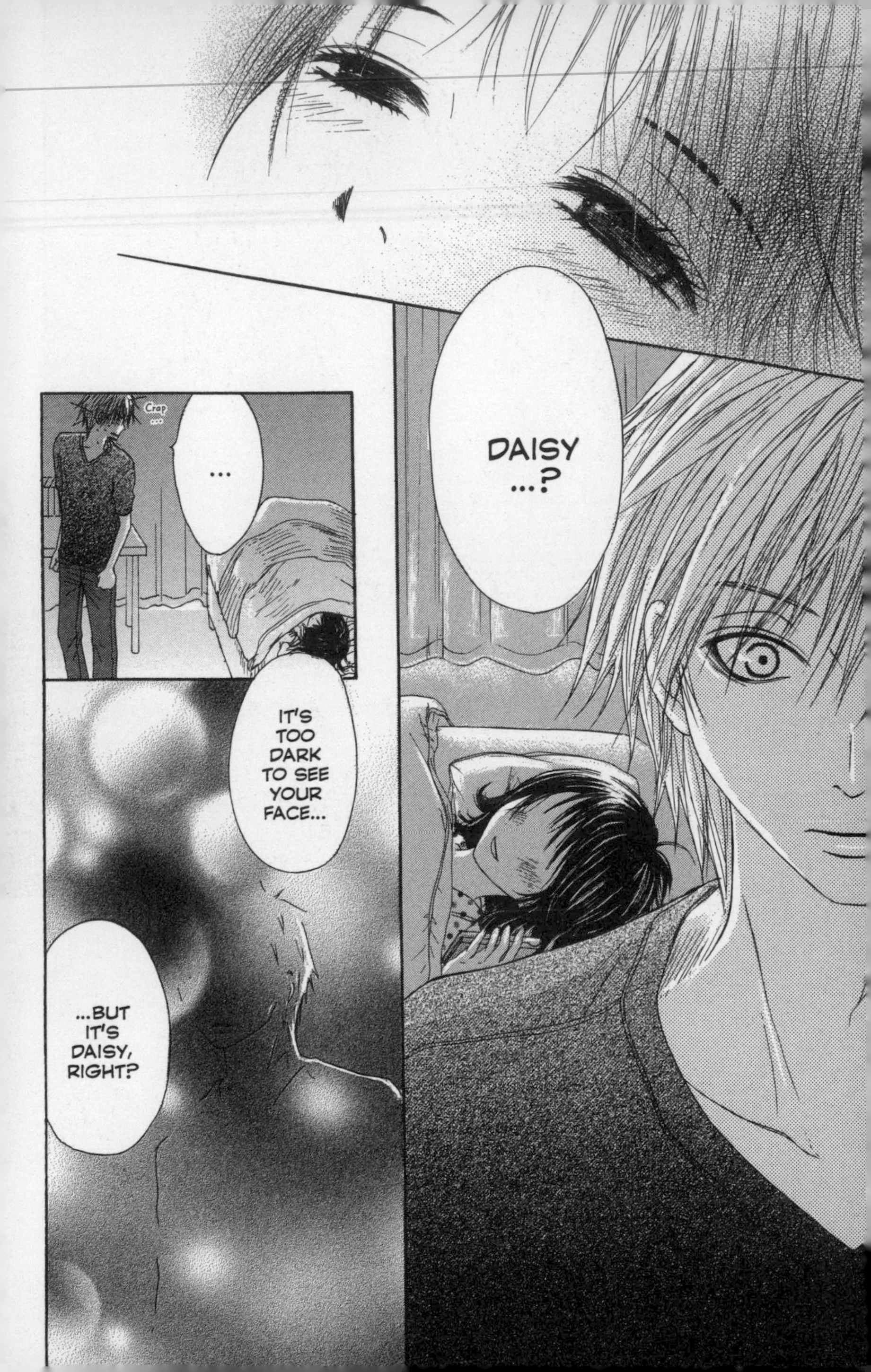
DAISY ...?
...
Crap ...
IT'S TOO DARK TO SEE YOUR FACE...
...BUT IT'S DAISY, RIGHT?

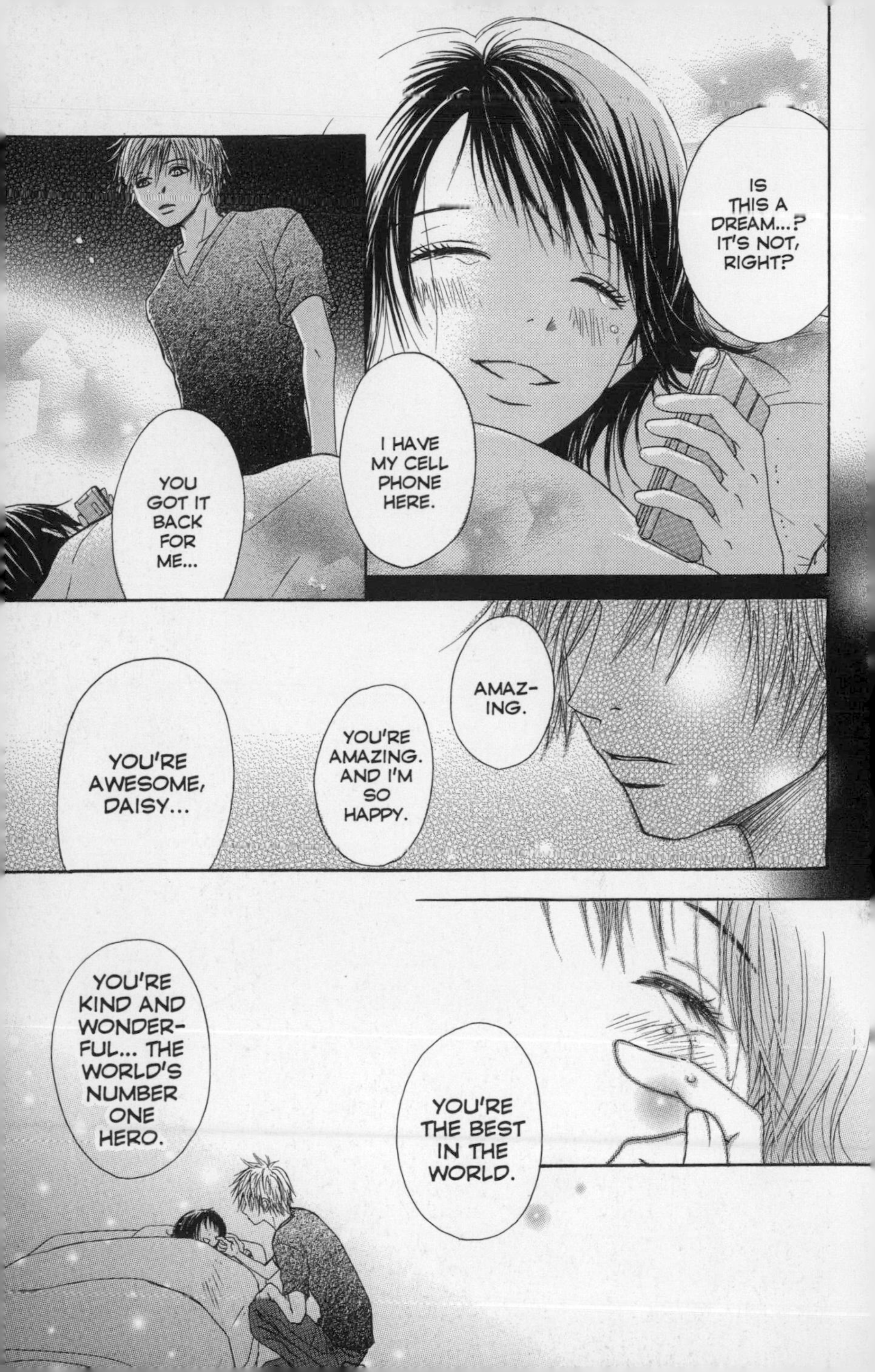
IS THIS A DREAM...? IT'S NOT, RIGHT?
I HAVE MY CELL PHONE HERE.
YOU GOT IT BACK FOR ME...
AMAZ-ING.
YOU'RE AMAZING. AND I'M SO HAPPY.
YOU'RE AWESOME, DAISY...
YOU'RE THE BEST IN THE WORLD.
YOU'RE KIND AND WONDER-FUL... THE WORLD'S NUMBER ONE HERO.

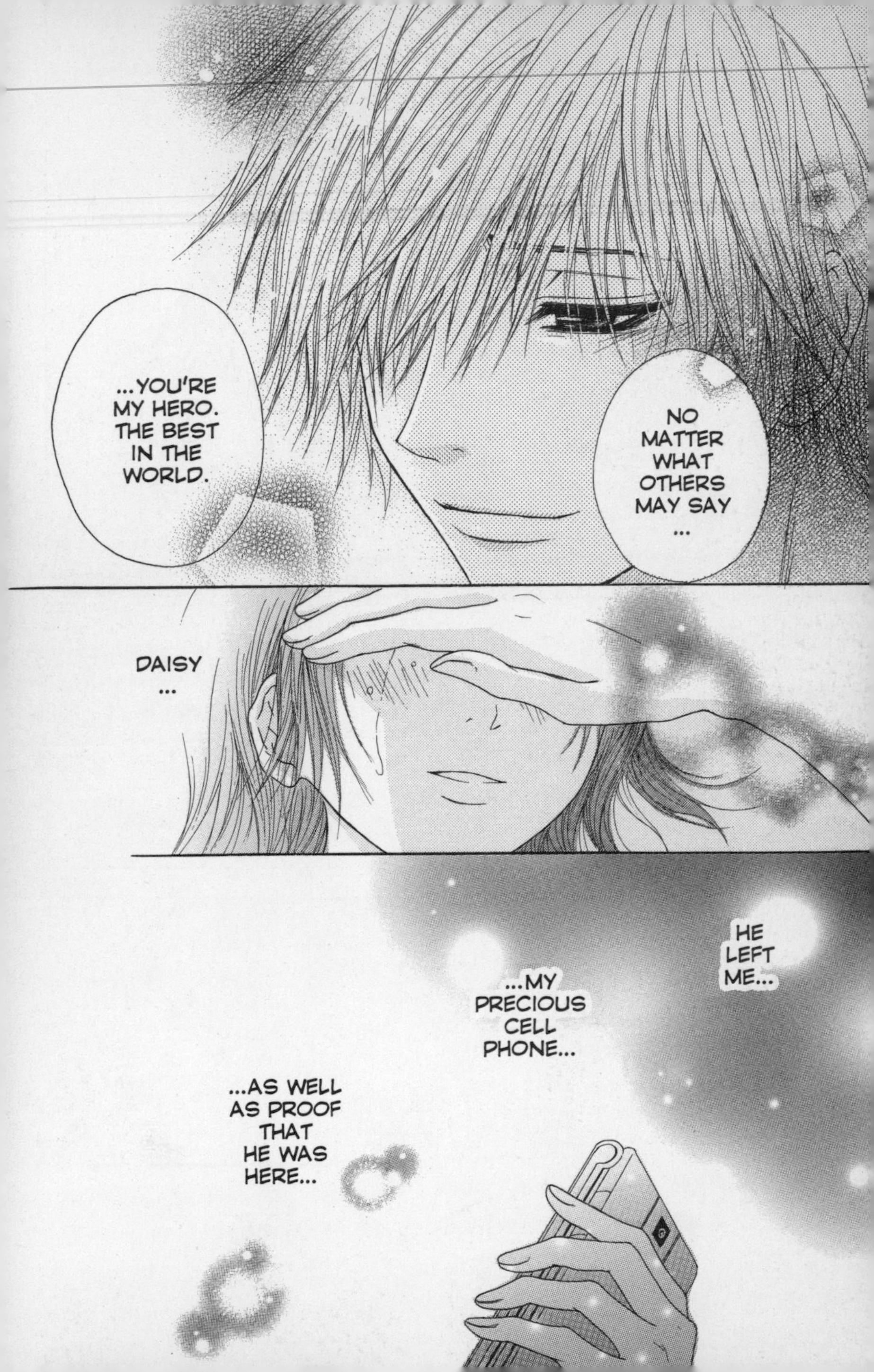
NO MATTER WHAT OTHERS MAY SAY ...
...YOU'RE MY HERO. THE BEST IN THE WORLD.
DAISY ...
HE LEFT ME...
...MY PRECIOUS CELL PHONE...
...AS WELL AS PROOF THAT HE WAS HERE...

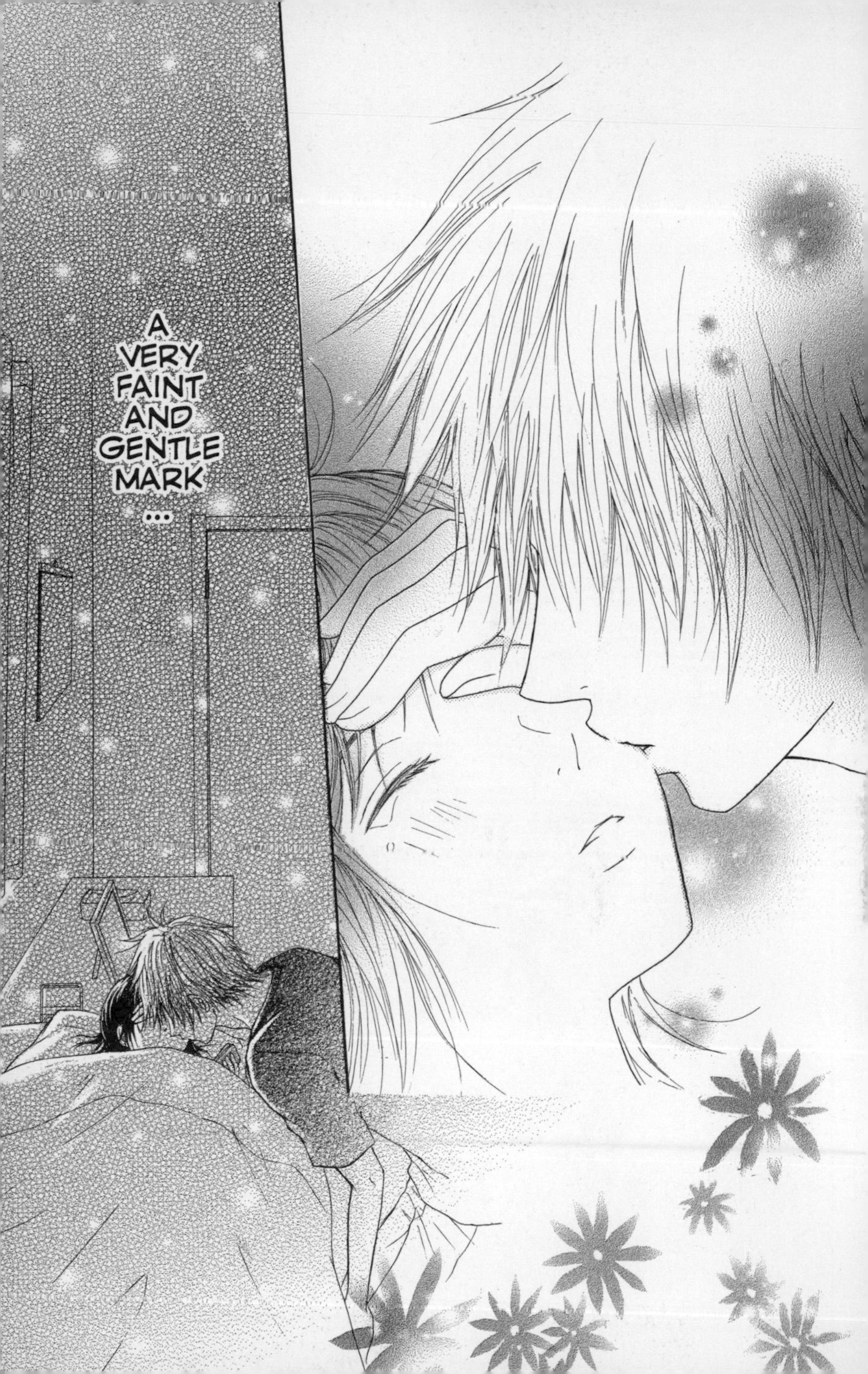
A VERY FAINT AND GENTLE MARK...

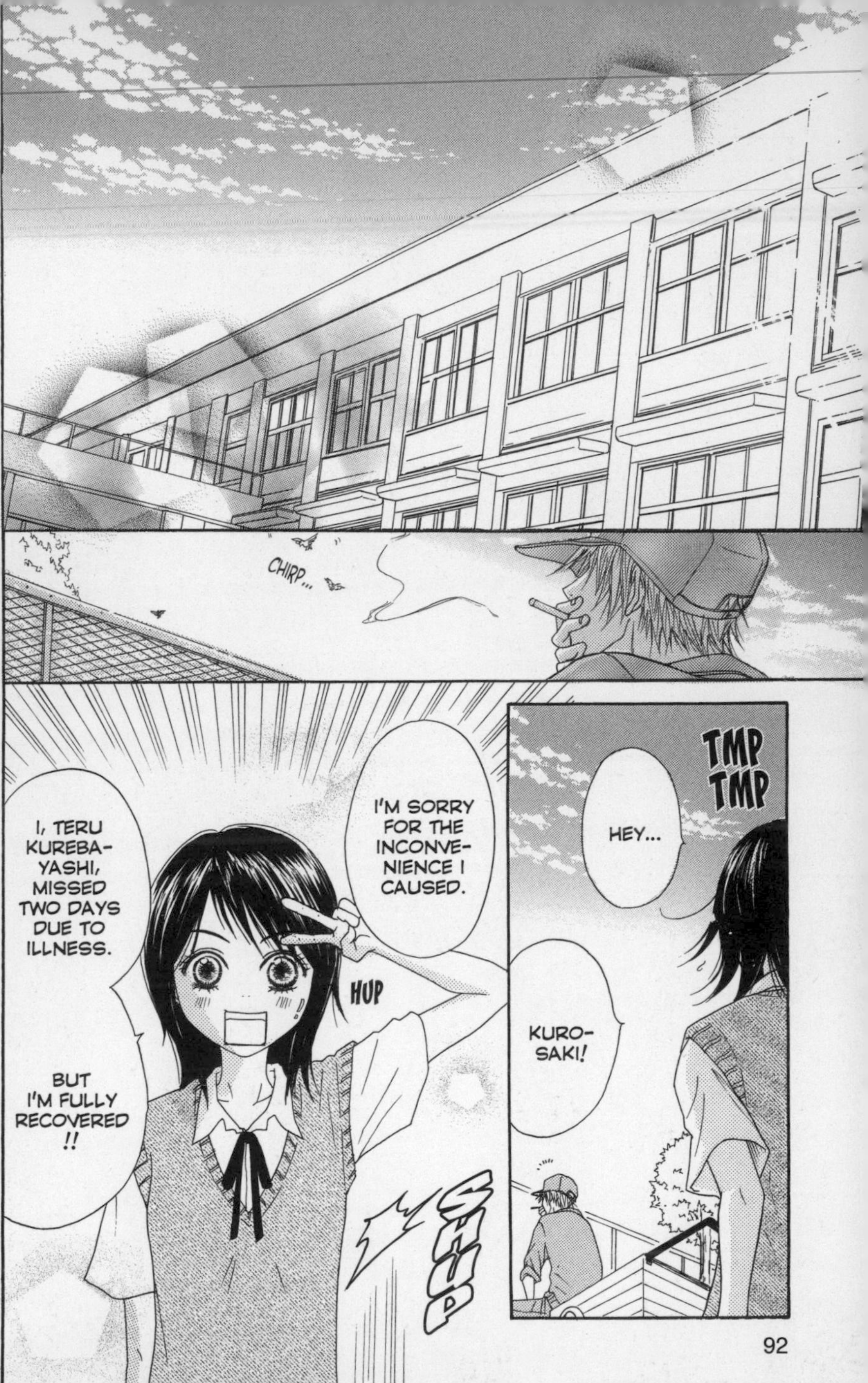
CHIRP...
TMP TMP
HEY...
KURO-SAKI!
I'M SORRY FOR THE INCONVENIENCE I CAUSED.
I, TERU KUREBAYASHI, MISSED TWO DAYS DUE TO ILLNESS.
HUP
BUT I'M FULLY RECOVERED!!
SHUP

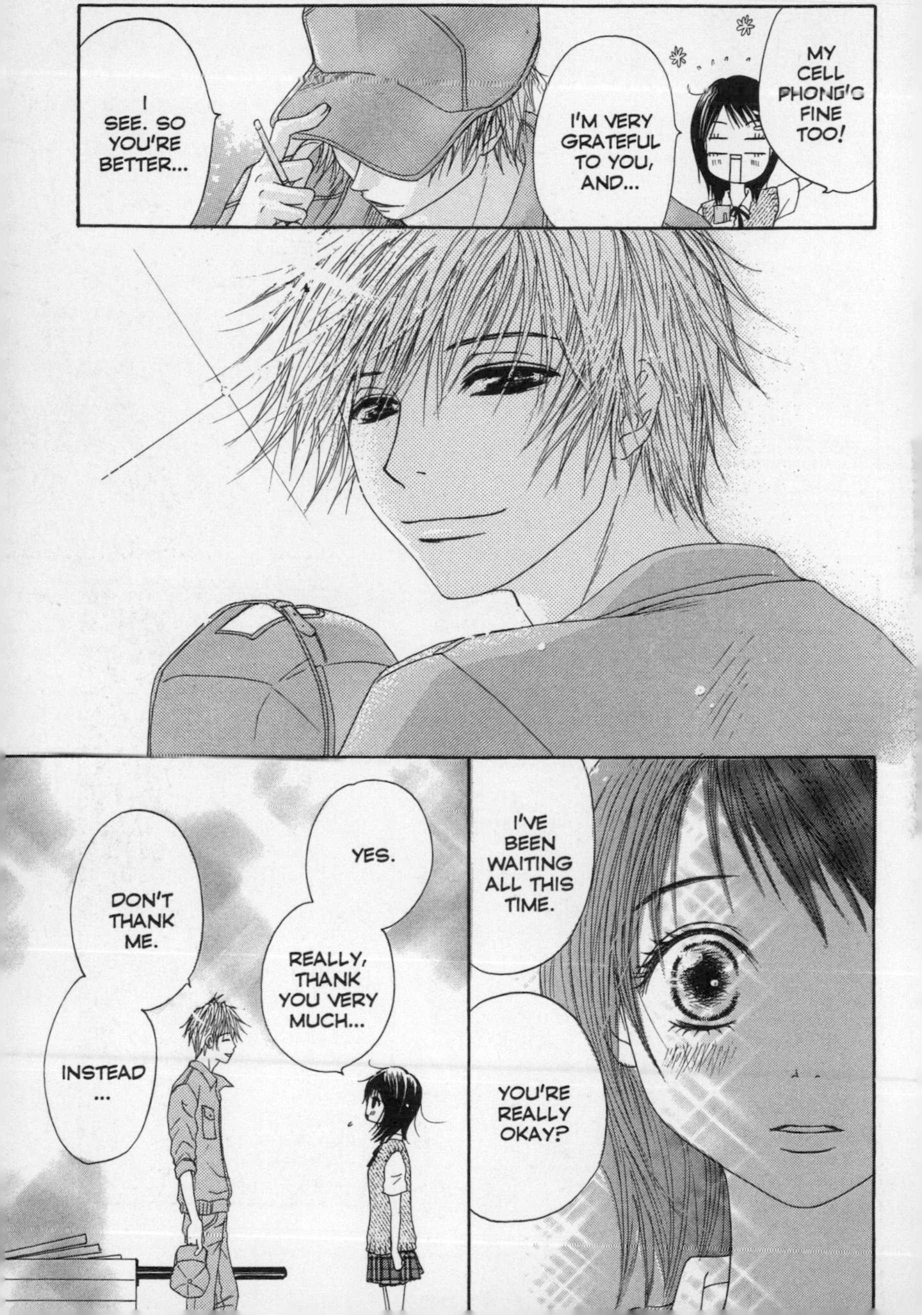
MY CELL PHONE'S FINE TOO!
I'M VERY GRATEFUL TO YOU, AND...
I SEE. SO YOU'RE BETTER...
I'VE BEEN WAITING ALL THIS TIME.
YOU'RE REALLY OKAY?
YES.
REALLY, THANK YOU VERY MUCH...
DON'T THANK ME.
INSTEAD...

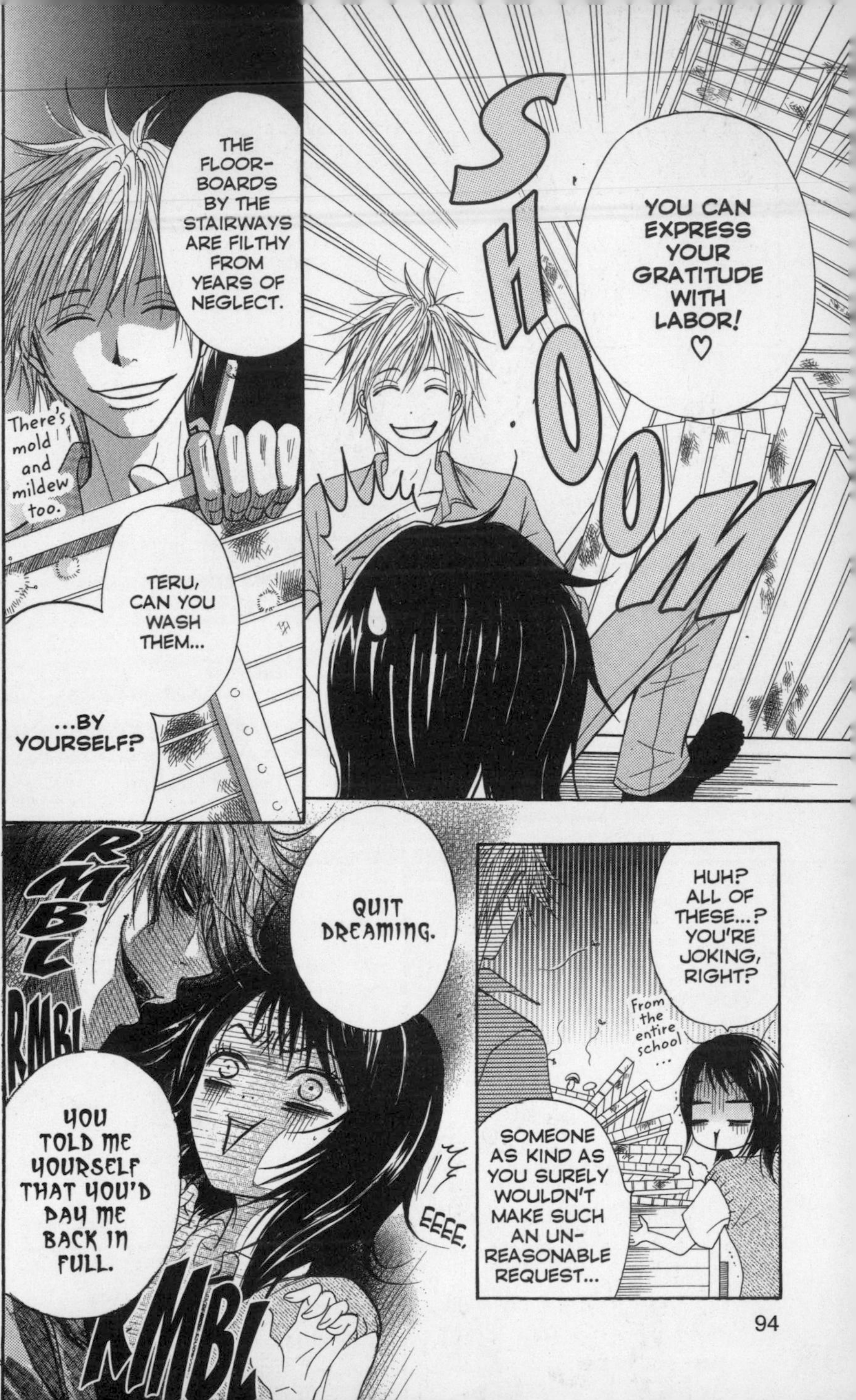
SHOOM
YOU CAN EXPRESS YOUR GRATITUDE WITH LABOR! ♡
THE FLOOR-BOARDS BY THE STAIRWAYS ARE FILTHY FROM YEARS OF NEGLECT.
There's mold and mildew too.
TERU, CAN YOU WASH THEM...
...BY YOURSELF?
HUH? ALL OF THESE...? YOU'RE JOKING, RIGHT?
From the entire school...
SOMEONE AS KIND AS YOU SURELY WOULDN'T MAKE SUCH AN UN-REASONABLE REQUEST...
QUIT DREAMING.
RMBL
RMBL
YOU TOLD ME YOURSELF THAT YOU'D PAY ME BACK IN FULL.
EEEE.
RMBL

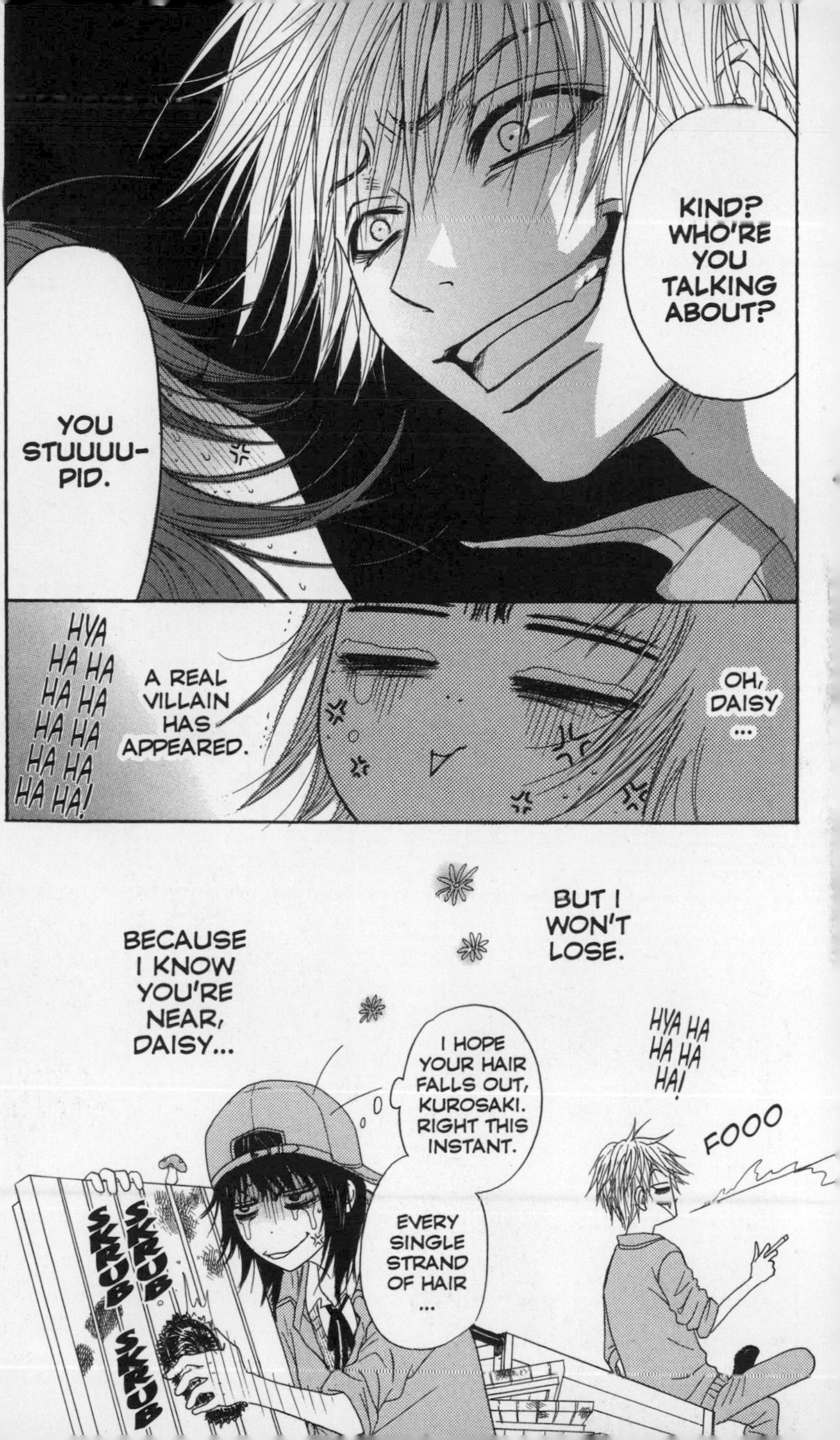
KIND? WHO'RE YOU TALKING ABOUT?
YOU STUUUU-PID.
OH, DAISY ...
A REAL VILLAIN HAS APPEARED.
HYA HA HA HA HA HA HA HA HA HA HA!
BUT I WON'T LOSE.
BECAUSE I KNOW YOU'RE NEAR, DAISY...
HYA HA HA HA HA!
FOOO
I HOPE YOUR HAIR FALLS OUT, KUROSAKI. RIGHT THIS INSTANT.
EVERY SINGLE STRAND OF HAIR ...
SKRUB SKRUB
SKRUB SKRUB

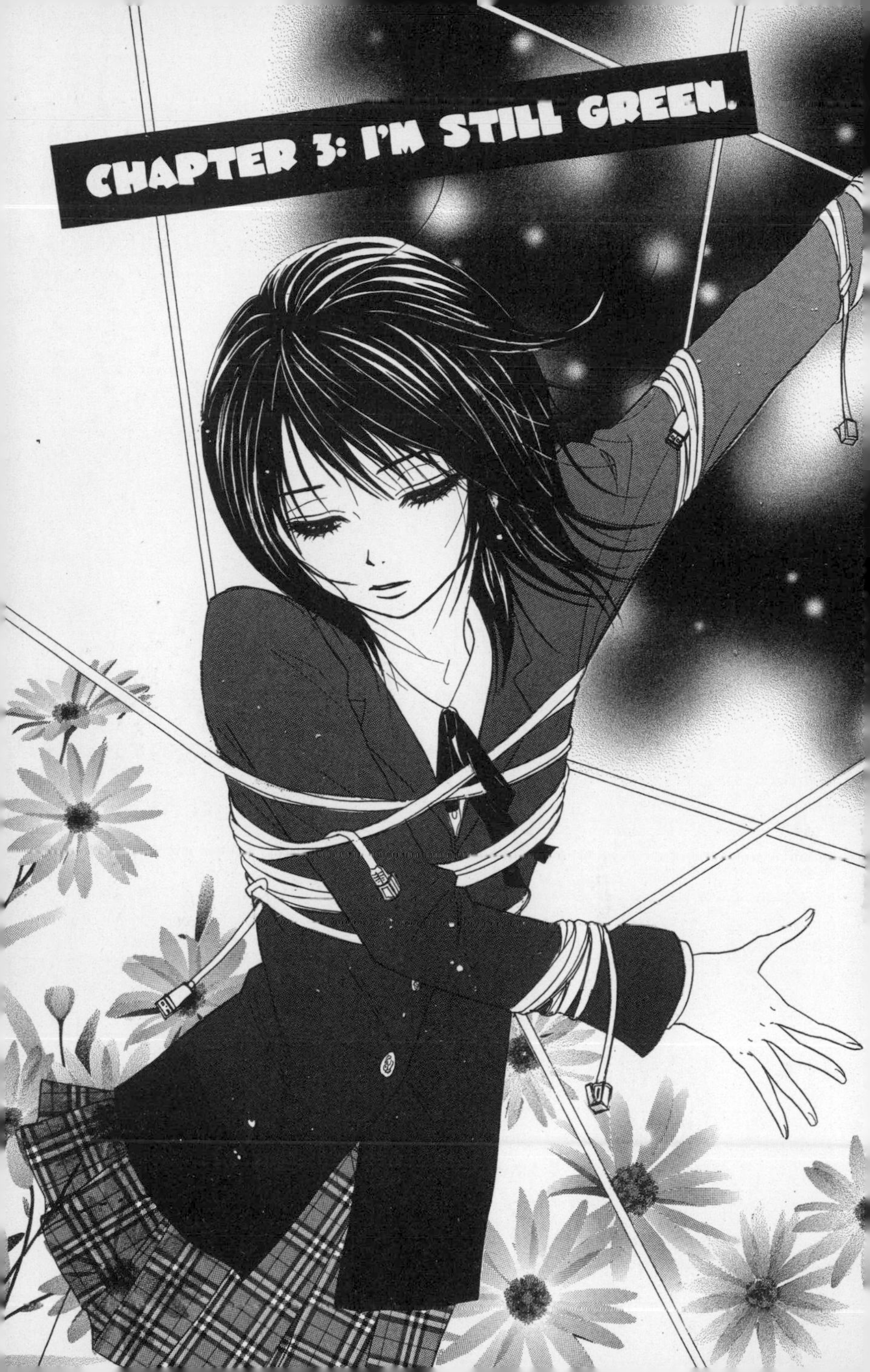
CHAPTER 3: I'M STILL GREEN.

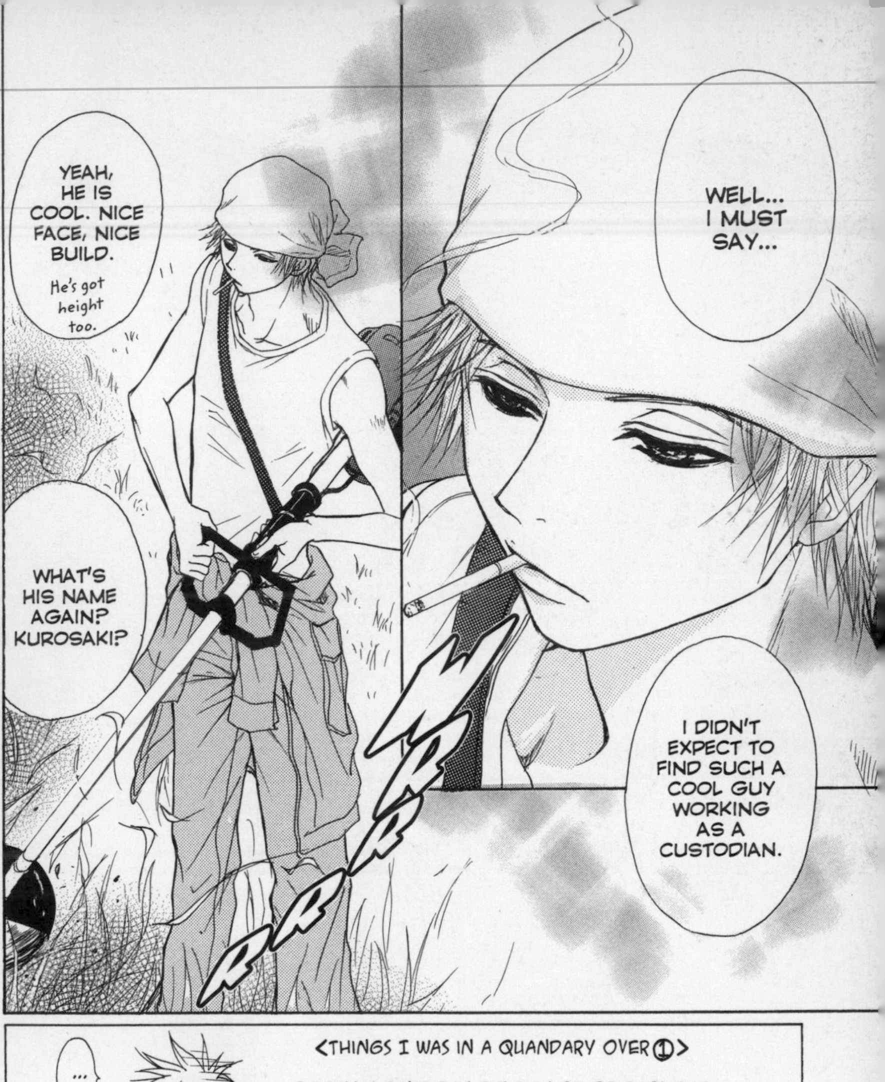
WELL... I MUST SAY...
I DIDN'T EXPECT TO FIND SUCH A COOL GUY WORKING AS A CUSTODIAN.
YEAH, HE IS COOL. NICE FACE, NICE BUILD.
He's got height too.
WHAT'S HIS NAME AGAIN? KUROSAKI?

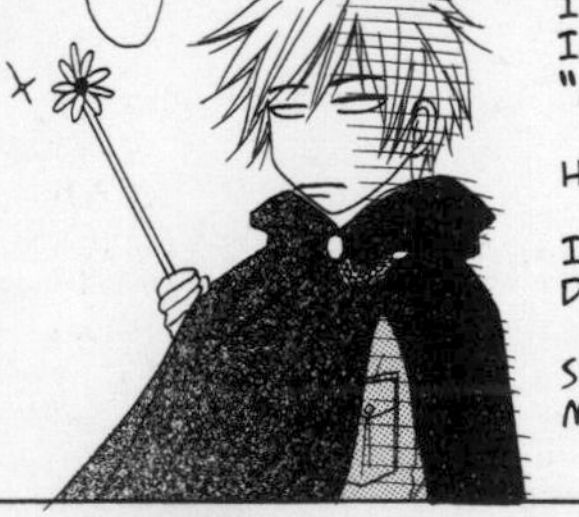
...

<THINGS I WAS IN A QUANDARY OVER ①>

I REALLY GAVE THIS TITLE A LOT OF THOUGHT. IN THE END, I HAD TWO TITLES, ONE OF WHICH WAS "MAGICIAN DAISY."

HMM... UM... I'M GLAD I DIDN'T MAKE THAT MISTAKE...

IN THE END, I RAN INTO A FELLOW MANGA ARTIST DURING THIS DILEMMA AND ASKED FOR HER ADVICE.

SHE SAID, "DENGEKI, DEFINITELY." SO THANK YOU, MS. Y-SUKO. IT WAS A CLOSE CALL.

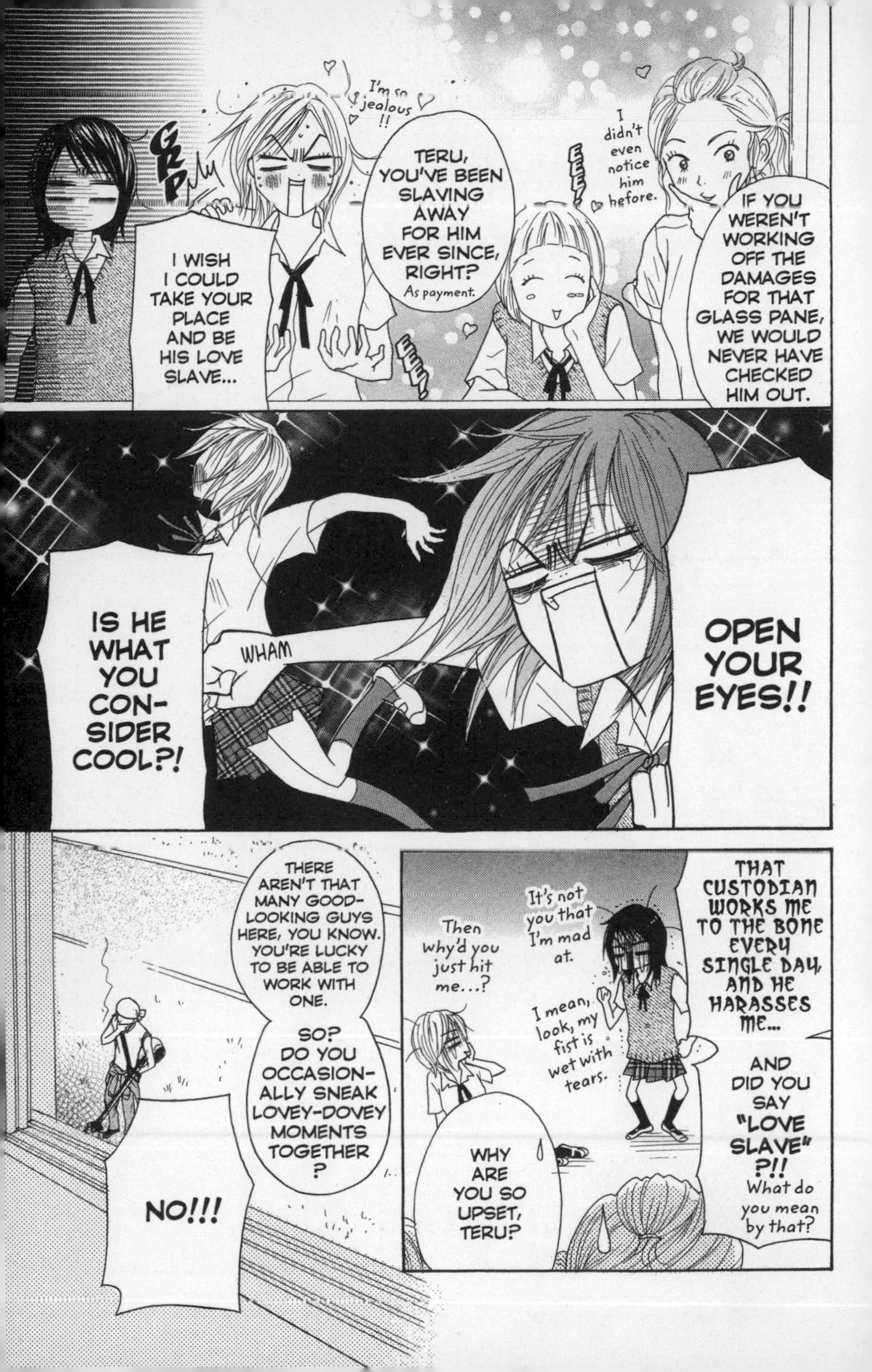
I didn't even notice him before.
IF YOU WEREN'T WORKING OFF THE DAMAGES FOR THAT GLASS PANE, WE WOULD NEVER HAVE CHECKED HIM OUT.
EEE
I'm so jealous!!
TERU, YOU'VE BEEN SLAVING AWAY FOR HIM EVER SINCE, RIGHT?
As payment.
GRP
I WISH I COULD TAKE YOUR PLACE AND BE HIS LOVE SLAVE...
OPEN YOUR EYES!!
WHAM
IS HE WHAT YOU CONSIDER COOL?!
THAT CUSTODIAN WORKS ME TO THE BONE EVERY SINGLE DAY, AND HE HARASSES ME...
AND DID YOU SAY "LOVE SLAVE"?!!
What do you mean by that?
It's not you that I'm mad at.
I mean, look, my fist is wet with tears.
Then why'd you just hit me...?
WHY ARE YOU SO UPSET, TERU?
THERE AREN'T THAT MANY GOOD-LOOKING GUYS HERE, YOU KNOW. YOU'RE LUCKY TO BE ABLE TO WORK WITH ONE.
SO? DO YOU OCCASIONALLY SNEAK LOVEY-DOVEY MOMENTS TOGETHER?
NO!!!

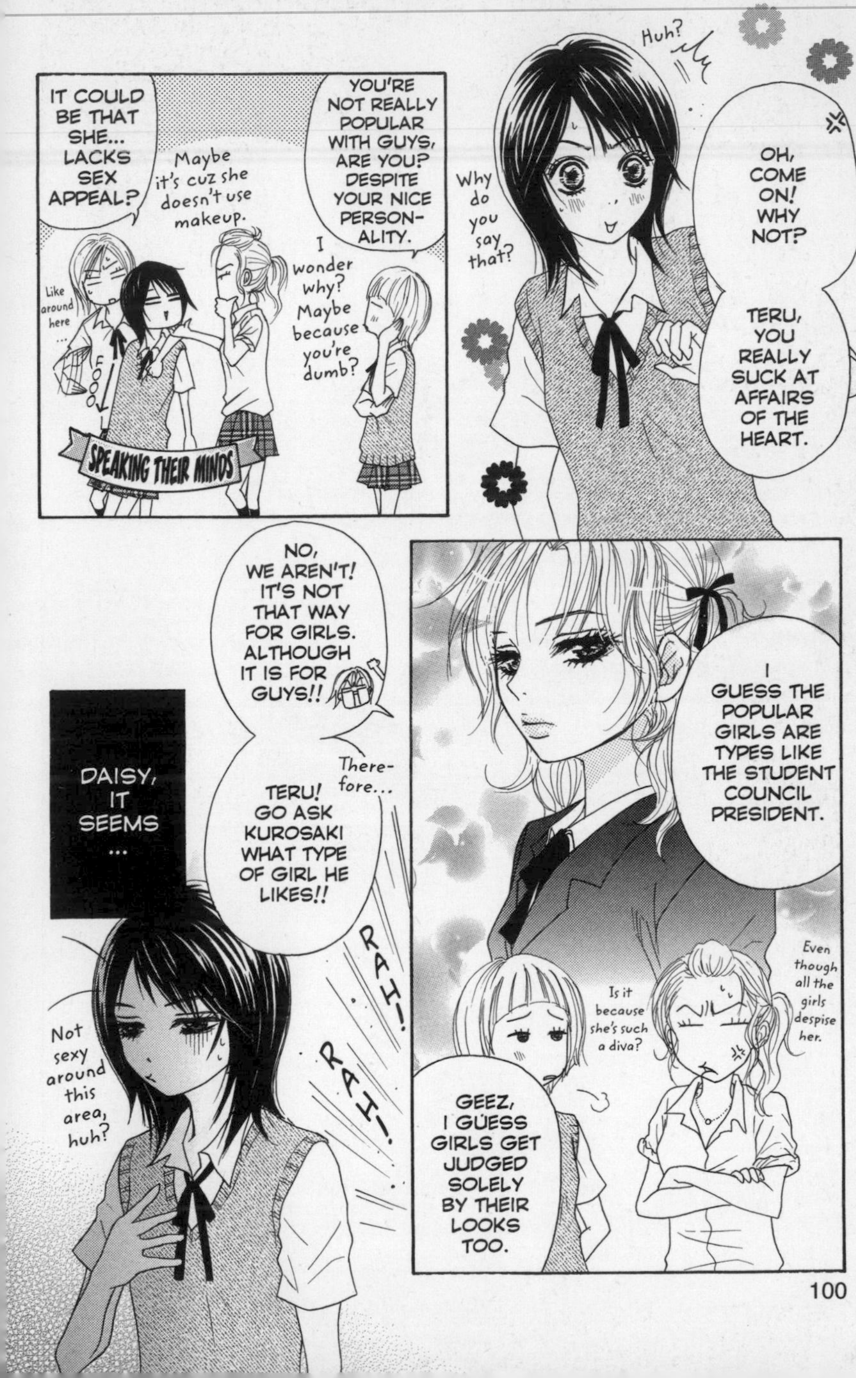
Huh?
OH, COME ON! WHY NOT?
TERU, YOU REALLY SUCK AT AFFAIRS OF THE HEART.
Why do you say that?
YOU'RE NOT REALLY POPULAR WITH GUYS, ARE YOU? DESPITE YOUR NICE PERSONALITY.
I wonder why? Maybe because you're dumb?
Maybe it's cuz she doesn't use makeup.
IT COULD BE THAT SHE... LACKS SEX APPEAL?
Like around here...
FOOO
SPEAKING THEIR MINDS
I GUESS THE POPULAR GIRLS ARE TYPES LIKE THE STUDENT COUNCIL PRESIDENT.
Even though all the girls despise her.
Is it because she's such a diva?
GEEZ, I GUESS GIRLS GET JUDGED SOLELY BY THEIR LOOKS TOO.
NO, WE AREN'T! IT'S NOT THAT WAY FOR GIRLS. ALTHOUGH IT IS FOR GUYS!!
There-fore...
TERU! GO ASK KUROSAKI WHAT TYPE OF GIRL HE LIKES!!
DAISY, IT SEEMS ...
RAH!
RAH!
Not sexy around this area, huh?

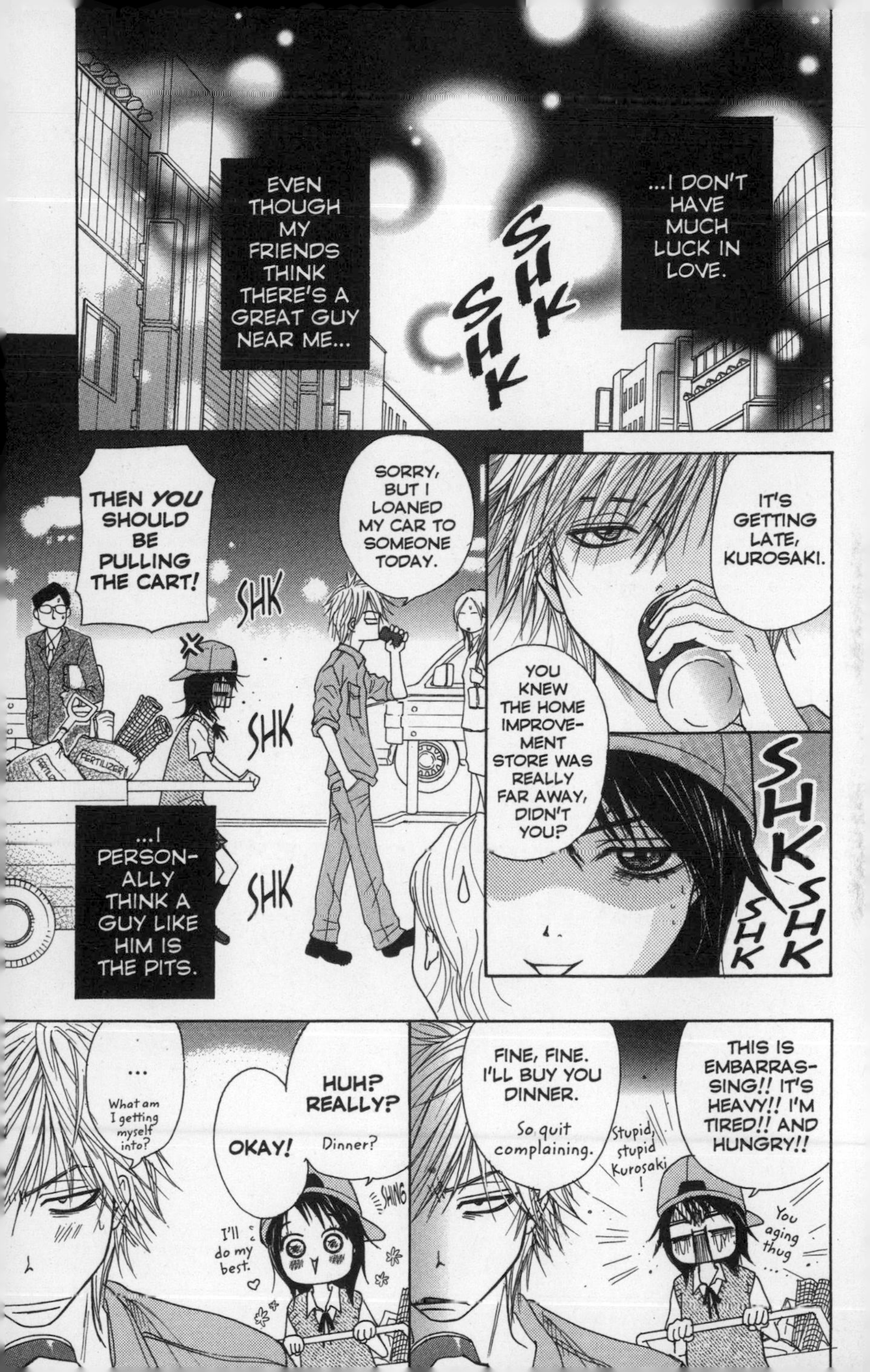
EVEN THOUGH MY FRIENDS THINK THERE'S A GREAT GUY NEAR ME...
SHK SHK
...I DON'T HAVE MUCH LUCK IN LOVE.
IT'S GETTING LATE, KUROSAKI.
YOU KNEW THE HOME IMPROVEMENT STORE WAS REALLY FAR AWAY, DIDN'T YOU?
SHK SHK SHK SHK
SORRY, BUT I LOANED MY CAR TO SOMEONE TODAY.
THEN *YOU* SHOULD BE PULLING THE CART!
FERTILIZER
SHK
SHK
SHK
...I PERSONALLY THINK A GUY LIKE HIM IS THE PITS.
THIS IS EMBARRASSING!! IT'S HEAVY!! I'M TIRED!! AND HUNGRY!!
You aging thug...
Stupid, stupid Kurosaki!
FINE, FINE. I'LL BUY YOU DINNER.
So quit complaining.
HUH? REALLY?
Dinner?
OKAY!
SHING
I'll do my best.
...
What am I getting myself into?

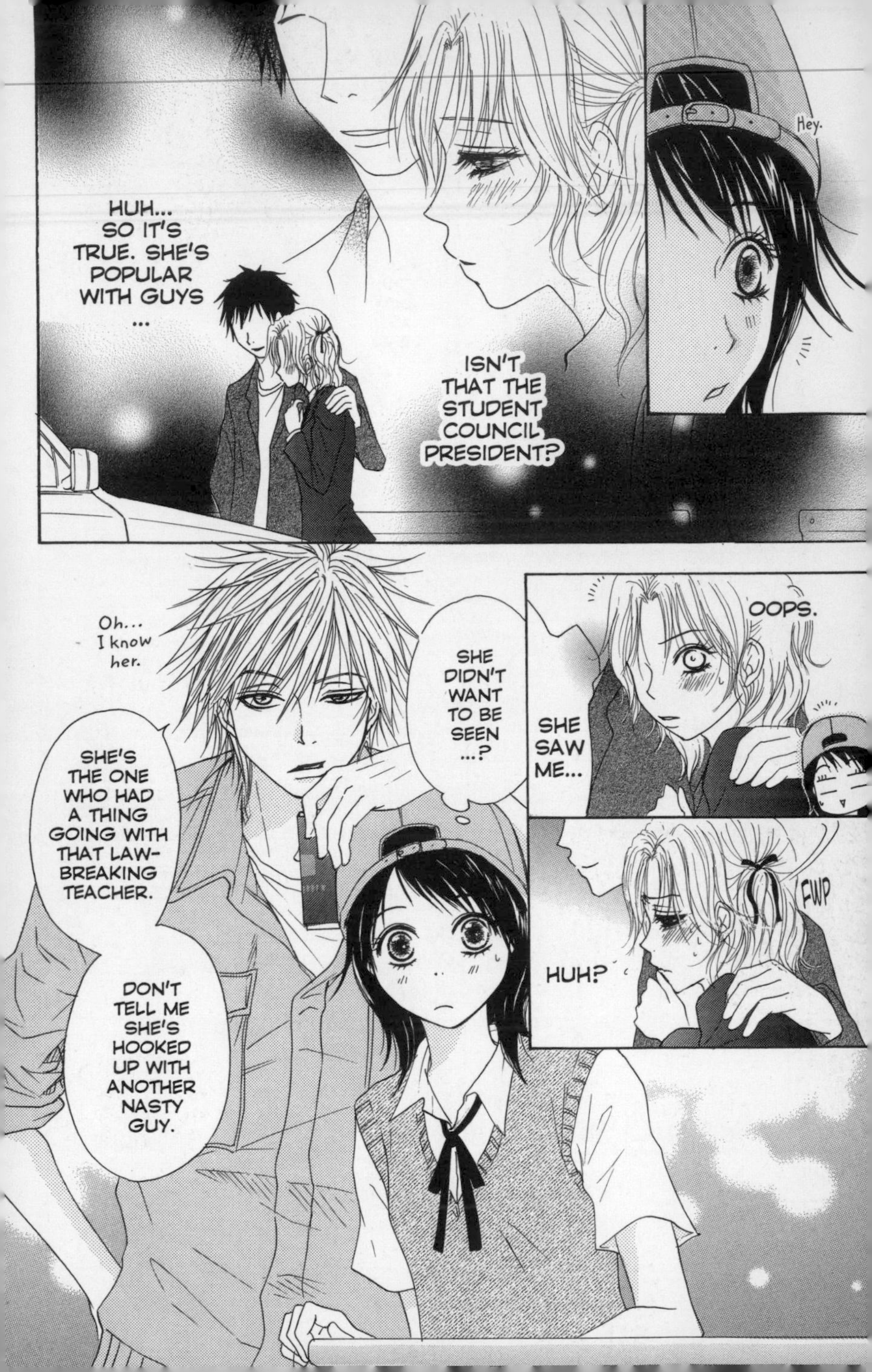
Hey.
ISN'T THAT THE STUDENT COUNCIL PRESIDENT?
HUH... SO IT'S TRUE. SHE'S POPULAR WITH GUYS ...
OOPS.
SHE SAW ME...
FWP
HUH?
SHE DIDN'T WANT TO BE SEEN ...?
Oh... I know her.
SHE'S THE ONE WHO HAD A THING GOING WITH THAT LAW-BREAKING TEACHER.
DON'T TELL ME SHE'S HOOKED UP WITH ANOTHER NASTY GUY.

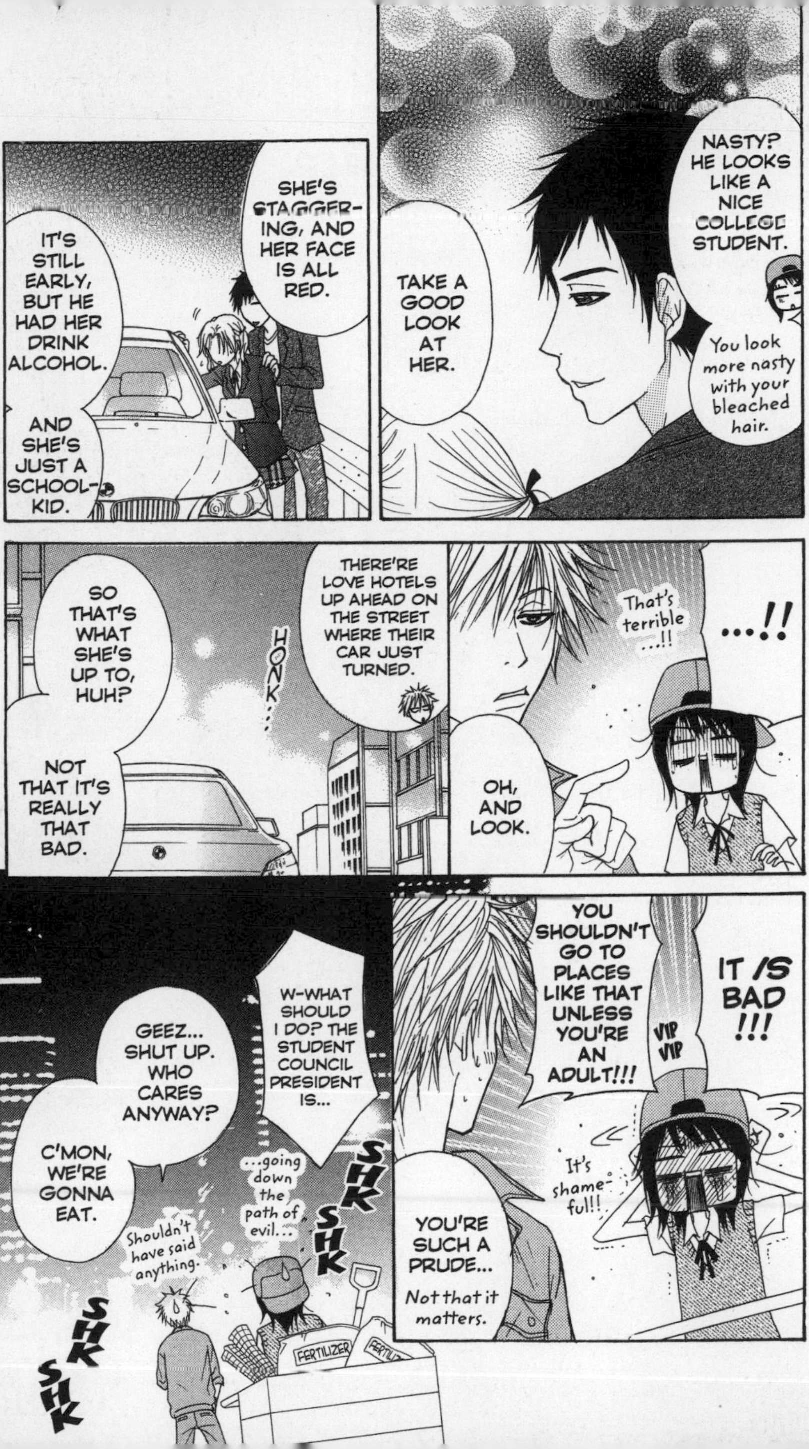
NASTY? HE LOOKS LIKE A NICE COLLEGE STUDENT.
You look more nasty with your bleached hair.
TAKE A GOOD LOOK AT HER.
SHE'S STAGGERING, AND HER FACE IS ALL RED.
IT'S STILL EARLY, BUT HE HAD HER DRINK ALCOHOL.
AND SHE'S JUST A SCHOOLKID.
...!!
That's terrible...!!
OH, AND LOOK.
THERE'RE LOVE HOTELS UP AHEAD ON THE STREET WHERE THEIR CAR JUST TURNED.
HONK...
SO THAT'S WHAT SHE'S UP TO, HUH?
NOT THAT IT'S REALLY THAT BAD.
IT IS BAD!!!
YOU SHOULDN'T GO TO PLACES LIKE THAT UNLESS YOU'RE AN ADULT!!!
VIP VIP
It's shameful!!
YOU'RE SUCH A PRUDE...
Not that it matters.
W-WHAT SHOULD I DO? THE STUDENT COUNCIL PRESIDENT IS...
...going down the path of evil...
SHK SHK
GEEZ... SHUT UP. WHO CARES ANYWAY?
C'MON, WE'RE GONNA EAT.
Shouldn't have said anything.
FERTILIZER
SHK SHK

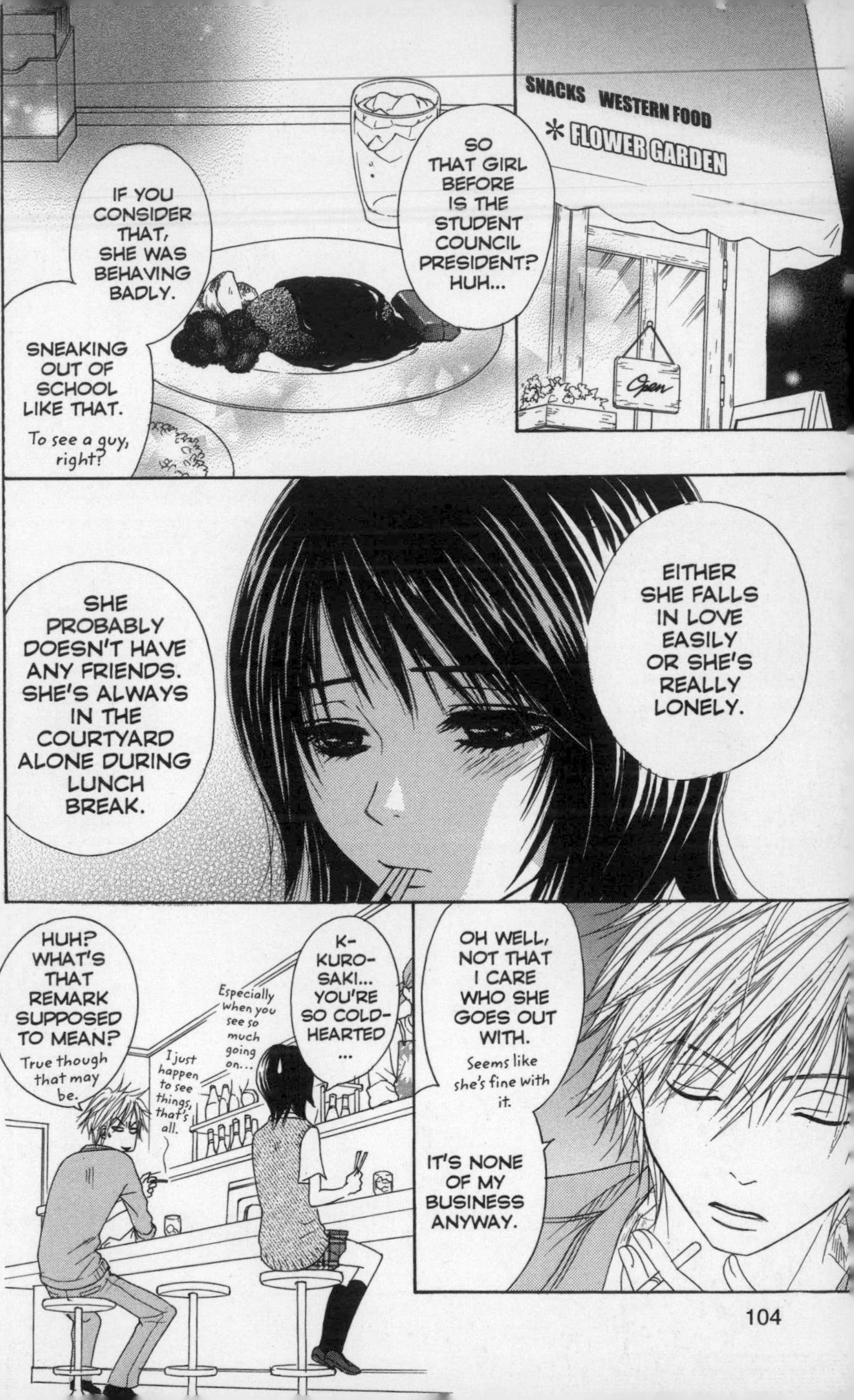
SNACKS WESTERN FOOD
* FLOWER GARDEN
Open
SO THAT GIRL BEFORE IS THE STUDENT COUNCIL PRESIDENT? HUH...
IF YOU CONSIDER THAT, SHE WAS BEHAVING BADLY.
SNEAKING OUT OF SCHOOL LIKE THAT.
To see a guy, right?
EITHER SHE FALLS IN LOVE EASILY OR SHE'S REALLY LONELY.
SHE PROBABLY DOESN'T HAVE ANY FRIENDS. SHE'S ALWAYS IN THE COURTYARD ALONE DURING LUNCH BREAK.
OH WELL, NOT THAT I CARE WHO SHE GOES OUT WITH.
Seems like she's fine with it.
IT'S NONE OF MY BUSINESS ANYWAY.
K-KURO-SAKI... YOU'RE SO COLD-HEARTED ...
Especially when you see so much going on...
HUH? WHAT'S THAT REMARK SUPPOSED TO MEAN?
True though that may be.
I just happen to see things, that's all.

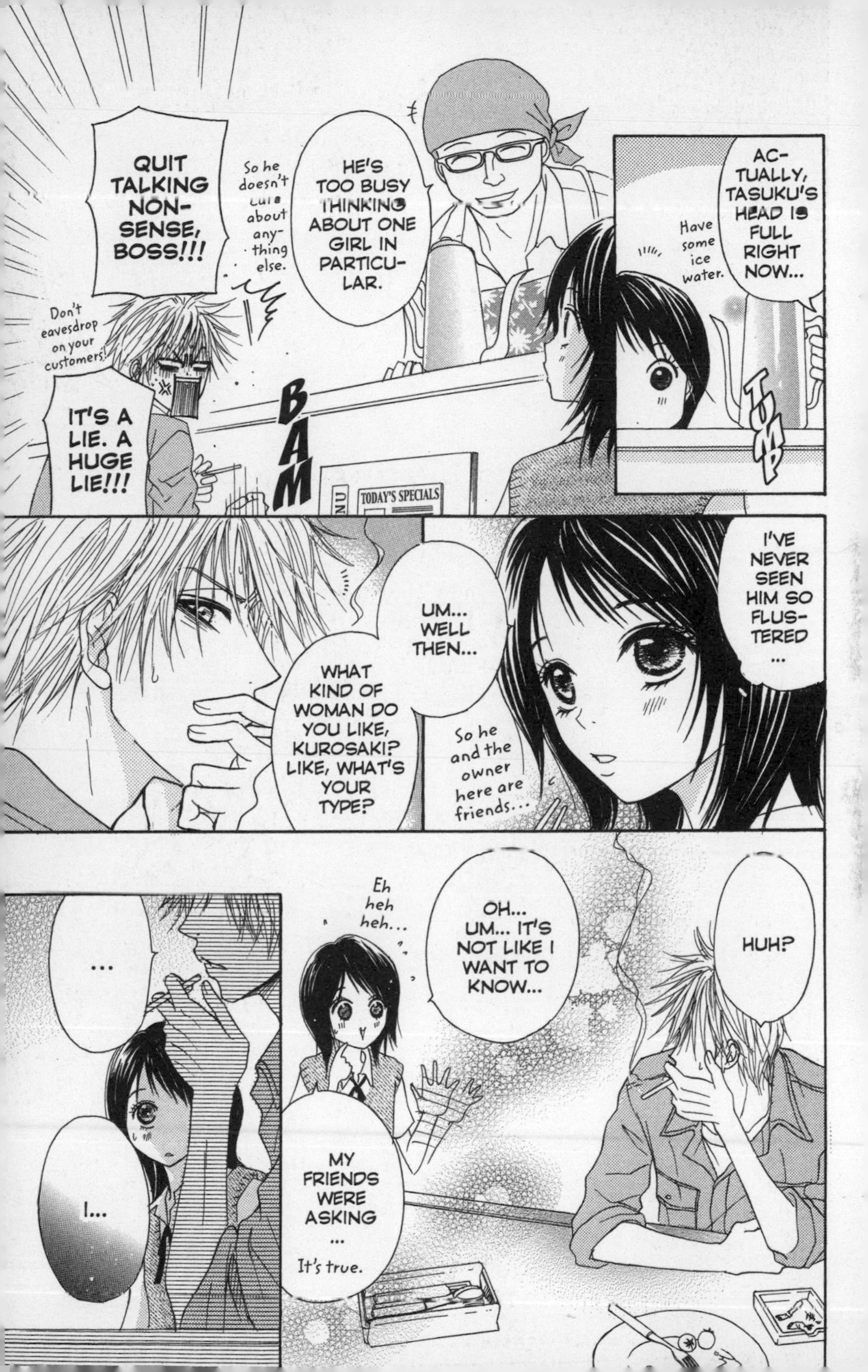

ACTUALLY, TASUKU'S HEAD IS FULL RIGHT NOW...
Have some ice water.
TUMP
HE'S TOO BUSY THINKING ABOUT ONE GIRL IN PARTICULAR.
So he doesn't care about anything else.
QUIT TALKING NONSENSE, BOSS!!!
Don't eavesdrop on your customers!
IT'S A LIE. A HUGE LIE!!!
BAM
TODAY'S SPECIALS
I'VE NEVER SEEN HIM SO FLUSTERED...
So he and the owner here are friends...
UM... WELL THEN...
WHAT KIND OF WOMAN DO YOU LIKE, KUROSAKI? LIKE, WHAT'S YOUR TYPE?
HUH?
OH... UM... IT'S NOT LIKE I WANT TO KNOW...
Eh heh heh...
MY FRIENDS WERE ASKING...
It's true.
...
I...

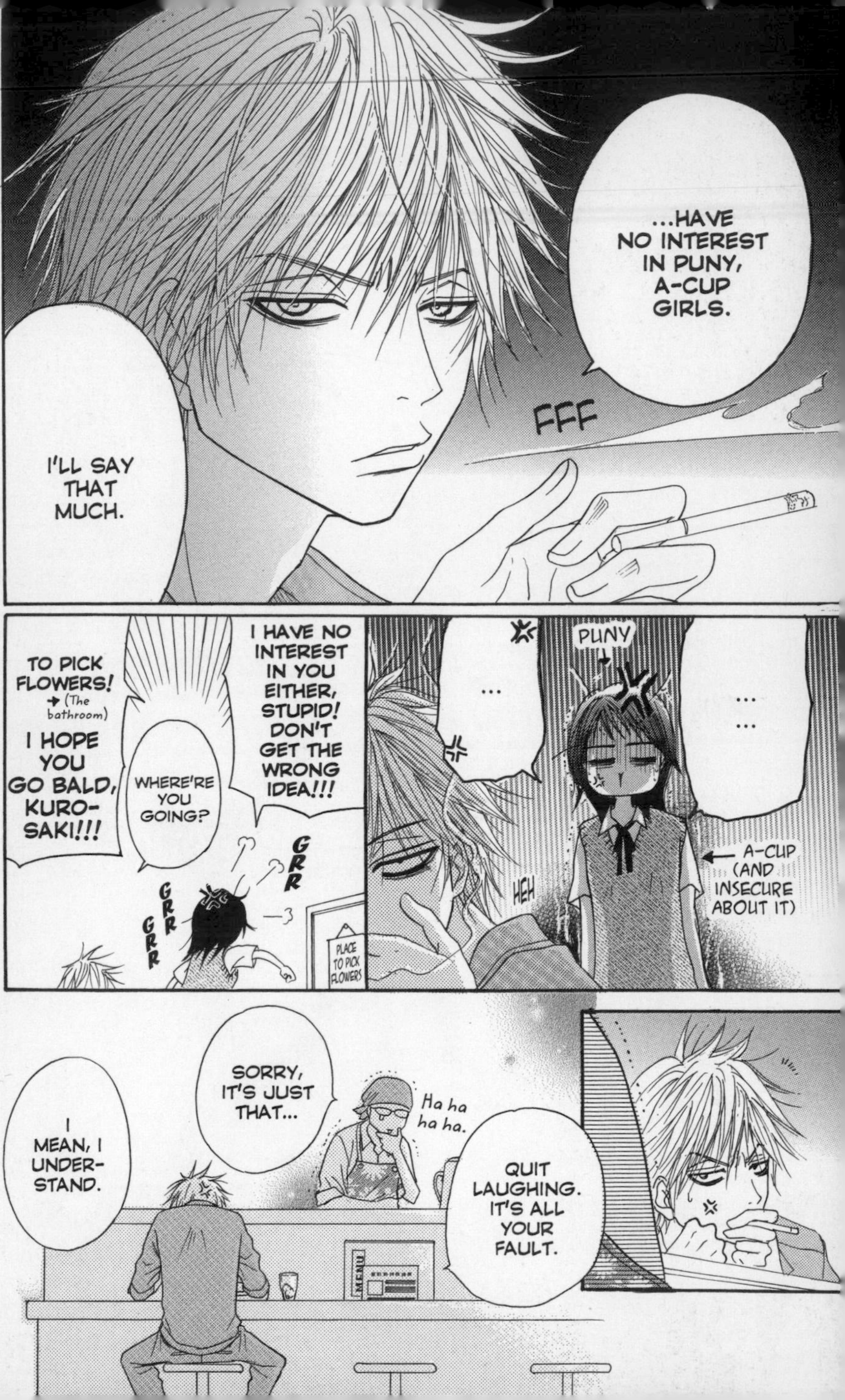
...HAVE NO INTEREST IN PUNY, A-CUP GIRLS.
FFF
I'LL SAY THAT MUCH.
... ...
PUNY
...
A-CUP (AND INSECURE ABOUT IT)
HEH
I HAVE NO INTEREST IN YOU EITHER, STUPID! DON'T GET THE WRONG IDEA!!!
WHERE'RE YOU GOING?
TO PICK FLOWERS!
(The bathroom)
I HOPE YOU GO BALD, KURO-SAKI!!!
GRR
GRR
GRR
PLACE TO PICK FLOWERS
QUIT LAUGHING. IT'S ALL YOUR FAULT.
Ha ha ha ha.
SORRY, IT'S JUST THAT...
I MEAN, I UNDERSTAND.
MENU

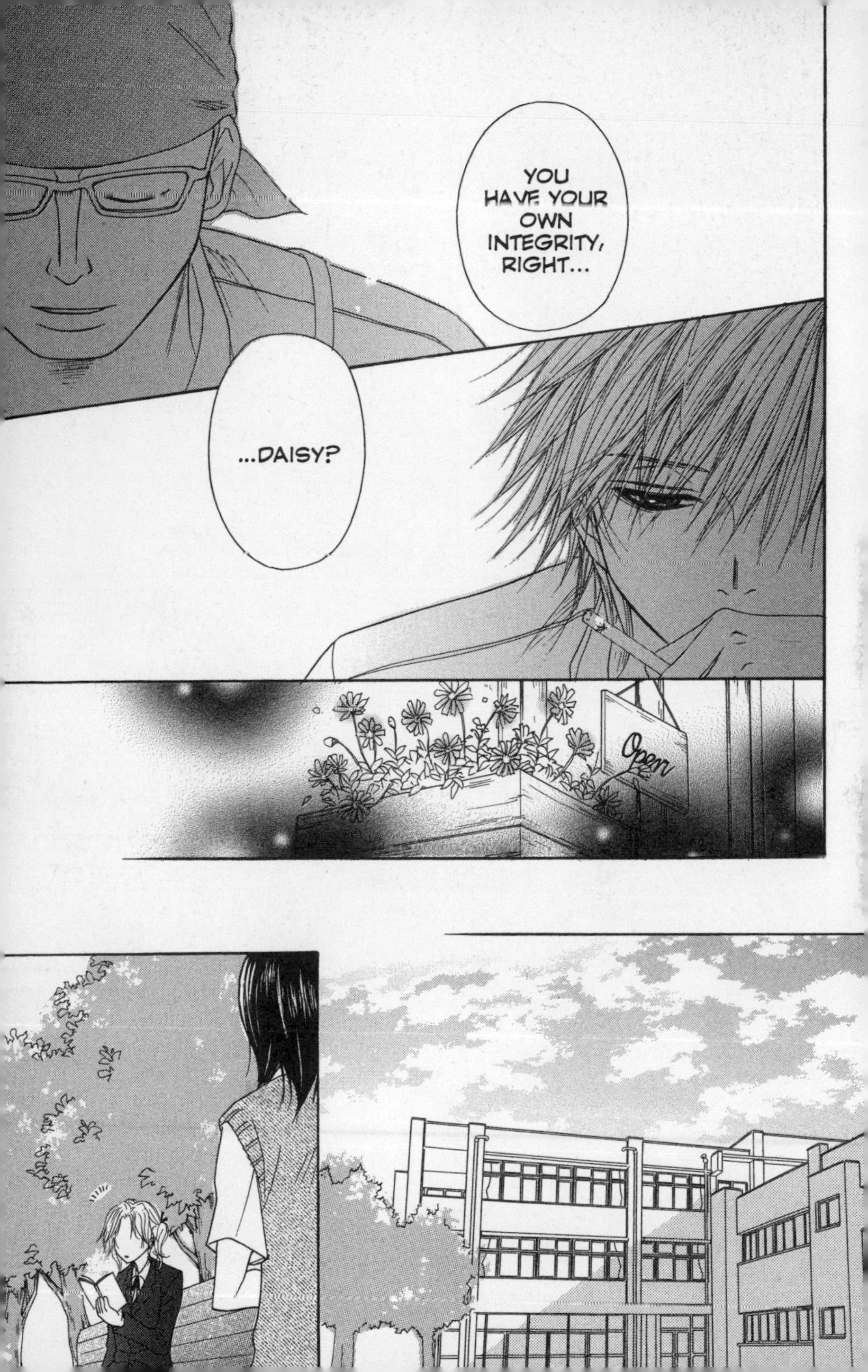
YOU HAVE YOUR OWN INTEGRITY, RIGHT...
...DAISY?
Open

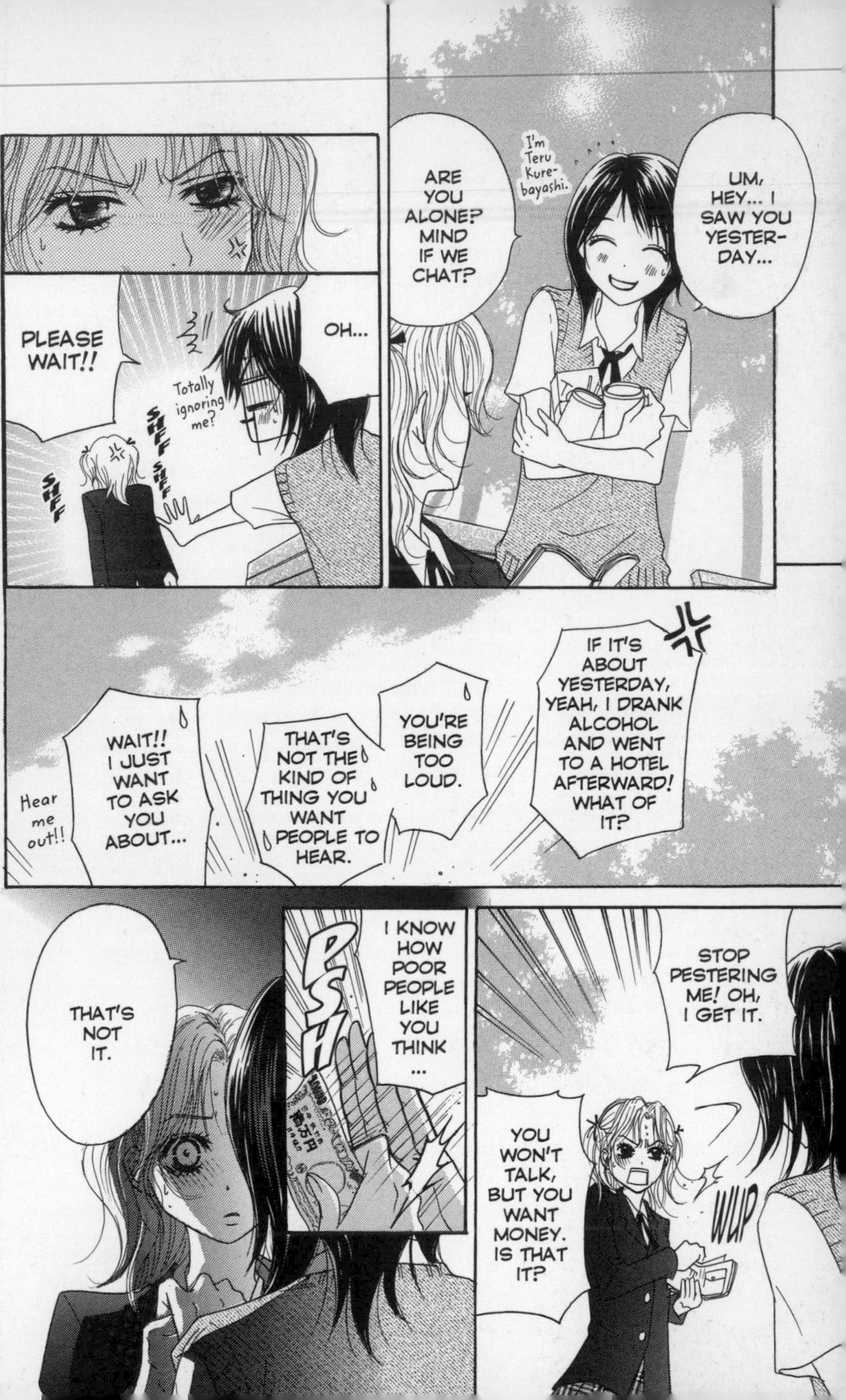
UM, HEY... I SAW YOU YESTERDAY...
I'm Teru Kurebayashi.
ARE YOU ALONE? MIND IF WE CHAT?
OH...
Totally ignoring me?
PLEASE WAIT!!
SHFF SHFF
SHFF
IF IT'S ABOUT YESTERDAY, YEAH, I DRANK ALCOHOL AND WENT TO A HOTEL AFTERWARD! WHAT OF IT?
YOU'RE BEING TOO LOUD.
THAT'S NOT THE KIND OF THING YOU WANT PEOPLE TO HEAR.
WAIT!! I JUST WANT TO ASK YOU ABOUT...
Hear me out!!
STOP PESTERING ME! OH, I GET IT.
YOU WON'T TALK, BUT YOU WANT MONEY. IS THAT IT?
WUP
PSH
I KNOW HOW POOR PEOPLE LIKE YOU THINK ...
THAT'S NOT IT.

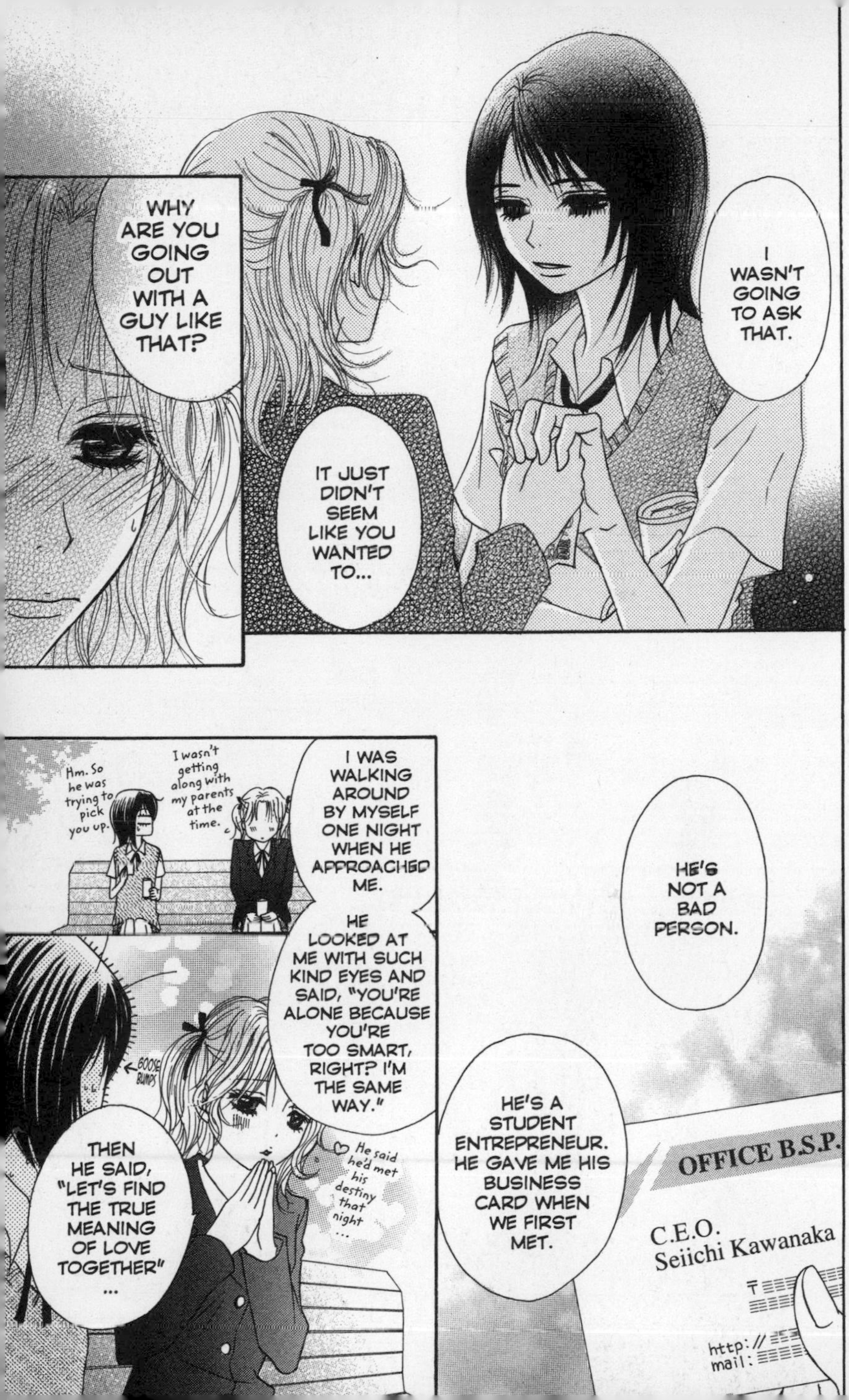
I WASN'T GOING TO ASK THAT.
IT JUST DIDN'T SEEM LIKE YOU WANTED TO...
WHY ARE YOU GOING OUT WITH A GUY LIKE THAT?
HE'S NOT A BAD PERSON.
HE'S A STUDENT ENTREPRENEUR. HE GAVE ME HIS BUSINESS CARD WHEN WE FIRST MET.
OFFICE B.S.P.
C.E.O.
Seiichi Kawanaka
http://
mail:
I WAS WALKING AROUND BY MYSELF ONE NIGHT WHEN HE APPROACHED ME.
I wasn't getting along with my parents at the time.
Hm. So he was trying to pick you up.
HE LOOKED AT ME WITH SUCH KIND EYES AND SAID, "YOU'RE ALONE BECAUSE YOU'RE TOO SMART, RIGHT? I'M THE SAME WAY."
He said he'd met his destiny that night...
GOOSE BUMPS
THEN HE SAID, "LET'S FIND THE TRUE MEANING OF LOVE TOGETHER"...

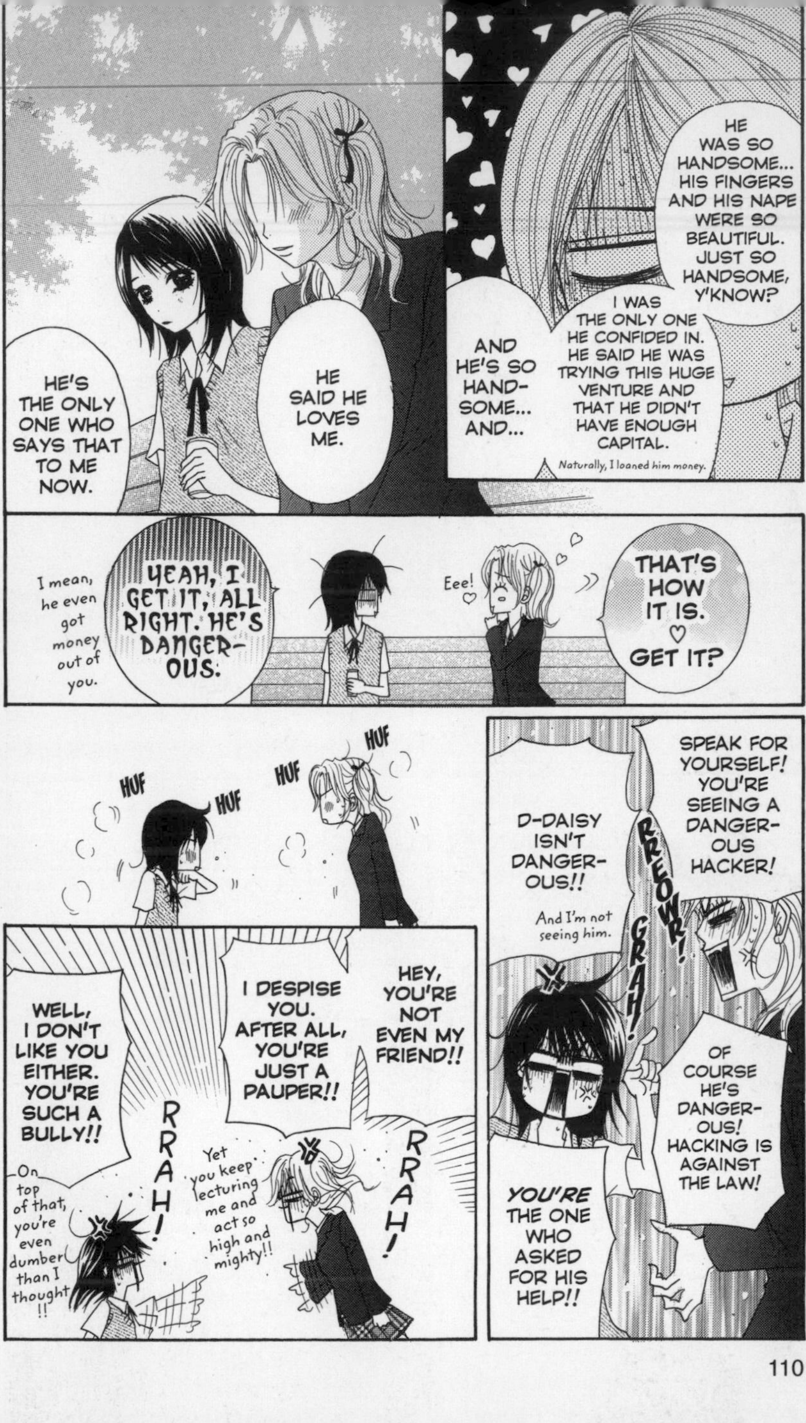
HE WAS SO HANDSOME... HIS FINGERS AND HIS NAPE WERE SO BEAUTIFUL. JUST SO HANDSOME, Y'KNOW?
I WAS THE ONLY ONE HE CONFIDED IN. HE SAID HE WAS TRYING THIS HUGE VENTURE AND THAT HE DIDN'T HAVE ENOUGH CAPITAL.
AND HE'S SO HAND-SOME... AND...
Naturally, I loaned him money.
HE SAID HE LOVES ME.
HE'S THE ONLY ONE WHO SAYS THAT TO ME NOW.
THAT'S HOW IT IS. ♡ GET IT?
Eee! ♡
YEAH, I GET IT, ALL RIGHT. HE'S DANGER-OUS.
I mean, he even got money out of you.
SPEAK FOR YOURSELF! YOU'RE SEEING A DANGER-OUS HACKER!
RREOWR!
D-DAISY ISN'T DANGER-OUS!!
And I'm not seeing him.
GRAH!
OF COURSE HE'S DANGER-OUS! HACKING IS AGAINST THE LAW!
YOU'RE THE ONE WHO ASKED FOR HIS HELP!!
HUF
HUF
HUF
HUF
HEY, YOU'RE NOT EVEN MY FRIEND!!
I DESPISE YOU. AFTER ALL, YOU'RE JUST A PAUPER!!
RRAH!
Yet you keep lecturing me and act so high and mighty!!
WELL, I DON'T LIKE YOU EITHER. YOU'RE SUCH A BULLY!!
RRAH!
On top of that, you're even dumber than I thought!!

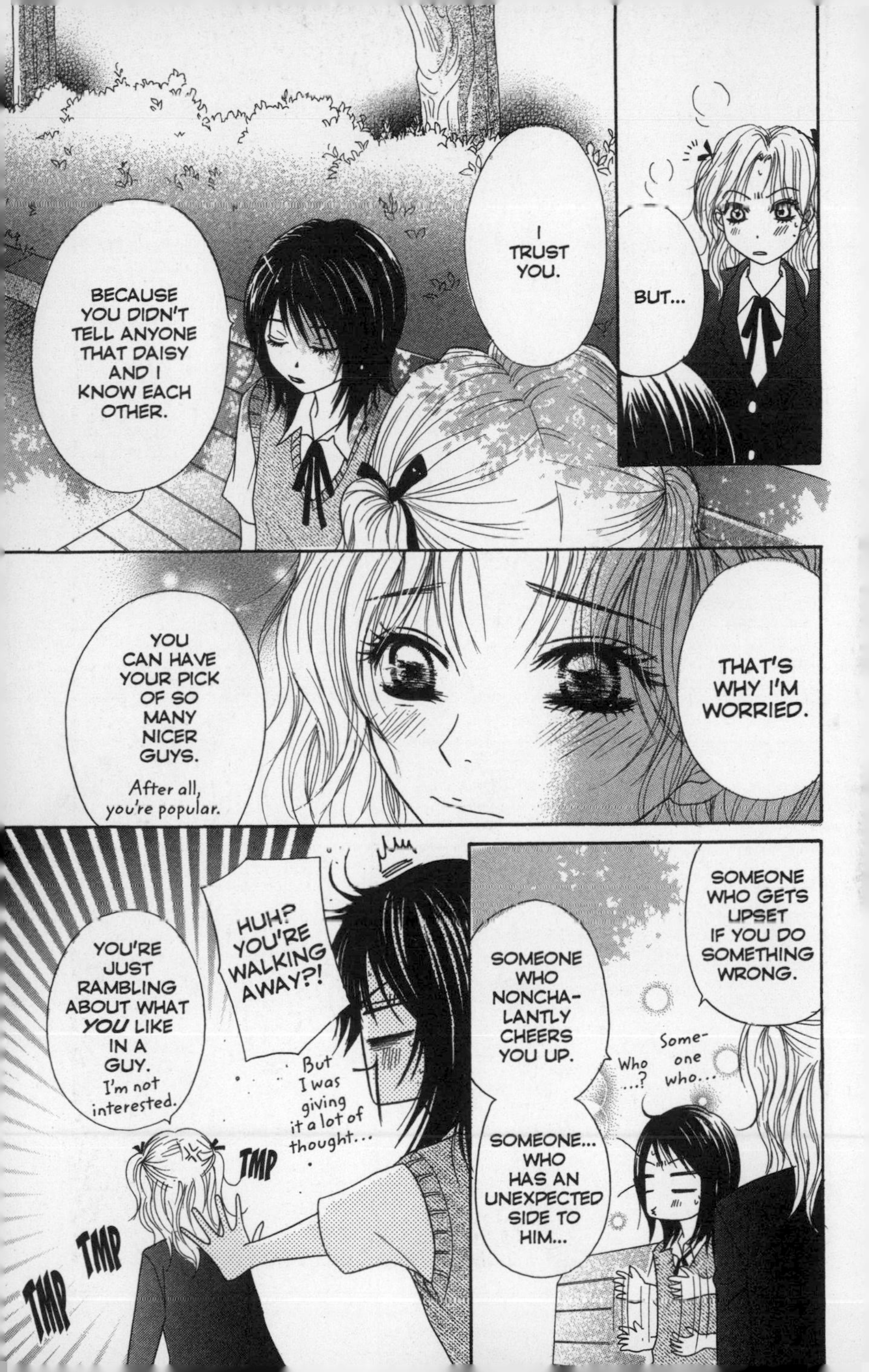
BUT...
I TRUST YOU.
BECAUSE YOU DIDN'T TELL ANYONE THAT DAISY AND I KNOW EACH OTHER.
THAT'S WHY I'M WORRIED.
YOU CAN HAVE YOUR PICK OF SO MANY NICER GUYS.
After all, you're popular.
SOMEONE WHO GETS UPSET IF YOU DO SOMETHING WRONG.
SOMEONE WHO NONCHALANTLY CHEERS YOU UP.
Someone who...
Who ...?
SOMEONE... WHO HAS AN UNEXPECTED SIDE TO HIM...
HUH? YOU'RE WALKING AWAY?!
But I was giving it a lot of thought...
YOU'RE JUST RAMBLING ABOUT WHAT YOU LIKE IN A GUY.
I'm not interested.
TMP
TMP
TMP

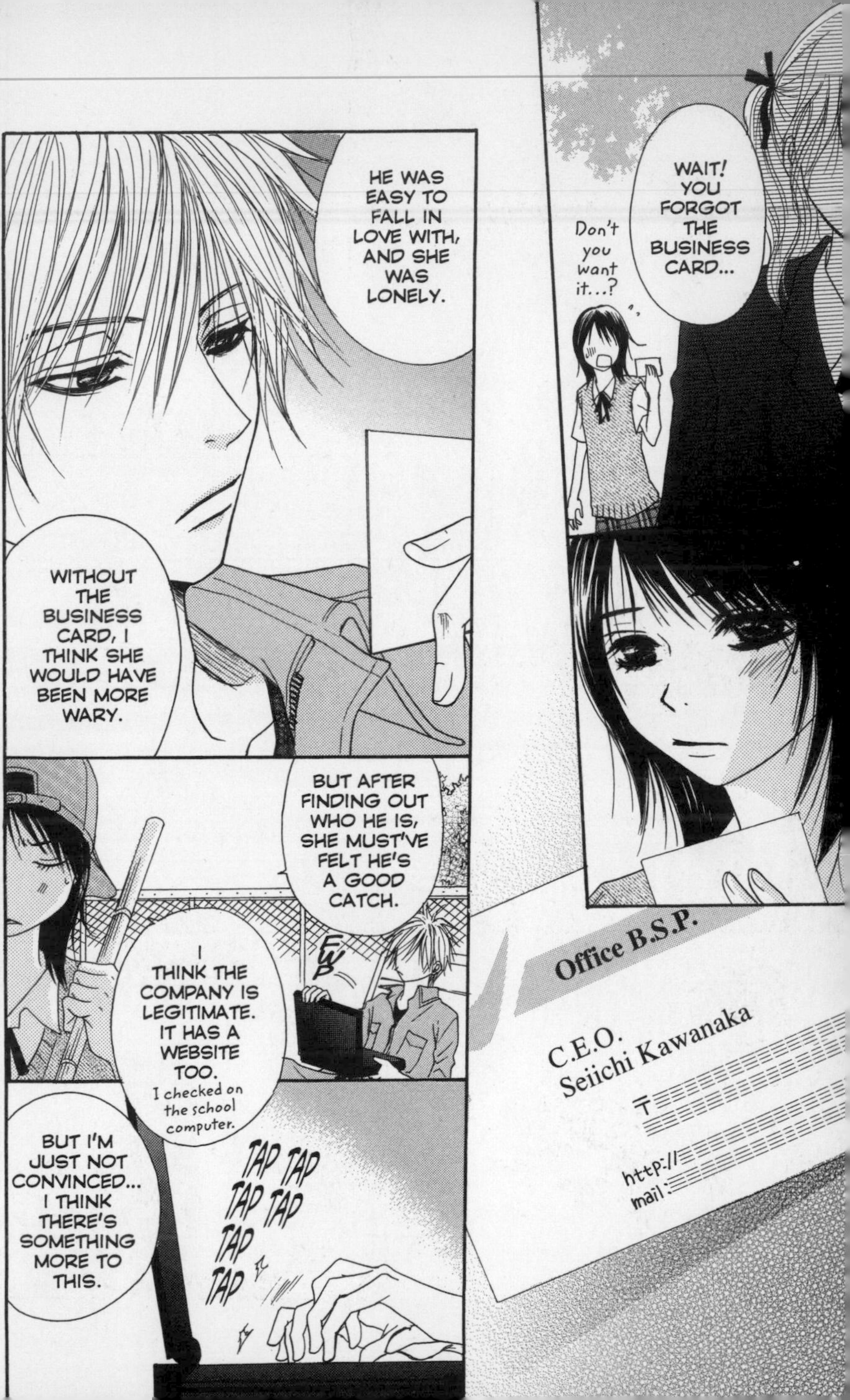
WAIT! YOU FORGOT THE BUSINESS CARD...
Don't you want it...?
Office B.S.P.
C.E.O.
Seiichi Kawanaka
〒
http://
mail:
HE WAS EASY TO FALL IN LOVE WITH, AND SHE WAS LONELY.
WITHOUT THE BUSINESS CARD, I THINK SHE WOULD HAVE BEEN MORE WARY.
BUT AFTER FINDING OUT WHO HE IS, SHE MUST'VE FELT HE'S A GOOD CATCH.
FWP
I THINK THE COMPANY IS LEGITIMATE. IT HAS A WEBSITE TOO.
I checked on the school computer.
TAP TAP TAP TAP TAP TAP
BUT I'M JUST NOT CONVINCED... I THINK THERE'S SOMETHING MORE TO THIS.

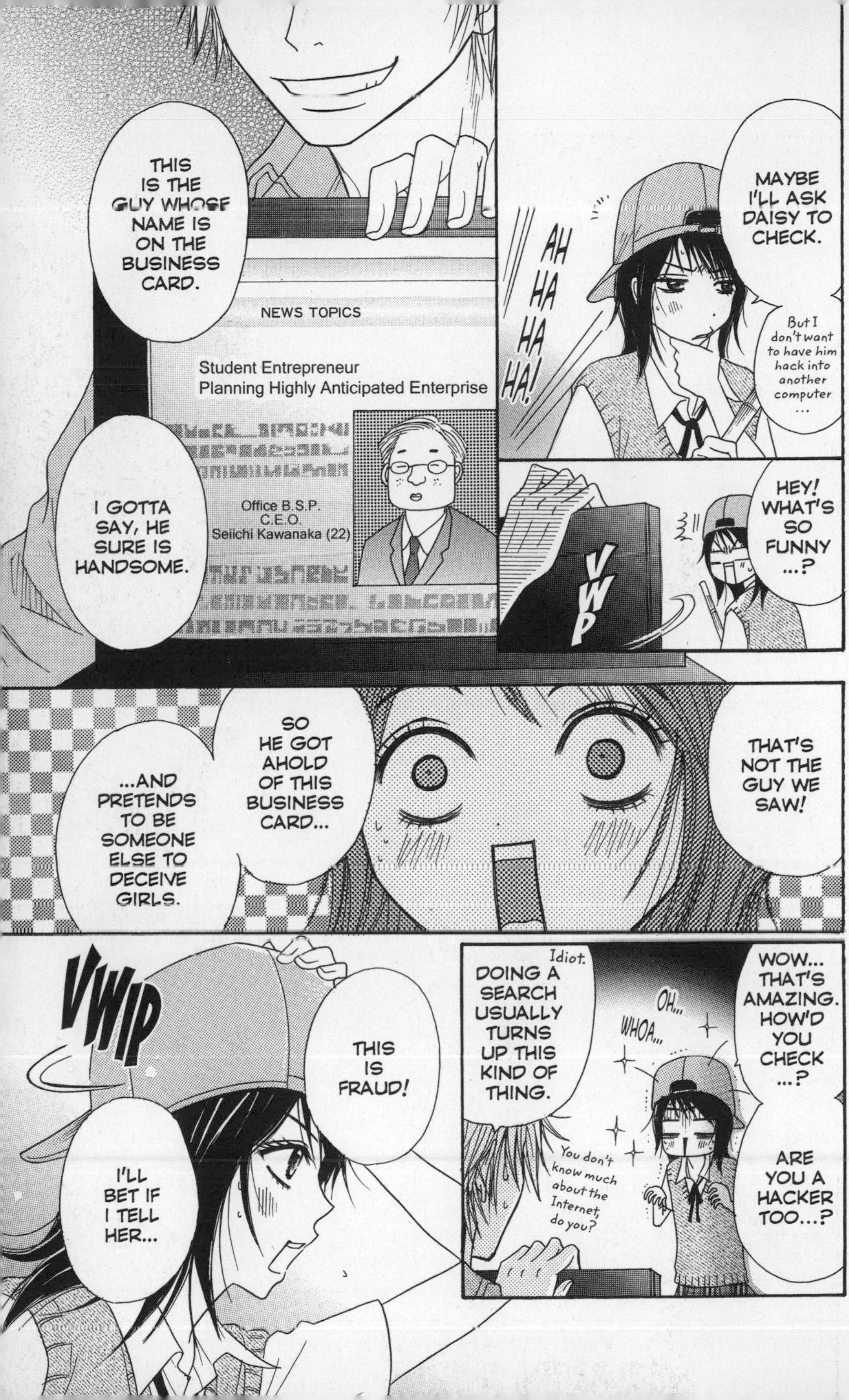
MAYBE I'LL ASK DAISY TO CHECK.
But I don't want to have him hack into another computer ...
AH HA HA HA HA!
HEY! WHAT'S SO FUNNY ...?
VWP
THIS IS THE GUY WHOSE NAME IS ON THE BUSINESS CARD.
NEWS TOPICS
Student Entrepreneur
Planning Highly Anticipated Enterprise
Office B.S.P.
C.E.O.
Seichi Kawanaka (22)
I GOTTA SAY, HE SURE IS HANDSOME.
THAT'S NOT THE GUY WE SAW!
SO HE GOT AHOLD OF THIS BUSINESS CARD...
...AND PRETENDS TO BE SOMEONE ELSE TO DECEIVE GIRLS.
WOW... THAT'S AMAZING. HOW'D YOU CHECK ...?
ARE YOU A HACKER TOO...?
OH...
WHOA...
Idiot.
DOING A SEARCH USUALLY TURNS UP THIS KIND OF THING.
You don't know much about the Internet, do you?
VWIP
THIS IS FRAUD!
I'LL BET IF I TELL HER...

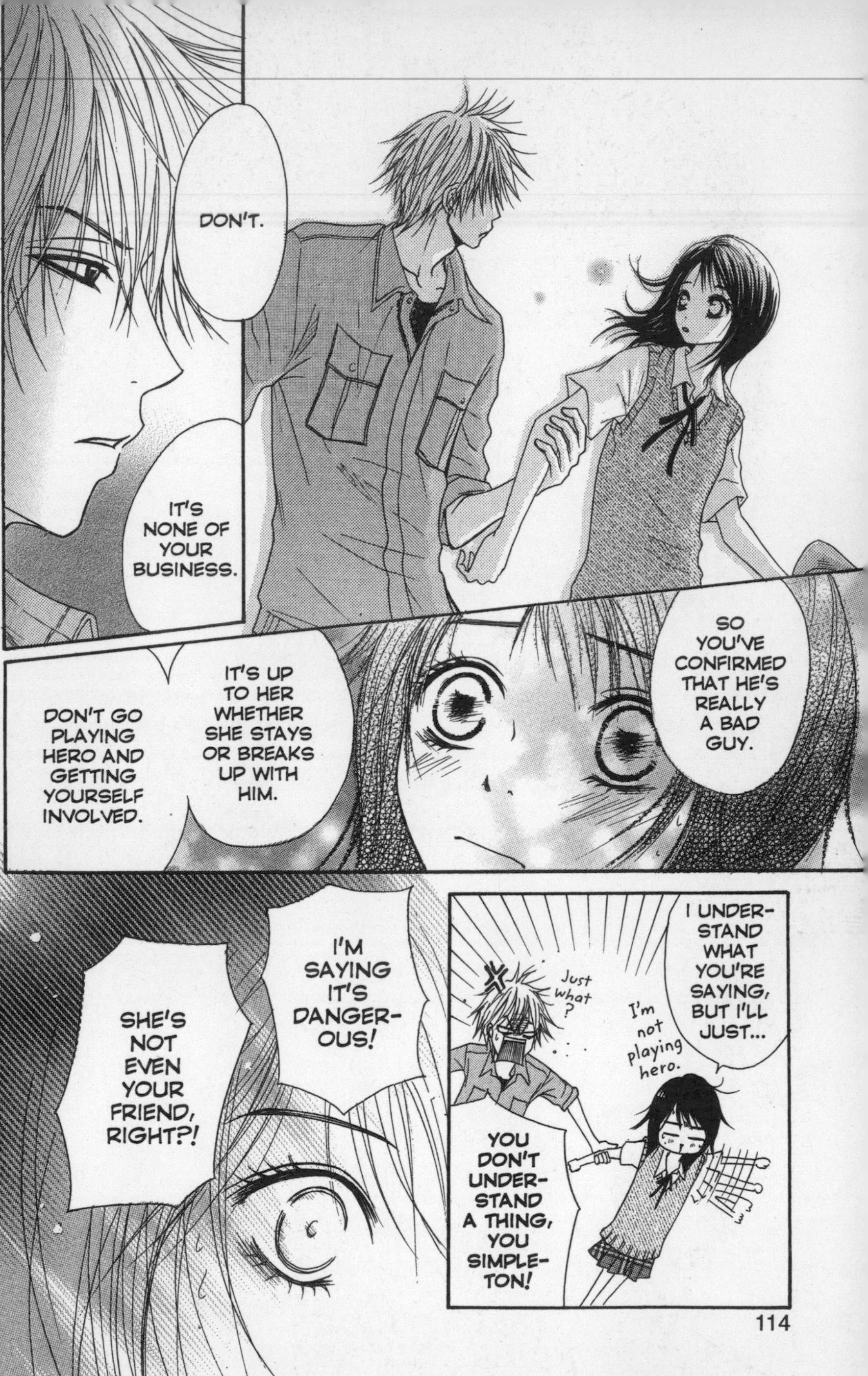
DON'T.
IT'S NONE OF YOUR BUSINESS.
SO YOU'VE CONFIRMED THAT HE'S REALLY A BAD GUY.
IT'S UP TO HER WHETHER SHE STAYS OR BREAKS UP WITH HIM.
DON'T GO PLAYING HERO AND GETTING YOURSELF INVOLVED.
I UNDER-STAND WHAT YOU'RE SAYING, BUT I'LL JUST...
I'm not playing hero.
Just what?
YOU DON'T UNDER-STAND A THING, YOU SIMPLE-TON!
I'M SAYING IT'S DANGER-OUS!
SHE'S NOT EVEN YOUR FRIEND, RIGHT?!

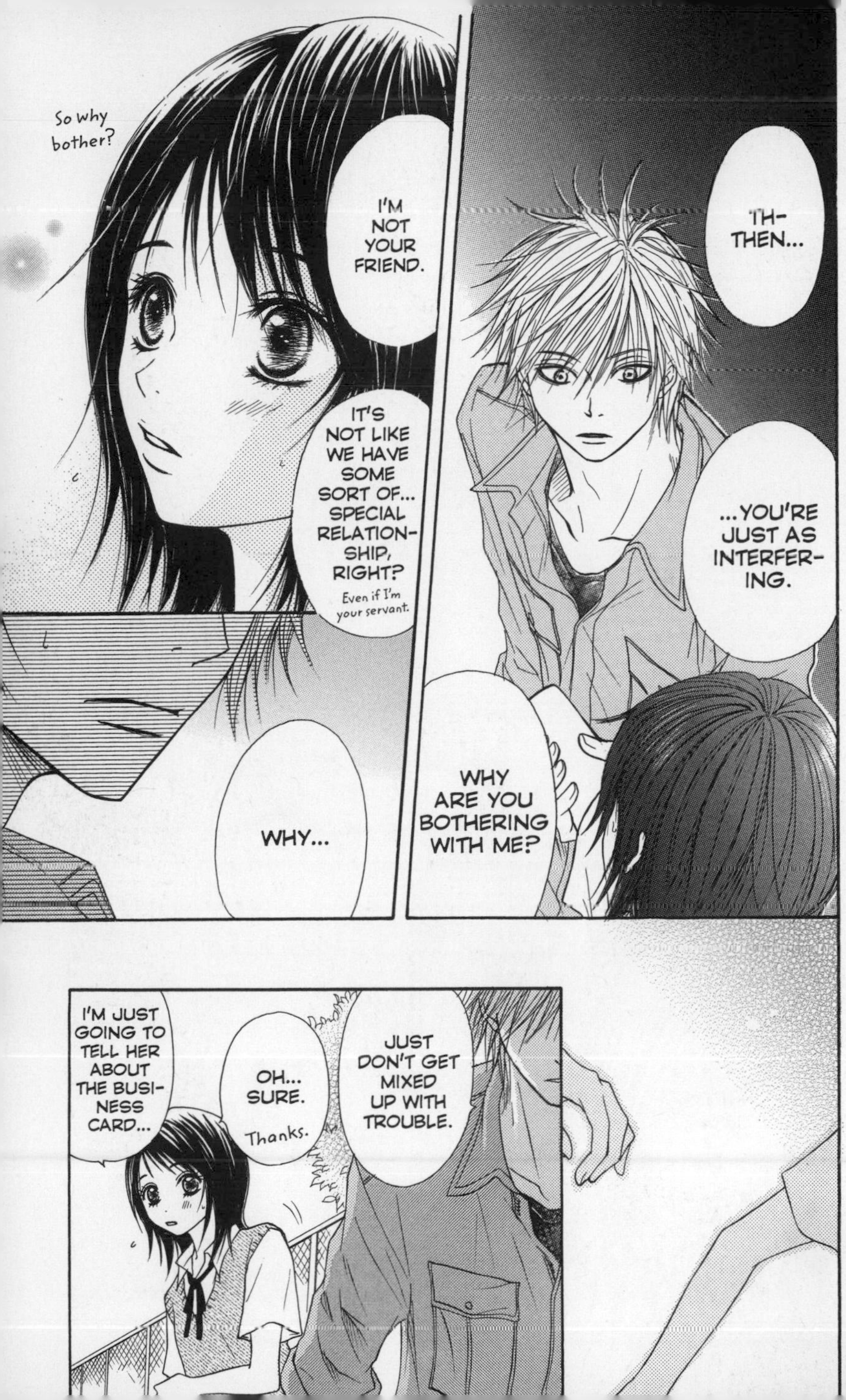
TH-THEN...
...YOU'RE JUST AS INTERFERING.
WHY ARE YOU BOTHERING WITH ME?
I'M NOT YOUR FRIEND.
IT'S NOT LIKE WE HAVE SOME SORT OF... SPECIAL RELATIONSHIP, RIGHT?
Even if I'm your servant.
So why bother?
WHY...
JUST DON'T GET MIXED UP WITH TROUBLE.
OH... SURE.
Thanks.
I'M JUST GOING TO TELL HER ABOUT THE BUSINESS CARD...

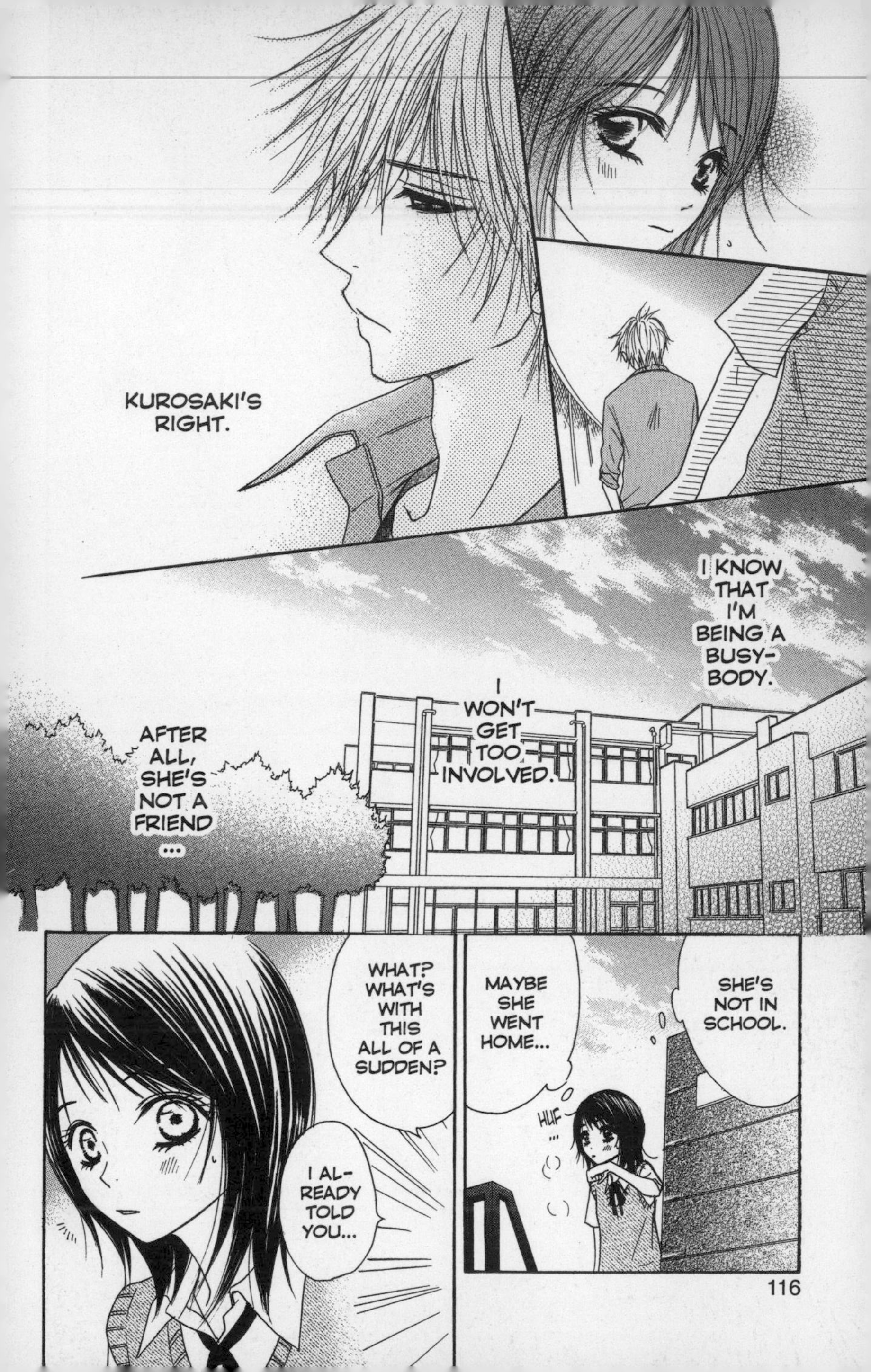
KUROSAKI'S RIGHT.
I KNOW THAT I'M BEING A BUSY-BODY.
I WON'T GET TOO INVOLVED.
AFTER ALL, SHE'S NOT A FRIEND...
SHE'S NOT IN SCHOOL.
MAYBE SHE WENT HOME...
HUF...
WHAT? WHAT'S WITH THIS ALL OF A SUDDEN?
I AL-READY TOLD YOU...

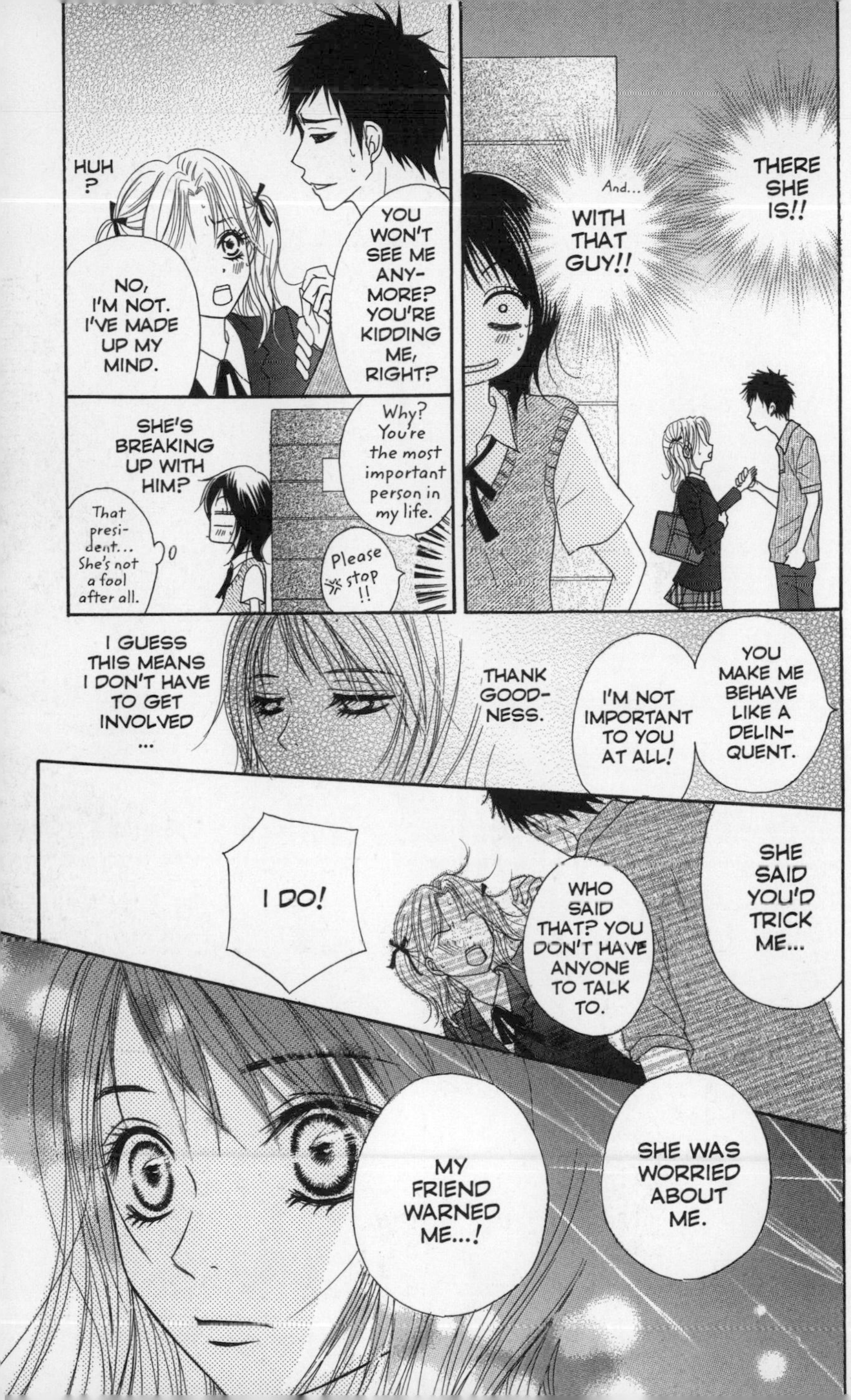
THERE SHE IS!!
And... WITH THAT GUY!!
YOU WON'T SEE ME ANYMORE? YOU'RE KIDDING ME, RIGHT?
HUH?
NO, I'M NOT. I'VE MADE UP MY MIND.
Why? You're the most important person in my life.
Please stop!!
SHE'S BREAKING UP WITH HIM?
That president... She's not a fool after all.
YOU MAKE ME BEHAVE LIKE A DELINQUENT.
I'M NOT IMPORTANT TO YOU AT ALL!
THANK GOODNESS.
I GUESS THIS MEANS I DON'T HAVE TO GET INVOLVED...
SHE SAID YOU'D TRICK ME...
WHO SAID THAT? YOU DON'T HAVE ANYONE TO TALK TO.
I DO!
SHE WAS WORRIED ABOUT ME.
MY FRIEND WARNED ME...!

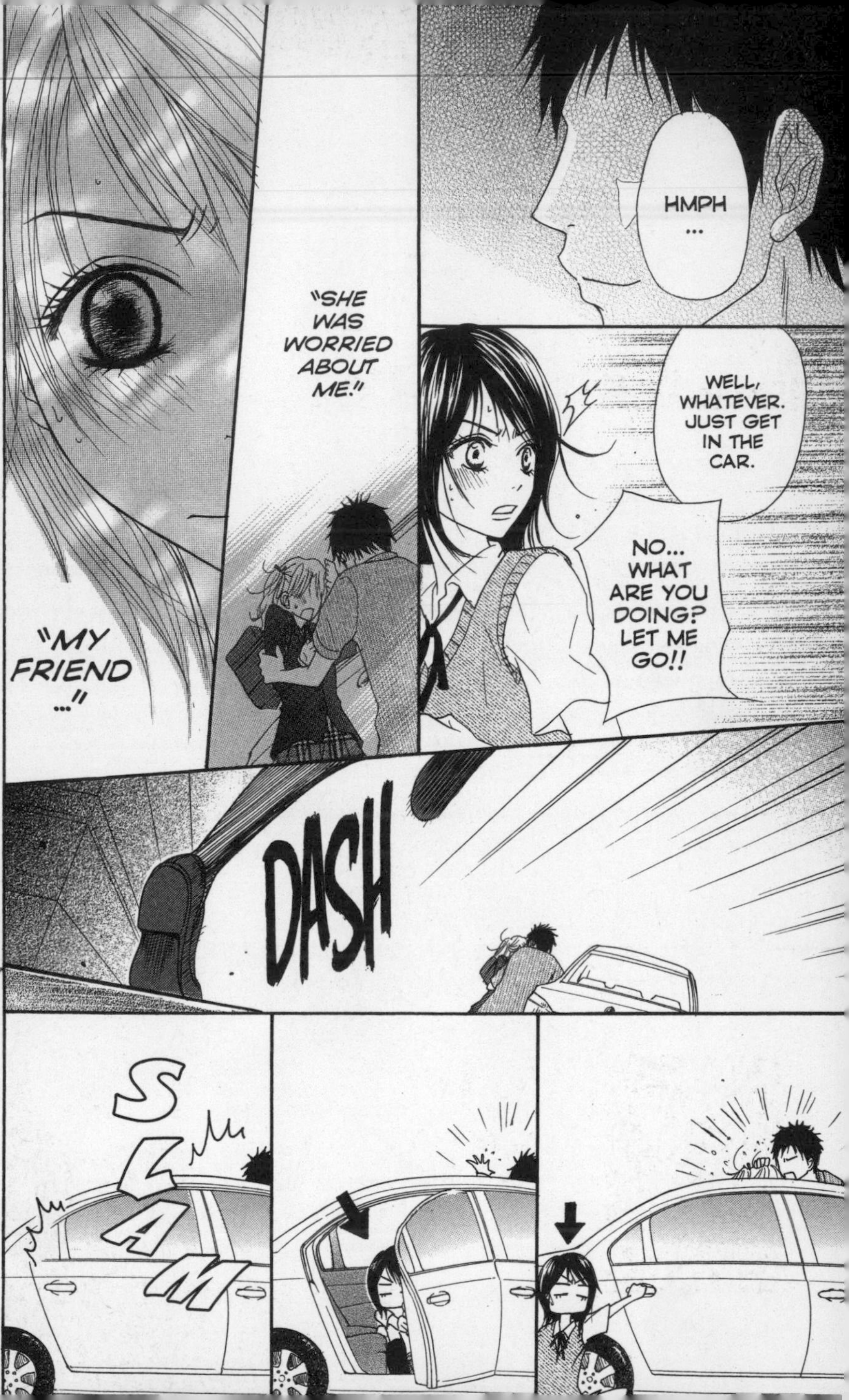
HMPH ...
WELL, WHATEVER. JUST GET IN THE CAR.
NO... WHAT ARE YOU DOING? LET ME GO!!
"SHE WAS WORRIED ABOUT ME."
"MY FRIEND ..."
DASH
SLAM

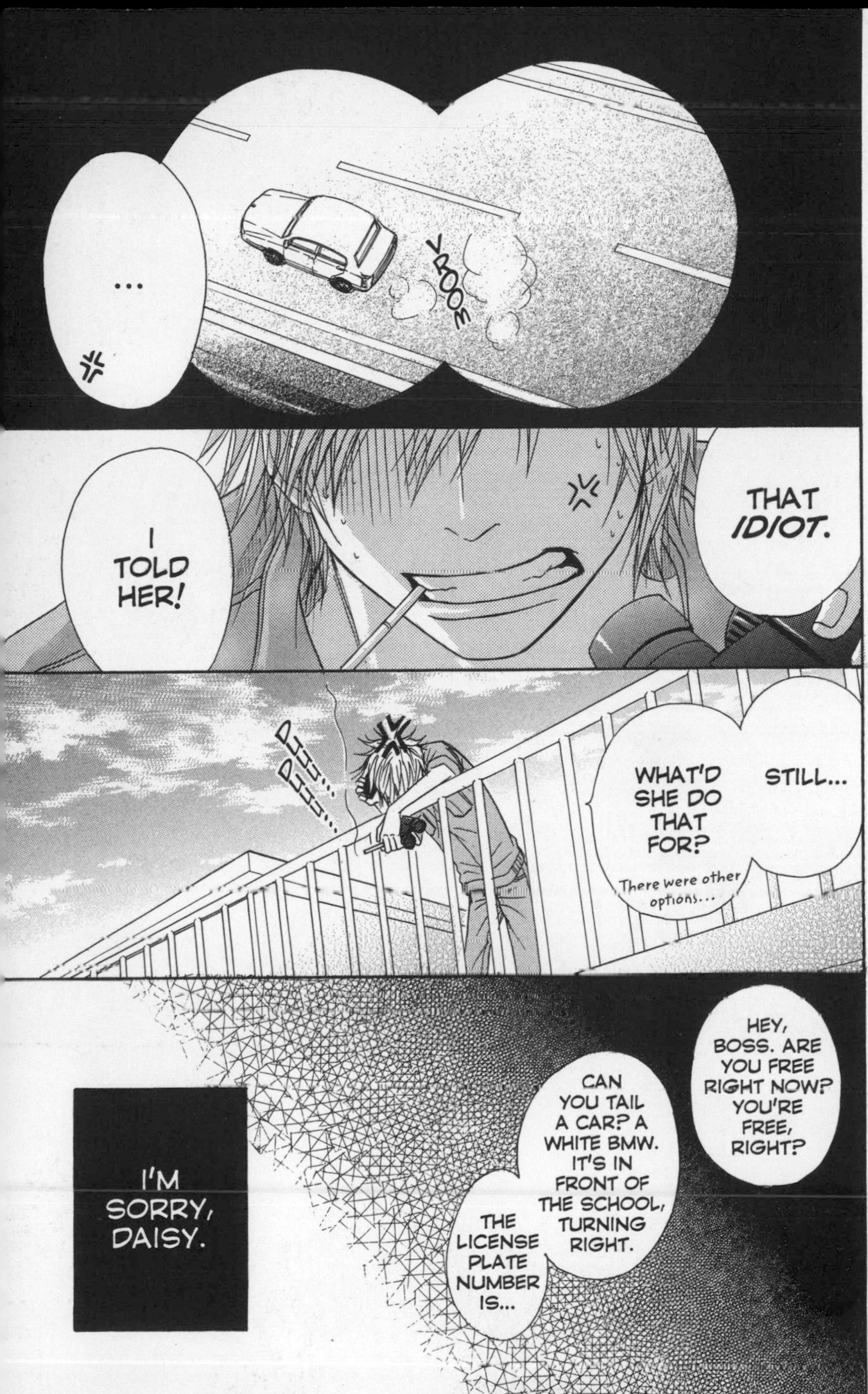
VROOOM
...
THAT IDIOT.
I TOLD HER!
STILL...
WHAT'D SHE DO THAT FOR?
There were other options...
HEY, BOSS. ARE YOU FREE RIGHT NOW? YOU'RE FREE, RIGHT?
CAN YOU TAIL A CAR? A WHITE BMW. IT'S IN FRONT OF THE SCHOOL, TURNING RIGHT.
THE LICENSE PLATE NUMBER IS...
I'M SORRY, DAISY.

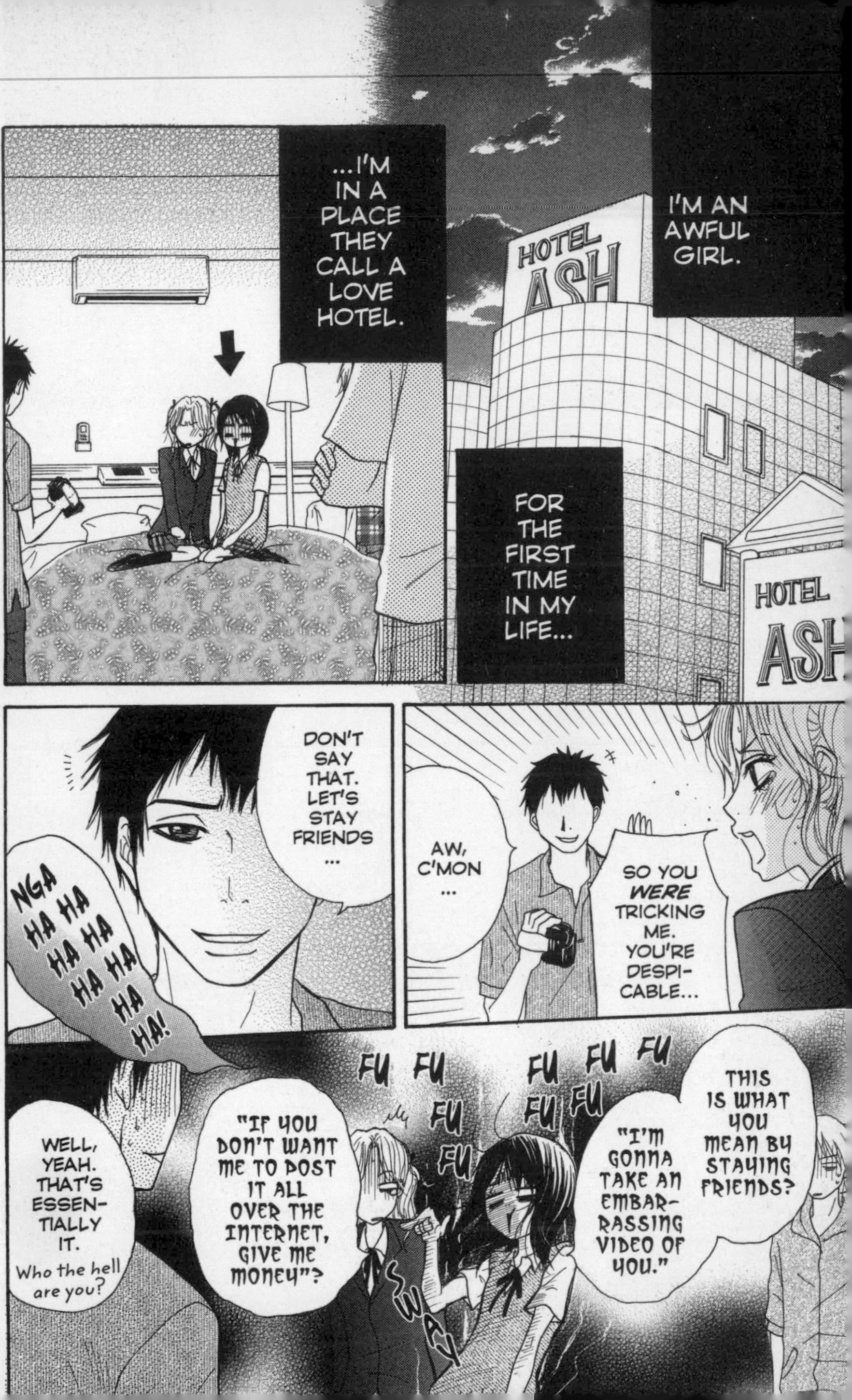
I'M AN AWFUL GIRL.
HOTEL ASH
FOR THE FIRST TIME IN MY LIFE...
HOTEL ASH
...I'M IN A PLACE THEY CALL A LOVE HOTEL.
SO YOU WERE TRICKING ME. YOU'RE DESPICABLE...
AW, C'MON...
DON'T SAY THAT. LET'S STAY FRIENDS...
NGA HA HA HA HA HA HA HA HA HA HA HA!
THIS IS WHAT YOU MEAN BY STAYING FRIENDS?
FU FU FU FU FU FU FU FU FU
"I'M GONNA TAKE AN EMBARRASSING VIDEO OF YOU."
"IF YOU DON'T WANT ME TO POST IT ALL OVER THE INTERNET, GIVE ME MONEY"?
SWAY
WELL, YEAH. THAT'S ESSENTIALLY IT.
Who the hell are you?

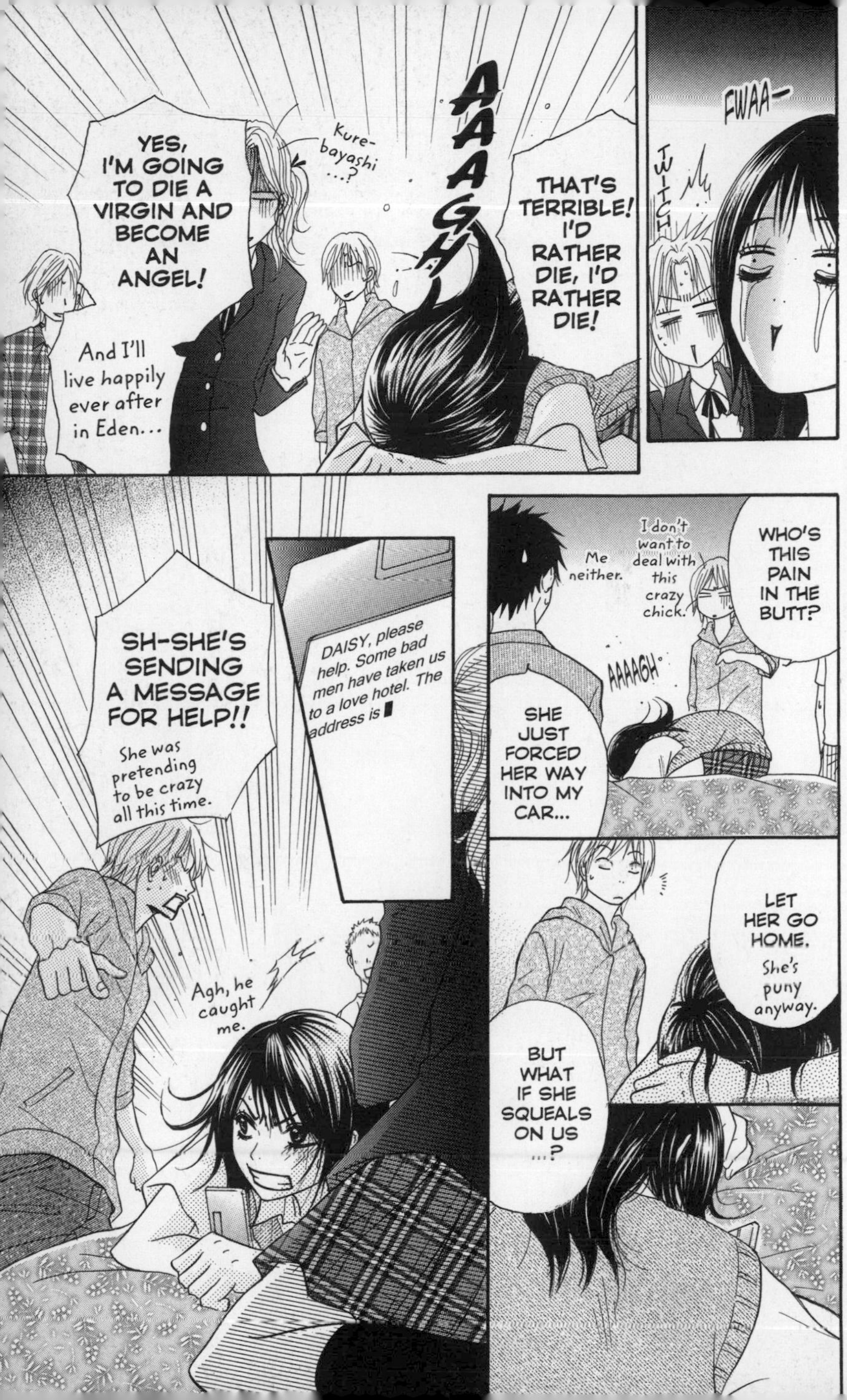
FWAA—
TWITCH
AAAAGH!
THAT'S TERRIBLE! I'D RATHER DIE, I'D RATHER DIE!
Kure-bayashi...?
YES, I'M GOING TO DIE A VIRGIN AND BECOME AN ANGEL!
And I'll live happily ever after in Eden...
WHO'S THIS PAIN IN THE BUTT?
I don't want to deal with this crazy chick.
Me neither.
AAAAGH
SHE JUST FORCED HER WAY INTO MY CAR...
LET HER GO HOME.
She's puny anyway.
BUT WHAT IF SHE SQUEALS ON US...?
SH-SHE'S SENDING A MESSAGE FOR HELP!!
She was pretending to be crazy all this time.
DAISY, please help. Some bad men have taken us to a love hotel. The address is
Agh, he caught me.

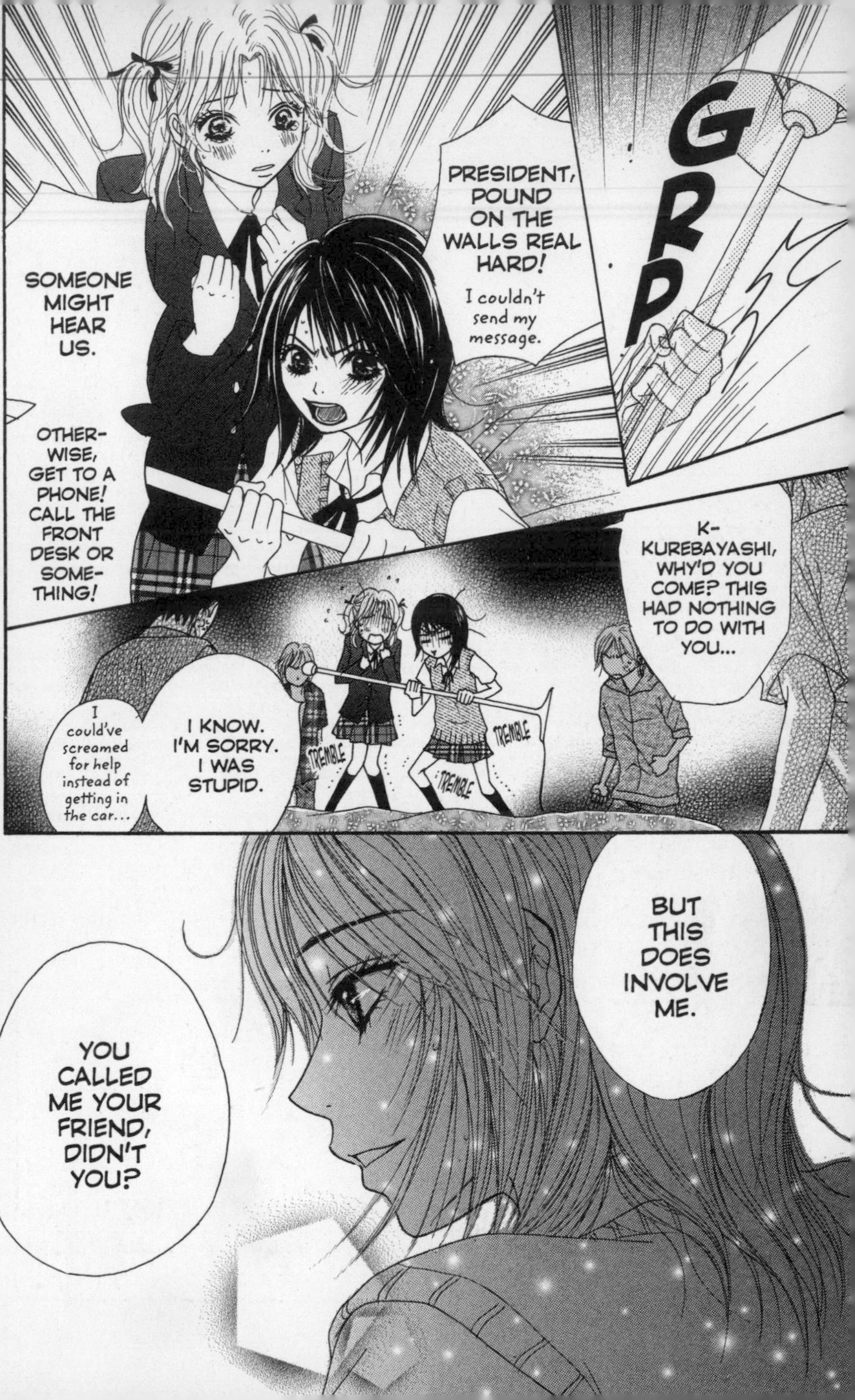
GRP
PRESIDENT, POUND ON THE WALLS REAL HARD!
I couldn't send my message.
SOMEONE MIGHT HEAR US.
OTHER-WISE, GET TO A PHONE! CALL THE FRONT DESK OR SOME-THING!
K-KUREBAYASHI, WHY'D YOU COME? THIS HAD NOTHING TO DO WITH YOU...
TREMBLE
TREMBLE
TREMBLE
I KNOW. I'M SORRY. I WAS STUPID.
I could've screamed for help instead of getting in the car...
BUT THIS DOES INVOLVE ME.
YOU CALLED ME YOUR FRIEND, DIDN'T YOU?

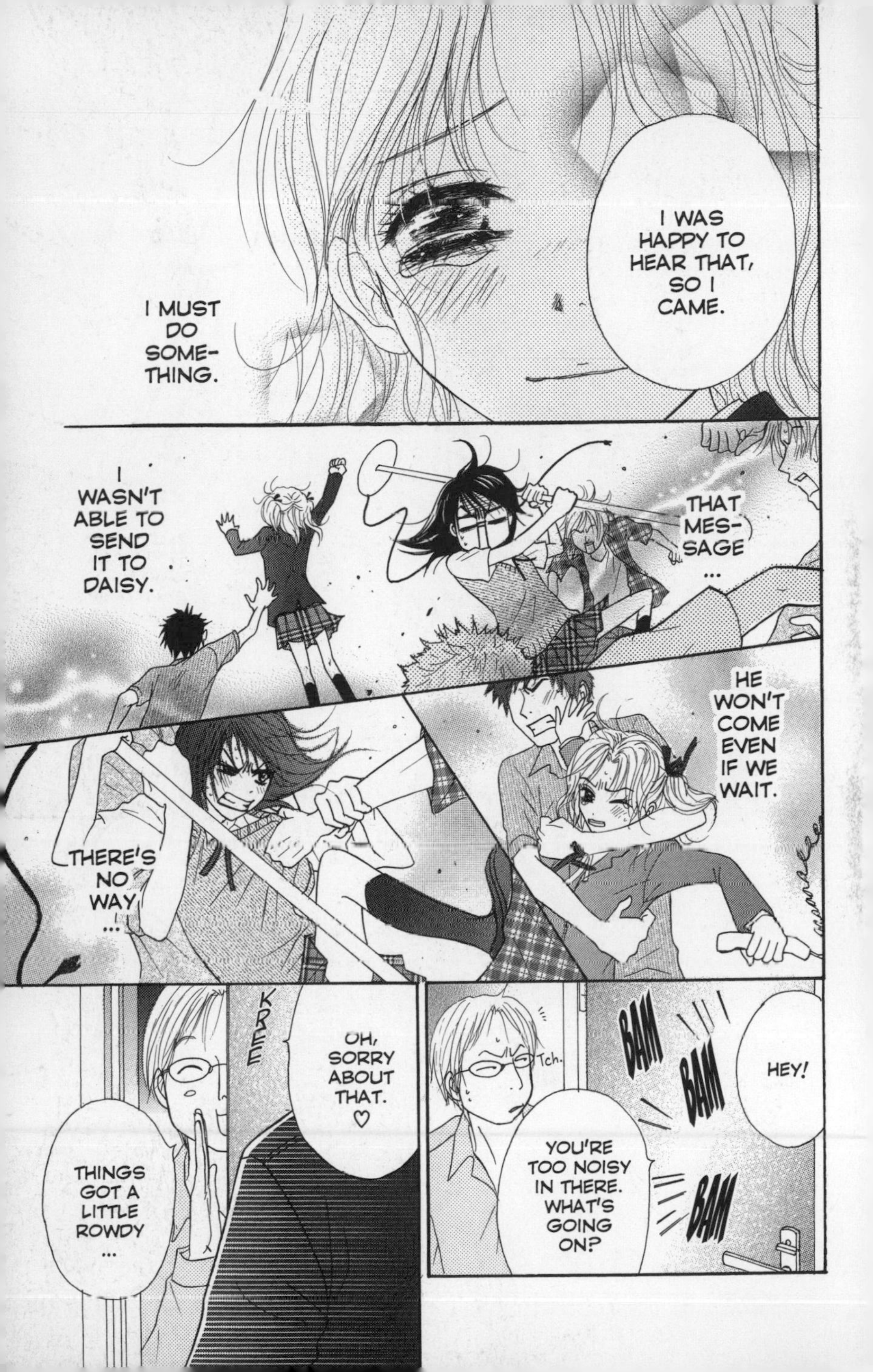
I WAS HAPPY TO HEAR THAT, SO I CAME.
I MUST DO SOME-THING.
THAT MES-SAGE...
I WASN'T ABLE TO SEND IT TO DAISY.
HE WON'T COME EVEN IF WE WAIT.
THERE'S NO WAY...
HEY!
BAM
BAM
BAM
Tch.
YOU'RE TOO NOISY IN THERE. WHAT'S GOING ON?
KREE
OH, SORRY ABOUT THAT. ♡
THINGS GOT A LITTLE ROWDY...

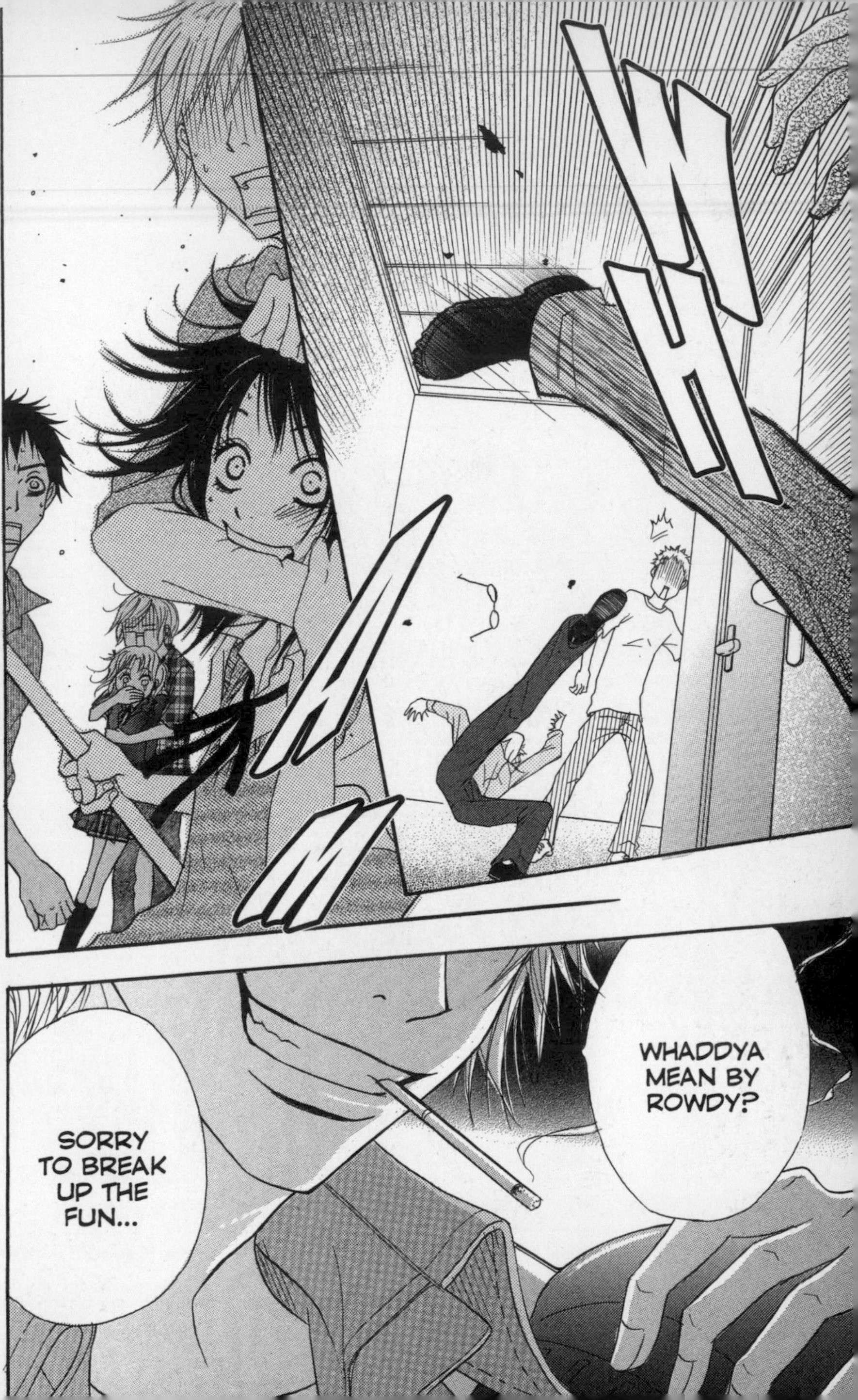
WHAM
WHADDYA MEAN BY ROWDY?
SORRY TO BREAK UP THE FUN...

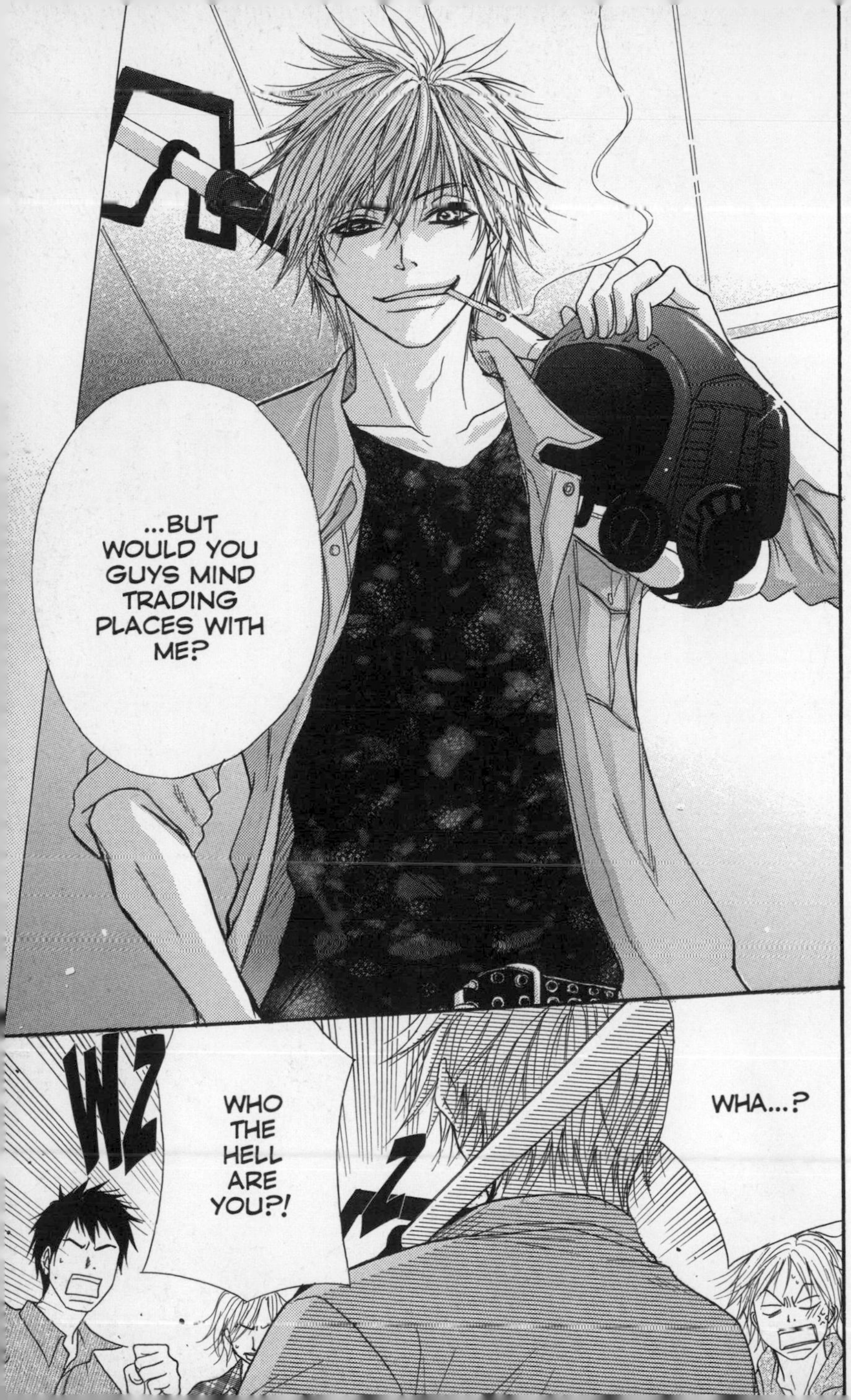
...BUT WOULD YOU GUYS MIND TRADING PLACES WITH ME?
WHA...?
WHO THE HELL ARE YOU?!
WZ

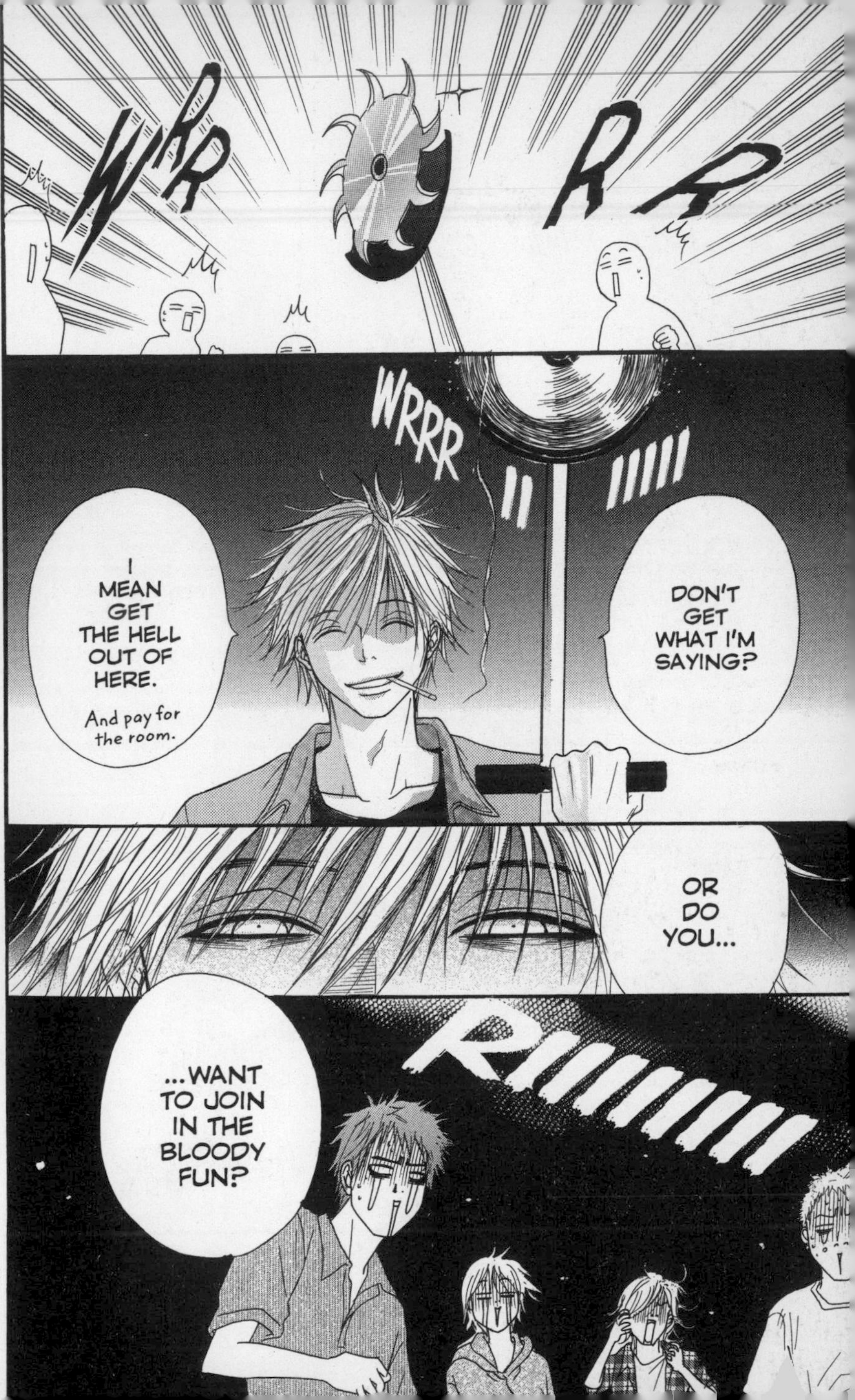
WRR
RRR
WRRR
DON'T GET WHAT I'M SAYING?
I MEAN GET THE HELL OUT OF HERE.
And pay for the room.
OR DO YOU...
RIIIIIII
...WANT TO JOIN IN THE BLOODY FUN?

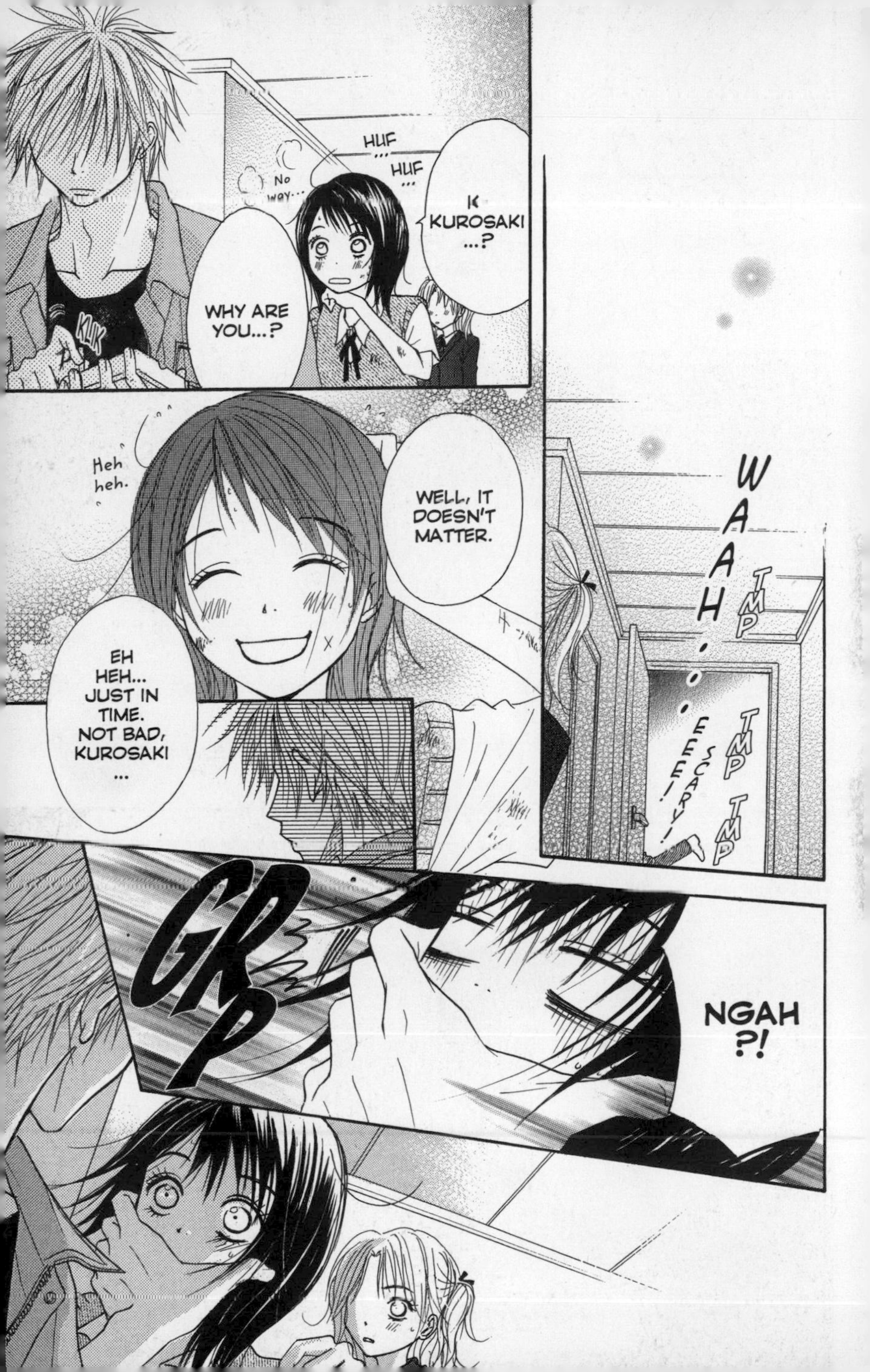

HUF ... HUF ...
K KUROSAKI ...?
No way...
WHY ARE YOU...?
KLIK
WAAAH...
EEEE! SCARY!
TMP TMP TMP TMP
WELL, IT DOESN'T MATTER.
Heh heh.
EH HEH... JUST IN TIME. NOT BAD, KUROSAKI ...
NGAH ?!
GRP

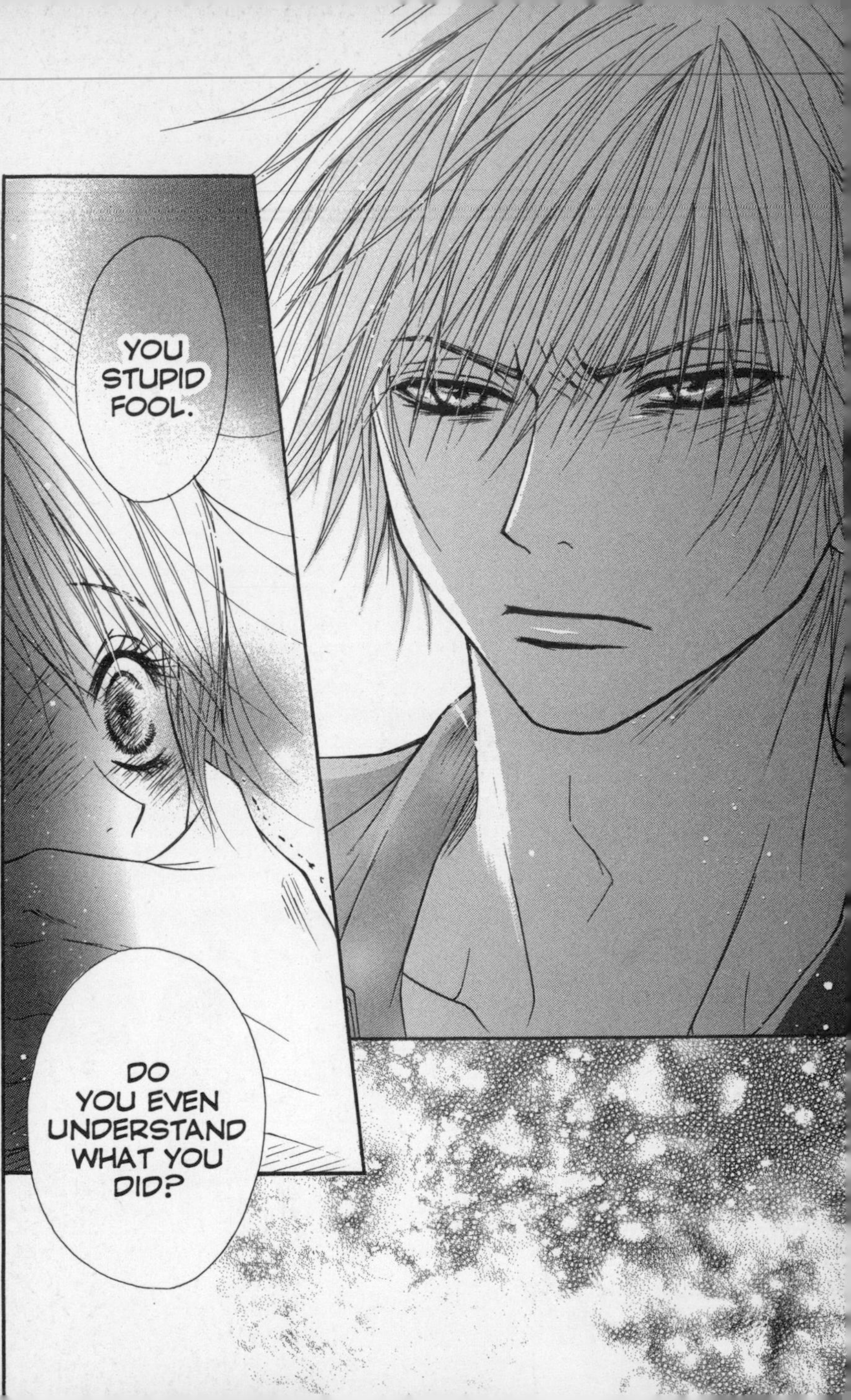
YOU STUPID FOOL.
DO YOU EVEN UNDERSTAND WHAT YOU DID?

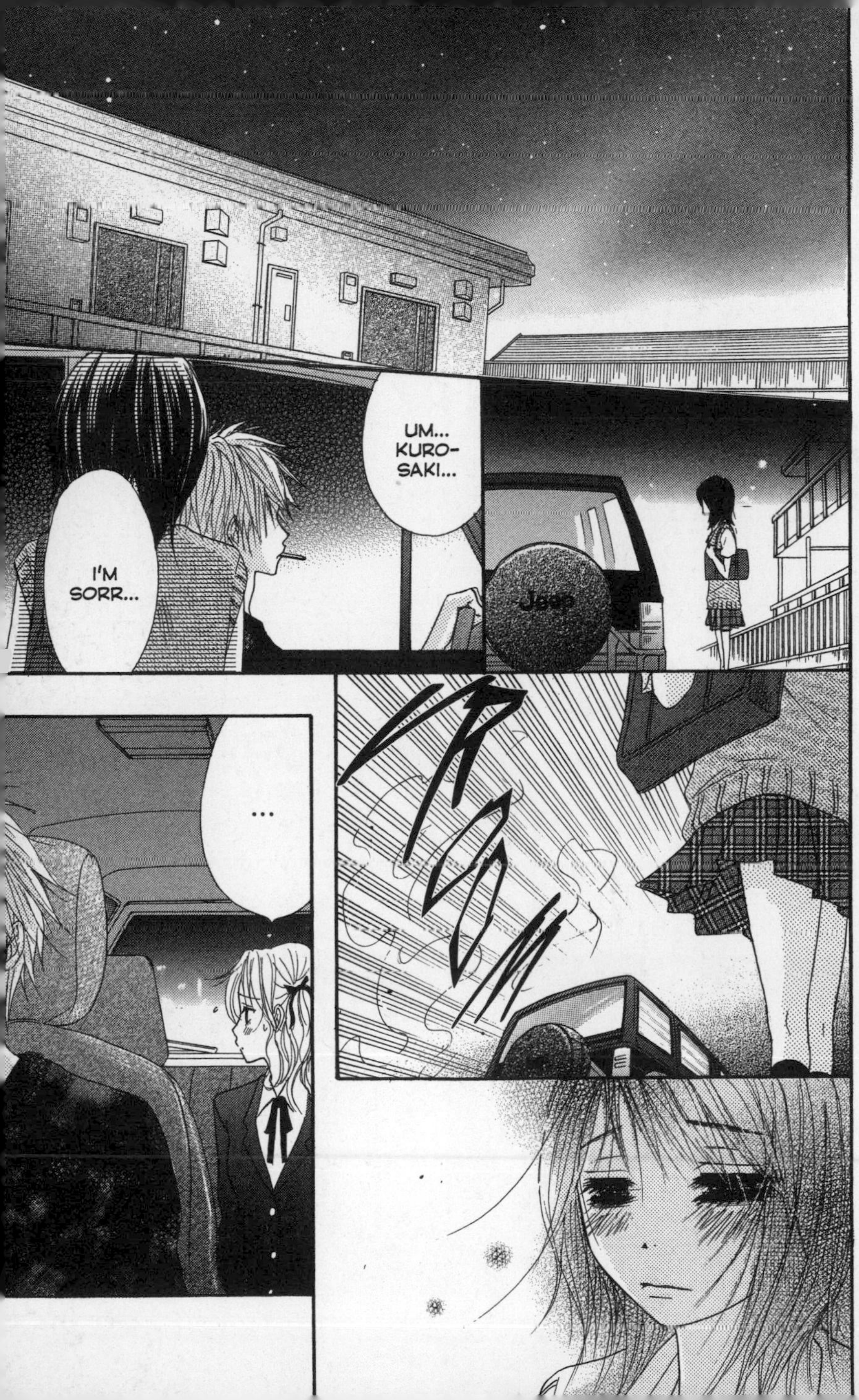
UM... KURO-SAKI...
I'M SORR...
VROOM
...

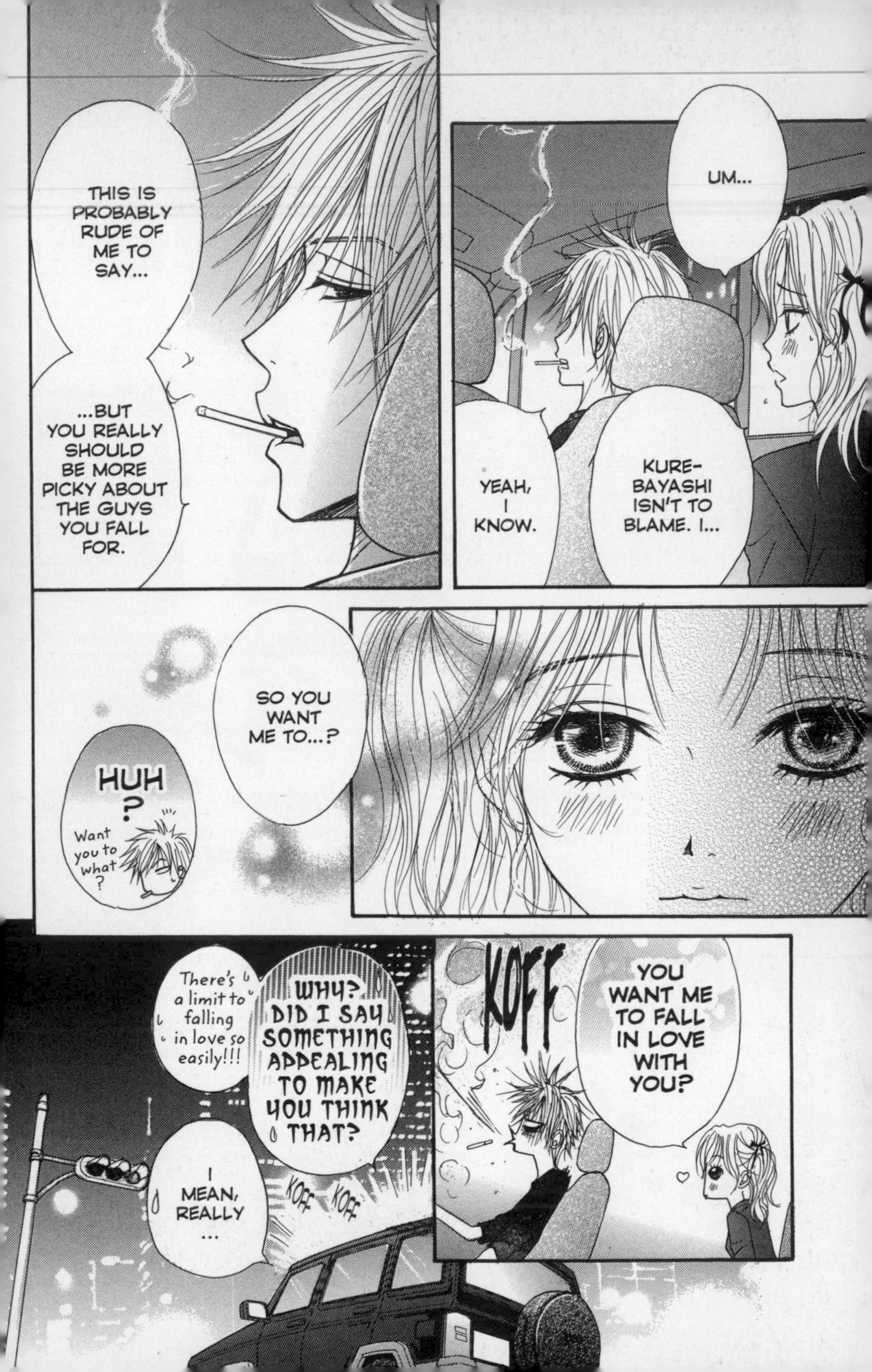
UM...
KURE-BAYASHI ISN'T TO BLAME. I...
YEAH, I KNOW.
THIS IS PROBABLY RUDE OF ME TO SAY...
...BUT YOU REALLY SHOULD BE MORE PICKY ABOUT THE GUYS YOU FALL FOR.
SO YOU WANT ME TO...?
HUH?
Want you to what?
YOU WANT ME TO FALL IN LOVE WITH YOU?
KOFF
WHY? DID I SAY SOMETHING APPEALING TO MAKE YOU THINK THAT?
There's a limit to falling in love so easily!!!
KOFF KOFF
I MEAN, REALLY ...

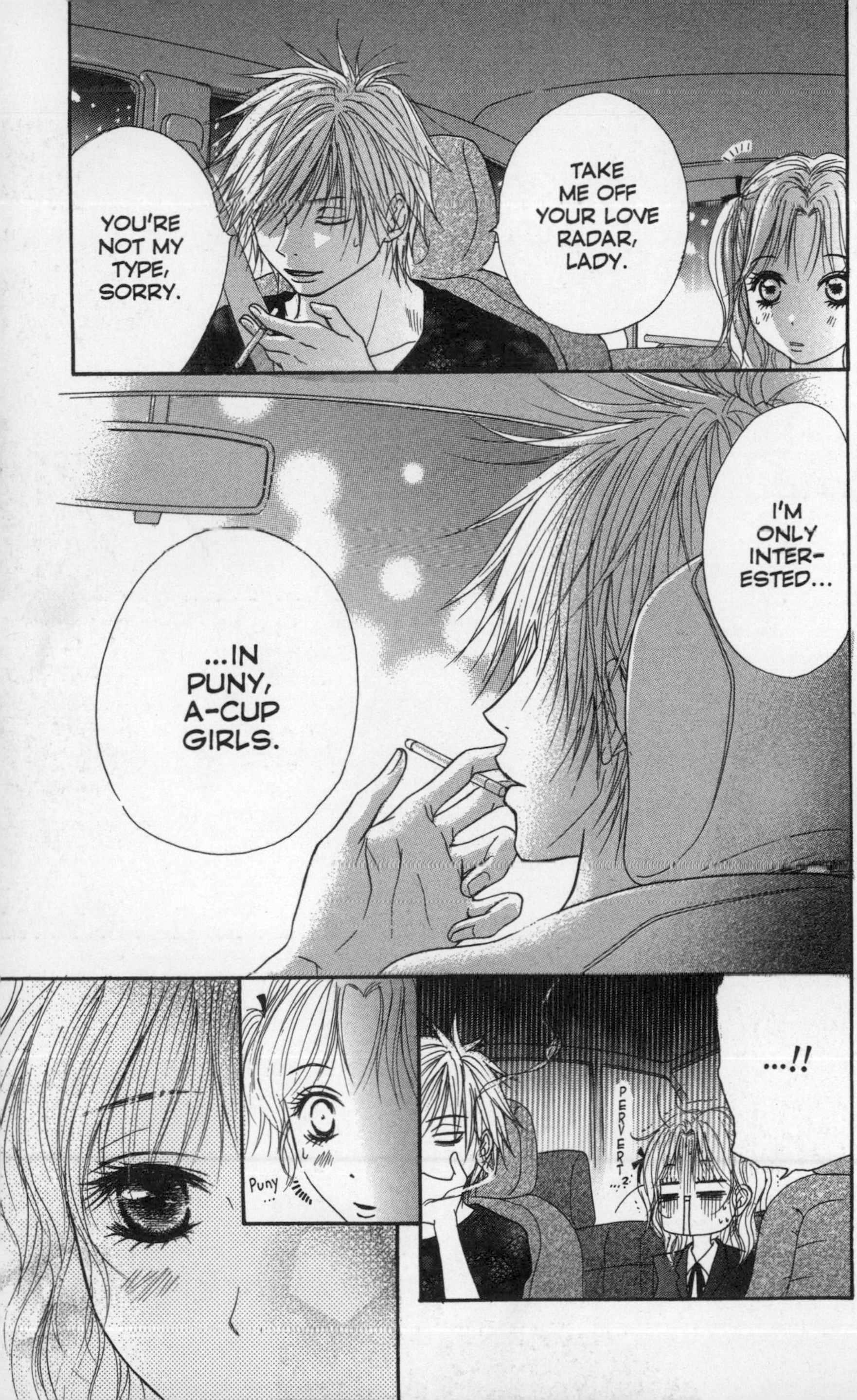
TAKE ME OFF YOUR LOVE RADAR, LADY.
YOU'RE NOT MY TYPE, SORRY.
I'M ONLY INTER-ESTED...
...IN PUNY, A-CUP GIRLS.
...!!
PERVERT...?
Puny...

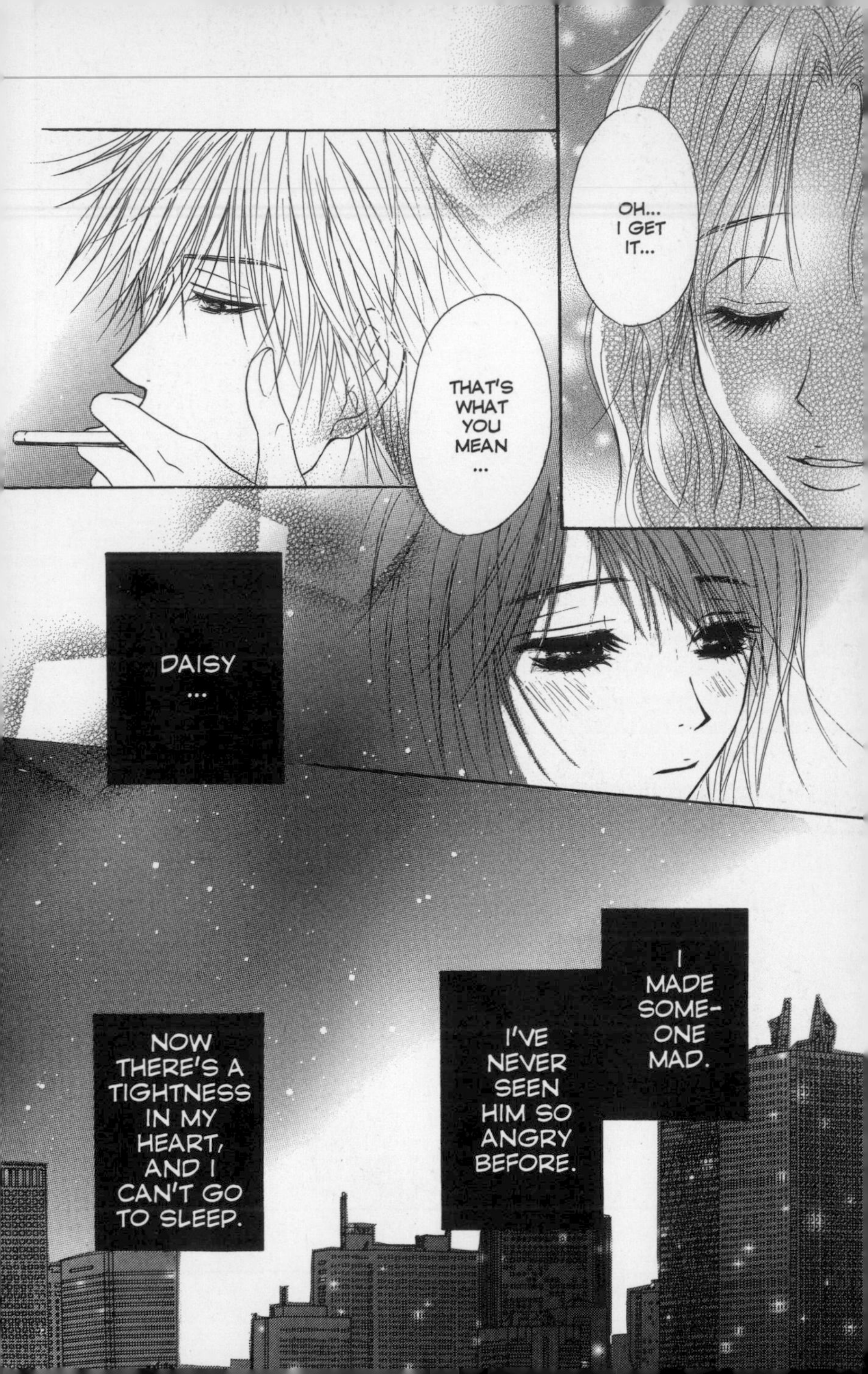
OH... I GET IT...
THAT'S WHAT YOU MEAN ...
DAISY ...
I MADE SOME-ONE MAD.
I'VE NEVER SEEN HIM SO ANGRY BEFORE.
NOW THERE'S A TIGHTNESS IN MY HEART, AND I CAN'T GO TO SLEEP.

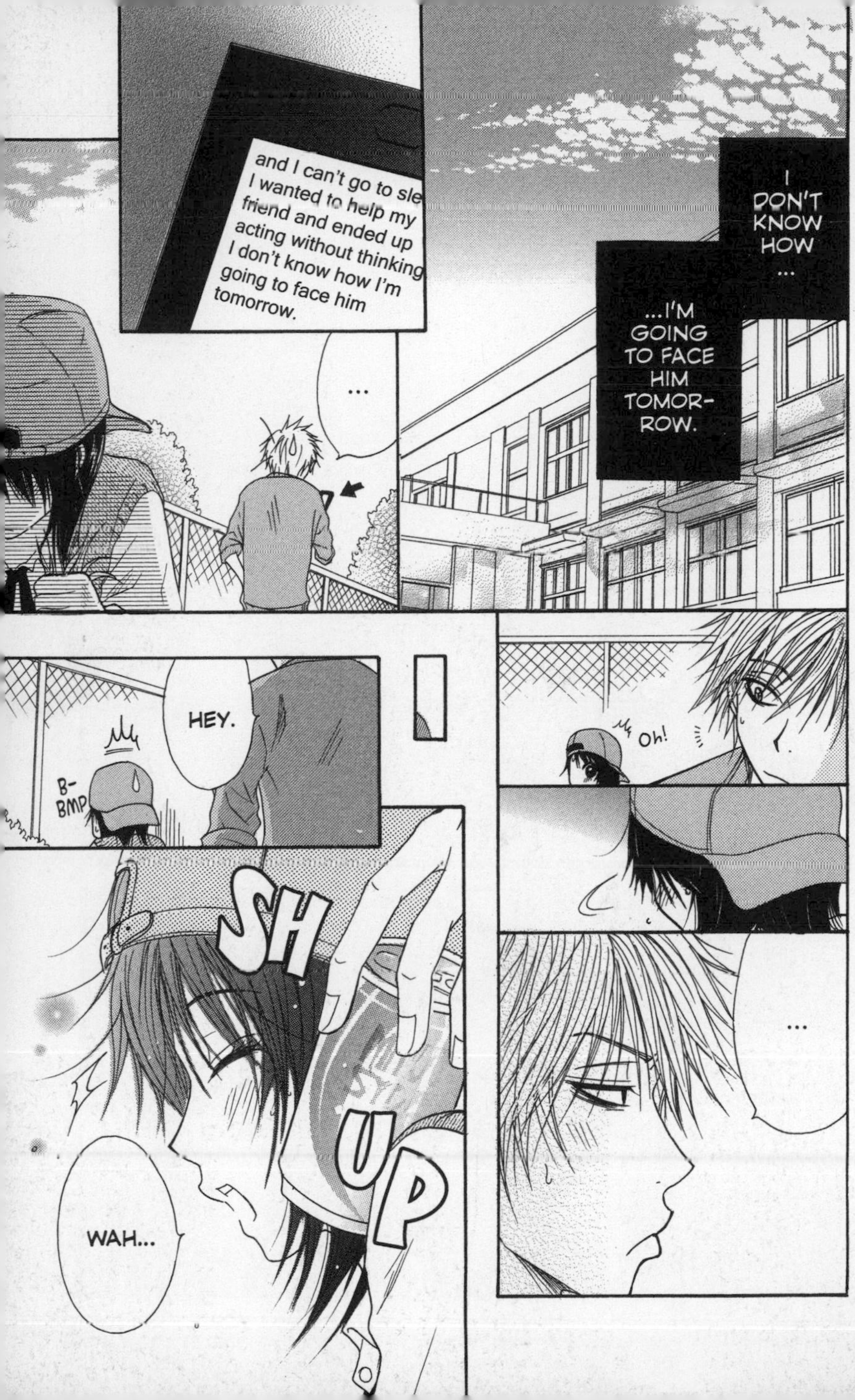

I DON'T KNOW HOW ...
...I'M GOING TO FACE HIM TOMOR-ROW.
and I can't go to sle
I wanted to help my
friend and ended up
acting without thinking
I don't know how I'm
going to face him
tomorrow.
...
Oh!
HEY.
B-BMP
...
SHUP
WAH...

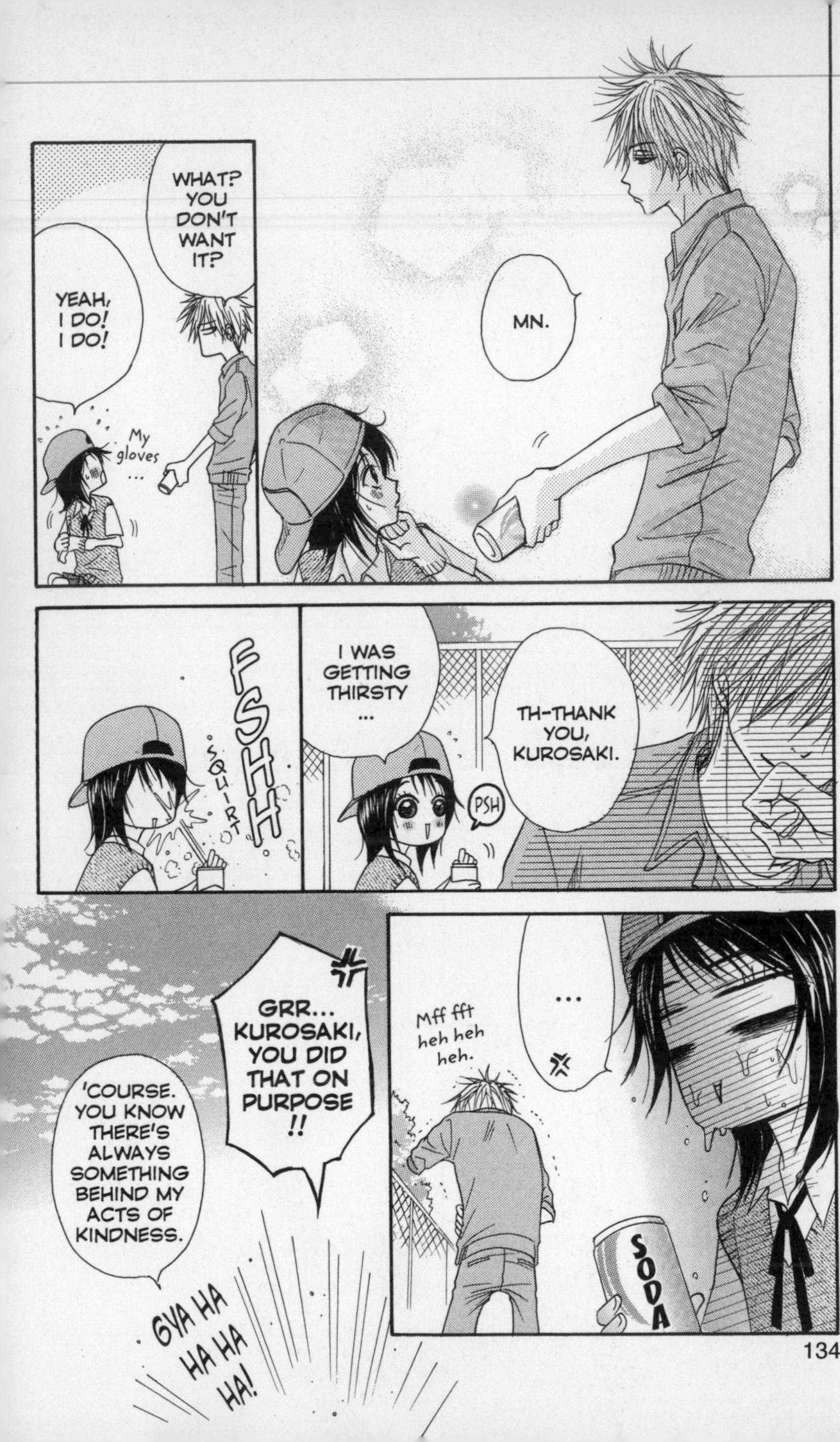
MN.
WHAT? YOU DON'T WANT IT?
YEAH, I DO! I DO!
My gloves ...
TH-THANK YOU, KUROSAKI.
PSH
I WAS GETTING THIRSTY ...
FSHH
SQUIRT
...
SODA
Mff fft heh heh heh.
GRR... KUROSAKI, YOU DID THAT ON PURPOSE !!
'COURSE. YOU KNOW THERE'S ALWAYS SOMETHING BEHIND MY ACTS OF KINDNESS.
GYA HA HA HA HA!

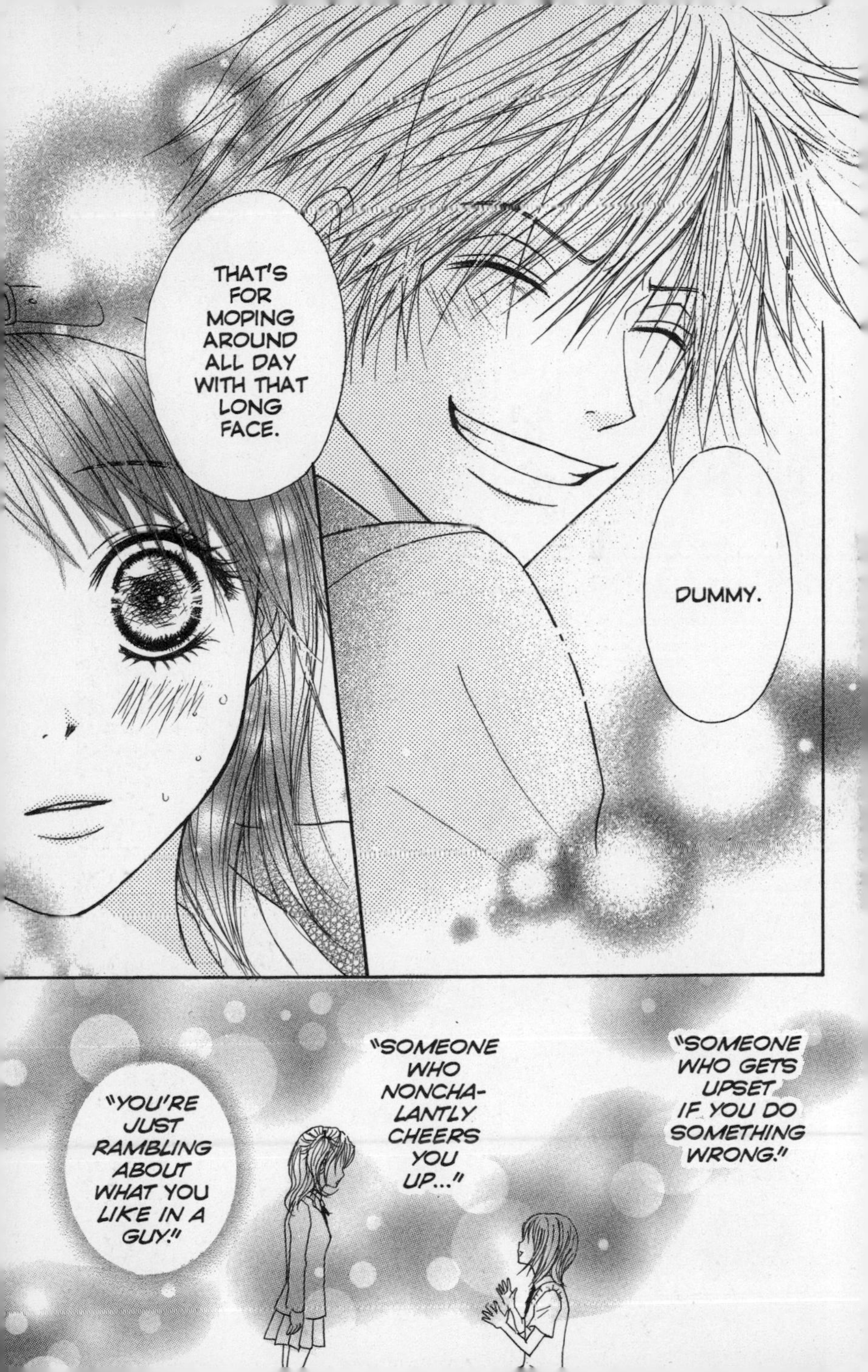
THAT'S FOR MOPING AROUND ALL DAY WITH THAT LONG FACE.
DUMMY.
"SOMEONE WHO GETS UPSET IF YOU DO SOMETHING WRONG."
"SOMEONE WHO NONCHA-LANTLY CHEERS YOU UP..."
"YOU'RE JUST RAMBLING ABOUT WHAT YOU LIKE IN A GUY."

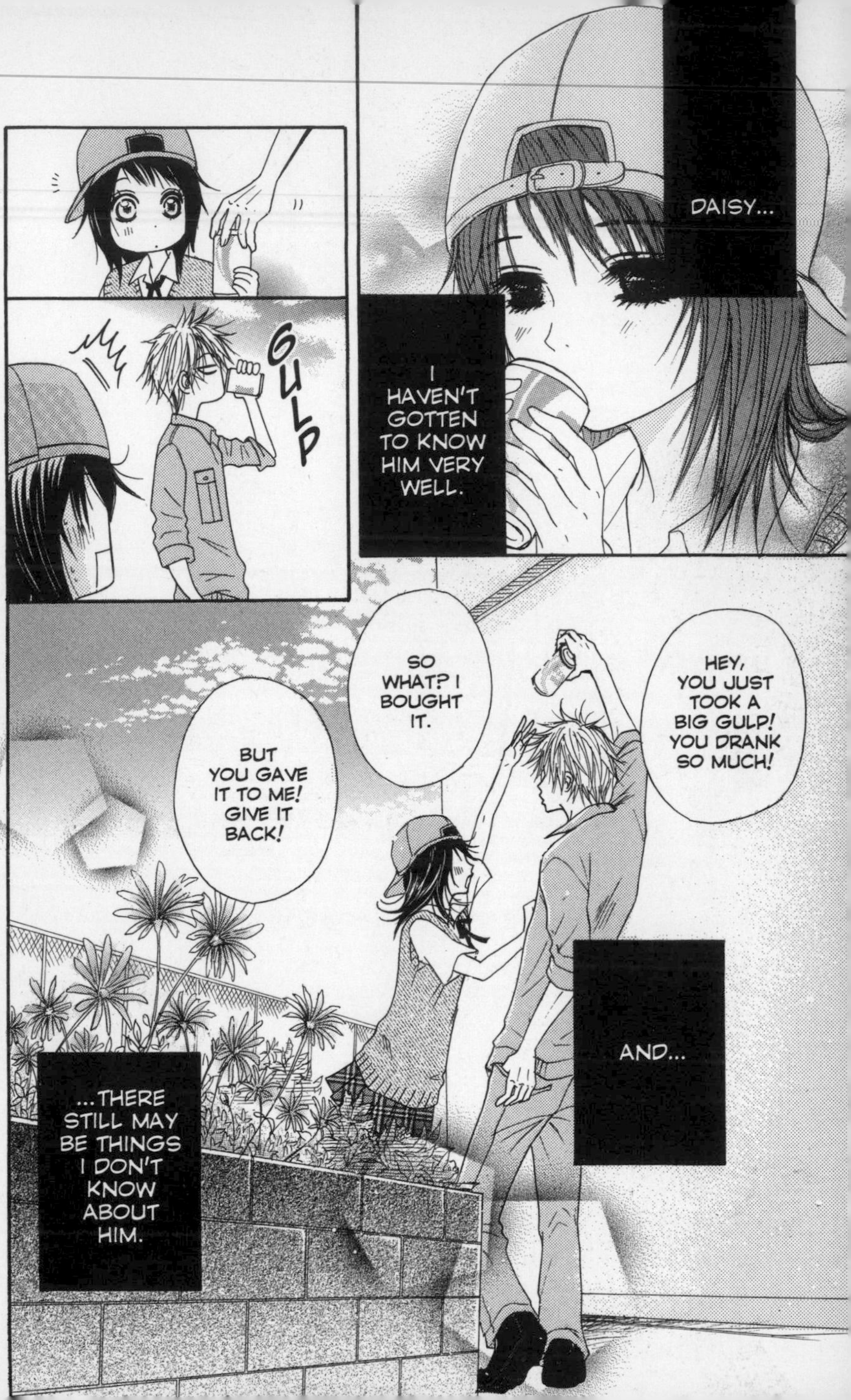
DAISY...
I HAVEN'T GOTTEN TO KNOW HIM VERY WELL.
GULP
HEY, YOU JUST TOOK A BIG GULP! YOU DRANK SO MUCH!
SO WHAT? I BOUGHT IT.
BUT YOU GAVE IT TO ME! GIVE IT BACK!
AND...
...THERE STILL MAY BE THINGS I DON'T KNOW ABOUT HIM.

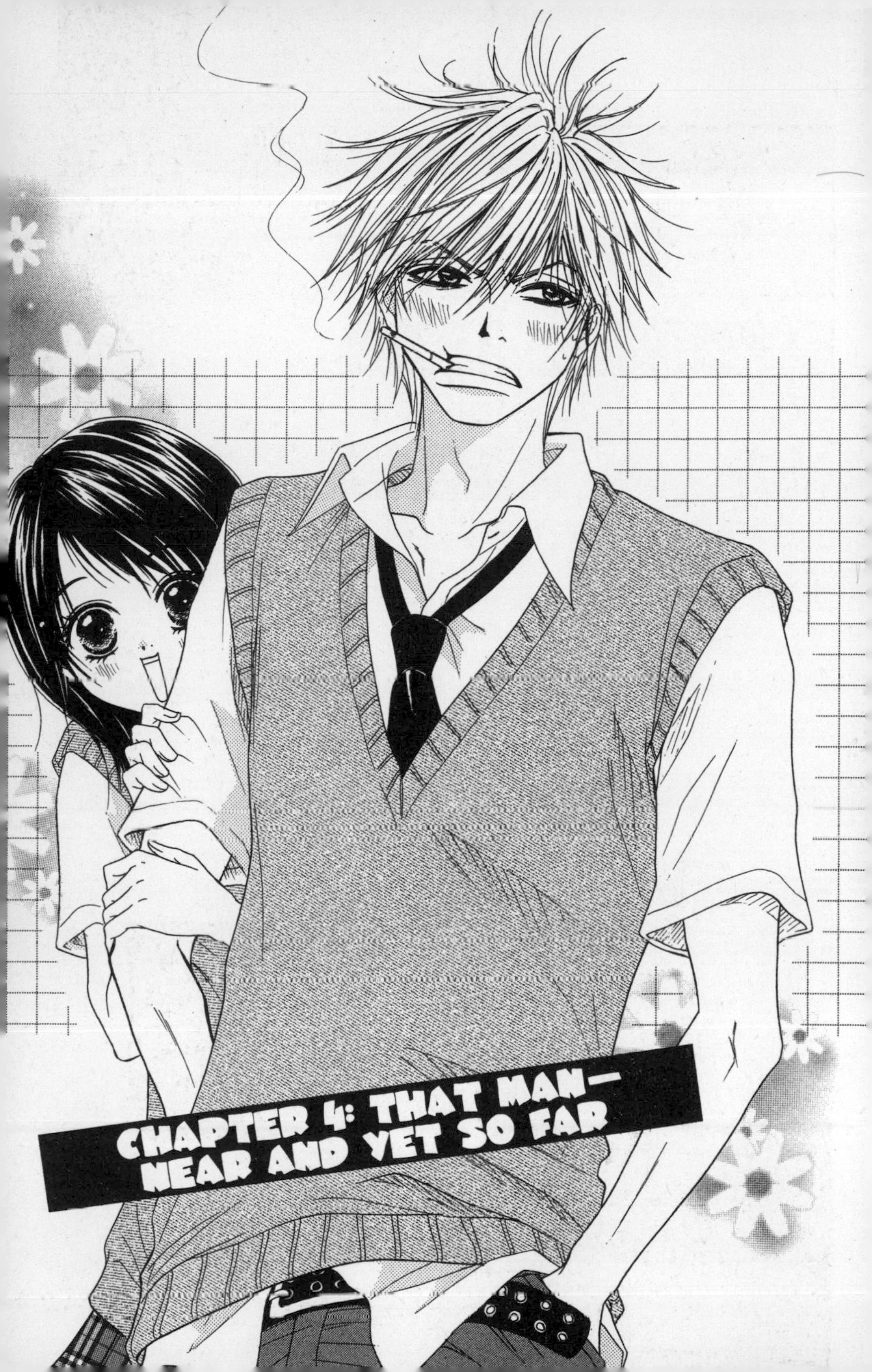
CHAPTER 4: THAT MAN—
NEAR AND YET SO FAR

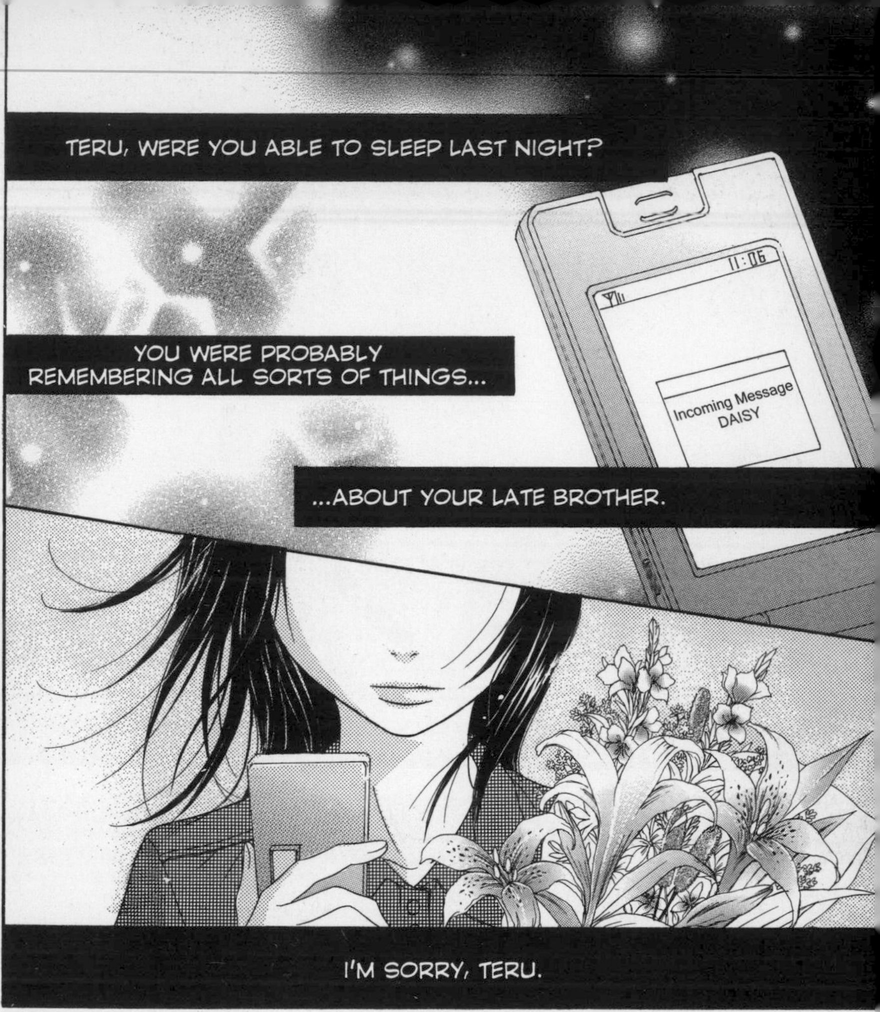
TERU, WERE YOU ABLE TO SLEEP LAST NIGHT?
11:06
Incoming Message
DAISY
YOU WERE PROBABLY REMEMBERING ALL SORTS OF THINGS...
...ABOUT YOUR LATE BROTHER.
I'M SORRY, TERU.

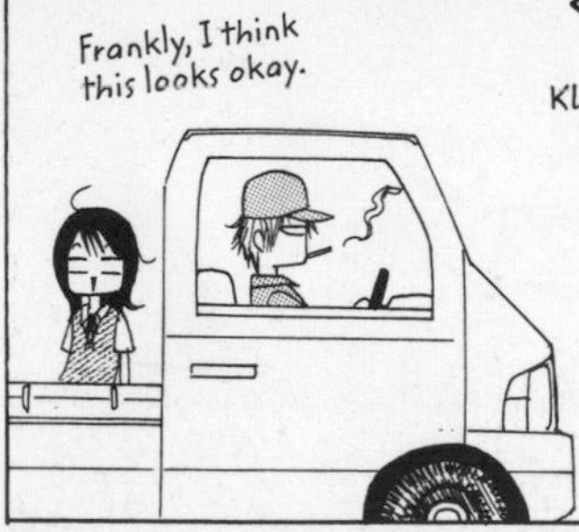
Frankly, I think this looks okay.

<THINGS I WAS IN A QUANDARY OVER ②>

KUROSAKI DRIVES A JEEP CHEROKEE (AN OLD MODEL). IN CHAPTER 2 WHEN I HAD TO DRAW HIS VEHICLE, I COULDN'T DECIDE WHETHER TO MAKE IT THAT OR A SMALL PICKUP TRUCK UNTIL THE VERY LAST MINUTE. AFTER MUCH THOUGHT, I DECIDED ON THE CHEROKEE... OH WELL... I GUESS IT WORKED OUT. IT'S MORE LIKE A SHOJO MANGA THIS WAY...

FOR THE CHEROKEE DATA, KUDOS TO MY KID SISTER AND HER HUSBAND. THANKS FOR ALL YOUR HELP. I'LL TREAT YOU TO RAMEN SOON.

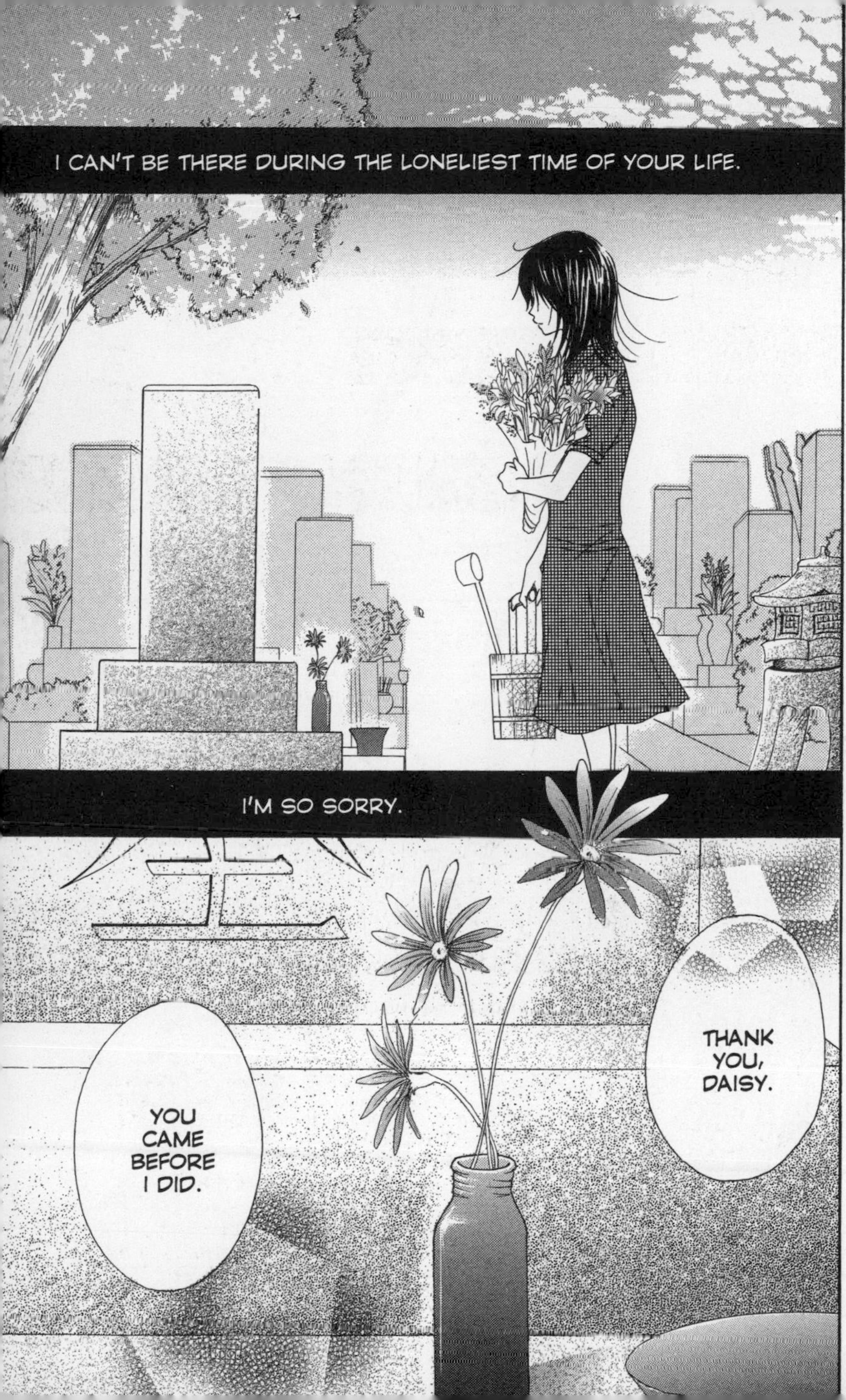
I CAN'T BE THERE DURING THE LONELIEST TIME OF YOUR LIFE.
I'M SO SORRY.
THANK YOU, DAISY.
YOU CAME BEFORE I DID.

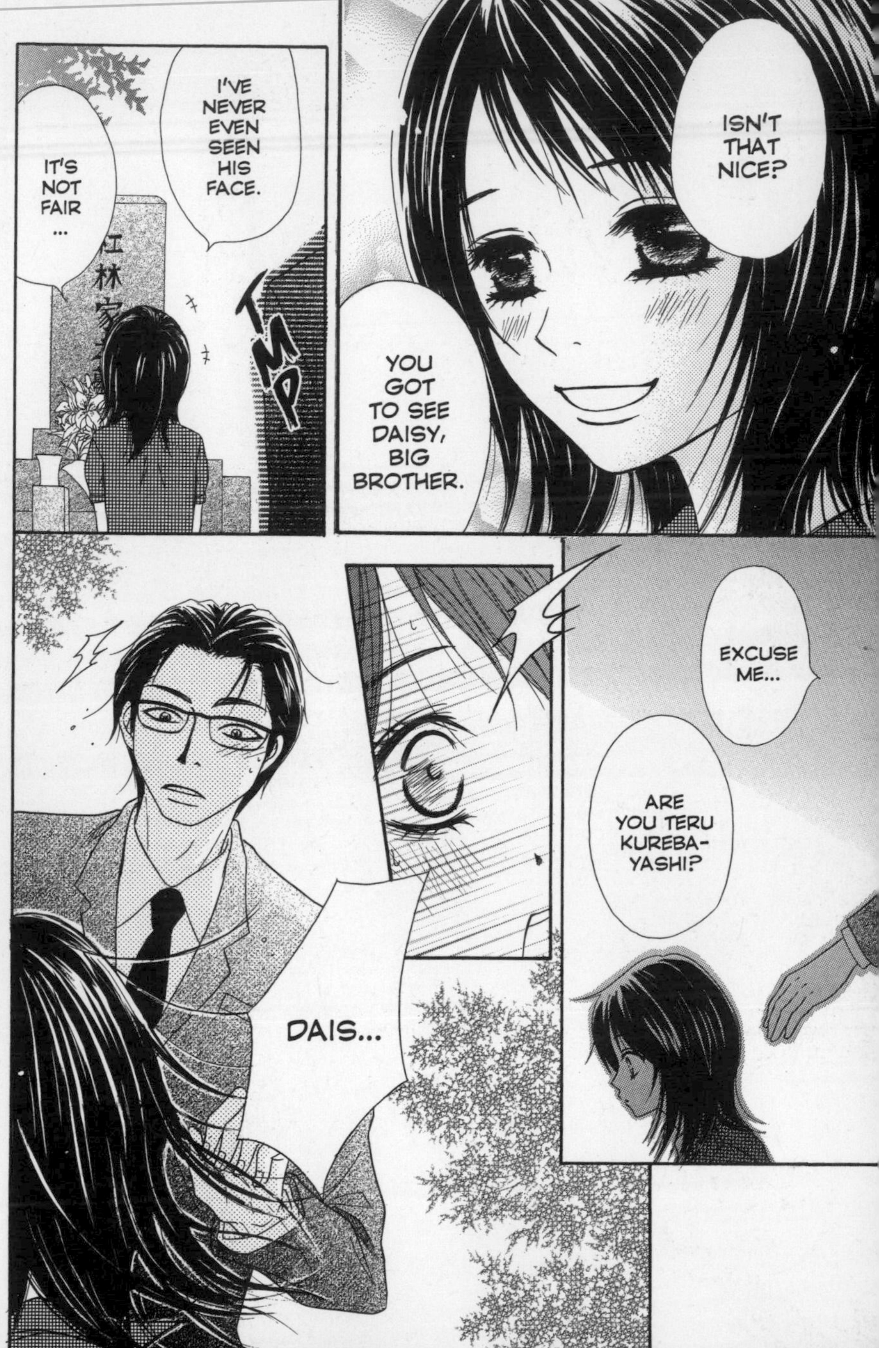
ISN'T THAT NICE?
YOU GOT TO SEE DAISY, BIG BROTHER.
I'VE NEVER EVEN SEEN HIS FACE.
IT'S NOT FAIR ...
TMP
EXCUSE ME...
ARE YOU TERU KUREBA-YASHI?
DAIS...

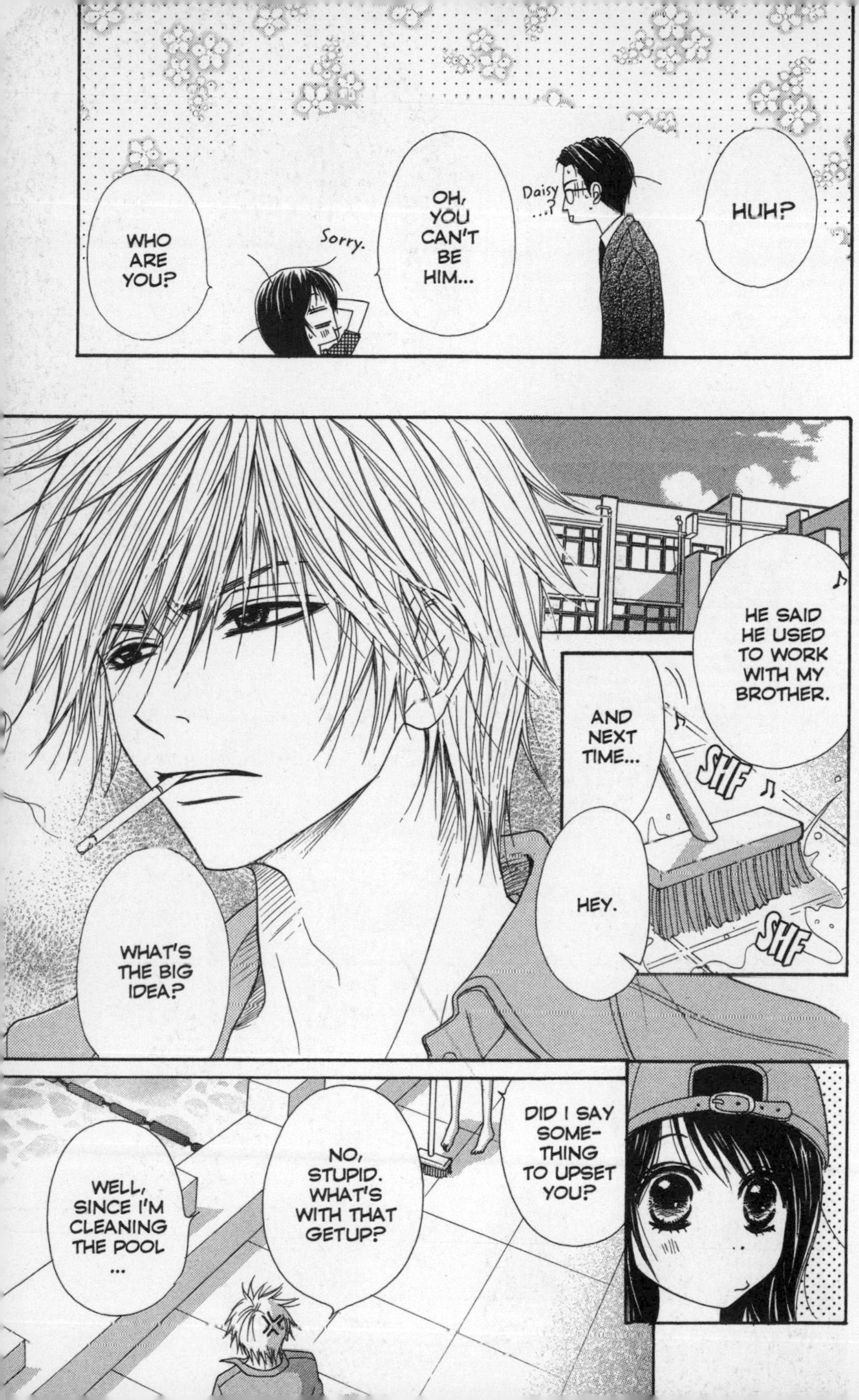
HUH?
Daisy ...?
OH, YOU CAN'T BE HIM...
Sorry.
WHO ARE YOU?
HE SAID HE USED TO WORK WITH MY BROTHER.
AND NEXT TIME...
SHF
SHF
HEY.
WHAT'S THE BIG IDEA?
DID I SAY SOME-THING TO UPSET YOU?
NO, STUPID. WHAT'S WITH THAT GETUP?
WELL, SINCE I'M CLEANING THE POOL ...

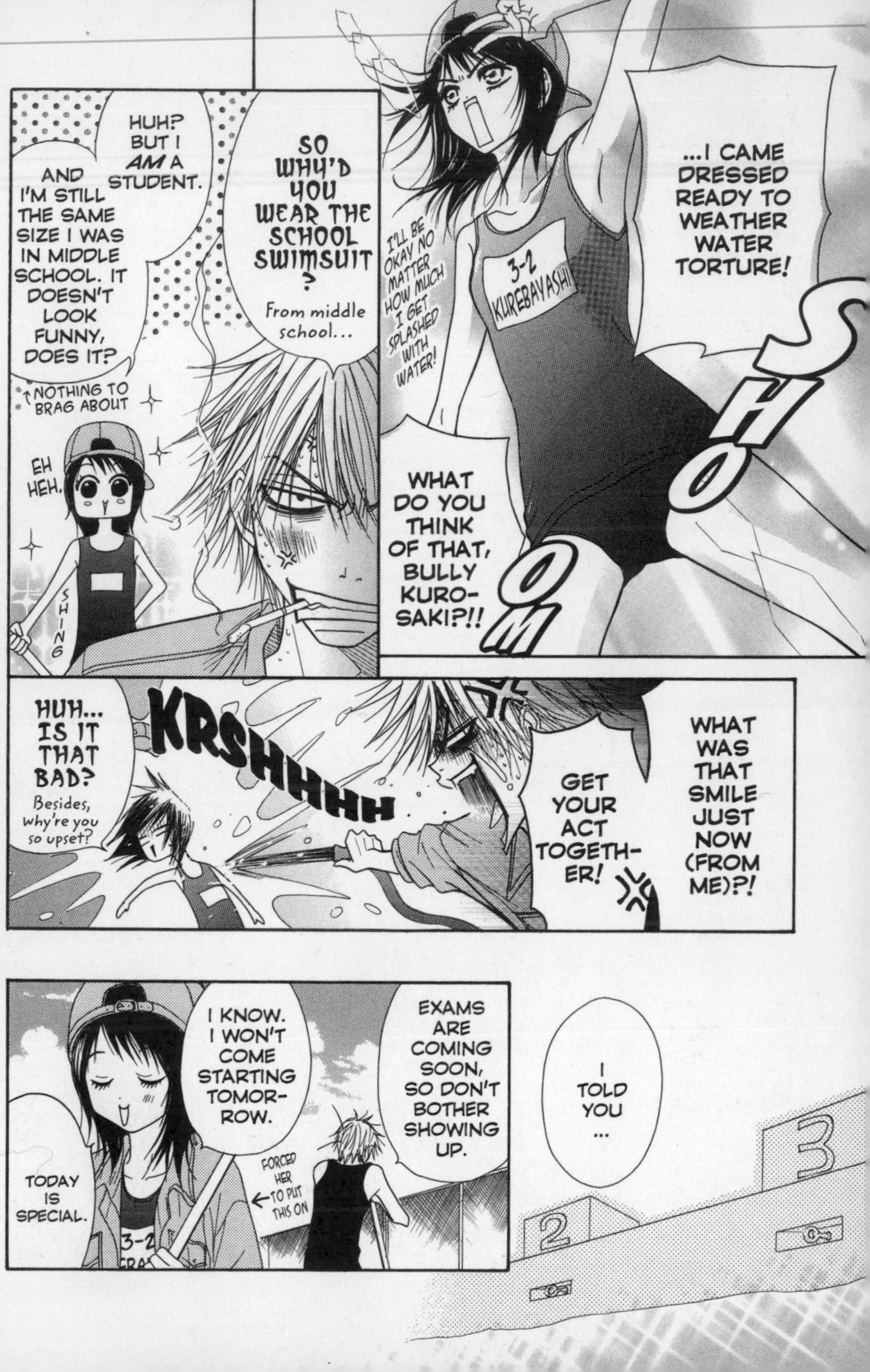
...I CAME DRESSED READY TO WEATHER WATER TORTURE!
I'LL BE OKAY NO MATTER HOW MUCH I GET SPLASHED WITH WATER!
3-2 KUREBAYASHI
SHOOM
WHAT DO YOU THINK OF THAT, BULLY KURO-SAKI?!!
SO WHY'D YOU WEAR THE SCHOOL SWIMSUIT?
From middle school...
HUH? BUT I AM A STUDENT.
AND I'M STILL THE SAME SIZE I WAS IN MIDDLE SCHOOL. IT DOESN'T LOOK FUNNY, DOES IT?
NOTHING TO BRAG ABOUT
EH HEH.
SHING
WHAT WAS THAT SMILE JUST NOW (FROM ME)?!
GET YOUR ACT TOGETH-ER!
KRSHHHHH
HUH... IS IT THAT BAD?
Besides, why're you so upset?
I TOLD YOU ...
EXAMS ARE COMING SOON, SO DON'T BOTHER SHOWING UP.
I KNOW. I WON'T COME STARTING TOMOR-ROW.
FORCED HER TO PUT THIS ON
TODAY IS SPECIAL.

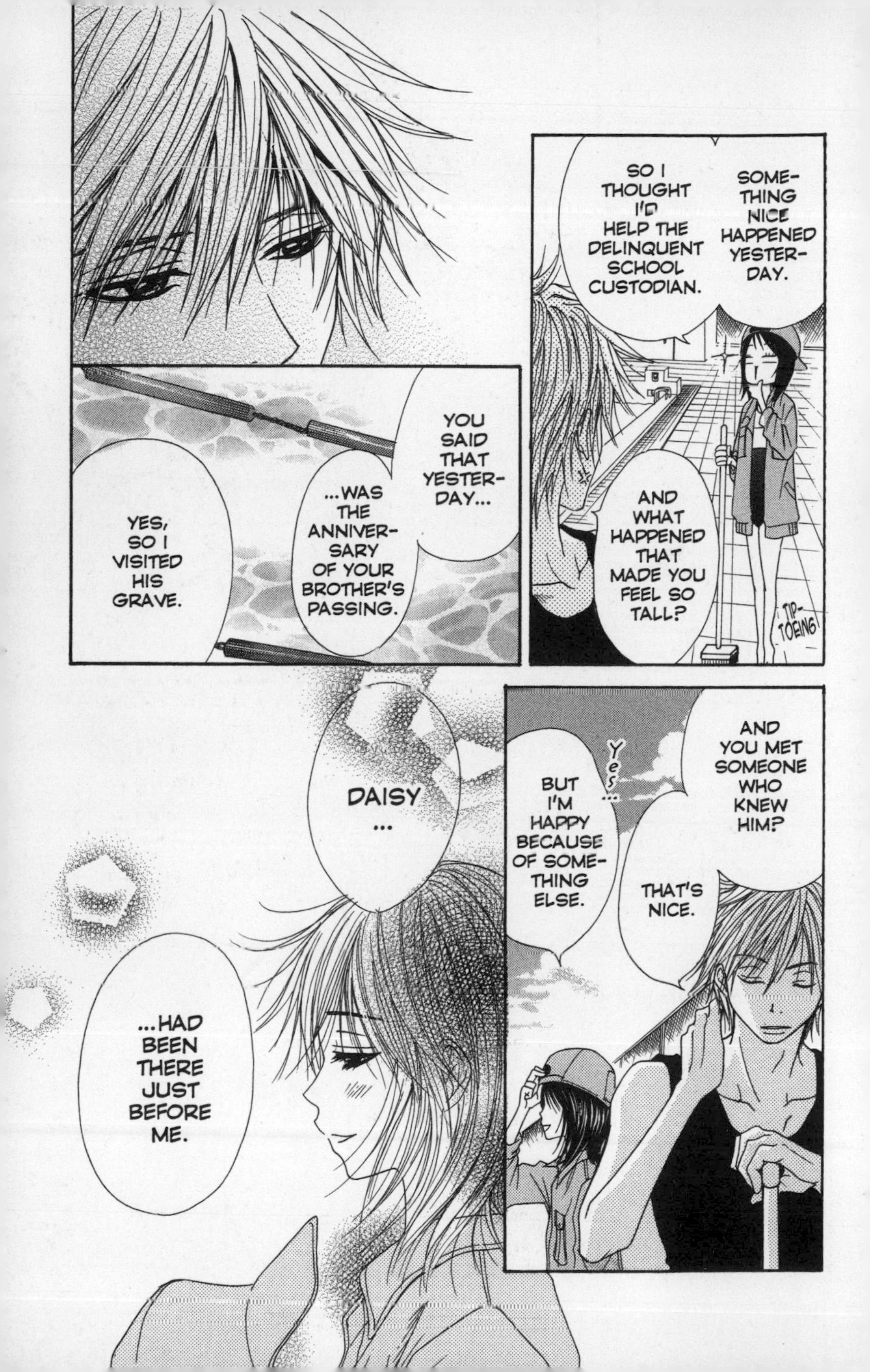
SOMETHING NICE HAPPENED YESTERDAY.
SO I THOUGHT I'D HELP THE DELINQUENT SCHOOL CUSTODIAN.
AND WHAT HAPPENED THAT MADE YOU FEEL SO TALL?
TIP-TOEING
YOU SAID THAT YESTERDAY...
...WAS THE ANNIVERSARY OF YOUR BROTHER'S PASSING.
YES, SO I VISITED HIS GRAVE.
AND YOU MET SOMEONE WHO KNEW HIM?
THAT'S NICE.
Yes...
BUT I'M HAPPY BECAUSE OF SOMETHING ELSE.
DAISY ...
...HAD BEEN THERE JUST BEFORE ME.

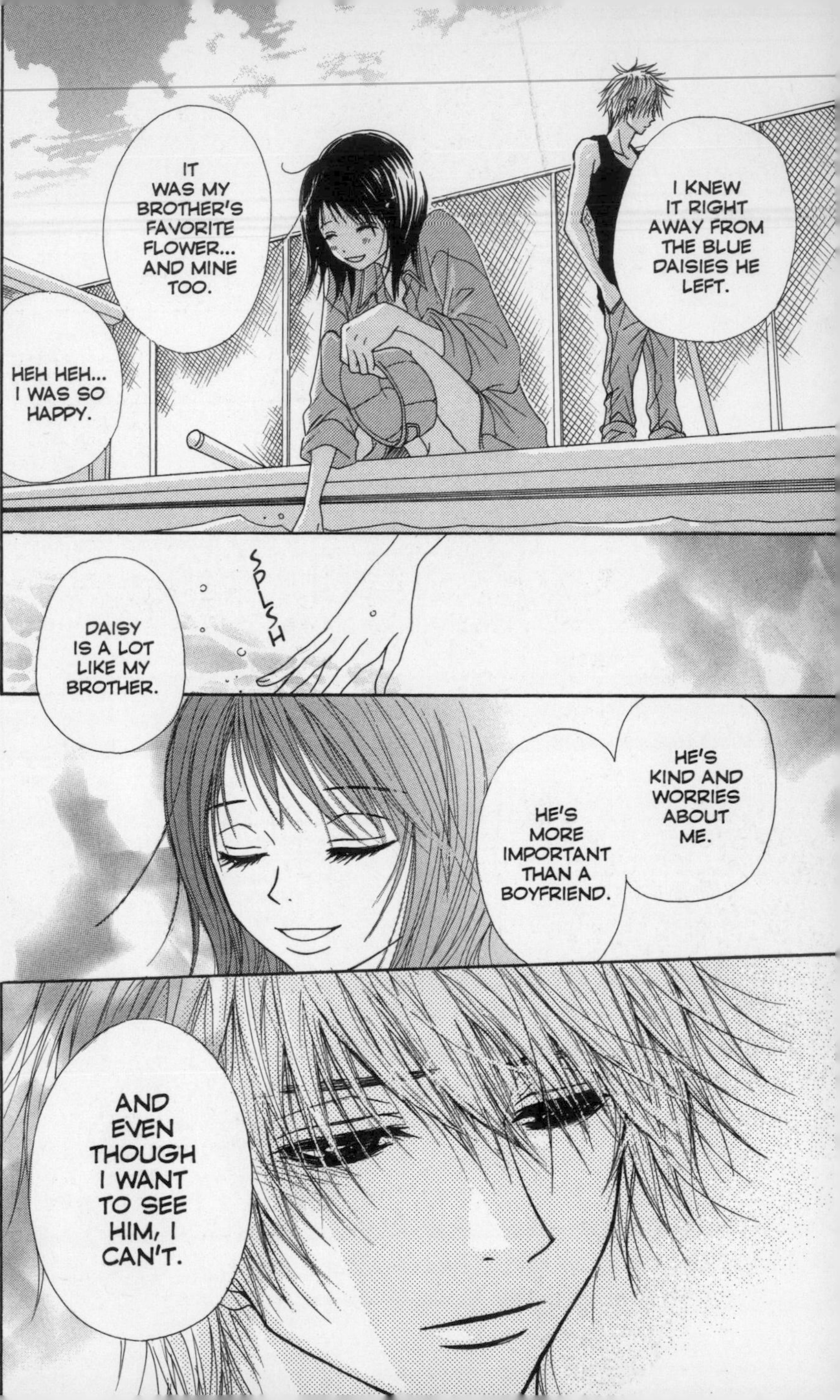
I KNEW IT RIGHT AWAY FROM THE BLUE DAISIES HE LEFT.
IT WAS MY BROTHER'S FAVORITE FLOWER... AND MINE TOO.
HEH HEH... I WAS SO HAPPY.
SPLSH
DAISY IS A LOT LIKE MY BROTHER.
HE'S KIND AND WORRIES ABOUT ME.
HE'S MORE IMPORTANT THAN A BOYFRIEND.
AND EVEN THOUGH I WANT TO SEE HIM, I CAN'T.

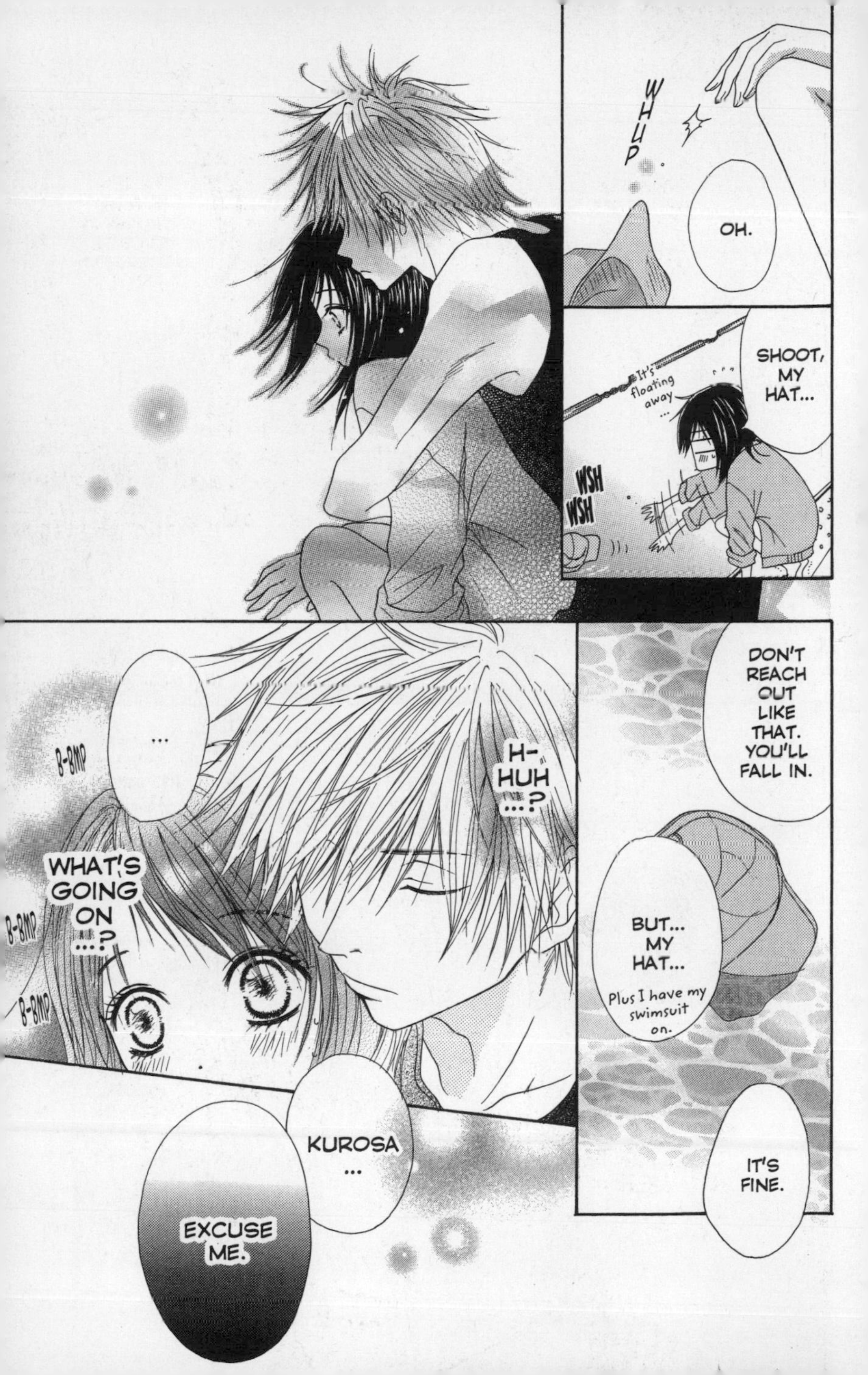
WHUP
OH.
It's floating away...
SHOOT, MY HAT...
WSH WSH
DON'T REACH OUT LIKE THAT. YOU'LL FALL IN.
BUT... MY HAT...
Plus I have my swimsuit on.
IT'S FINE.
H-HUH...?
...
B-BMP
WHAT'S GOING ON...?
B-BMP
B-BMP
KUROSA...
EXCUSE ME.

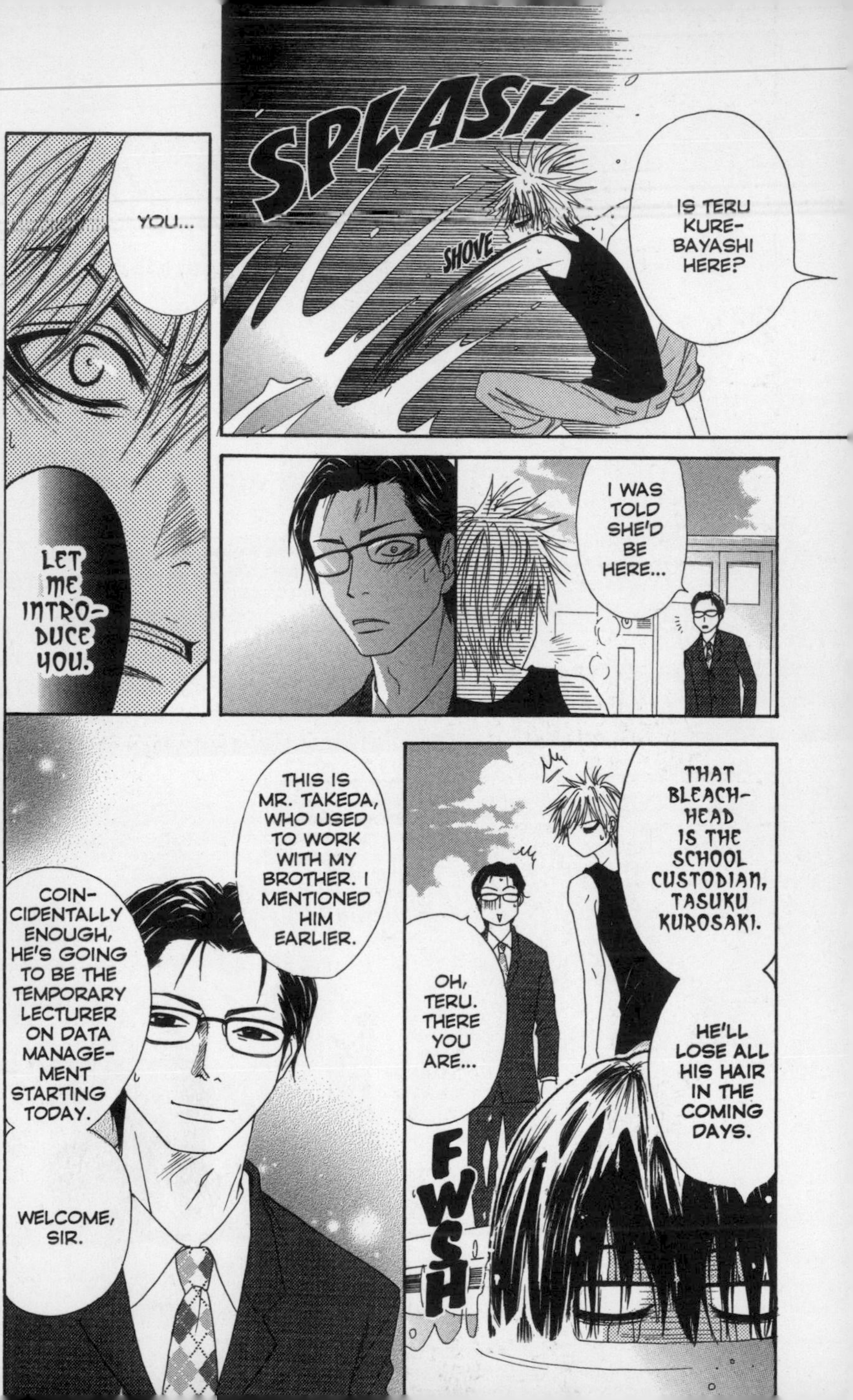
IS TERU KURE-BAYASHI HERE?
SPLASH
SHOVE
I WAS TOLD SHE'D BE HERE...
YOU...
LET ME INTRO-DUCE YOU.
THAT BLEACH-HEAD IS THE SCHOOL CUSTODIAN, TASUKU KUROSAKI.
HE'LL LOSE ALL HIS HAIR IN THE COMING DAYS.
OH, TERU. THERE YOU ARE...
FWSH
THIS IS MR. TAKEDA, WHO USED TO WORK WITH MY BROTHER. I MENTIONED HIM EARLIER.
COIN-CIDENTALLY ENOUGH, HE'S GOING TO BE THE TEMPORARY LECTURER ON DATA MANAGE-MENT STARTING TODAY.
WELCOME, SIR.

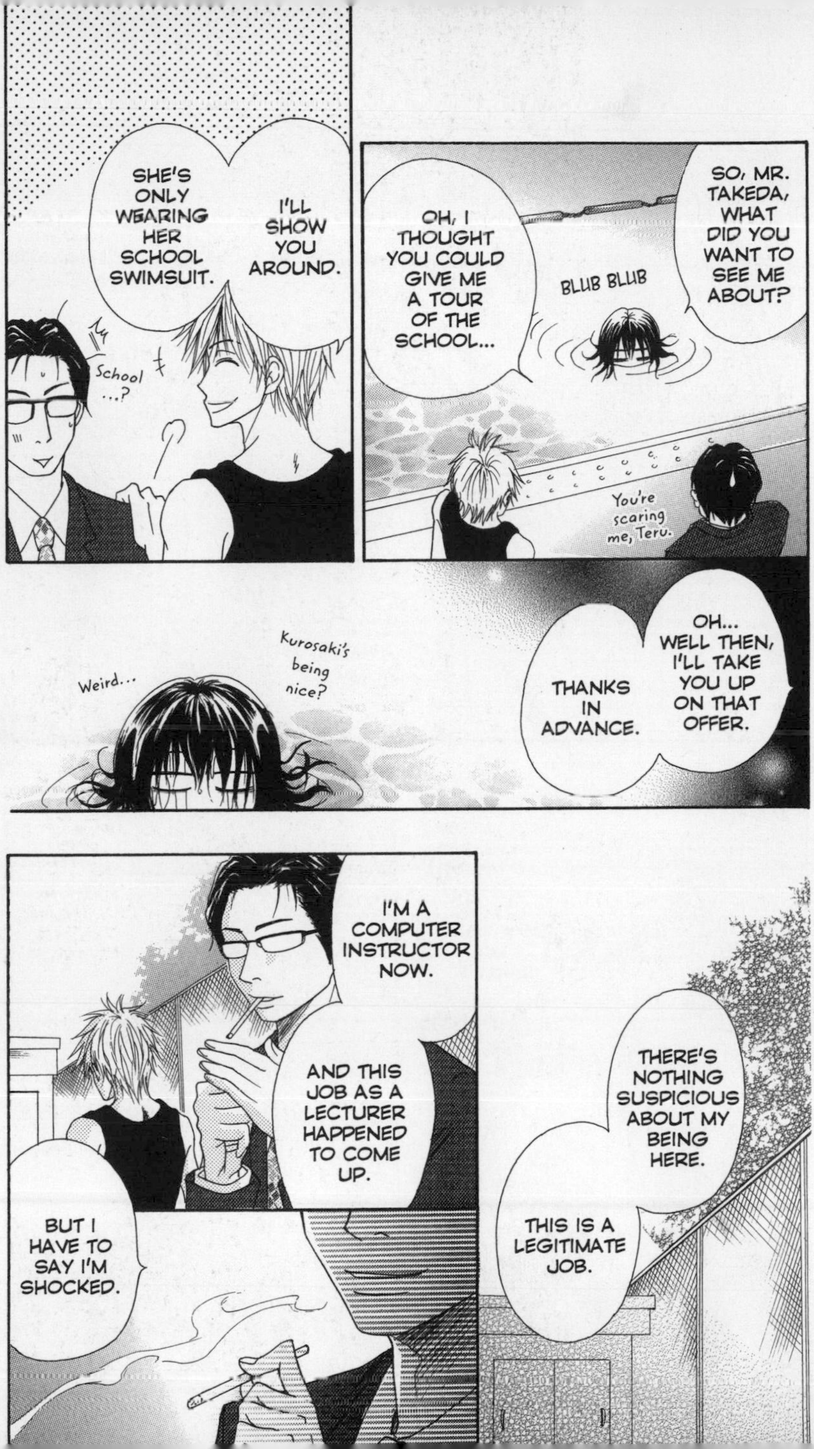
SO, MR. TAKEDA, WHAT DID YOU WANT TO SEE ME ABOUT?
BLUB BLUB
OH, I THOUGHT YOU COULD GIVE ME A TOUR OF THE SCHOOL...
You're scaring me, Teru.
I'LL SHOW YOU AROUND.
SHE'S ONLY WEARING HER SCHOOL SWIMSUIT.
School ...?
OH... WELL THEN, I'LL TAKE YOU UP ON THAT OFFER.
THANKS IN ADVANCE.
Kurosaki's being nice?
Weird...
THERE'S NOTHING SUSPICIOUS ABOUT MY BEING HERE.
THIS IS A LEGITIMATE JOB.
I'M A COMPUTER INSTRUCTOR NOW.
AND THIS JOB AS A LECTURER HAPPENED TO COME UP.
BUT I HAVE TO SAY I'M SHOCKED.

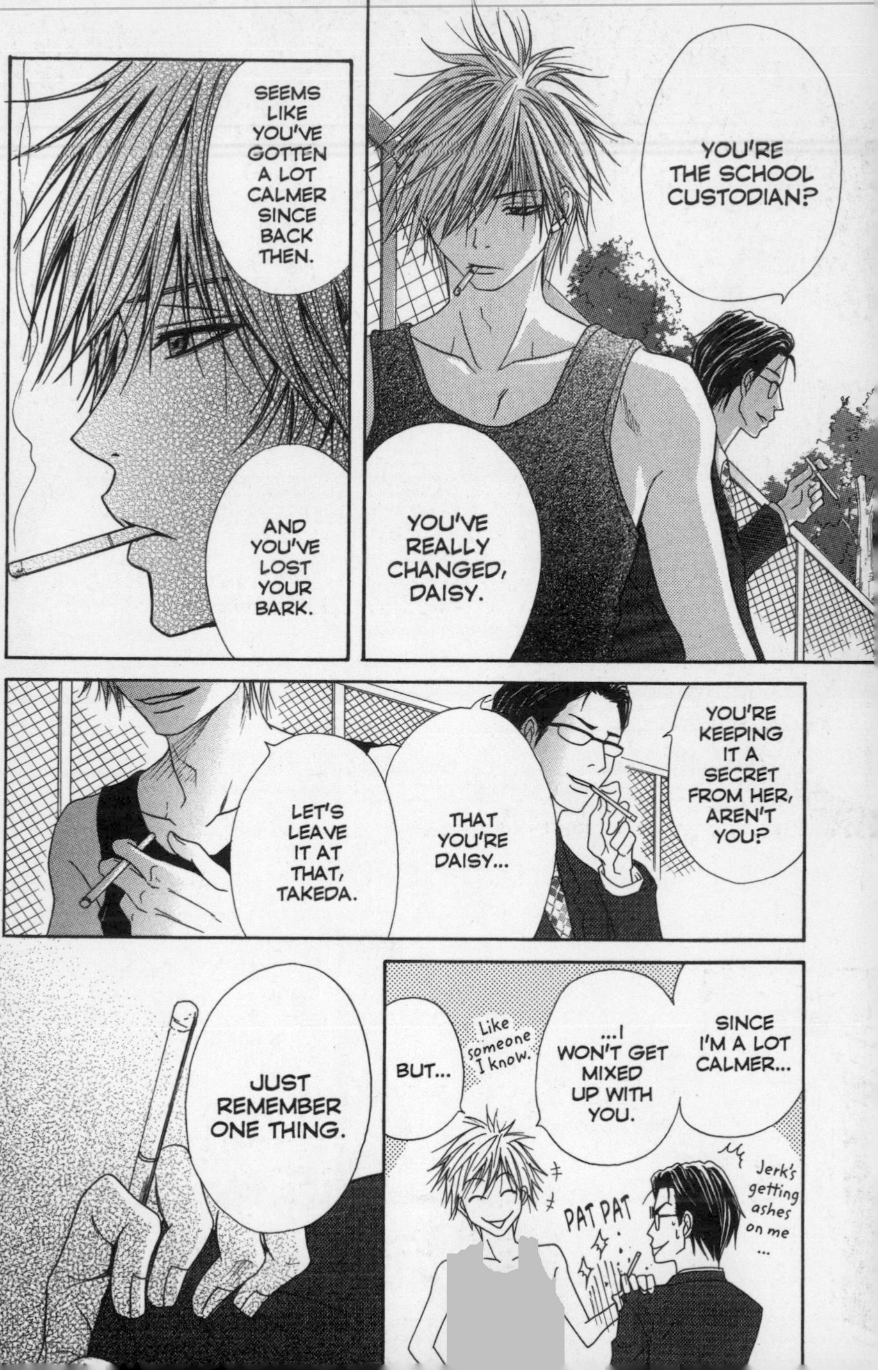
YOU'RE THE SCHOOL CUSTODIAN?
YOU'VE REALLY CHANGED, DAISY.
SEEMS LIKE YOU'VE GOTTEN A LOT CALMER SINCE BACK THEN.
AND YOU'VE LOST YOUR BARK.
YOU'RE KEEPING IT A SECRET FROM HER, AREN'T YOU?
THAT YOU'RE DAISY...
LET'S LEAVE IT AT THAT, TAKEDA.
SINCE I'M A LOT CALMER...
...I WON'T GET MIXED UP WITH YOU.
Like someone I know.
BUT...
Jerk's getting ashes on me ...
PAT PAT
JUST REMEMBER ONE THING.

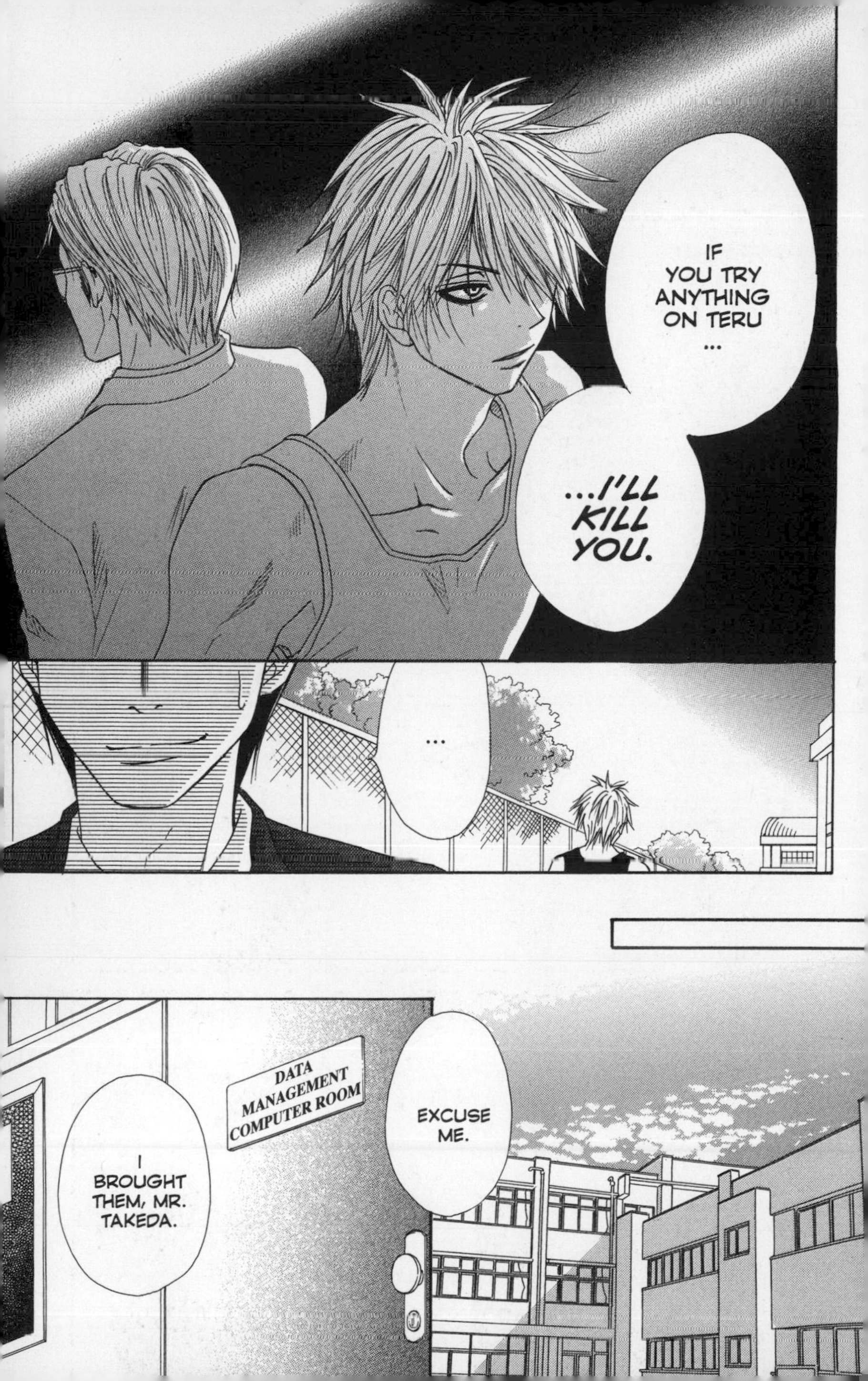
IF YOU TRY ANYTHING ON TERU ...
...I'LL KILL YOU.
...
EXCUSE ME.
DATA MANAGEMENT COMPUTER ROOM
I BROUGHT THEM, MR. TAKEDA.

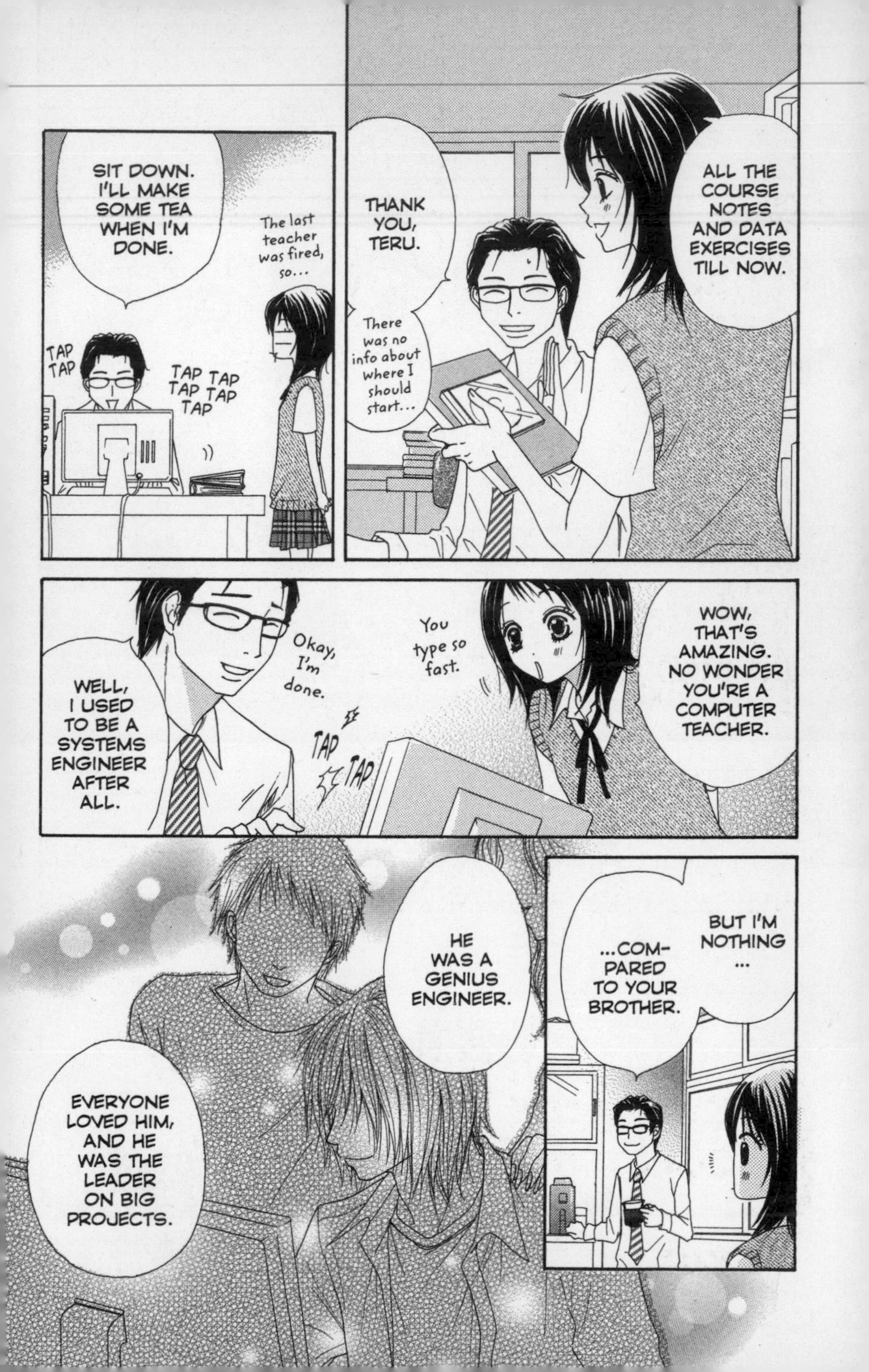

ALL THE COURSE NOTES AND DATA EXERCISES TILL NOW.
THANK YOU, TERU.
There was no info about where I should start...
The last teacher was fired, so...
SIT DOWN. I'LL MAKE SOME TEA WHEN I'M DONE.
TAP TAP TAP TAP TAP
TAP TAP
WOW, THAT'S AMAZING. NO WONDER YOU'RE A COMPUTER TEACHER.
You type so fast.
Okay, I'm done.
TAP TAP
WELL, I USED TO BE A SYSTEMS ENGINEER AFTER ALL.
BUT I'M NOTHING ...
...COM-PARED TO YOUR BROTHER.
HE WAS A GENIUS ENGINEER.
EVERYONE LOVED HIM, AND HE WAS THE LEADER ON BIG PROJECTS.

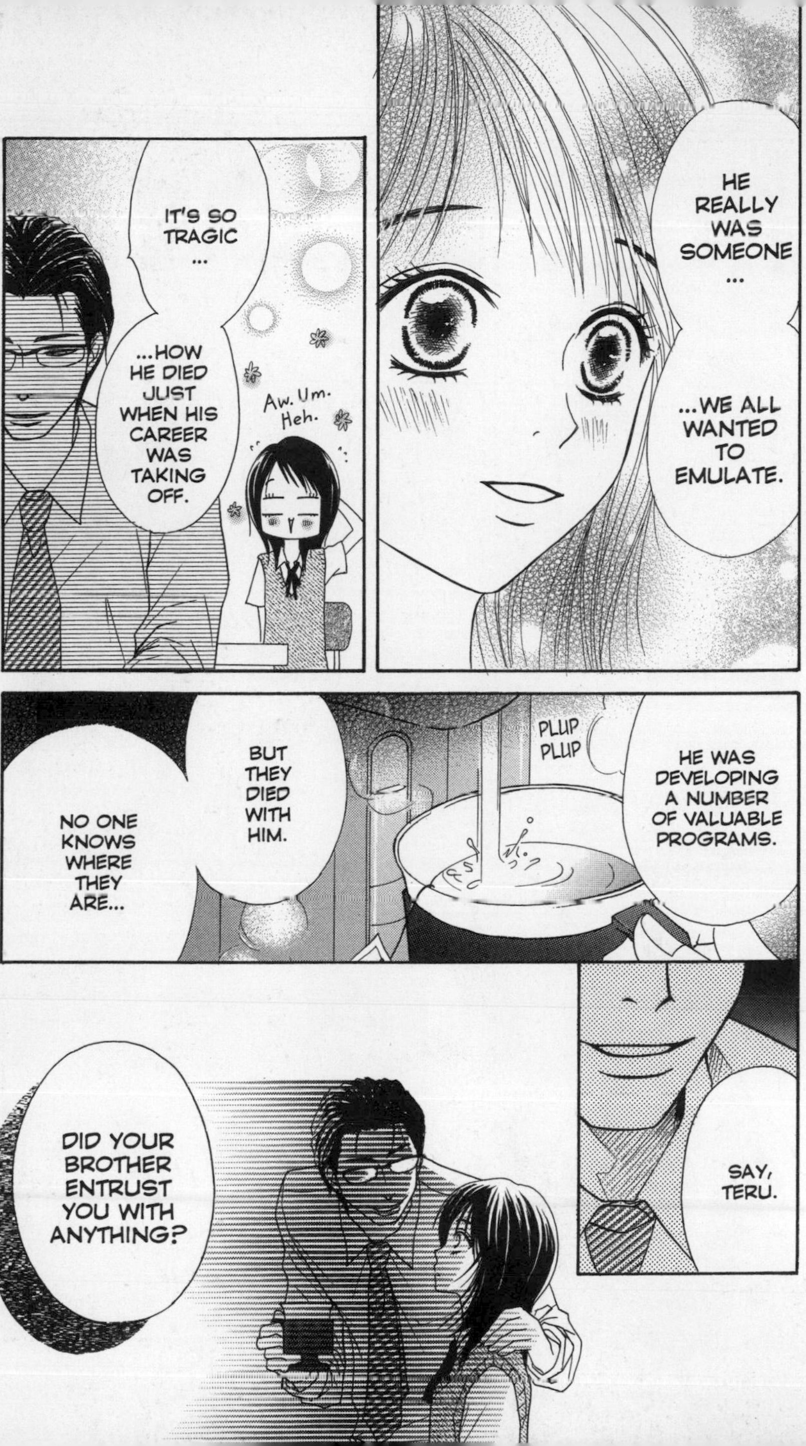
HE REALLY WAS SOMEONE ...
...WE ALL WANTED TO EMULATE.
IT'S SO TRAGIC ...
...HOW HE DIED JUST WHEN HIS CAREER WAS TAKING OFF.
Aw. Um. Heh.
HE WAS DEVELOPING A NUMBER OF VALUABLE PROGRAMS.
PLUP PLUP
BUT THEY DIED WITH HIM.
NO ONE KNOWS WHERE THEY ARE...
SAY, TERU.
DID YOUR BROTHER ENTRUST YOU WITH ANYTHING?

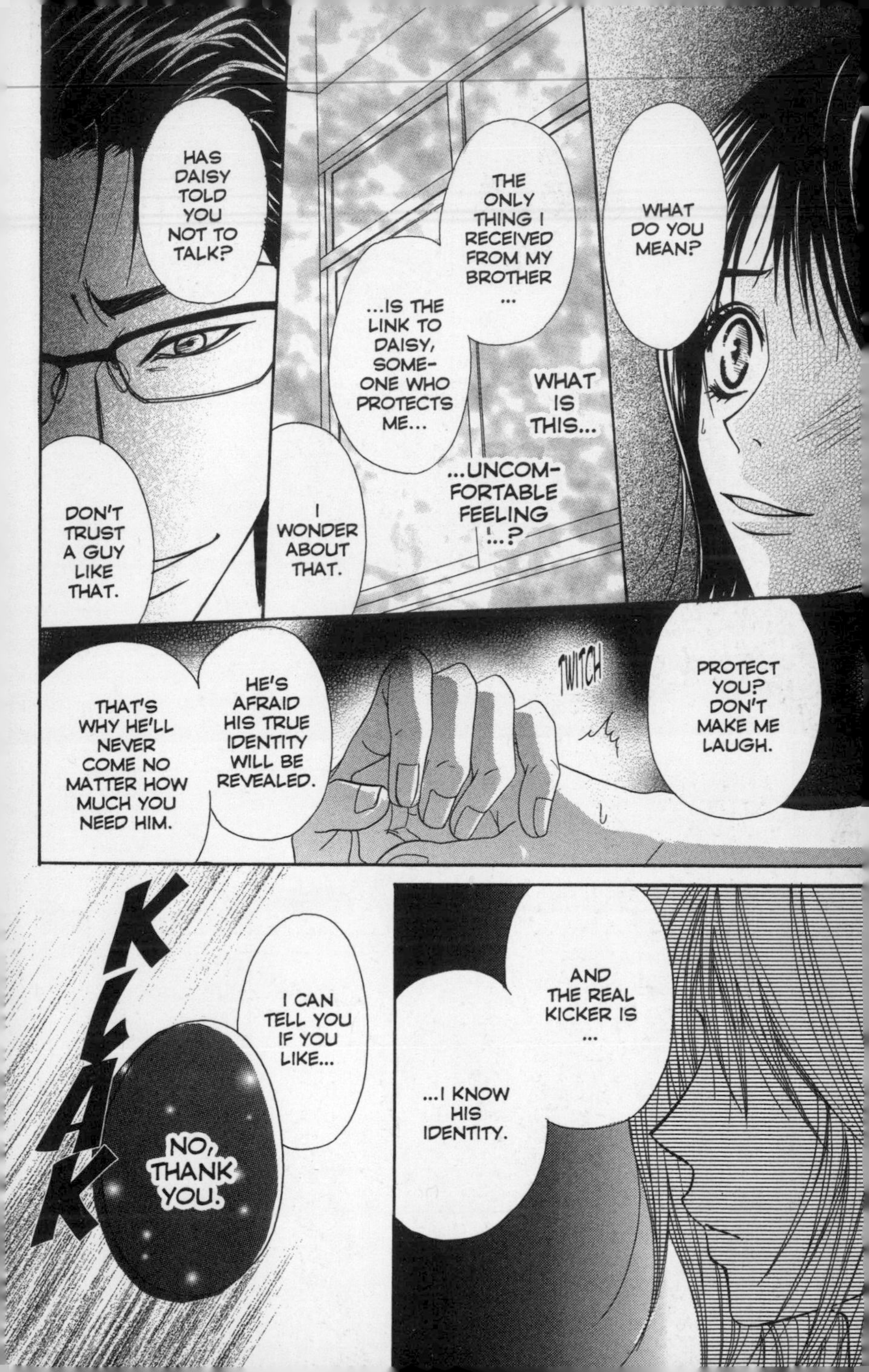
WHAT DO YOU MEAN?
THE ONLY THING I RECEIVED FROM MY BROTHER ...
...IS THE LINK TO DAISY, SOME-ONE WHO PROTECTS ME...
WHAT IS THIS...
...UNCOM-FORTABLE FEELING ...?
I WONDER ABOUT THAT.
HAS DAISY TOLD YOU NOT TO TALK?
DON'T TRUST A GUY LIKE THAT.
PROTECT YOU? DON'T MAKE ME LAUGH.
TWITCH
HE'S AFRAID HIS TRUE IDENTITY WILL BE REVEALED.
THAT'S WHY HE'LL NEVER COME NO MATTER HOW MUCH YOU NEED HIM.
AND THE REAL KICKER IS ...
...I KNOW HIS IDENTITY.
I CAN TELL YOU IF YOU LIKE...
KLAK
NO, THANK YOU.

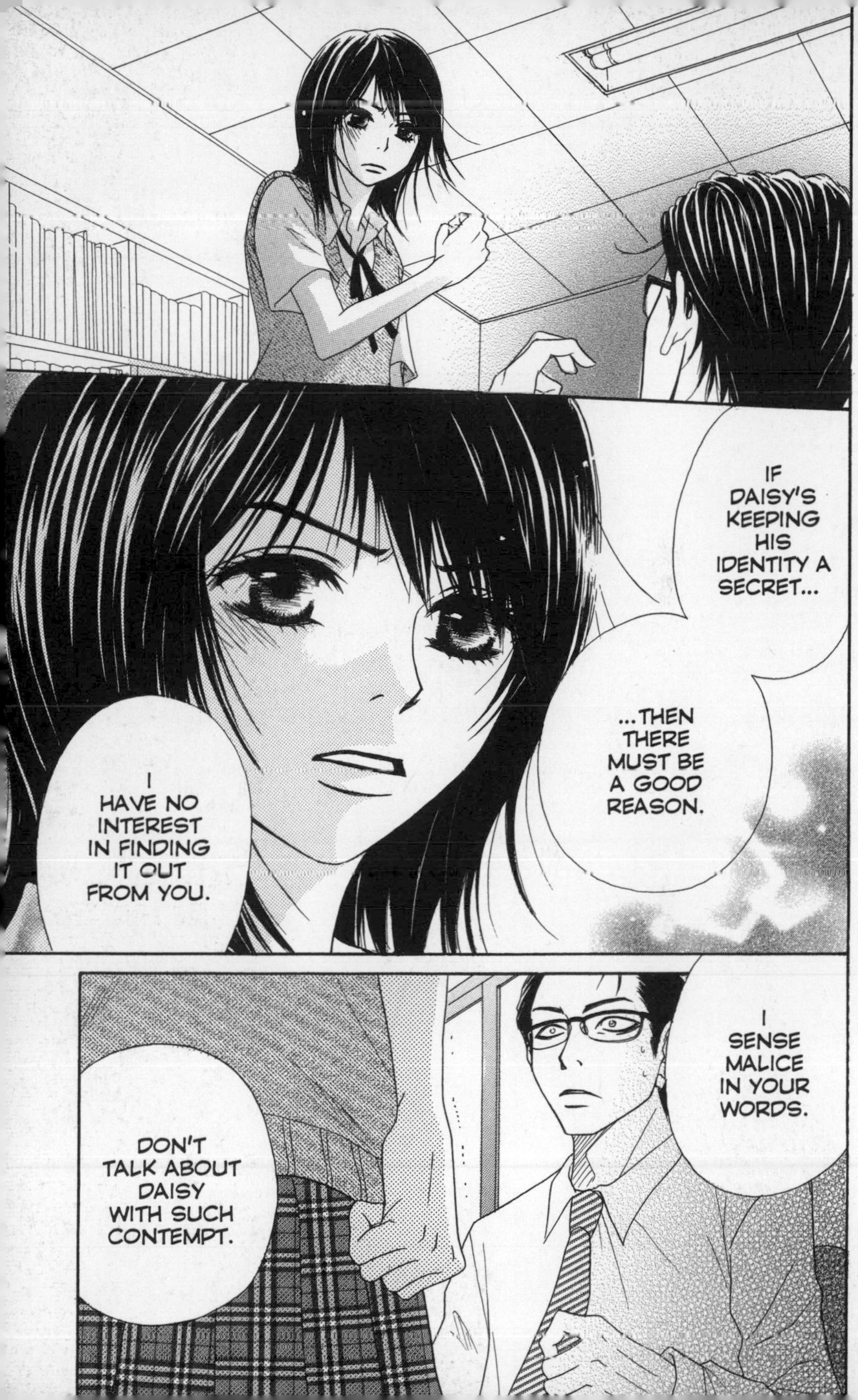
IF DAISY'S KEEPING HIS IDENTITY A SECRET...
...THEN THERE MUST BE A GOOD REASON.
I HAVE NO INTEREST IN FINDING IT OUT FROM YOU.
I SENSE MALICE IN YOUR WORDS.
DON'T TALK ABOUT DAISY WITH SUCH CONTEMPT.

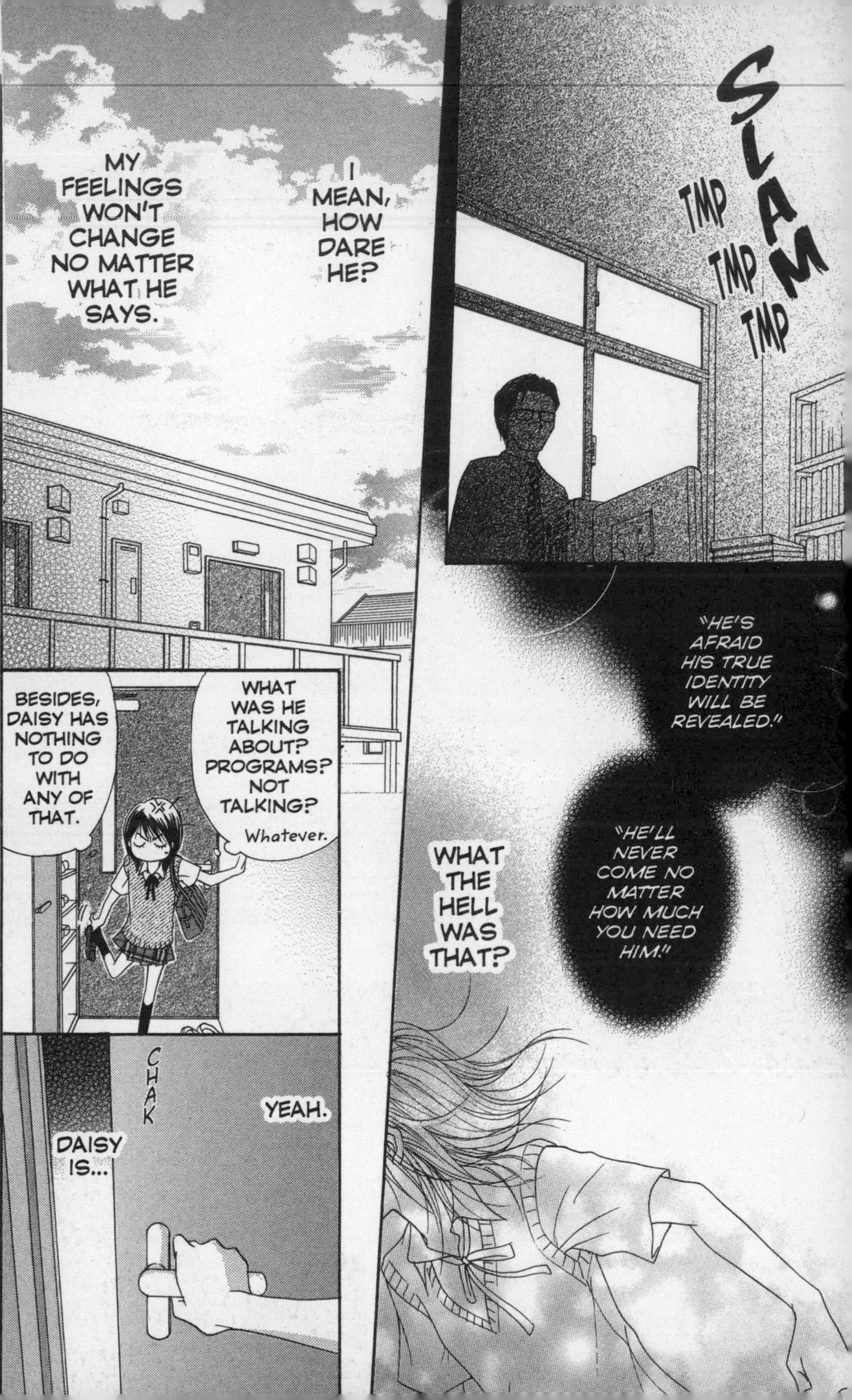
SLAM
TMP
TMP
TMP
"HE'S AFRAID HIS TRUE IDENTITY WILL BE REVEALED."
"HE'LL NEVER COME NO MATTER HOW MUCH YOU NEED HIM."
WHAT THE HELL WAS THAT?
I MEAN, HOW DARE HE?
MY FEELINGS WON'T CHANGE NO MATTER WHAT HE SAYS.
WHAT WAS HE TALKING ABOUT? PROGRAMS? NOT TALKING?
Whatever.
BESIDES, DAISY HAS NOTHING TO DO WITH ANY OF THAT.
CHAK
YEAH.
DAISY IS...

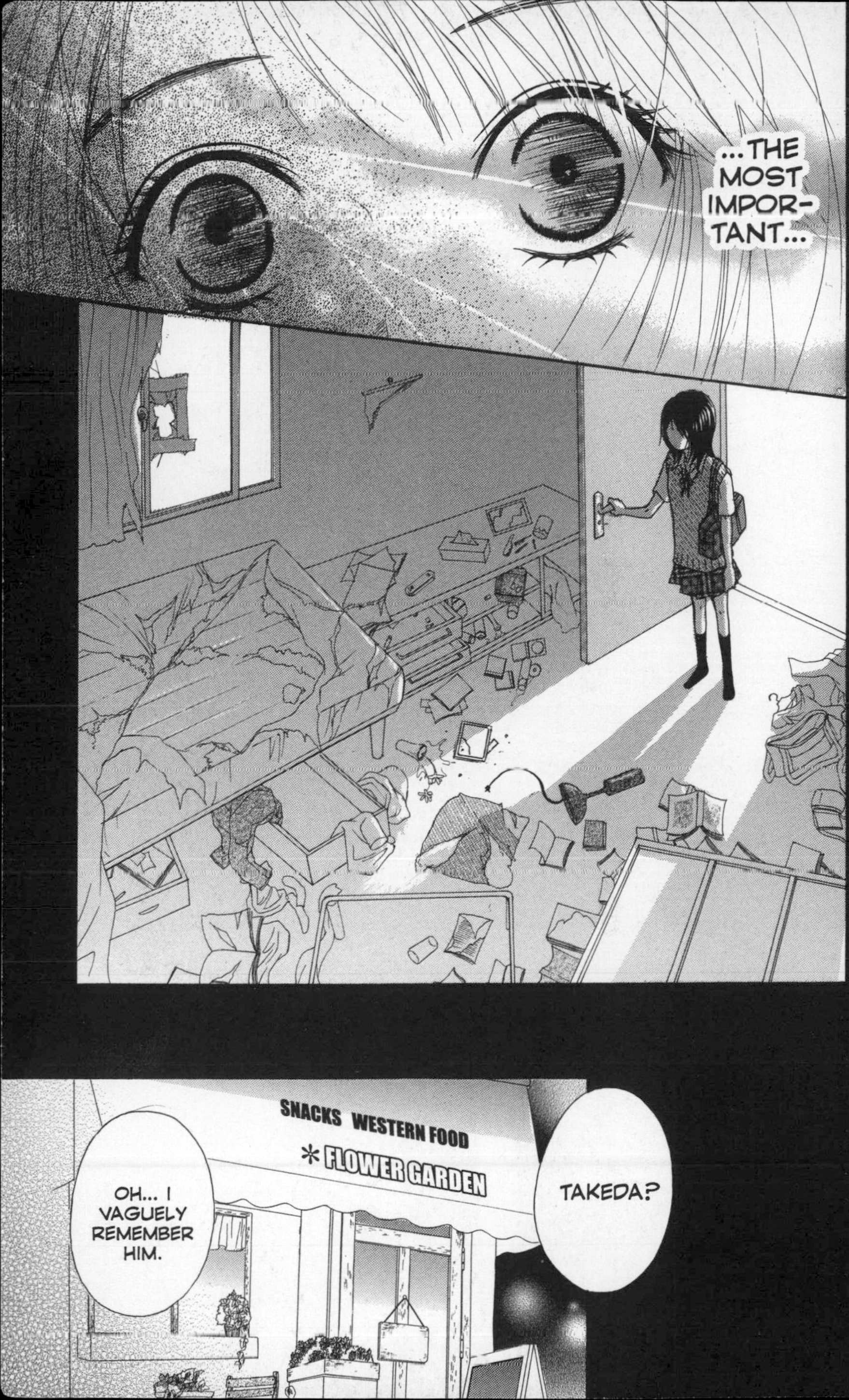
...THE MOST IMPOR-TANT...
SNACKS WESTERN FOOD
FLOWER GARDEN
TAKEDA?
OH... I VAGUELY REMEMBER HIM.

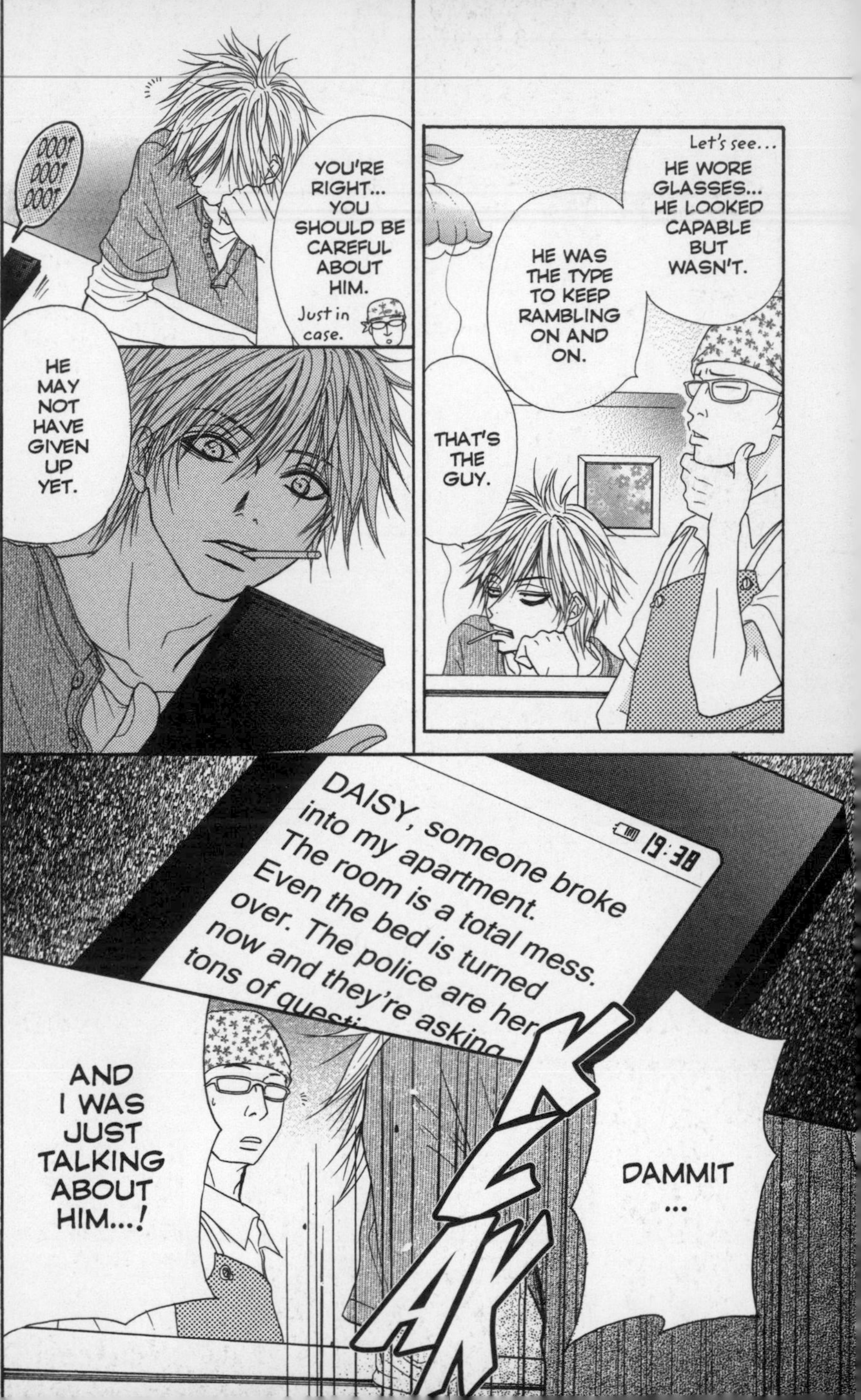
Let's see...
HE WORE GLASSES... HE LOOKED CAPABLE BUT WASN'T.
HE WAS THE TYPE TO KEEP RAMBLING ON AND ON.
THAT'S THE GUY.
DOOT DOOT DOOT
YOU'RE RIGHT... YOU SHOULD BE CAREFUL ABOUT HIM.
Just in case.
HE MAY NOT HAVE GIVEN UP YET.
19:38
DAISY, someone broke into my apartment. The room is a total mess. Even the bed is turned over. The police are her now and they're asking tons of questi
KLAK
DAMMIT...
AND I WAS JUST TALKING ABOUT HIM...!

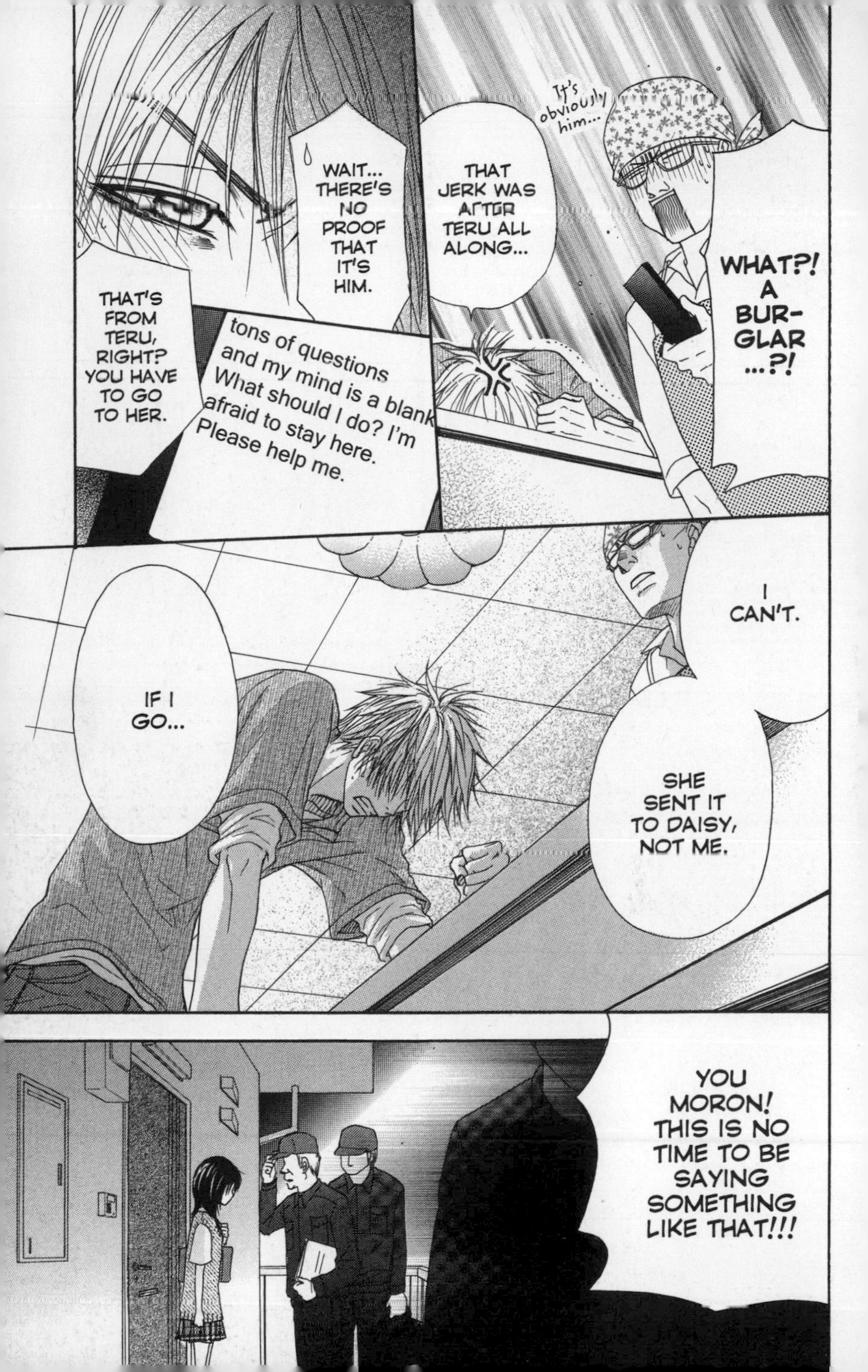
WHAT?! A BURGLAR...?!
It's obviously him...
THAT JERK WAS AFTER TERU ALL ALONG...
WAIT... THERE'S NO PROOF THAT IT'S HIM.
THAT'S FROM TERU, RIGHT? YOU HAVE TO GO TO HER.
tons of questions and my mind is a blank What should I do? I'm afraid to stay here. Please help me.
I CAN'T.
SHE SENT IT TO DAISY, NOT ME.
IF I GO...
YOU MORON! THIS IS NO TIME TO BE SAYING SOMETHING LIKE THAT!!!

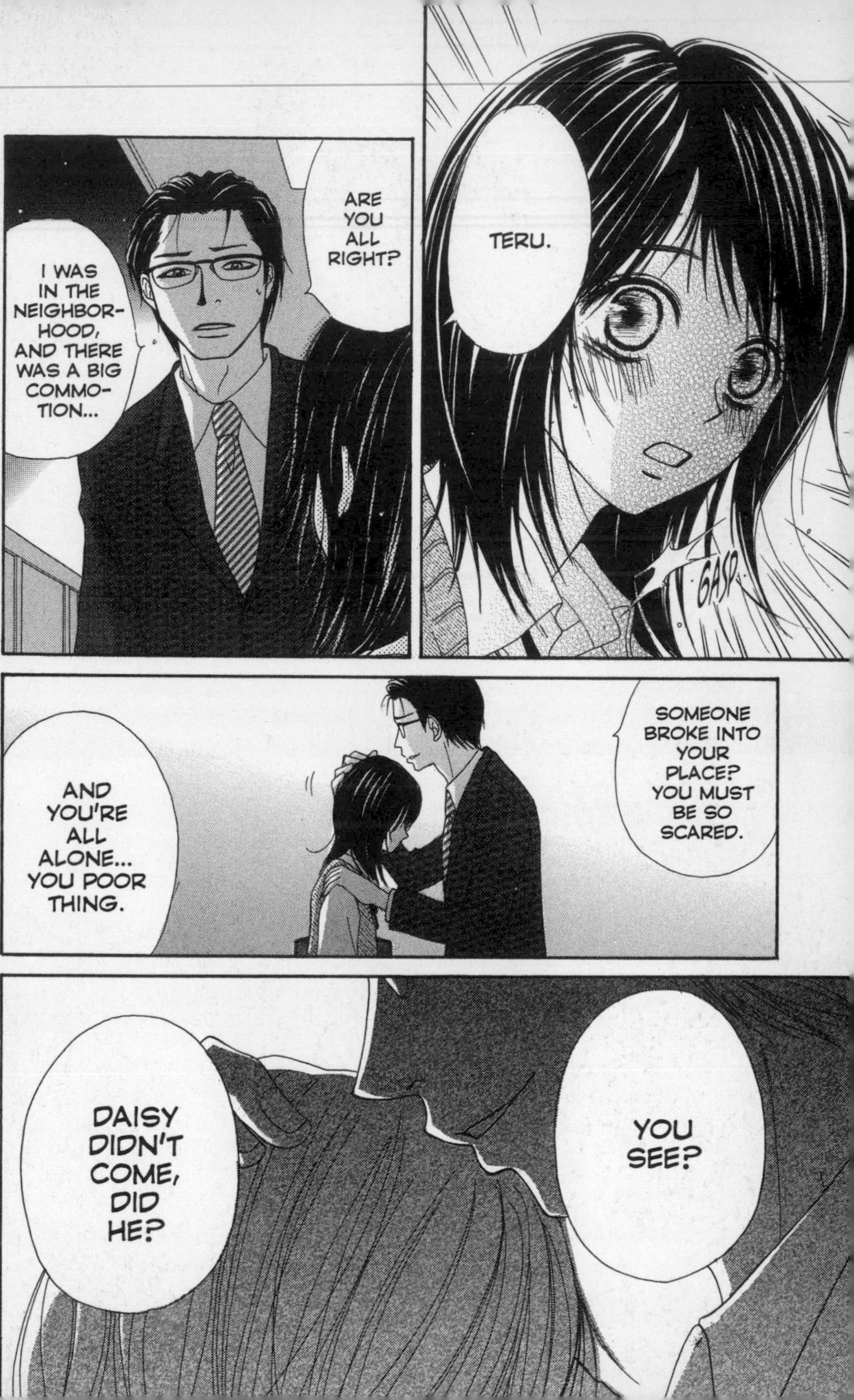
TERU.
GASP
ARE YOU ALL RIGHT?
I WAS IN THE NEIGHBORHOOD, AND THERE WAS A BIG COMMOTION...
SOMEONE BROKE INTO YOUR PLACE? YOU MUST BE SO SCARED.
AND YOU'RE ALL ALONE... YOU POOR THING.
YOU SEE?
DAISY DIDN'T COME, DID HE?

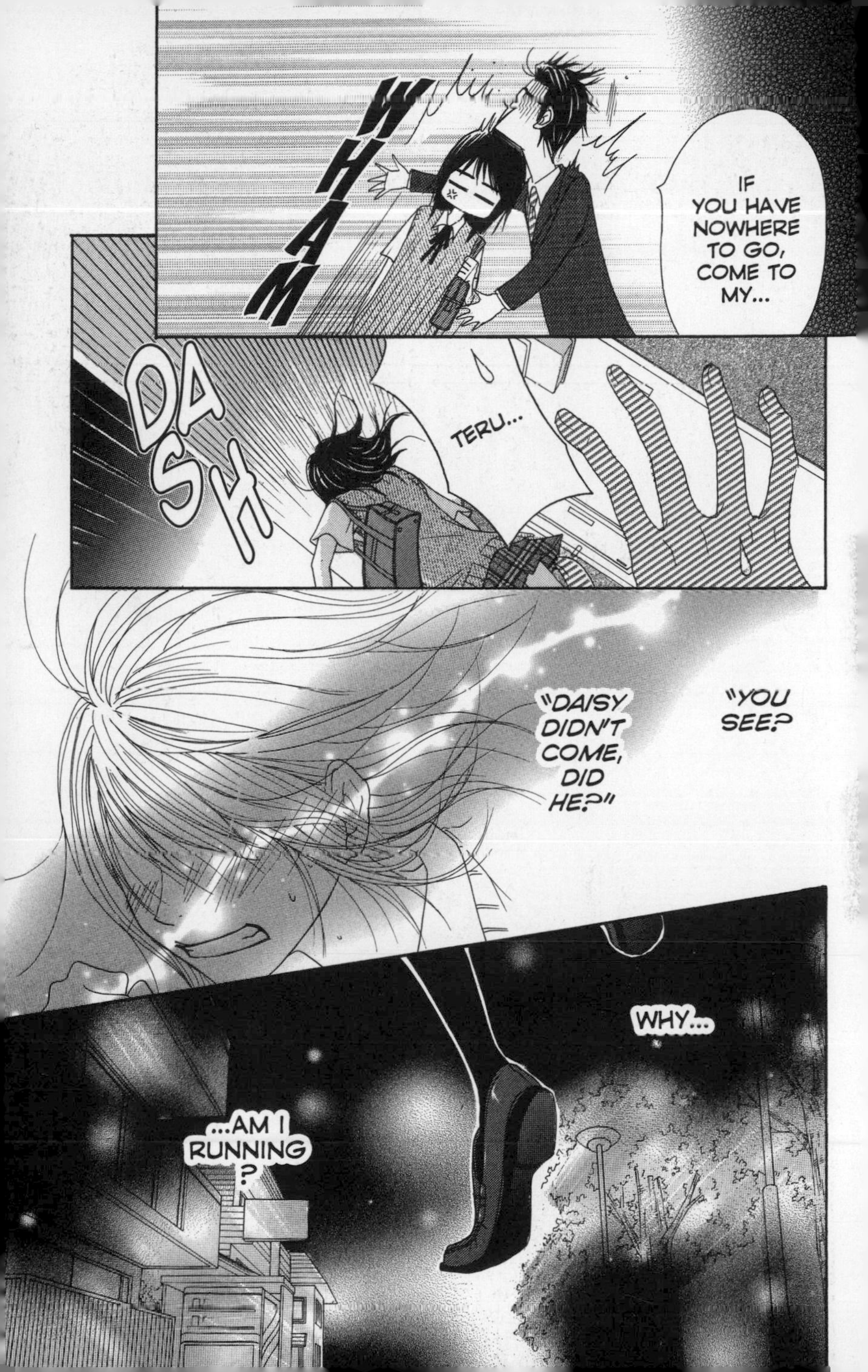
IF YOU HAVE NOWHERE TO GO, COME TO MY...
WHAM
TERU...
DASH
"YOU SEE?
"DAISY DIDN'T COME, DID HE?"
WHY...
...AM I RUNNING?

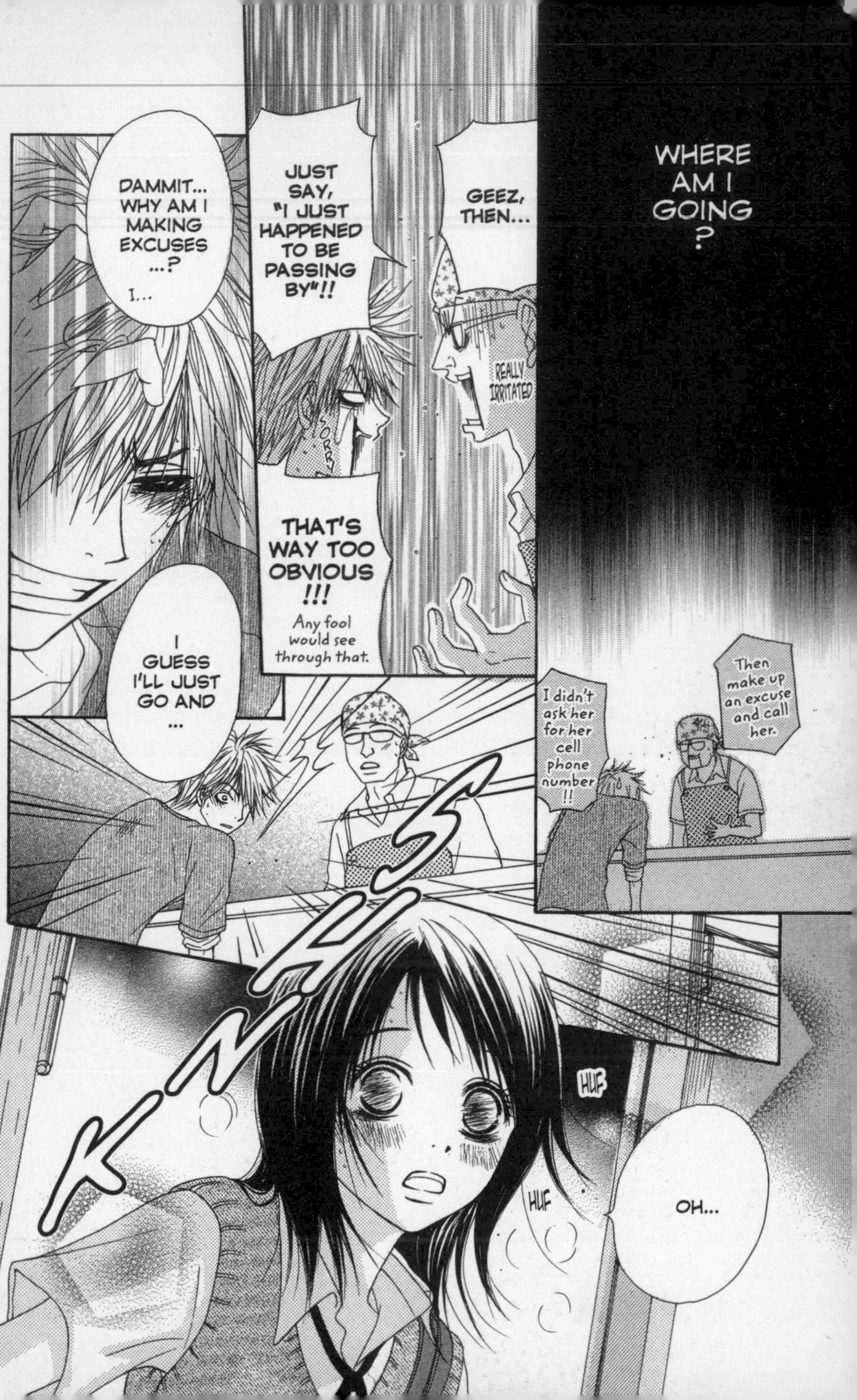
WHERE AM I GOING?
Then make up an excuse and call her.
I didn't ask her for her cell phone number!!
GEEZ, THEN...
REALLY IRRITATED
JUST SAY, "I JUST HAPPENED TO BE PASSING BY"!!
SORRY
THAT'S WAY TOO OBVIOUS!!!
Any fool would see through that.
DAMMIT... WHY AM I MAKING EXCUSES ...?
I...
I GUESS I'LL JUST GO AND ...
K-N-H-S
HUF
HUF
OH...

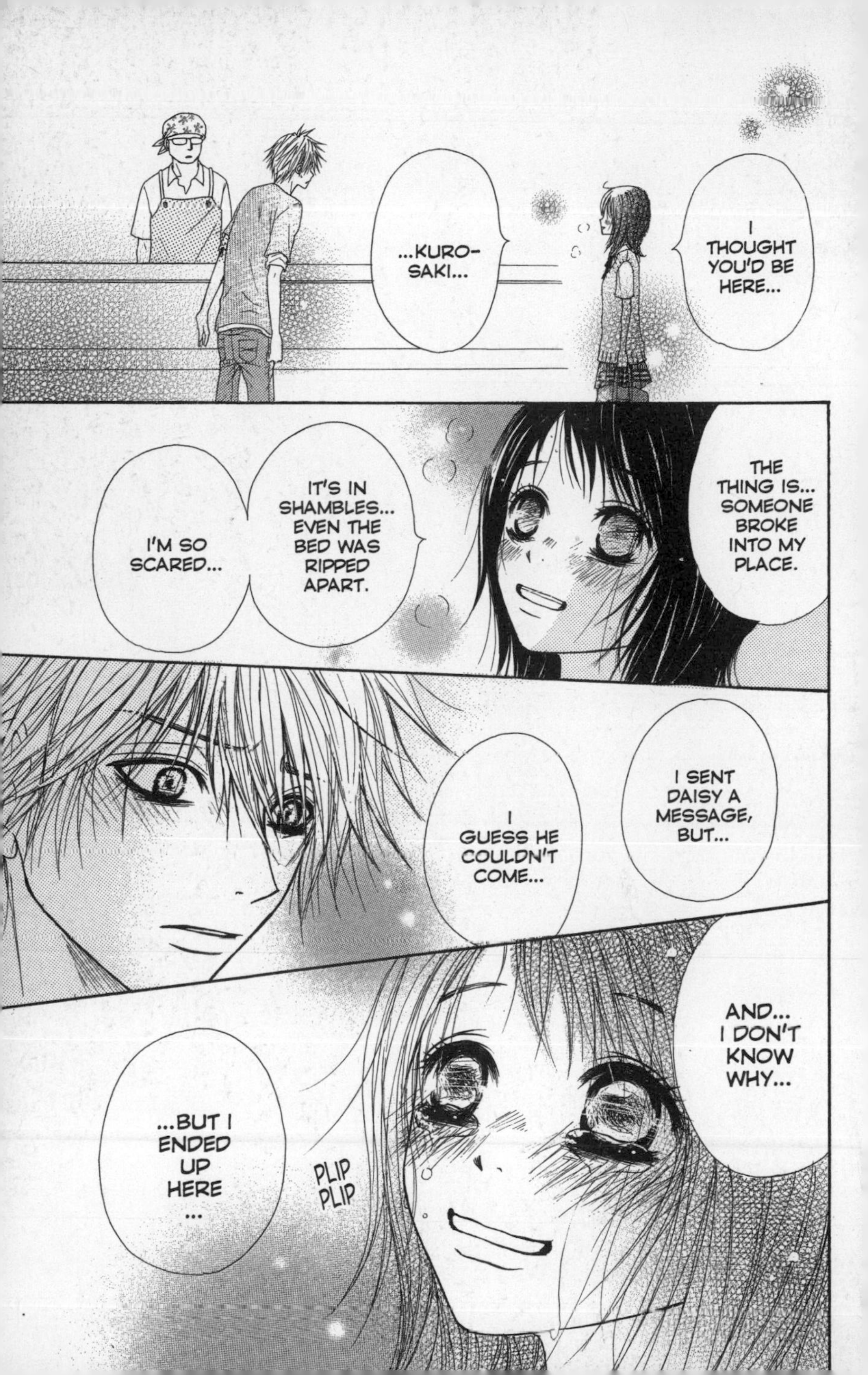
I THOUGHT YOU'D BE HERE...
...KURO-SAKI...
THE THING IS... SOMEONE BROKE INTO MY PLACE.
IT'S IN SHAMBLES... EVEN THE BED WAS RIPPED APART.
I'M SO SCARED...
I SENT DAISY A MESSAGE, BUT...
I GUESS HE COULDN'T COME...
AND... I DON'T KNOW WHY...
PLIP PLIP
...BUT I ENDED UP HERE...

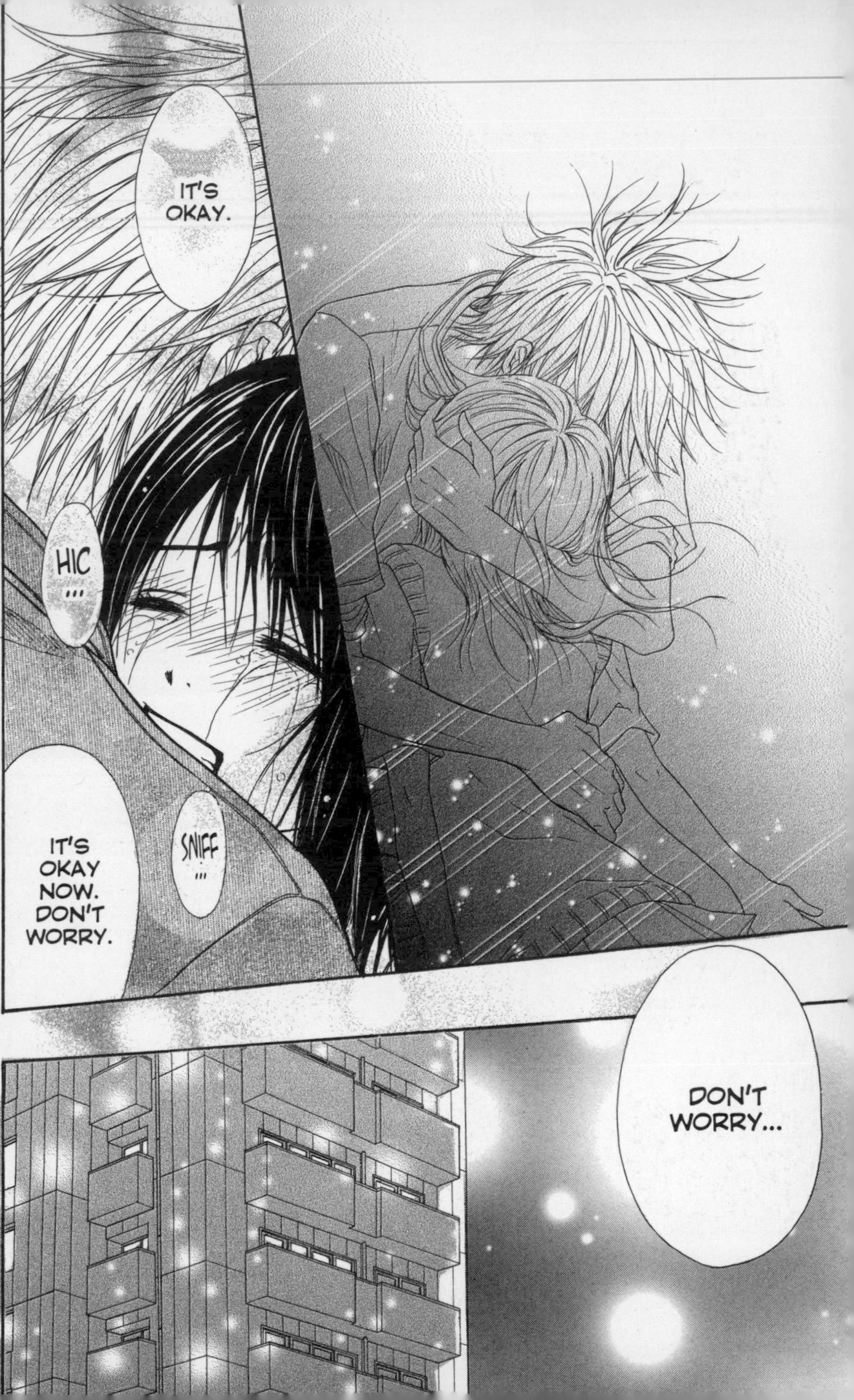
IT'S OKAY.
HIC ...
SNIFF ...
IT'S OKAY NOW. DON'T WORRY.
DON'T WORRY...

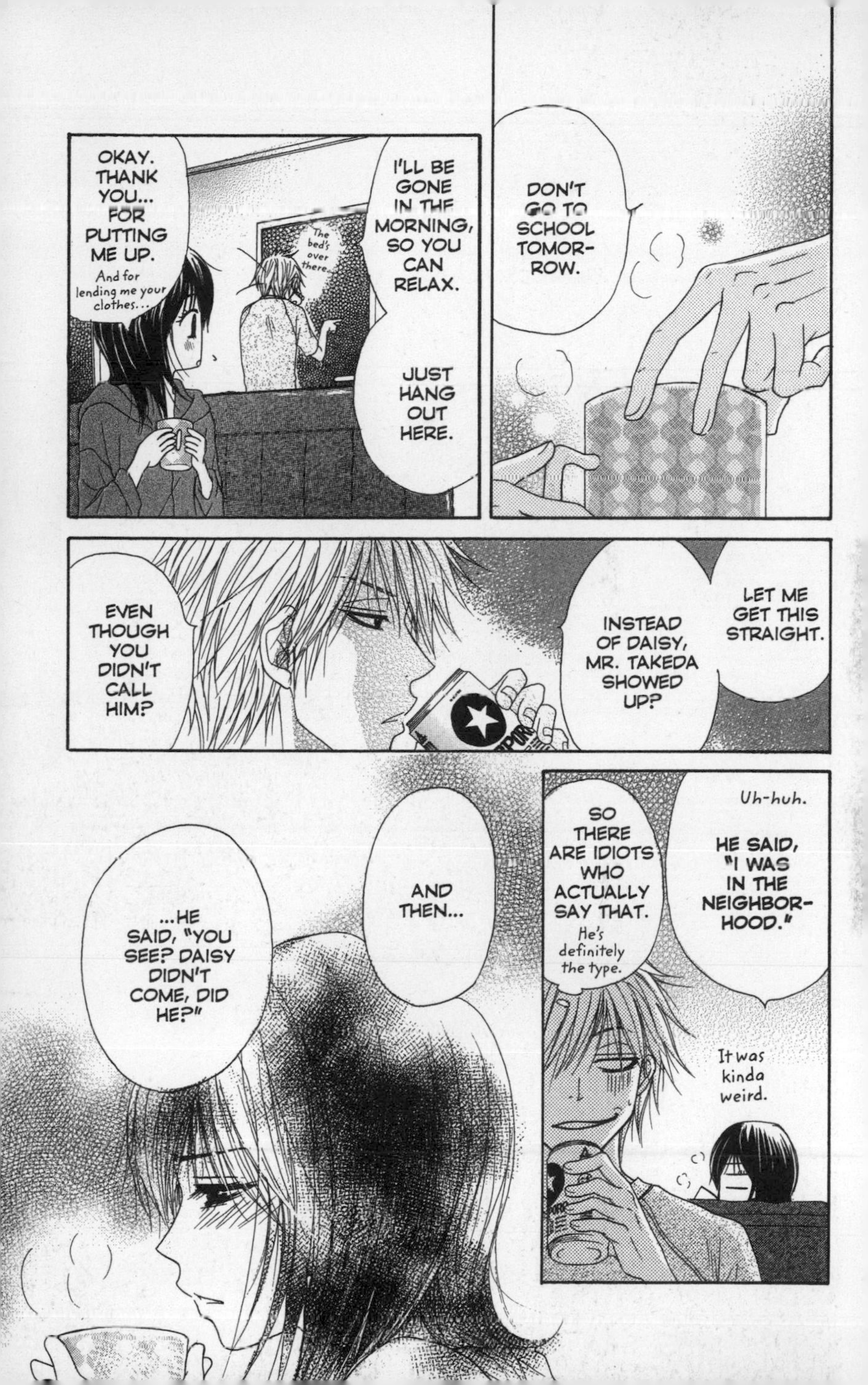
DON'T GO TO SCHOOL TOMORROW.
I'LL BE GONE IN THE MORNING, SO YOU CAN RELAX.
The bed's over there.
JUST HANG OUT HERE.
OKAY. THANK YOU... FOR PUTTING ME UP.
And for lending me your clothes...
LET ME GET THIS STRAIGHT.
INSTEAD OF DAISY, MR. TAKEDA SHOWED UP?
EVEN THOUGH YOU DIDN'T CALL HIM?
Uh-huh.
HE SAID, "I WAS IN THE NEIGHBORHOOD."
SO THERE ARE IDIOTS WHO ACTUALLY SAY THAT.
He's definitely the type.
It was kinda weird.
AND THEN...
...HE SAID, "YOU SEE? DAISY DIDN'T COME, DID HE?"

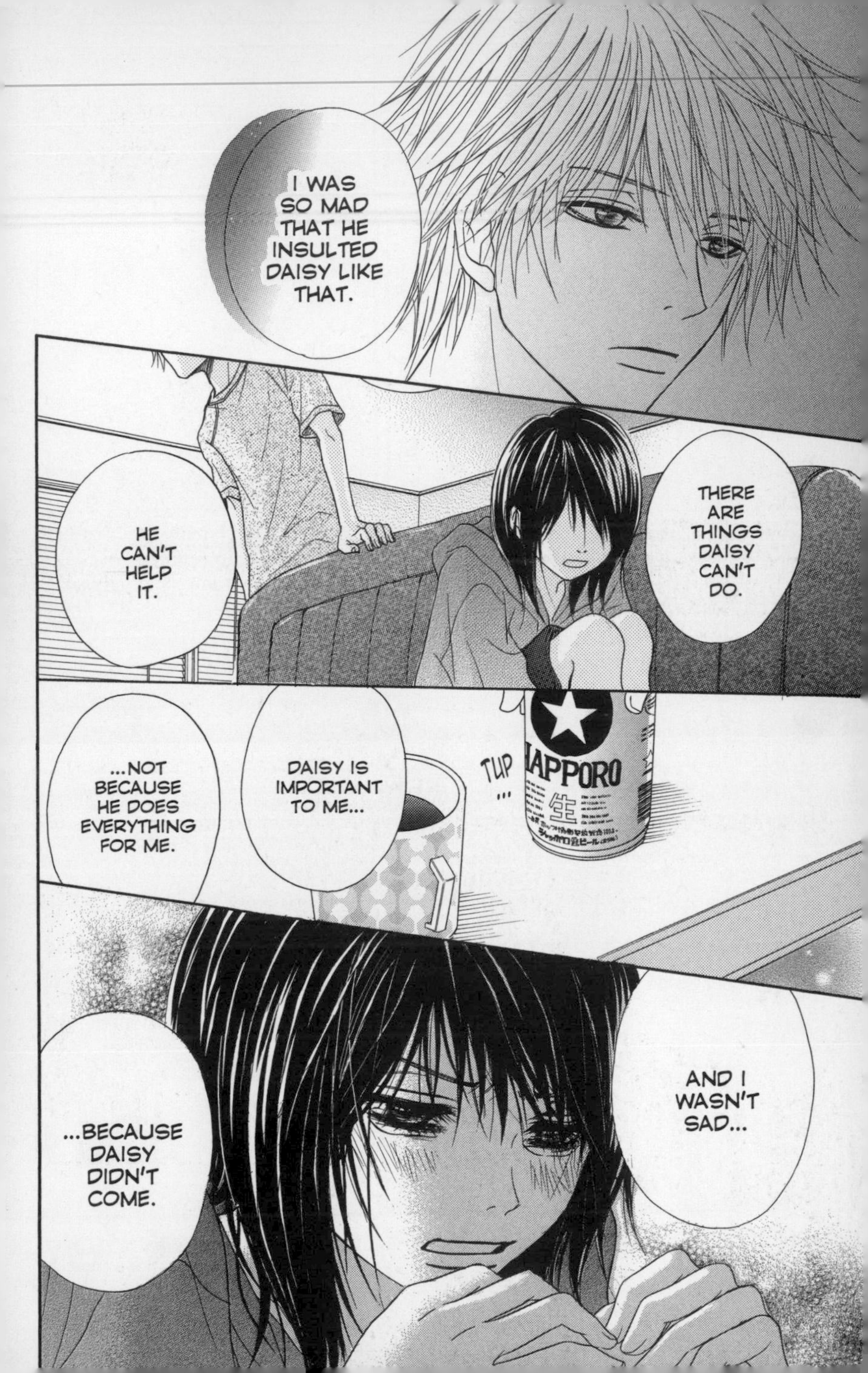
I WAS SO MAD THAT HE INSULTED DAISY LIKE THAT.
THERE ARE THINGS DAISY CAN'T DO.
HE CAN'T HELP IT.
TUP...
DAISY IS IMPORTANT TO ME...
...NOT BECAUSE HE DOES EVERYTHING FOR ME.
AND I WASN'T SAD...
...BECAUSE DAISY DIDN'T COME.

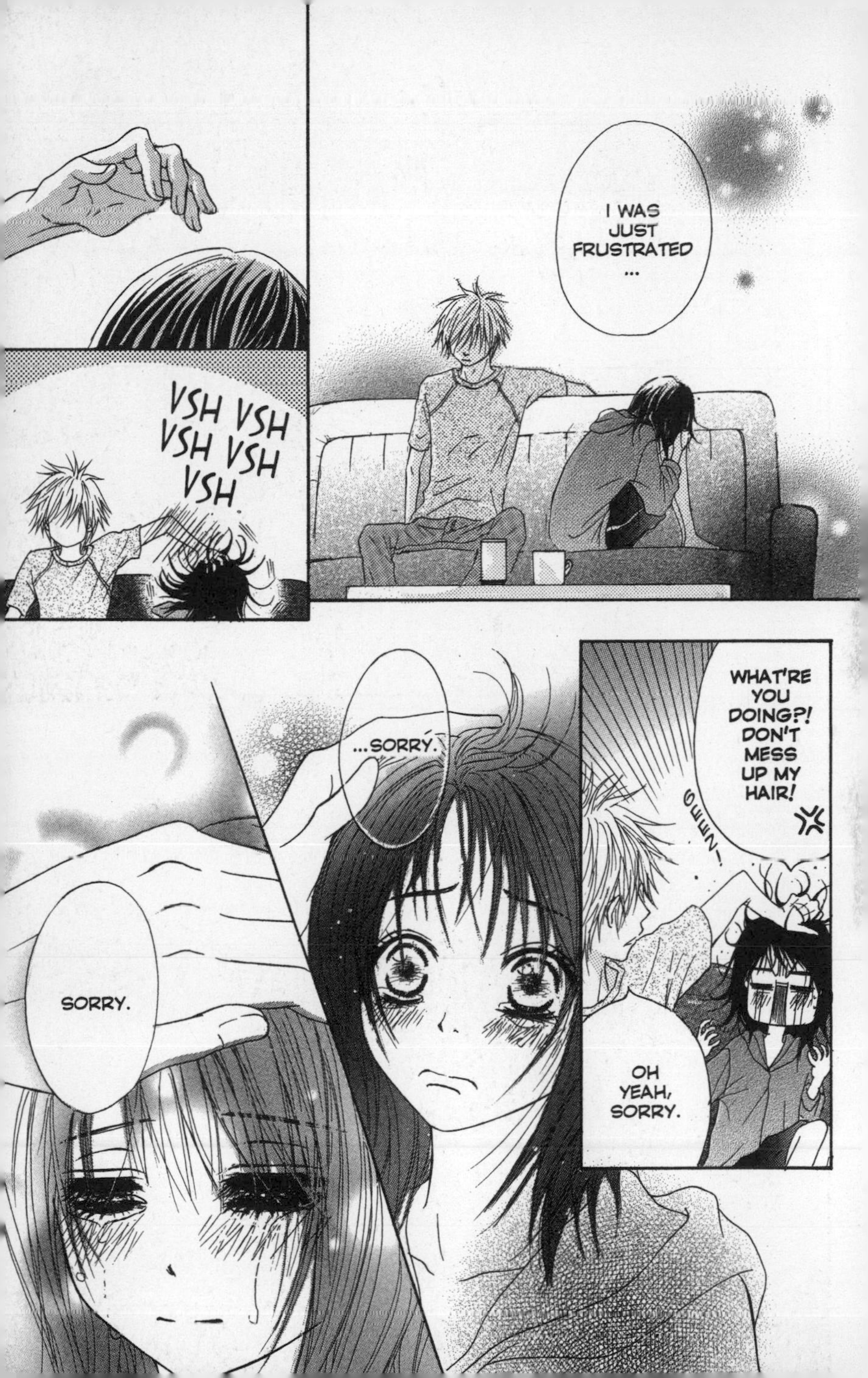
I WAS JUST FRUSTRATED ...
VSH VSH VSH VSH VSH
WHAT'RE YOU DOING?! DON'T MESS UP MY HAIR!
GWEEN-!
OH YEAH, SORRY.
...SORRY.
SORRY.

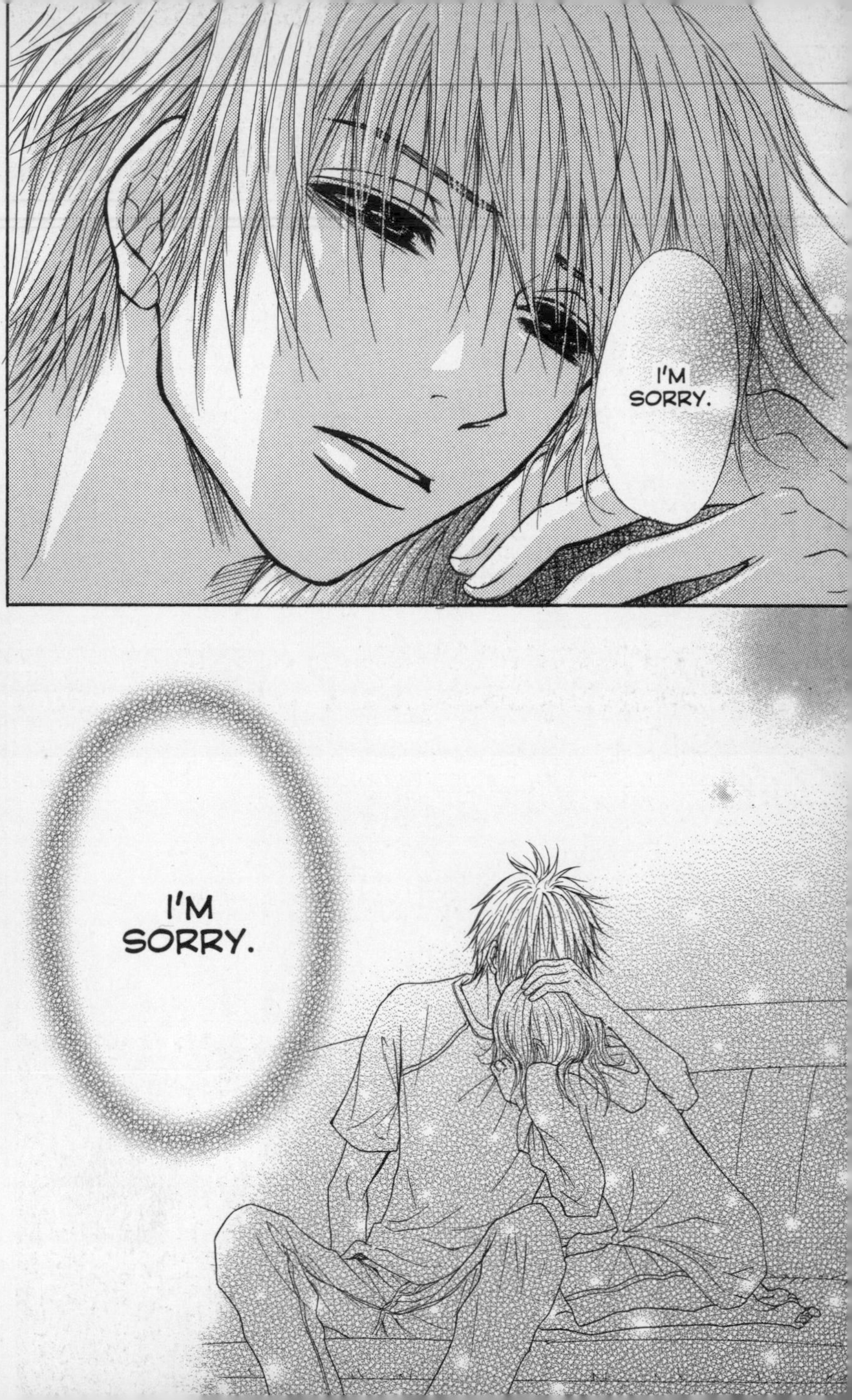
I'M SORRY.
I'M SORRY.

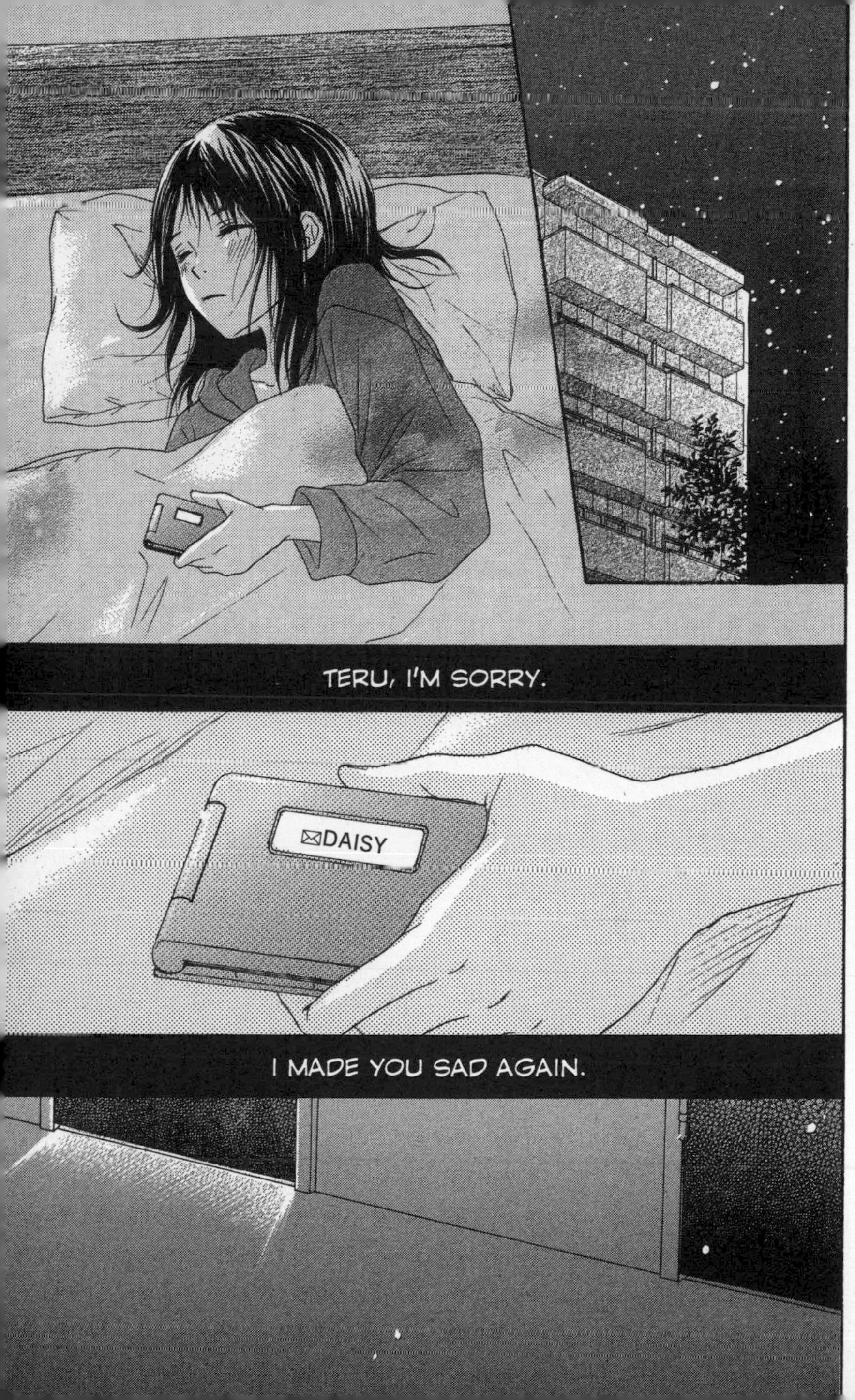
TERU, I'M SORRY.
DAISY
I MADE YOU SAD AGAIN.

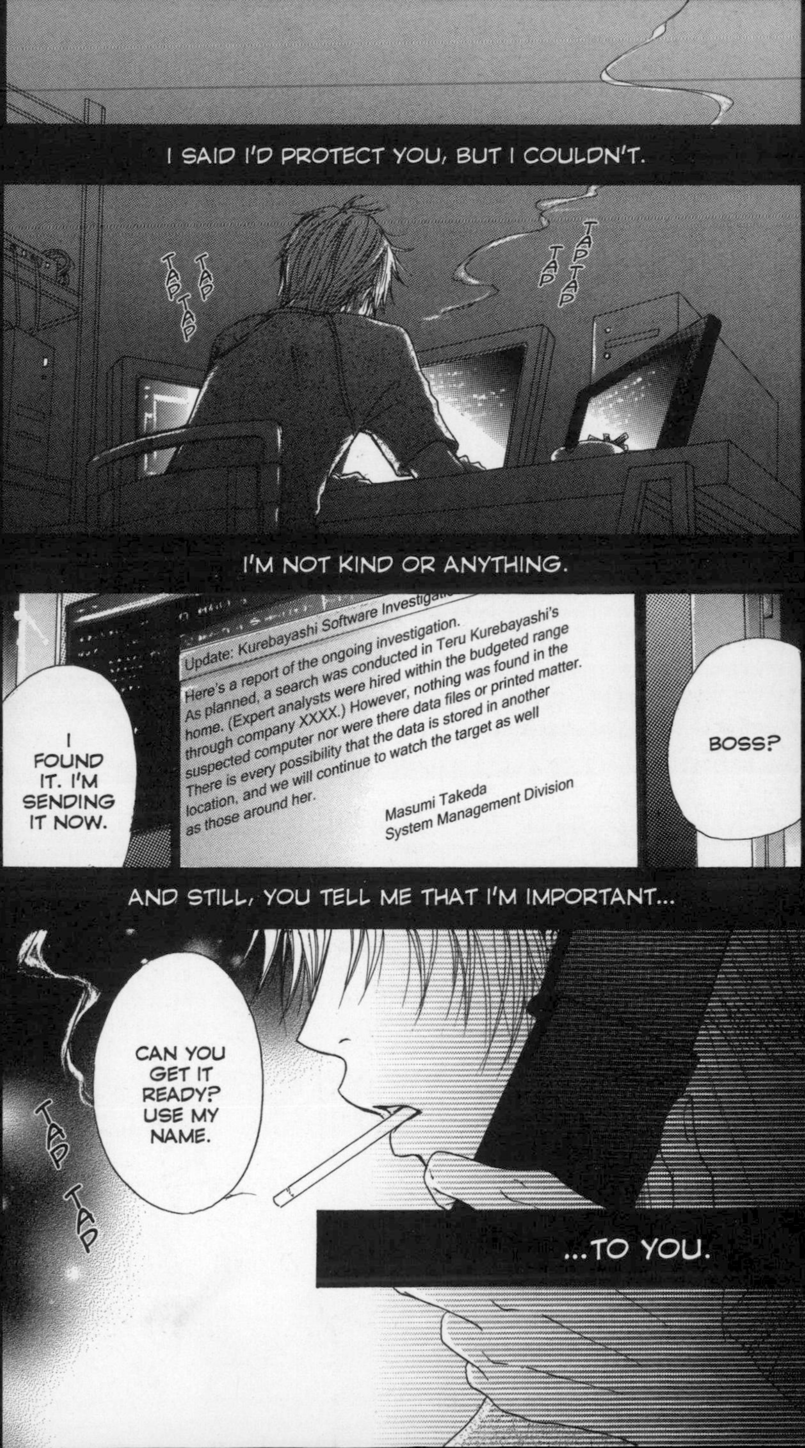
I SAID I'D PROTECT YOU, BUT I COULDN'T.
TAP TAPTAP
TAP TAPTAP
I'M NOT KIND OR ANYTHING.
BOSS?
Kurebayashi Software Investig
Update: Kurebayashi Software Investigation.
Here's a report of the ongoing investigation.
As planned, a search was conducted in Teru Kurebayashi's home. (Expert analysts were hired within the budgeted range through company XXXX.) However, nothing was found in the suspected computer nor were there data files or printed matter. There is every possibility that the data is stored in another location, and we will continue to watch the target as well as those around her.
Masumi Takeda
System Management Division
I FOUND IT. I'M SENDING IT NOW.
AND STILL, YOU TELL ME THAT I'M IMPORTANT...
CAN YOU GET IT READY? USE MY NAME.
TAP TAP
...TO YOU.

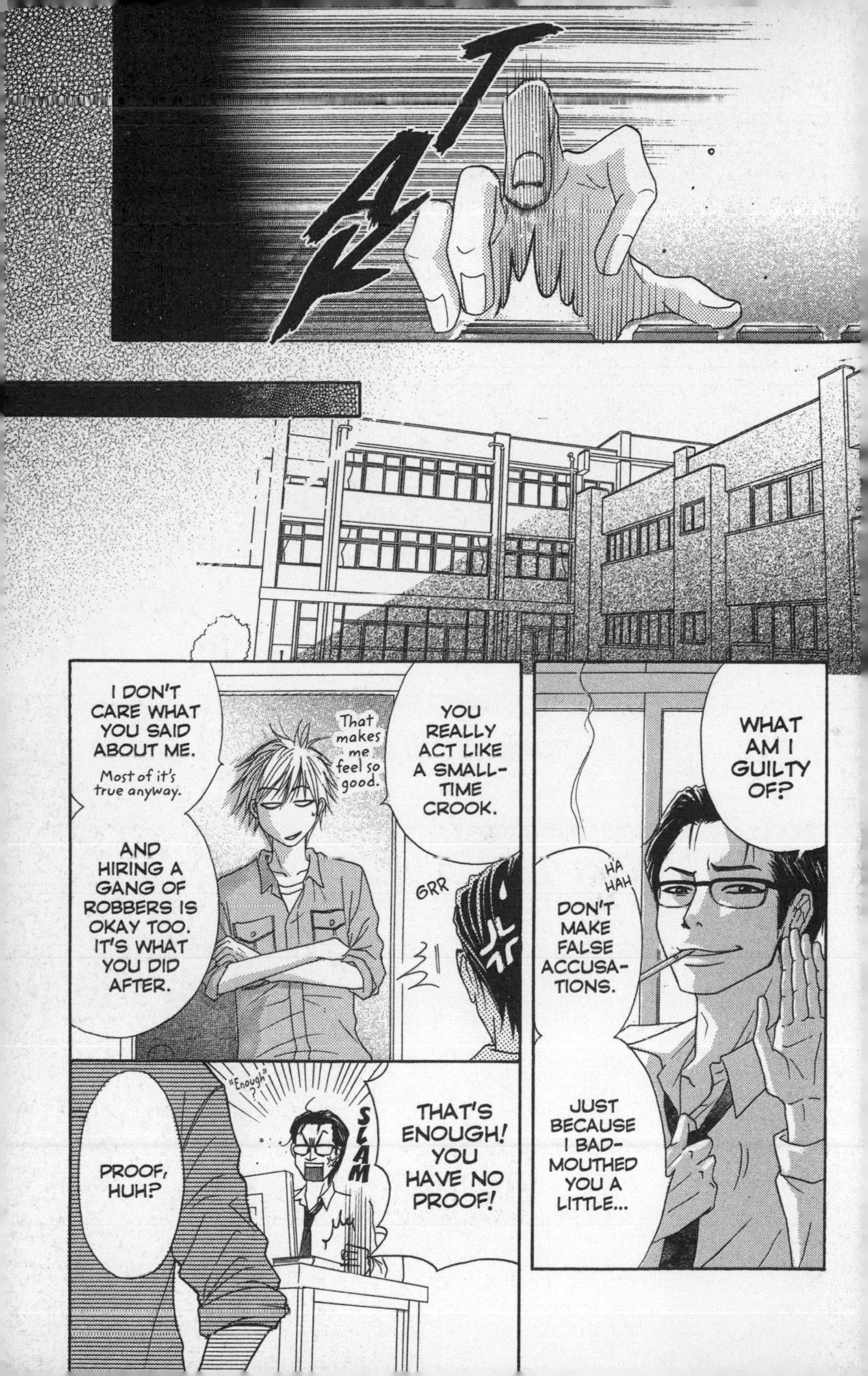
WHAT AM I GUILTY OF?
HA HAH
DON'T MAKE FALSE ACCUSA-TIONS.
JUST BECAUSE I BAD-MOUTHED YOU A LITTLE...
YOU REALLY ACT LIKE A SMALL-TIME CROOK.
That makes me feel so good.
GRR
I DON'T CARE WHAT YOU SAID ABOUT ME.
Most of it's true anyway.
AND HIRING A GANG OF ROBBERS IS OKAY TOO. IT'S WHAT YOU DID AFTER.
THAT'S ENOUGH! YOU HAVE NO PROOF!
SLAM
"Enough"?
PROOF, HUH?

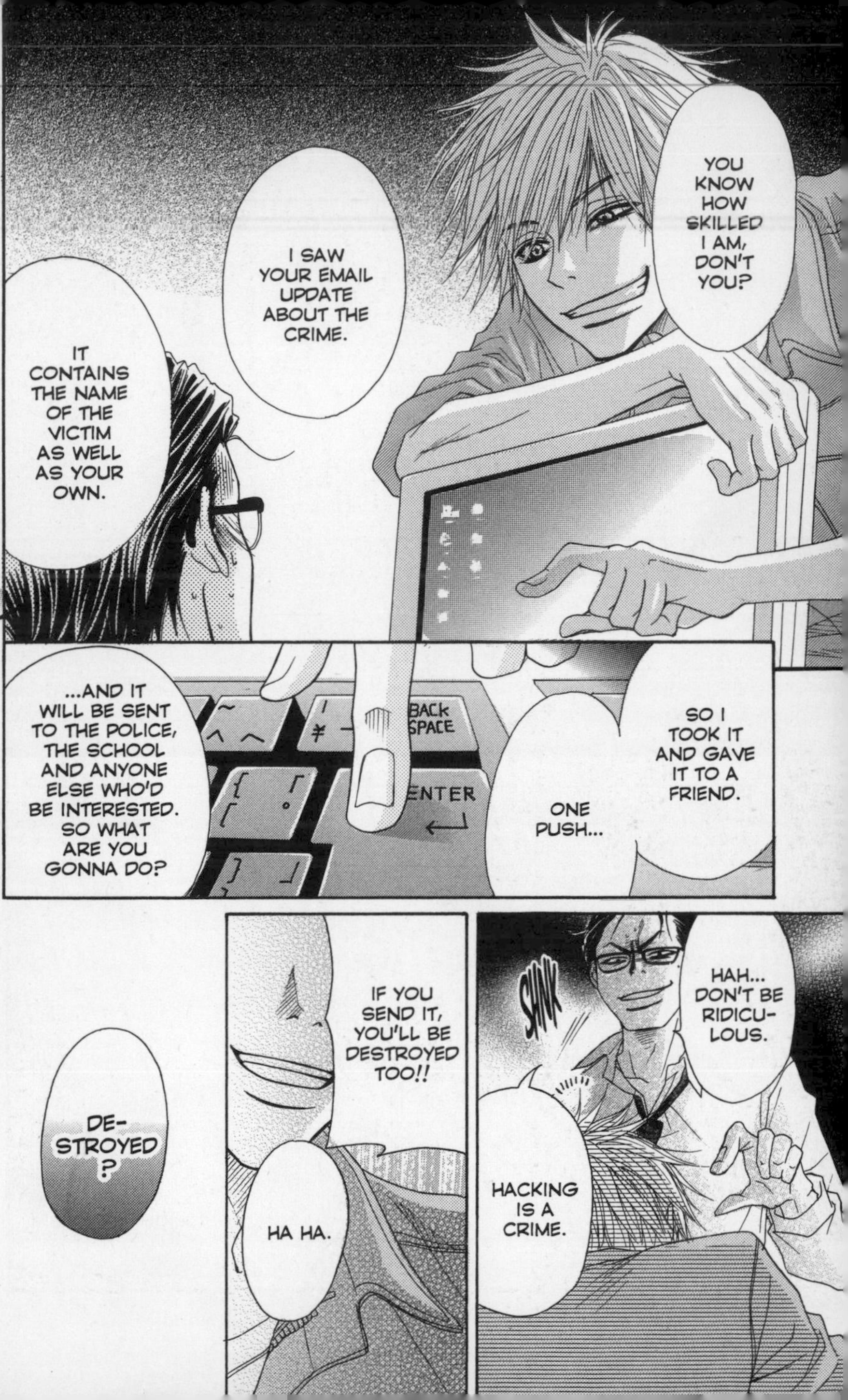
YOU KNOW HOW SKILLED I AM, DON'T YOU?
I SAW YOUR EMAIL UPDATE ABOUT THE CRIME.
IT CONTAINS THE NAME OF THE VICTIM AS WELL AS YOUR OWN.
SO I TOOK IT AND GAVE IT TO A FRIEND.
ONE PUSH...
BACK SPACE
ENTER
...AND IT WILL BE SENT TO THE POLICE, THE SCHOOL AND ANYONE ELSE WHO'D BE INTERESTED. SO WHAT ARE YOU GONNA DO?
HAH... DON'T BE RIDICULOUS.
SHINK
HACKING IS A CRIME.
IF YOU SEND IT, YOU'LL BE DESTROYED TOO!!
HA HA.
DE-STROYED?

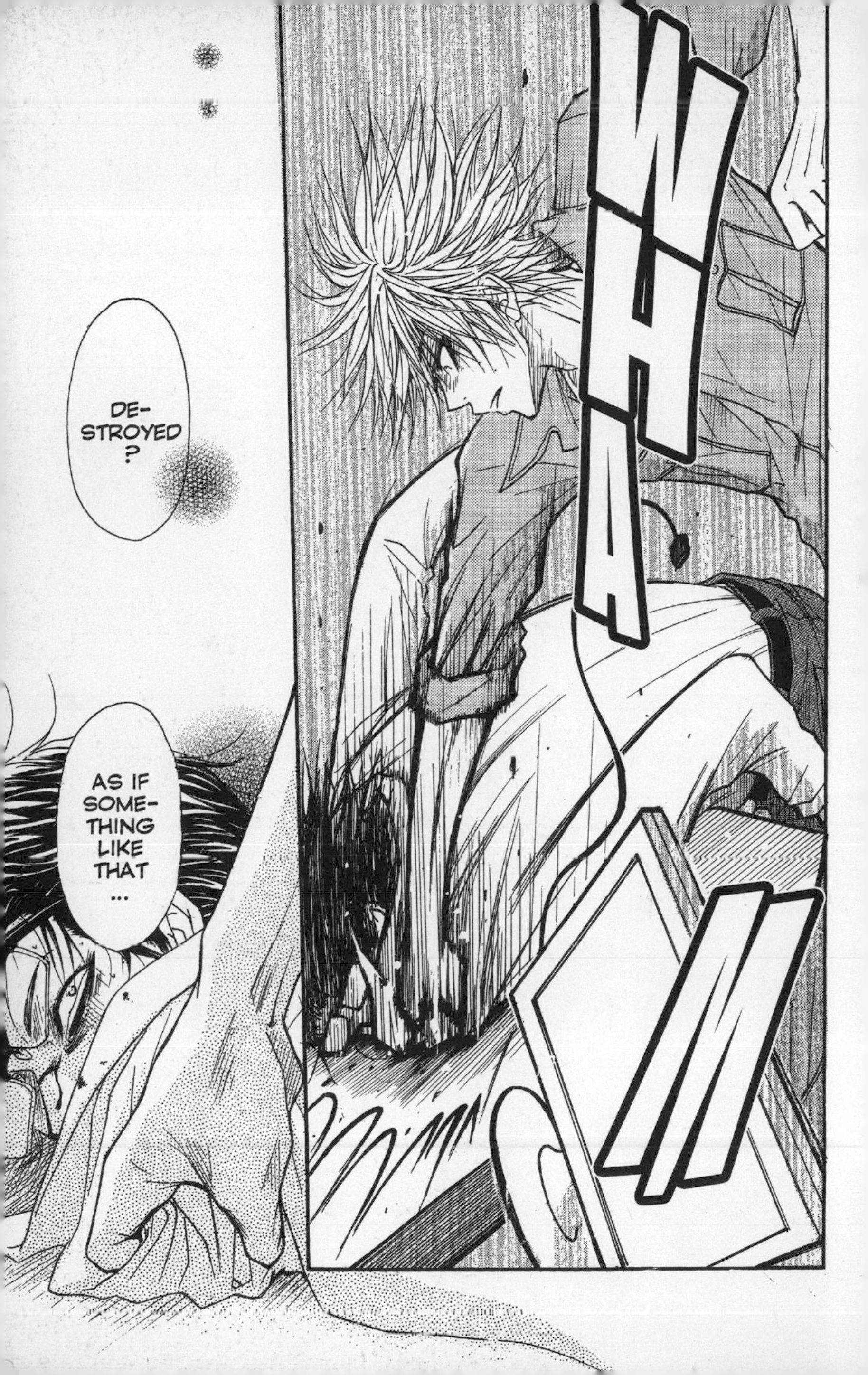
WHAM
DE-STROYED?
AS IF SOMETHING LIKE THAT...

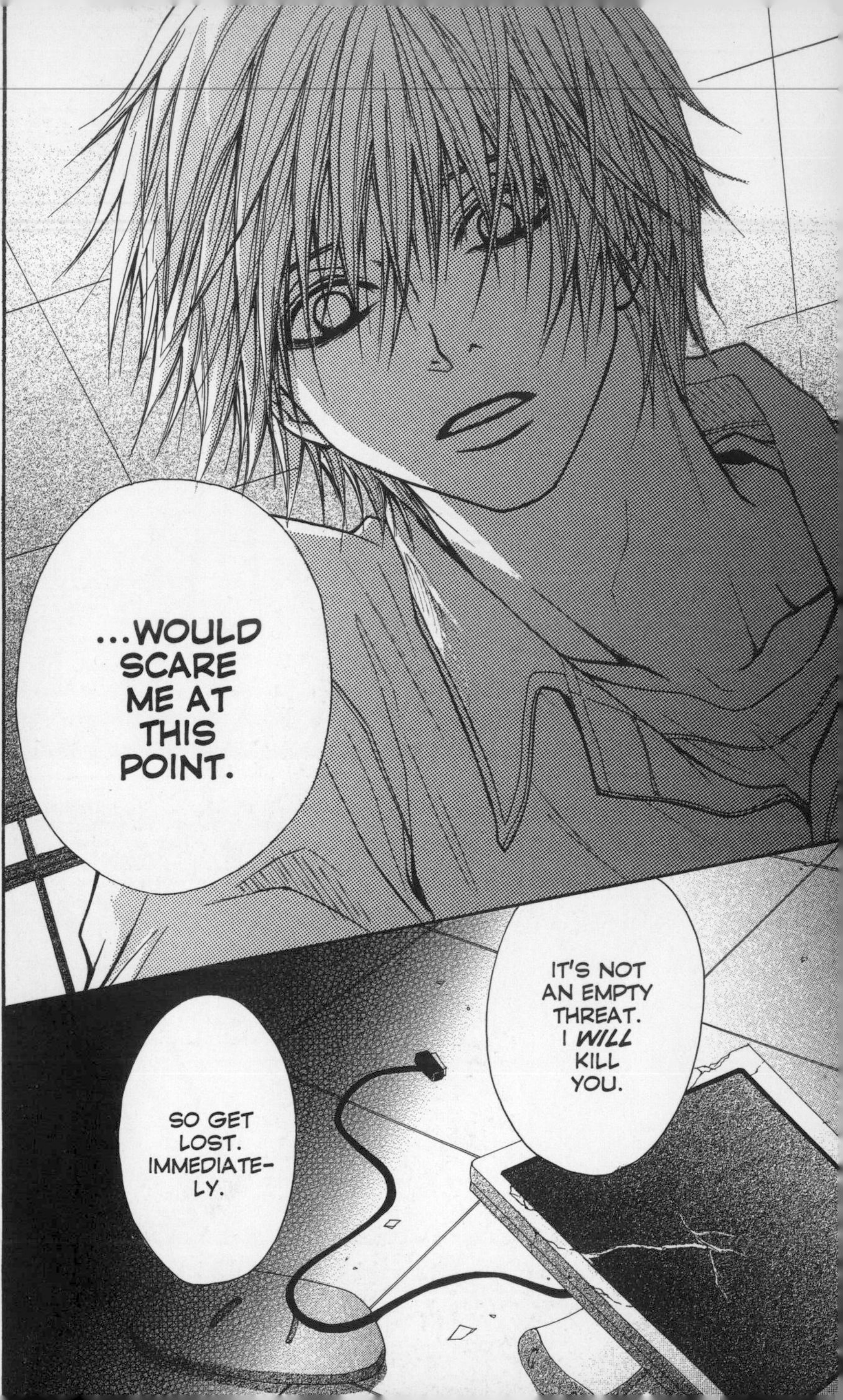
...WOULD SCARE ME AT THIS POINT.
IT'S NOT AN EMPTY THREAT. I *WILL* KILL YOU.
SO GET LOST. IMMEDIATE-LY.

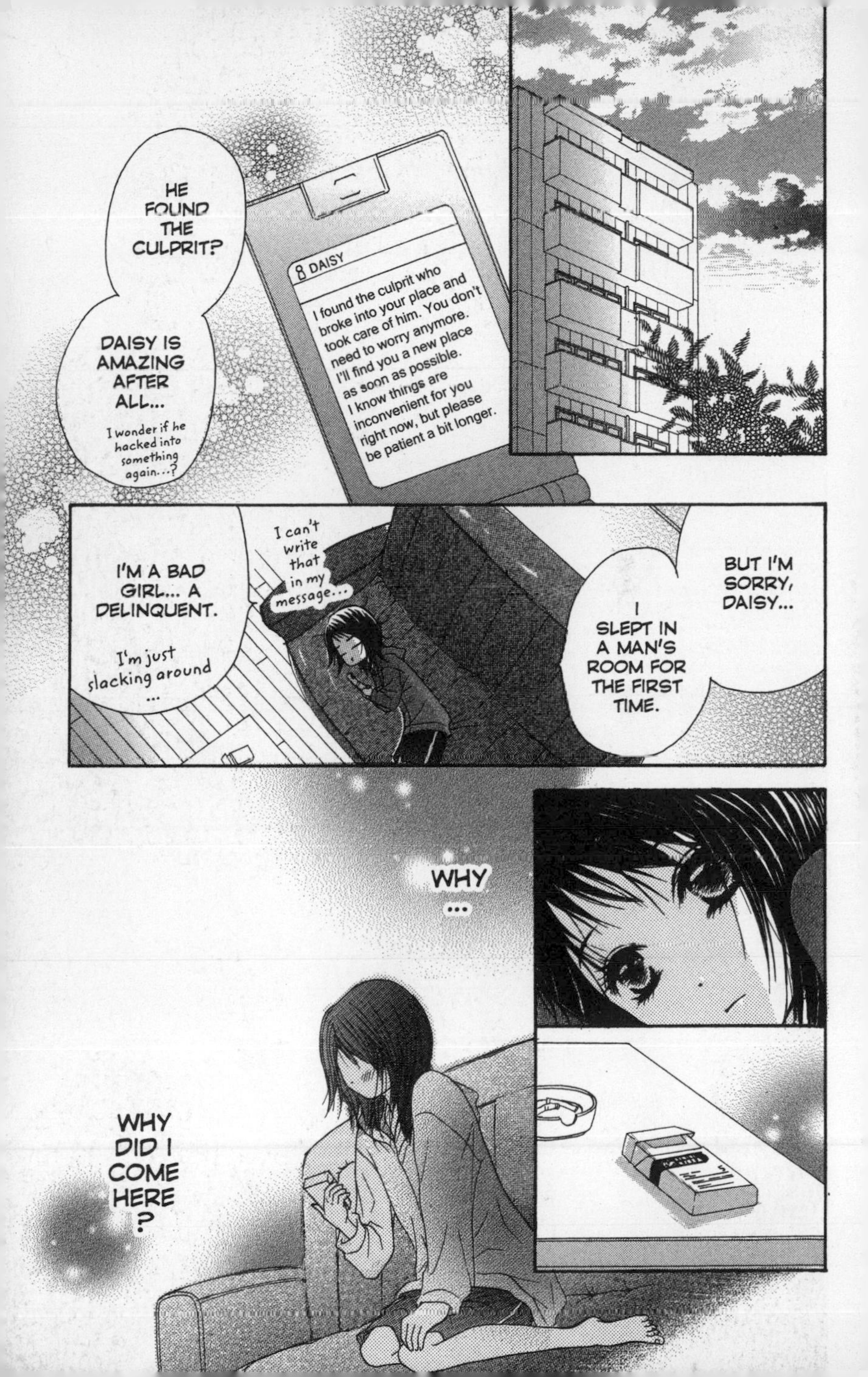
DAISY
I found the culprit who broke into your place and took care of him. You don't need to worry anymore. I'll find you a new place as soon as possible. I know things are inconvenient for you right now, but please be patient a bit longer.
HE FOUND THE CULPRIT?
DAISY IS AMAZING AFTER ALL...
I wonder if he hacked into something again...?
BUT I'M SORRY, DAISY...
I SLEPT IN A MAN'S ROOM FOR THE FIRST TIME.
I can't write that in my message...
I'M A BAD GIRL... A DELINQUENT.
I'm just slacking around ...
WHY ...
WHY DID I COME HERE ?

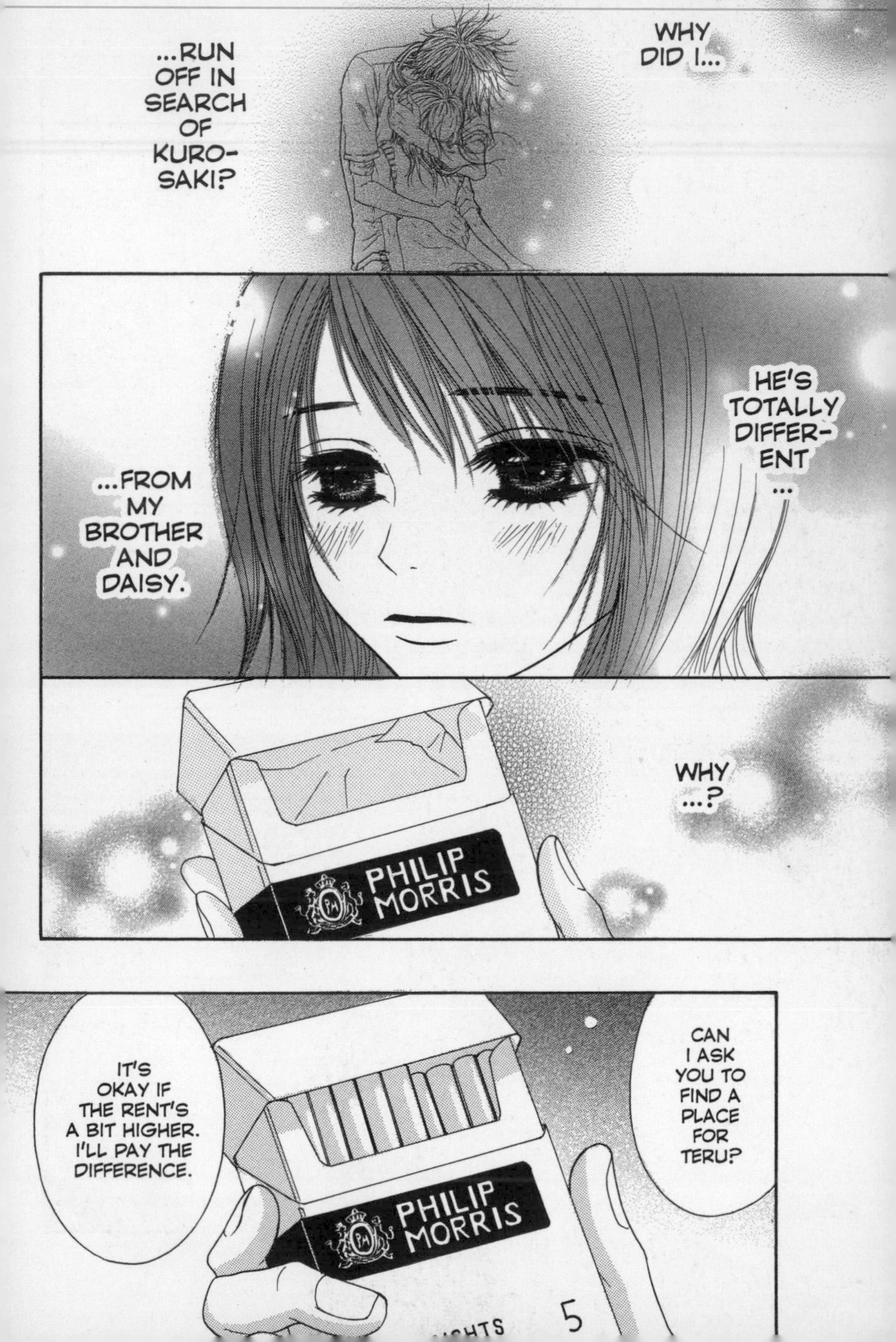

WHY DID I...
...RUN OFF IN SEARCH OF KURO-SAKI?
HE'S TOTALLY DIFFER-ENT...
...FROM MY BROTHER AND DAISY.
WHY...?
PHILIP MORRIS
CAN I ASK YOU TO FIND A PLACE FOR TERU?
IT'S OKAY IF THE RENT'S A BIT HIGHER. I'LL PAY THE DIFFERENCE.
PHILIP MORRIS

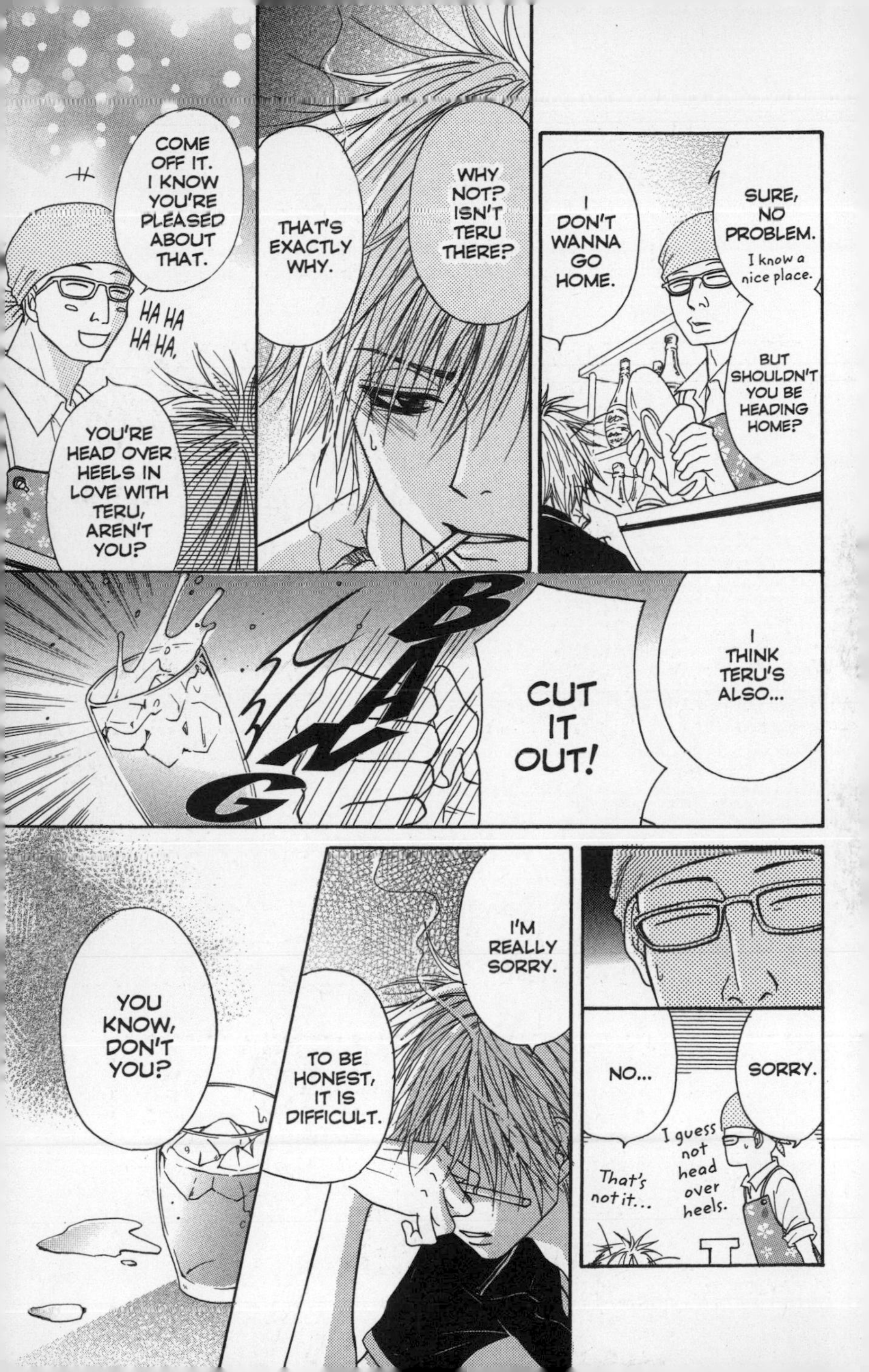

SURE, NO PROBLEM.
I know a nice place.
BUT SHOULDN'T YOU BE HEADING HOME?
I DON'T WANNA GO HOME.
WHY NOT? ISN'T TERU THERE?
THAT'S EXACTLY WHY.
COME OFF IT. I KNOW YOU'RE PLEASED ABOUT THAT.
HA HA HA HA.
YOU'RE HEAD OVER HEELS IN LOVE WITH TERU, AREN'T YOU?
I THINK TERU'S ALSO...
CUT IT OUT!
BANG
SORRY.
I guess not head over heels.
NO...
That's not it...
I'M REALLY SORRY.
TO BE HONEST, IT IS DIFFICULT.
YOU KNOW, DON'T YOU?

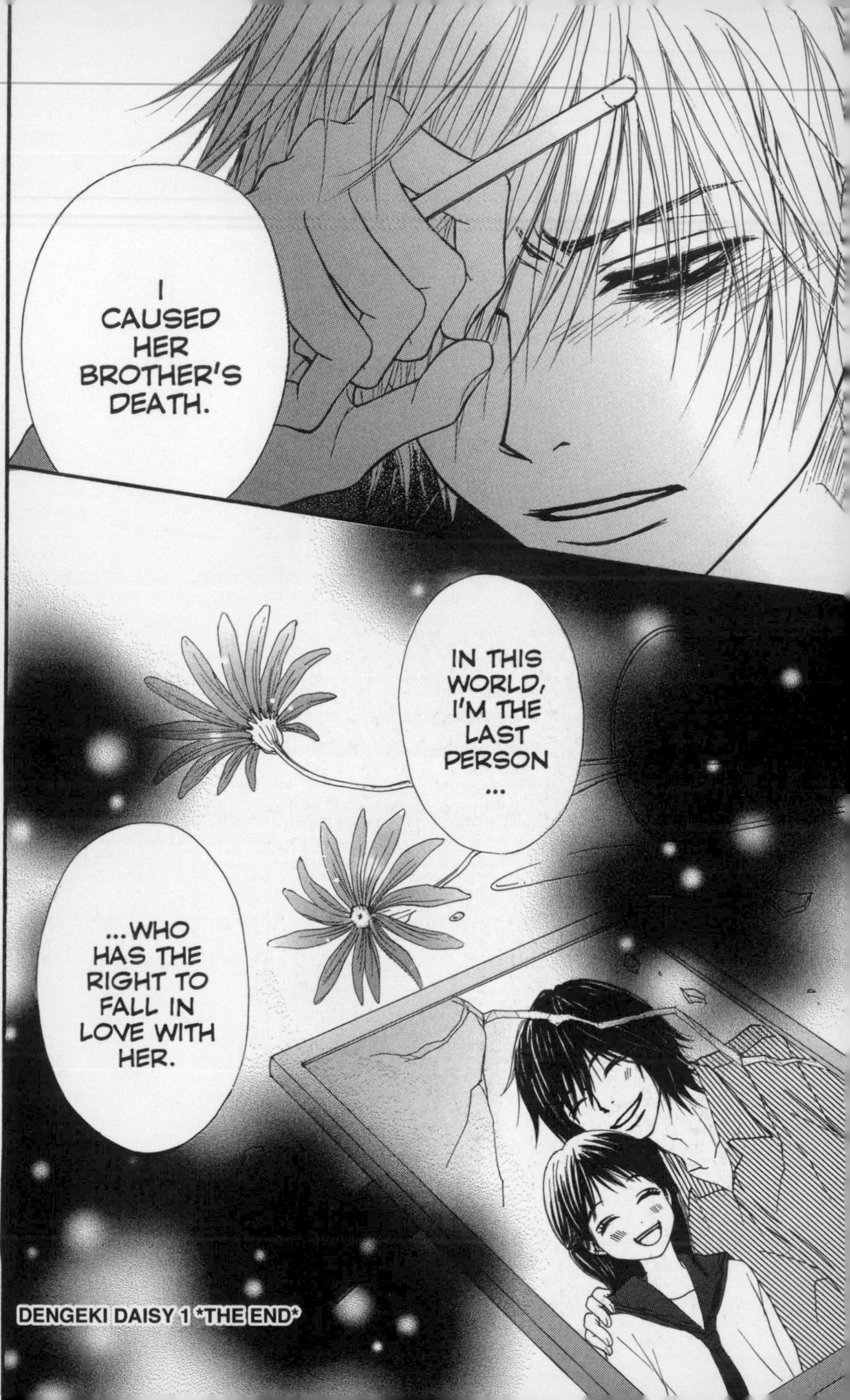
I CAUSED HER BROTHER'S DEATH.
IN THIS WORLD, I'M THE LAST PERSON ...
...WHO HAS THE RIGHT TO FALL IN LOVE WITH HER.
DENGEKI DAISY 1 *THE END*

WARNING

THE NEXT SECTION IS SORT OF LIKE A *DENGEKI DAISY* SIDE STORY THAT I CREATED FOR *DELUXE BETSUCOMI*.

PLEASE BE WARNED THAT:

* IT IS NOT A CONTINUATION OF CHAPTER 4 (WHICH ENDED A COUPLE OF PAGES AGO).
* IT HAS NOTHING TO DO WITH THE MAIN STORY (MAYBE JUST A LITTLE).
* THEY HAVEN'T DONE IT.

THAT IS ALL.

BUT ACTUALLY, I'M SORRY. PLEASE FORGIVE ME. PLEASE HELP ME.

IF THIS SIDE STORY IS YOUR INTRODUCTION TO *DENGEKI DAISY*, YOU'VE MISUNDERSTOOD 98 PERCENT OF IT. SO PLEASE READ WHAT'S BEEN PUBLISHED BEFORE THIS. OUT LOUD. THREE TIMES.

DENGEKI
SOME-THING
Let me see!
? ? ?
Why can't I read it?

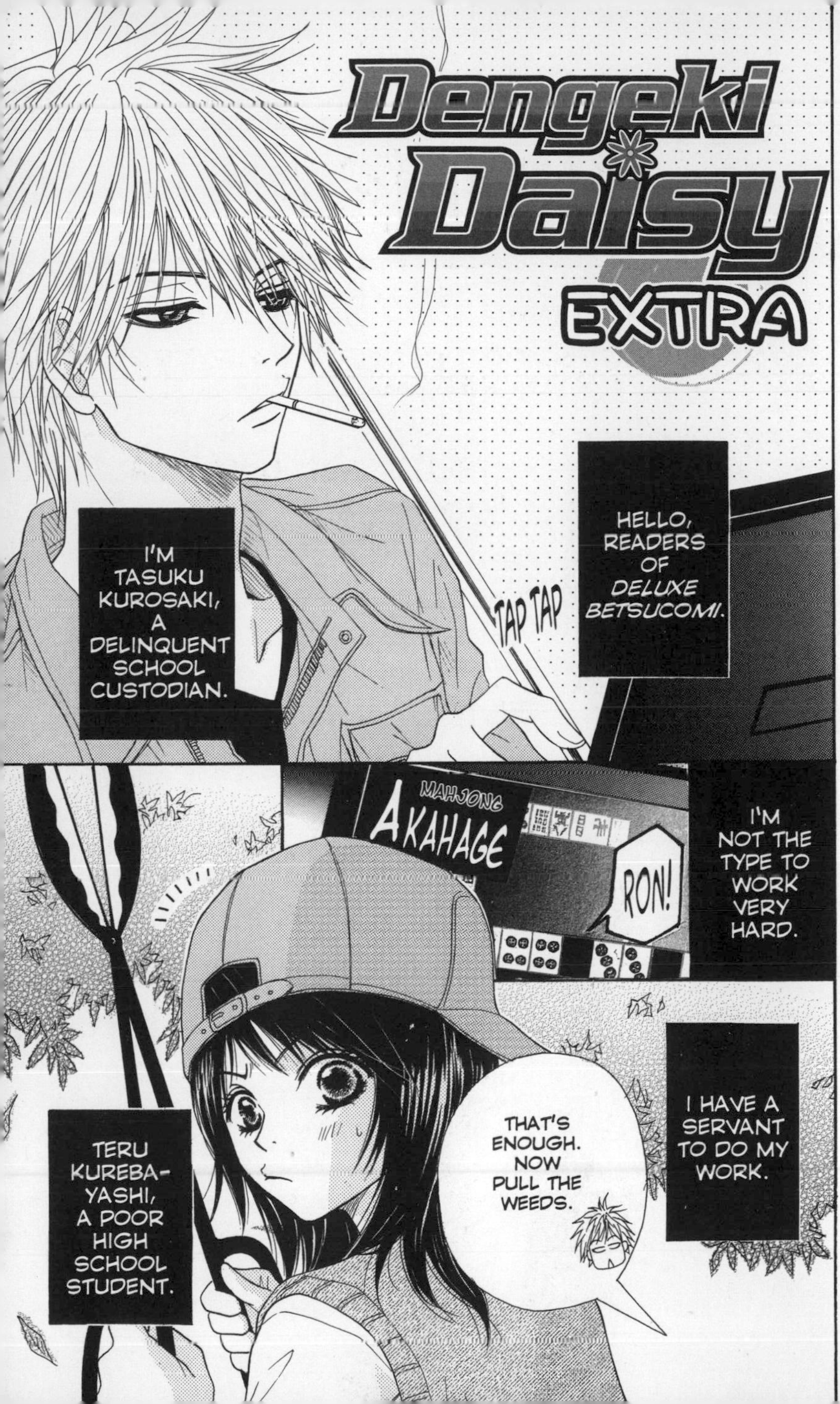
Dengeki Daisy
EXTRA
HELLO, READERS OF DELUXE BETSUCOMI.
TAP TAP
I'M TASUKU KUROSAKI, A DELINQUENT SCHOOL CUSTODIAN.
I'M NOT THE TYPE TO WORK VERY HARD.
MAHJONG AKAHAGE
RON!
I HAVE A SERVANT TO DO MY WORK.
THAT'S ENOUGH. NOW PULL THE WEEDS.
TERU KUREBA-YASHI, A POOR HIGH SCHOOL STUDENT.

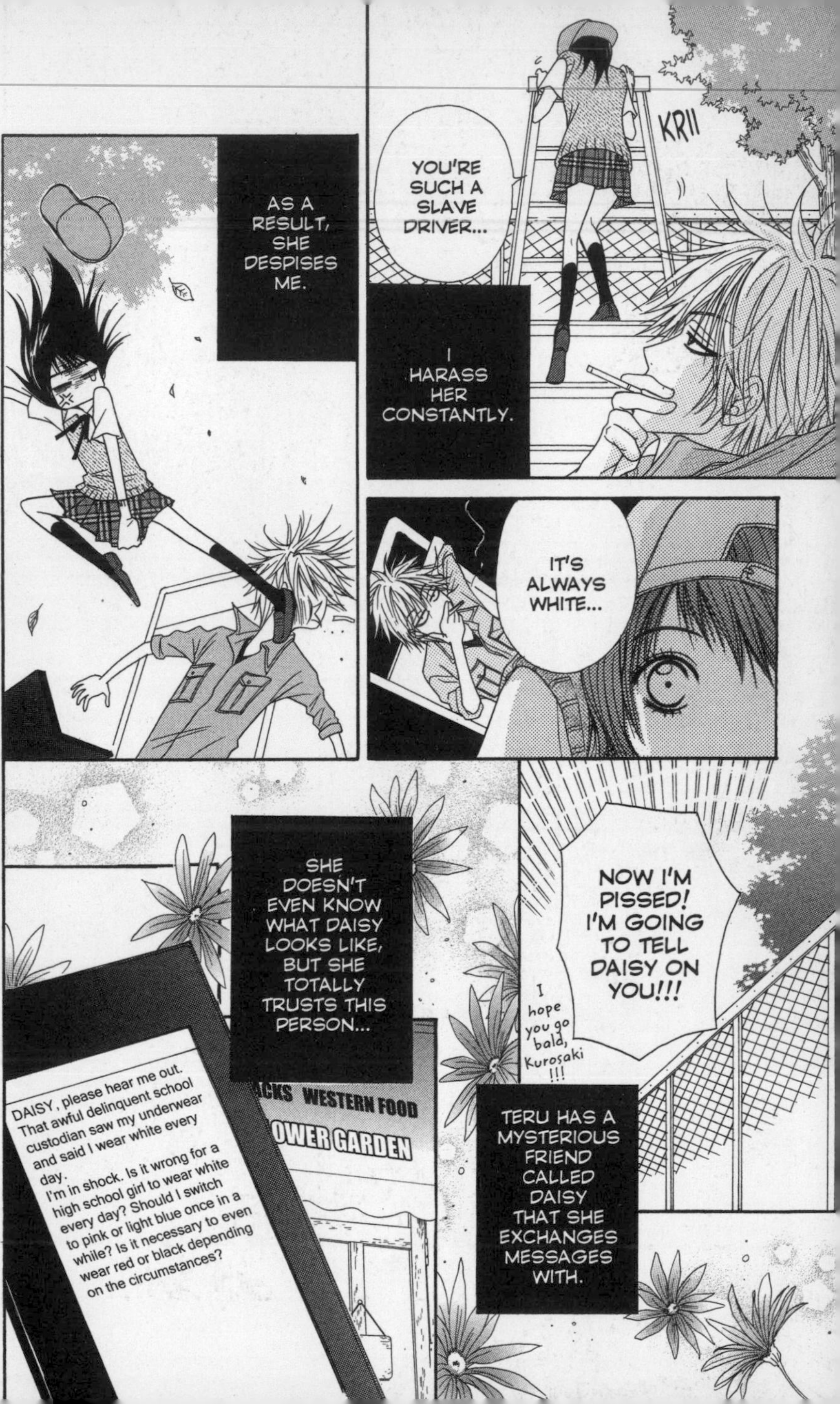
KRII
YOU'RE SUCH A SLAVE DRIVER...
I HARASS HER CONSTANTLY.
IT'S ALWAYS WHITE...
AS A RESULT, SHE DESPISES ME.
NOW I'M PISSED! I'M GOING TO TELL DAISY ON YOU!!!
I hope you go bald, Kurosaki!!!
TERU HAS A MYSTERIOUS FRIEND CALLED DAISY THAT SHE EXCHANGES MESSAGES WITH.
SHE DOESN'T EVEN KNOW WHAT DAISY LOOKS LIKE, BUT SHE TOTALLY TRUSTS THIS PERSON...
WESTERN FOOD
DAISY, please hear me out. That awful delinquent school custodian saw my underwear and said I wear white every day.
I'm in shock. Is it wrong for a high school girl to wear white every day? Should I switch to pink or light blue once in a while? Is it necessary to even wear red or black depending on the circumstances?

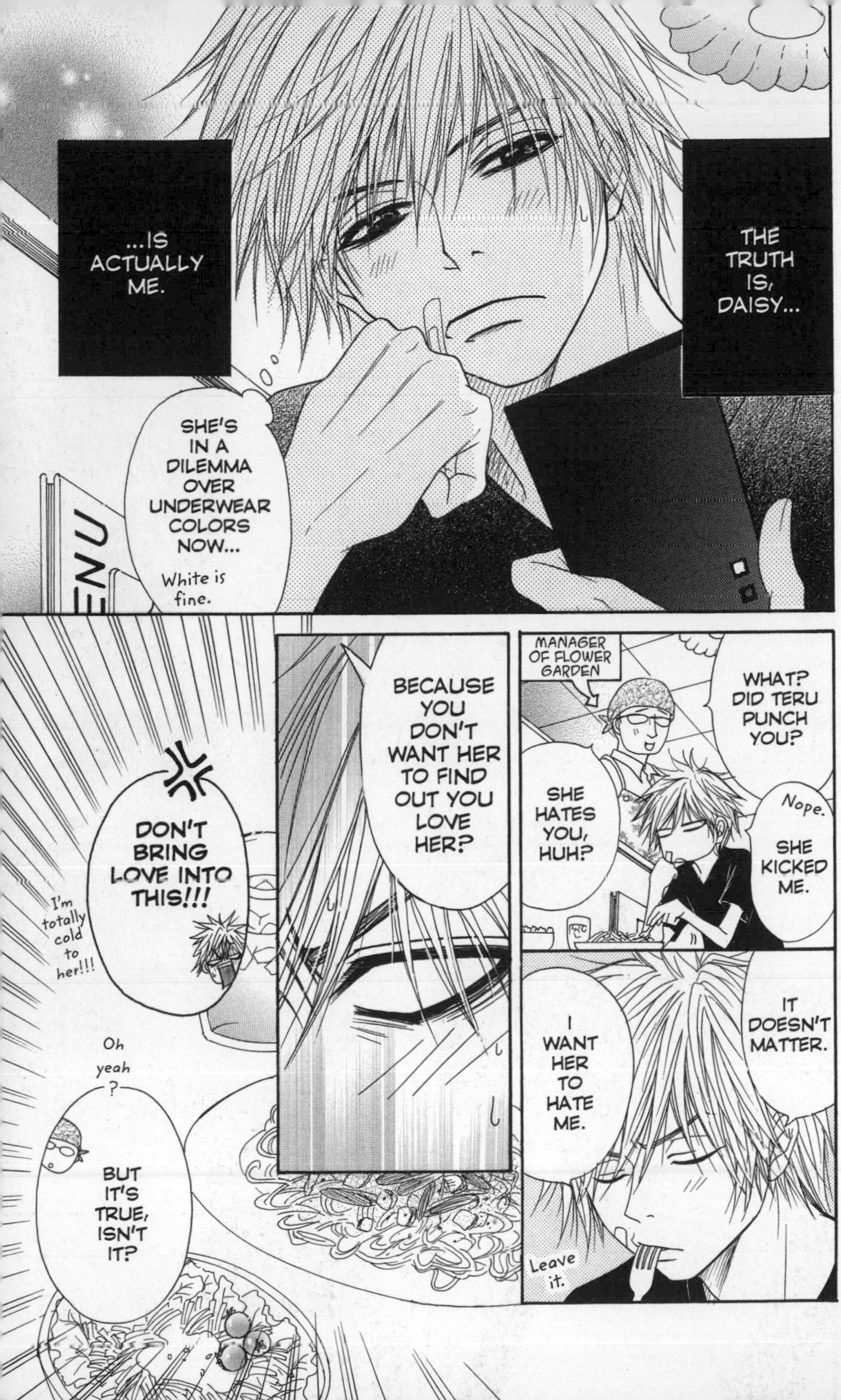
THE TRUTH IS, DAISY...
...IS ACTUALLY ME.
SHE'S IN A DILEMMA OVER UNDERWEAR COLORS NOW...
White is fine.
MANAGER OF FLOWER GARDEN
WHAT? DID TERU PUNCH YOU?
Nope.
SHE KICKED ME.
SHE HATES YOU, HUH?
IT DOESN'T MATTER.
I WANT HER TO HATE ME.
Leave it.
BECAUSE YOU DON'T WANT HER TO FIND OUT YOU LOVE HER?
DON'T BRING LOVE INTO THIS!!!
I'm totally cold to her!!!
Oh yeah?
BUT IT'S TRUE, ISN'T IT?

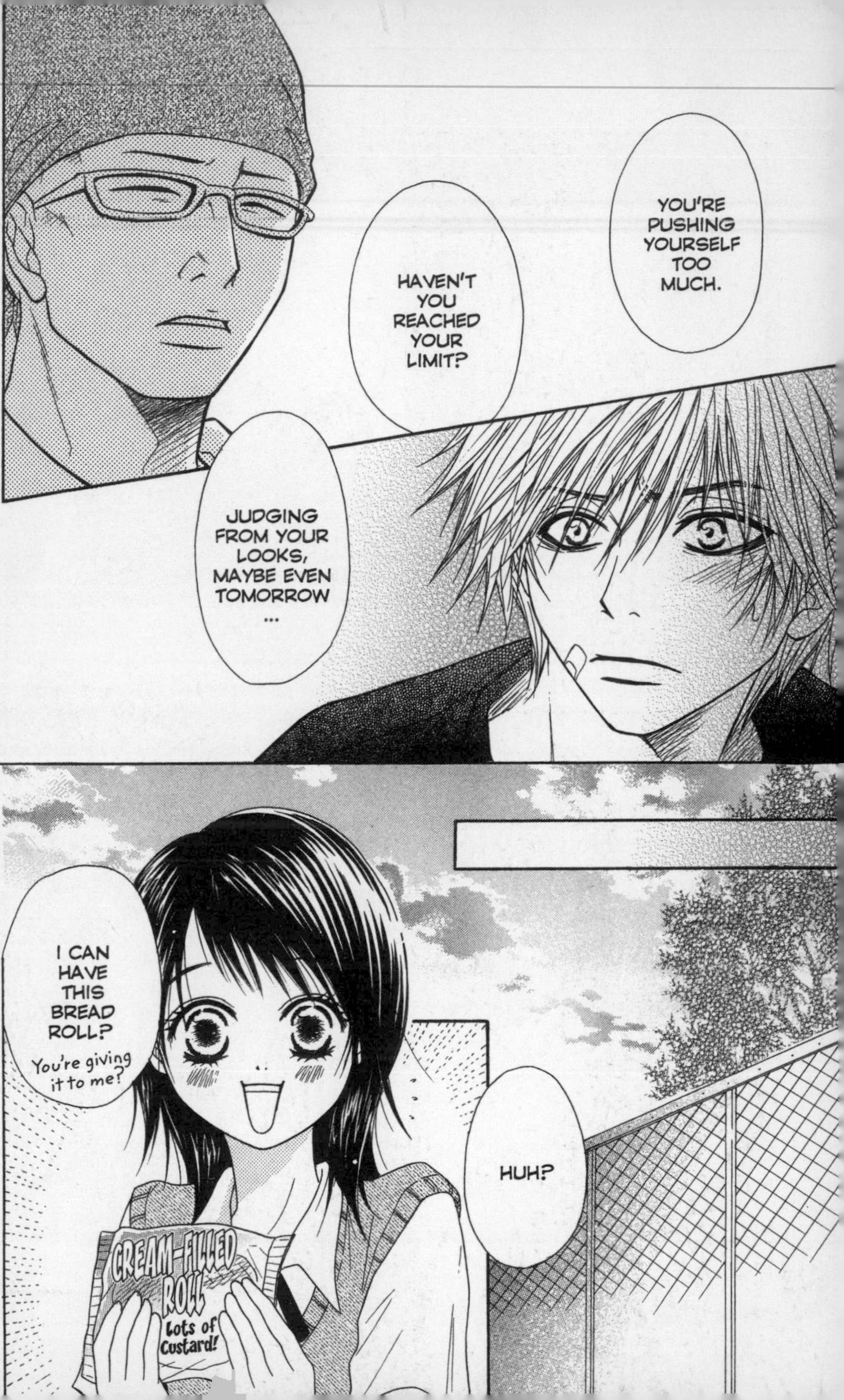
YOU'RE PUSHING YOURSELF TOO MUCH.
HAVEN'T YOU REACHED YOUR LIMIT?
JUDGING FROM YOUR LOOKS, MAYBE EVEN TOMORROW ...
I CAN HAVE THIS BREAD ROLL?
You're giving it to me?
HUH?
CREAM-FILLED ROLL
Lots of Custard!

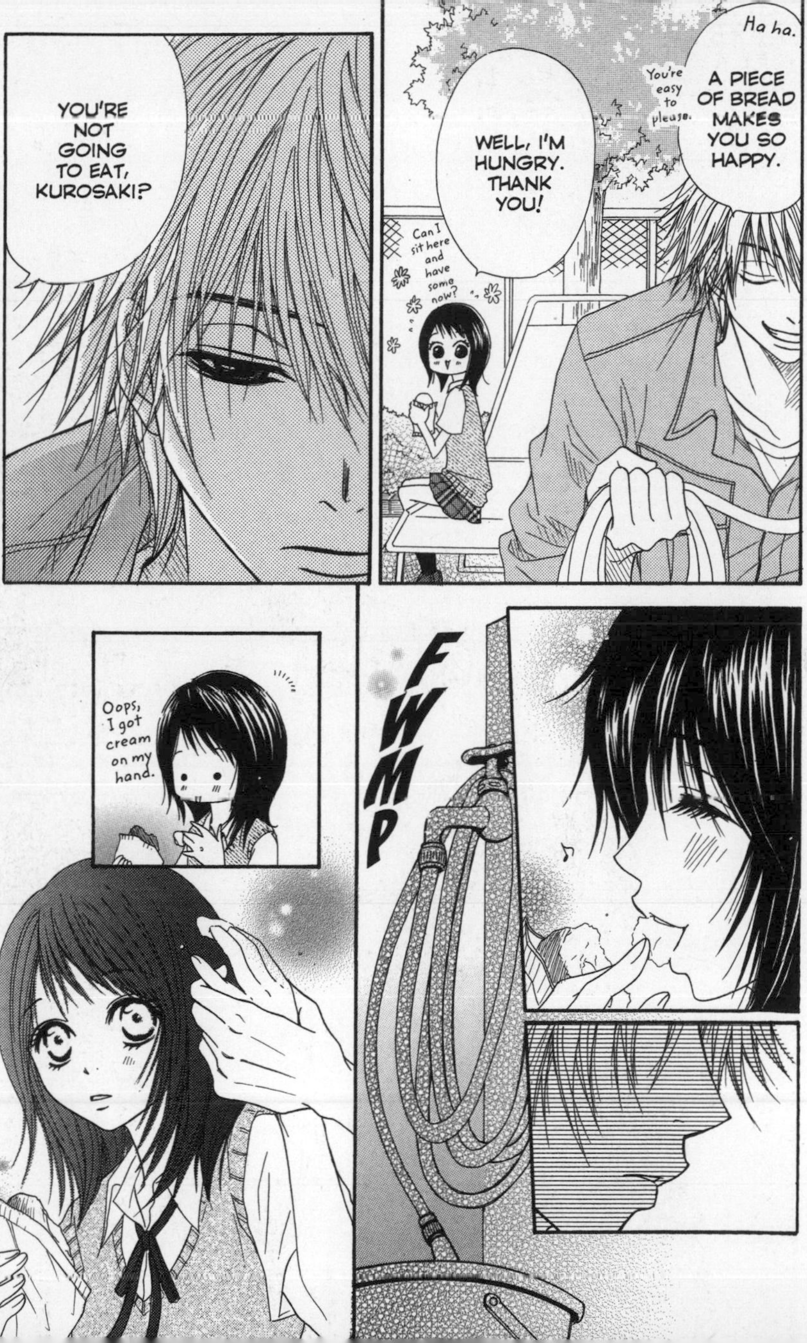
Ha ha.
A PIECE OF BREAD MAKES YOU SO HAPPY.
You're easy to please.
WELL, I'M HUNGRY. THANK YOU!
Can I sit here and have some now?
YOU'RE NOT GOING TO EAT, KUROSAKI?
FWMP
Oops, I got cream on my hand.

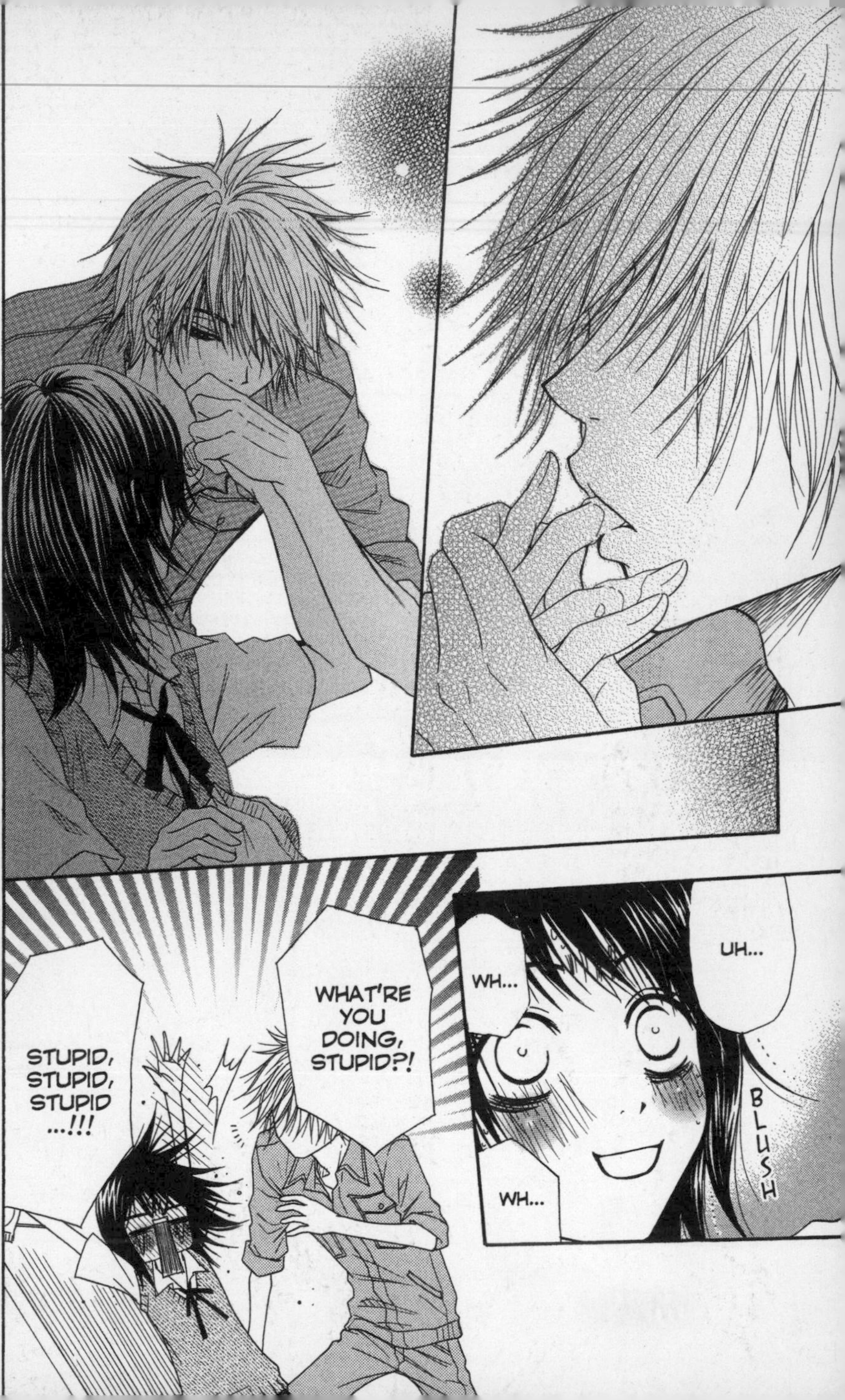
UH...
WH...
BLUSH
WH...
WHAT'RE YOU DOING, STUPID?!
STUPID, STUPID, STUPID ...!!!

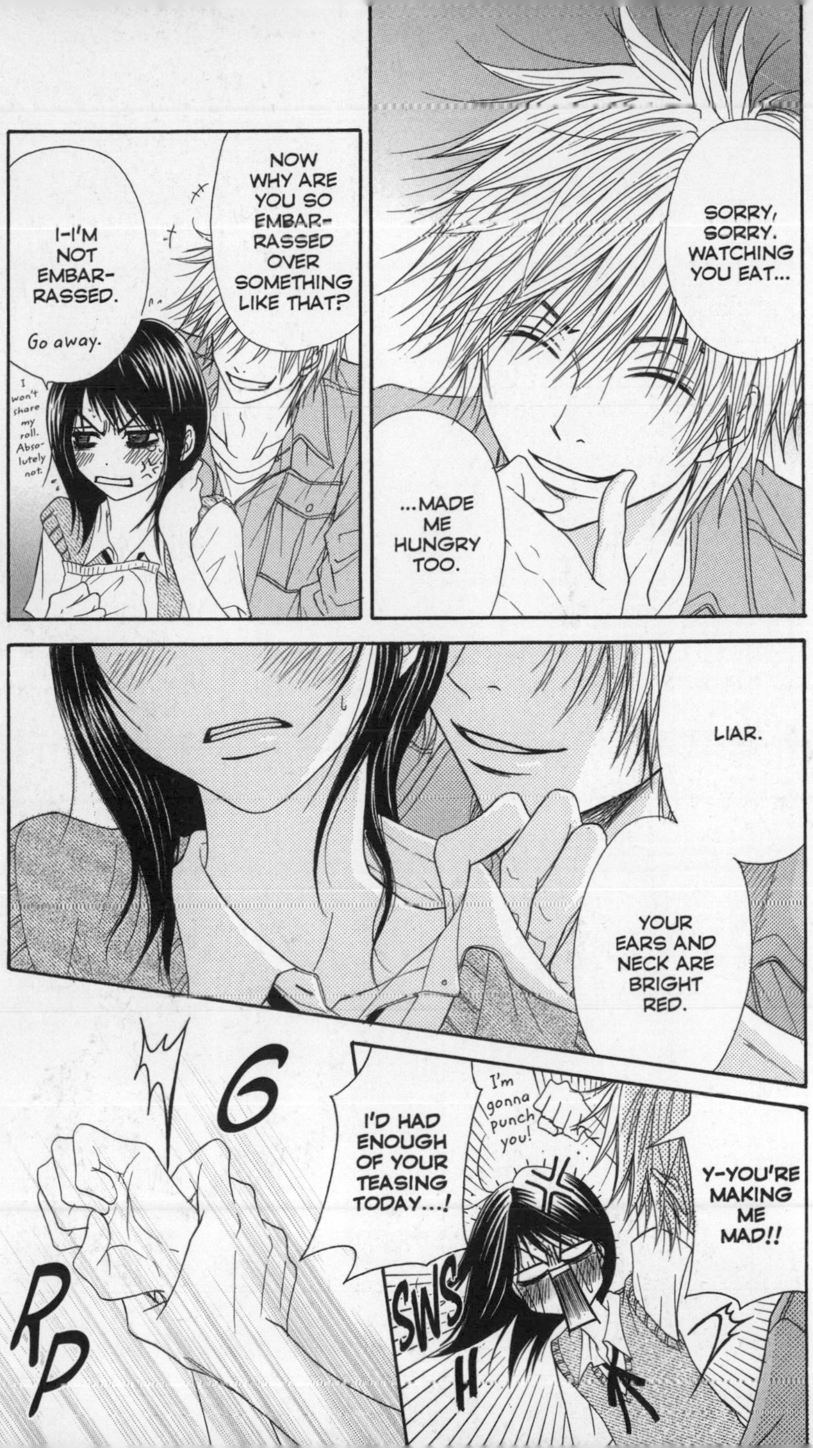
SORRY, SORRY. WATCHING YOU EAT...
...MADE ME HUNGRY TOO.
NOW WHY ARE YOU SO EMBAR-RASSED OVER SOMETHING LIKE THAT?
I-I'M NOT EMBAR-RASSED.
Go away.
I won't share my roll. Abso-lutely not.
LIAR.
YOUR EARS AND NECK ARE BRIGHT RED.
Y-YOU'RE MAKING ME MAD!!
I'm gonna punch you!
SWSH
I'D HAD ENOUGH OF YOUR TEASING TODAY...!
G
RP

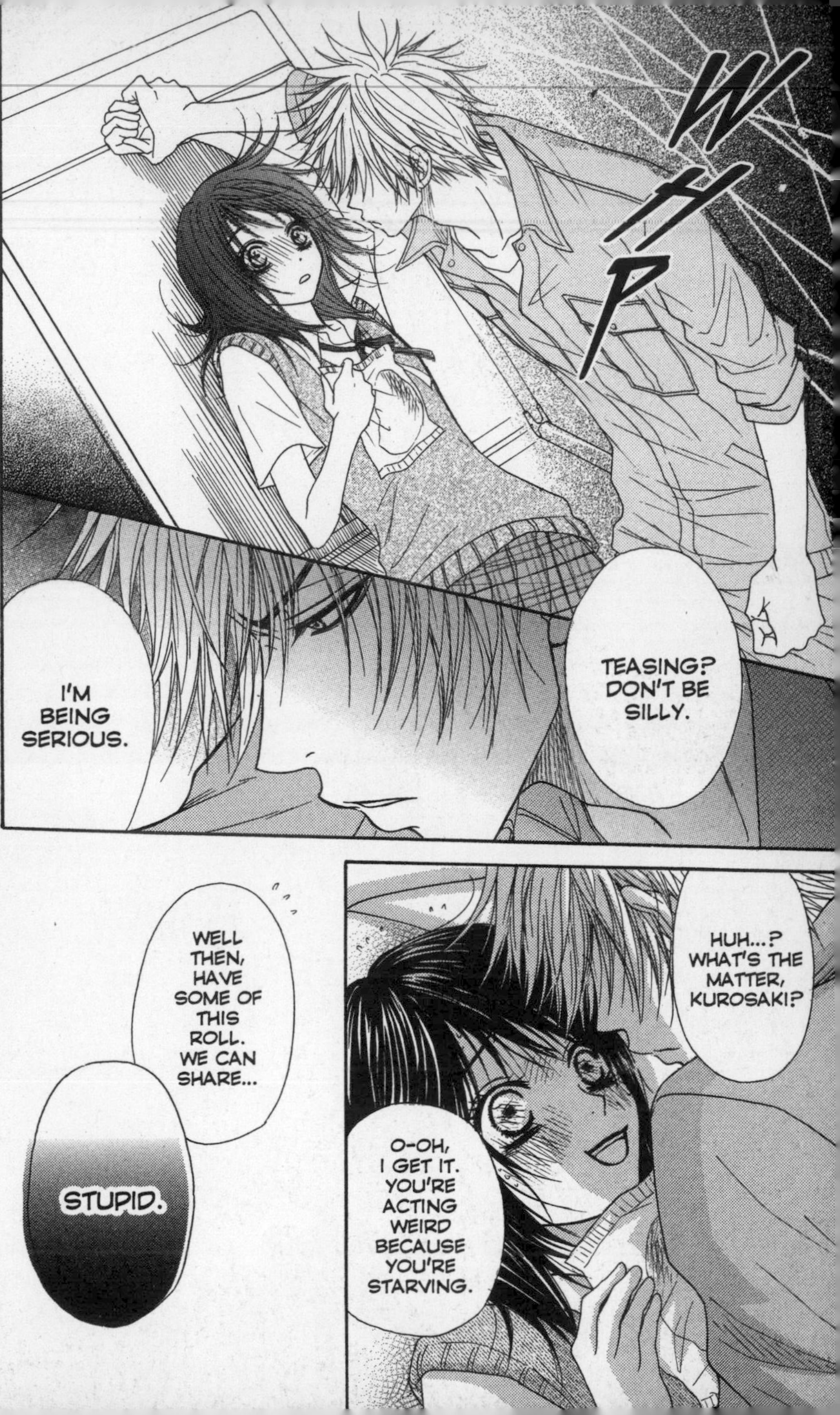
WHIP
TEASING? DON'T BE SILLY.
I'M BEING SERIOUS.
HUH...? WHAT'S THE MATTER, KUROSAKI?
O-OH, I GET IT. YOU'RE ACTING WEIRD BECAUSE YOU'RE STARVING.
WELL THEN, HAVE SOME OF THIS ROLL. WE CAN SHARE...
STUPID.

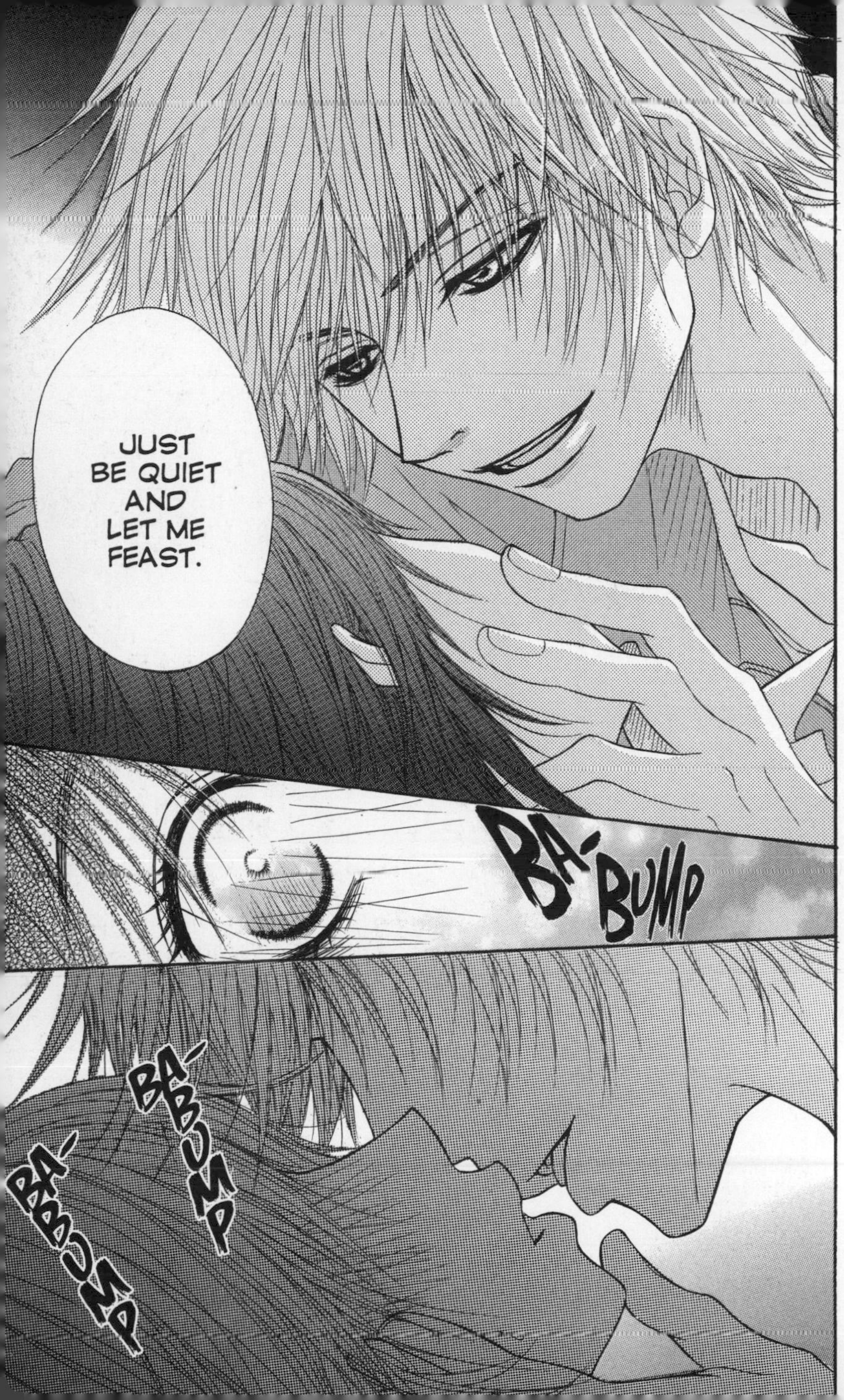
JUST BE QUIET AND LET ME FEAST.
BA-BUMP
BA-BUMP
BA-BUMP

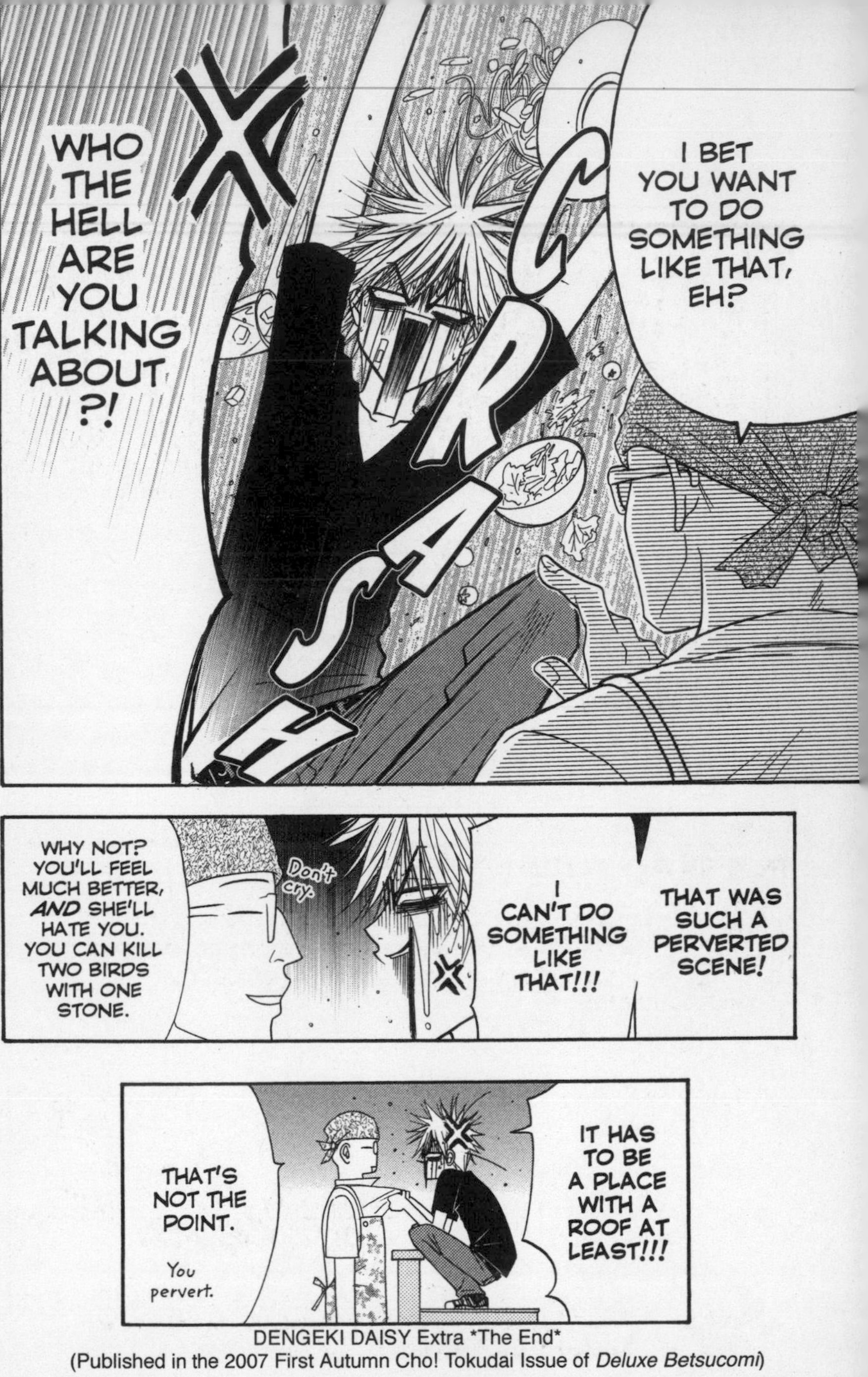
I BET YOU WANT TO DO SOMETHING LIKE THAT, EH?
CRASH
WHO THE HELL ARE YOU TALKING ABOUT?!
THAT WAS SUCH A PERVERTED SCENE!
I CAN'T DO SOMETHING LIKE THAT!!!
Don't cry.
WHY NOT? YOU'LL FEEL MUCH BETTER, AND SHE'LL HATE YOU. YOU CAN KILL TWO BIRDS WITH ONE STONE.
IT HAS TO BE A PLACE WITH A ROOF AT LEAST!!!
THAT'S NOT THE POINT.
You pervert.

DENGEKI DAISY Extra *The End*
(Published in the 2007 First Autumn Cho! Tokudai Issue of *Deluxe Betsucomi*)

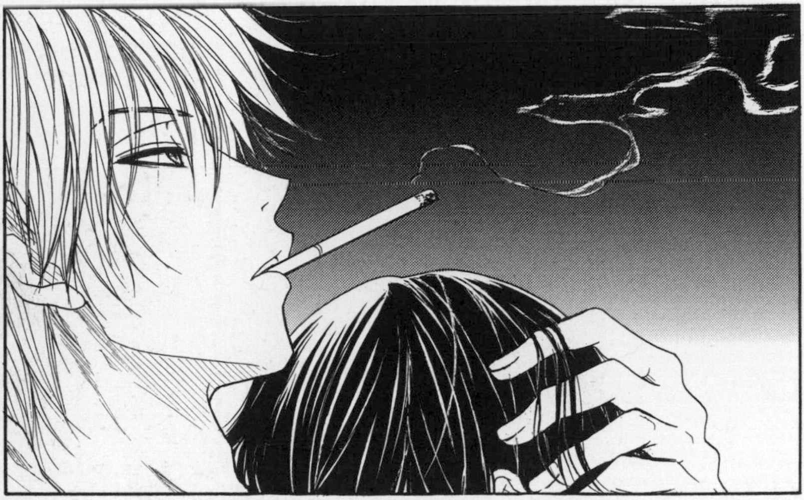

I DREW WHAT I THOUGHT WOULD BE THE MOST HILARIOUS PICTURE AFTER READING THAT STUPID SIDE STORY.

THIS IS THE END OF VOLUME 1 OF *DENGEKI DAISY.*

I HOPE THAT YOU WILL CONTINUE TO FOLLOW THE ESCAPADES OF THE PUNY A-CUP HIGH SCHOOL GIRL AND THE LOLICON DELINQUENT CUSTODIAN. LET'S MEET AGAIN IN VOLUME 2!! (I'M SURE THERE WILL BE A SECOND VOLUME!!!)

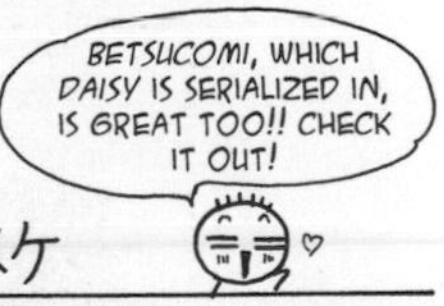
BETSUCOMI, WHICH DAISY IS SERIALIZED IN, IS GREAT TOO!! CHECK IT OUT!

最富　キョウスケ

KYOUSUKE MOTOMI

THANKS ······· Tomo / Yuh / Nao / Yuka / Tomoko / Nagisa / Yasuko / Miku / Kaco
Kakuko / Yuhka // Junko ······· and "Natsuko".

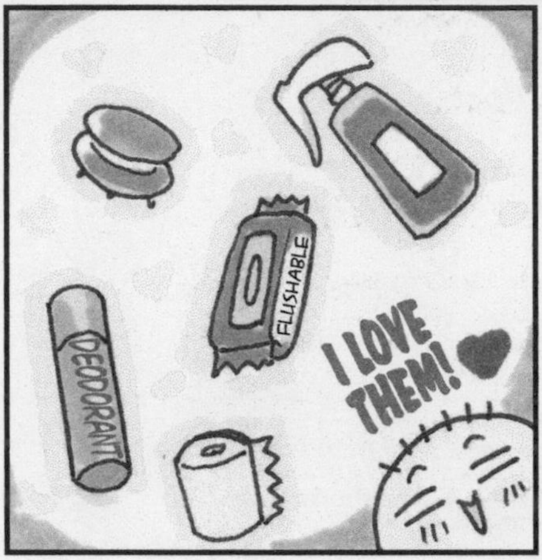
FLUSHABLE
DEODORANT
I LOVE THEM!

I like drugstores. Lately, I've been enjoying buying all sorts of toiletries. I get a thrill when new scents appear on the market.

-Kyousuke Motomi

Born on August 1, Kyousuke Motomi debuted in *Deluxe Betsucomi* with *Hetakuso Kyupiddo* (No-Good Cupid) in 2002. She is the creator of *Otokomae! Biizu Kurabu* (Handsome! Beads Club), and her latest work *Dengeki Daisy* is currently being serialized in *Betsucomi*. Motomi enjoys sleeping, tea ceremonies and reading Haruki Murakami.

DENGEKI DAISY

VOL. 1
Shojo Beat Edition

STORY AND ART BY
KYOUSUKE MOTOMI

© 2007 Kyousuke MOTOMI/Shogakukan
All rights reserved.
Original Japanese edition "DENGEKI DAISY"
published by SHOGAKUKAN Inc.

Translation & Adaptation/JN Productions
Touch-up Art & Lettering/Rina Mapa
Design/Yukiko Whitley
Editor/Amy Yu

Printed in the U.S.A.

Published by VIZ Media, LLC
P.O. Box 77010
San Francisco, CA 94107

10 9 8 7 6 5 4
First printing, July 2010
Fourth printing, January 2011

www.viz.com   www.shojobeat.com